D1171889

ENGLISH BIOGRAPHY
BEFORE 1700

ENGLISH BIOGRAPHY
BEFORE 1700

BY

DONALD A. STAUFFER
D. PHIL. OXON.

NEW YORK
RUSSELL & RUSSELL · INC
1964

COPYRIGHT, 1930

BY THE PRESIDENT AND FELLOWS OF HARVARD COLLEGE

REISSUED, 1964, BY RUSSELL & RUSSELL, INC.

BY ARRANGEMENT WITH HARVARD UNIVERSITY PRESS

L. C. CATALOG CARD NO: 64—10712

920.002
S 798e
111311

PRINTED IN THE UNITED STATES OF AMERICA

INTRODUCTION

THE aim of this study is to consider, historically and critically, the art of English biography from the earliest times to the year 1700. English biography has here been arbitrarily defined as including all lives written by Englishmen, whatever the subject or the language of the works may be. Thus, Dryden's *Life of Plutarch* is treated at some length, although Plutarch was not an Englishman; and the *Magna Vita Sancti Hugonis* receives considerable notice, although Adam of Eynsham did not write in English. Nor has the term Englishman been narrowly limited, especially in the centuries after the Conquest. The standard has been approximately the same as that of the Dictionary of National Biography, so that an Anglicized Frenchman such as Bernard André of Toulouse is discussed.

It is not the purpose of this survey to present new facts in the lives of individuals, but new facts in the history of biography. No adequate work is at the present time available which surveys English biography during these years as a branch of literature. Where such major fields as lyric poetry, drama, romance, and the beginnings of the English novel have been scrutinized, and even such minor forms as the ballad or the picaresque novel have received attention, biography in England as a branch of literature has remained practically untouched. This essay is intended as a step toward the history of an important section in English letters.

The method of this study has been to give in the bibliography all extant pieces of English biography before the year 1700, and to describe the more important items in some detail in the text. The problem of presentation, where the field itself is so broad and the period covered so extended, has not been without difficulties. No arrangement is perfect. A strict chronological account without the grouping of allied biographies would have rendered this essay unreadable and meaningless. The method of division here used has been adopted for the sake of convenience and clarity. The arrangement in the first two chapters, covering the mediaeval period and the English Renaissance, is roughly chronological. The seventeenth century is more complex. Two forms — the lives of churchmen and the autobiographies — represent coherent and important developments, and these, together with the secular, intimate lives, are discussed in three parallel chapters. Izaak Walton is of such interest in his own right as to demand separate consideration. The text treats only biographies that are of intrinsic worth or that represent a significant popular development. In order to relieve the reader from details too overpowering, descriptions of biographies of secondary importance are relegated to the bibliography, which consequently becomes, in certain respects, a *catalogue raisonné*. A chronological table of the principal biographies has also been added at the end; and cross references, in the few cases where they are necessary, have been given in the text. This constitutes the historical survey.

But in addition, each separate biography is considered in relation to life-writing in general. Its salient traits, its original contributions to the art of biography, and its literary value have therefore been noticed, and these qualities have been illustrated throughout by direct quotations. In the final chapter, an attempt has been made to draw together the threads of the separate divisions; to place biography more definitely in its relation to allied forms such as history or the novel, the preface or the character sketch; and also to determine what the early biographers themselves considered as the ideal in life-writing. This constitutes the critical survey.

The extent of this study has made the complete and detailed examination of any single work impossible, and the focus throughout has been upon biography by Englishmen considered as a part of English literature, rather than upon any individual piece. The works themselves have been read in the original editions except where otherwise stated. There has been no attempt to deal adequately with biographies yet remaining in manuscript.

The historical surveys have been developed by frequent illustrations from original biographies. In these quotations, the spelling, punctuation, and capitalization of the originals have been preserved.[1]

The first part of the bibliography is a subject-and-author index of English biographies before 1700. The date of the first edition is given, and where this differs widely from the time when it was written, the date of composition is also included. The better subsequent editions of important biographies are mentioned, and rudimentary descriptions of the biographies are introduced when significant items are not discussed in the text. It need hardly be stated that the bibliography is not complete. Many minor titles, and doubtless more than a few biographies of genuine interest, must have

---

1. Contractions have been expanded, italics have been disregarded, and typographical antiquities such as "i," "u," and "y" have been usually rendered by their modern equivalents "j," "v," and "th."

been overlooked, but it is hoped that the study will prove of value as pioneer work in a varied and fertile field. The last part of the bibliography gives the more important secondary authorities, those works written after 1700 which have furnished historical, or critical, or bibliographical aid.

An introduction is not the place to present conclusions, and the reader is referred to the final critical chapter for an analysis of English biography before 1700. One or two points only should be stated here. Two facts of particular interest may be noted: the prevalence, in almost all periods, of numerous attempts at biography, and the extreme rarity of successful ventures. Few forms are so exacting. The ideal biographer must be endowed with industry, sympathy, judgment, and some literary capacity, qualities diverse and seldom united in one person. On the other hand, his creative imagination must be held in severe check. Where the novelist, the poet, the dramatist may allow his fancy to wander as it list, the biographer is continually bound by what has happened. He works as an historian, not a philosopher. From this arises the ironical paradox that the ordinary biographer is unable to make his heroes live, because they have lived; their actual existence prevents him from rendering their lives convincing. He takes breathing figures and makes of them stone effigies. This results chiefly from what may be called the historical overweight in biography. The narrative is occupied with those events in the life of an individual which concern society rather than the individual himself. The counsel of the greatest of classical biographers is neglected: "Nor is it in the most distinguished achievements that man's personality may be best discerned; an act of

small note, a short saying, a jest will distinguish the real
character better than the greatest sieges and most de-
cisive battles." It is not altogether fortunate that men
of national importance have been the principal subjects
for written memorials. Biographical values might have
been better realized had more writers known, as Dr.
Johnson knew, that "there has rarely passed a life of
which a judicious and faithful narrative would not be
useful."

Nevertheless, in spite of the rarity of good biographies, there are more of them in the period under study
than is commonly supposed. This essay will have attained one of its aims if it can draw attention to such
lesser-known biographies as the lives of Hugh of Lincoln, Sir John Perrott, Henry Burton, Charles Croke,
and Lady Anne Halkett, and help to place them by the
side of more famous works such as Cavendish's *Wolsey*,
Roper's *More*, and Walton's lives.

Another aim of this study will be achieved if the
reader is brought to realize that biography was a
flourishing and a diversified branch of English literature
before 1700. At some period prior to this date, almost
every type of life-writing had been practiced — impersonal, political, ethical, malicious, encomiastic, romantic, intimate, mystical, satirical, documented, subjective, voluminously Boswellian. Biography formed an
important part of the literature in England during the
Middle Ages. The Latin saints' lives show a maturity
in form and expression which entitles them to a more
honorable place in the literary history of the English
people than they have as yet received. With the growth
of the English language as a poetic vehicle, biography
adds to its ethical examples of holy living furnished by

x INTRODUCTION

the saints' lives a further field for speculation in the mediaeval idea of Fortune's wheel and the fall of the great, a theme which occupies metrical biographers from Lydgate to Storer and Drayton. Later, under the manifold influences of the Renaissance, and with the development of English prose, biography becomes more diverse, and in the period between 1550 and 1700 may be found the rudiments of those types which flower in succeeding centuries. To a general consideration of the roots of English biography, of royal and ecclesiastical lives, of the beginnings of autobiographical writings, of the encyclopedic collections that foreshadow the modern search for knowledge for its own sake, and of those shorter and simpler annals that mark the beginning of intimate life-writing and earn for biography a place as a branch of literature, the following pages will be devoted.

For valuable suggestions and criticism, the writer is indebted to Dr. P. S. Allen, President of Corpus Christi College, Oxford, to Mr. George Gordon, President of Magdalen, to Mr. Kenneth Sisam of the Clarendon Press, to Professors Robert K. Root, Morris W. Croll, and Duane R. Stuart of Princeton University, and particularly to Professor D. Nichol Smith of the University of Oxford.

Princeton, New Jersey
March 31, 1930

CONTENTS

CHAPTER I

THE MEDIAEVAL PERIOD — 700-1500

CONTENTS

CHAPTER IV

IZAAK WALTON

CHAPTER V

INTIMATE BIOGRAPHY

CHAPTER VI

THE AUTOBIOGRAPHY

CHAPTER VII

A CRITICAL SURVEY

CONTENTS

ENGLISH BIOGRAPHY

Thus one generation succeeds another, both in their lives, recreations, hopes, fears, and deaths.

Izaak Walton,
Life of Sir Henry Wotton

I

THE MEDIAEVAL PERIOD
700–1500

Put not your hope in your worldly good.
SIR DAVID LYNDSAYE

THIS chapter will treat biographies written in England from the time of Bede to the time of Sir Thomas More. The eight centuries between 700 and 1500 will thus be viewed at a glance. Such brevity does not imply a lack of life histories written during the mediaeval period. It indicates, however, that biography as an art was static in the Middle Ages. The Latin models for the chroniclers and hagiographers were fixed, and developments or modifications in the practice of writing lives were rare.

Mediaeval English biography, therefore, will here be described as something comparatively solid, permanent, and unchanging, as a background for the diversity and richness of the biographies written in England after the Renaissance.

The biographies of the Middle Ages are self-contained. Their relation to modern life-writing is slight and may adequately be considered in an introductory chapter. Yet in themselves mediaeval lives are impressive because of their mass and their uniform cast and purpose. They are interesting in their own right, entirely apart from their relation to later methods of composing lives. They reflect the corporate spirit and the faith of the

Middle Ages: their heroes are ideal figures rather than individuals; the lives are didactic.

The subjects for mediaeval English biography may be found among the leaders in church and state. The two first forms of biography in England, therefore, are devotional and historical. And of the two, the devotional biography is by far the more important, and the saint's life becomes the typical biographical form of the Middle Ages.

A saint's life is a moral biography. Since it deals with the history of a holy man, it is unsuccessful if it is not edifying, and imperfect if it does not teach Christian virtue and strengthen Christian faith. The mediaeval biographers, particularly those at a distance from their subject, were conscious of a difference between a saint and an ordinary man. The professional duties of the saint, if they may be so designated, consisted not only in living in the most exemplary and pious fashion, but also in performing miracles, in healing the sick, in foretelling the future, and in giving varied and miraculous signs of holiness. Considered as a work of art, therefore, no piece of hagiography is complete without supernatural anecdotes, for without such divine favor, a saint is not a saint, but a mere virtuous man.

Viewed as a dispassionate and objective chronicle, however, the saint's life meets with little sympathy to-day. The curing of a paralytic, which the mediaeval mind ascribed to God, is now explained as an emotional stimulus causing a physiological reflex, and ultimately, it is believed, may be reduced to the interaction of ions. Between the sceptical modern and the credulous mediaeval attitudes there is a gulf apparently so wide that a discussion of saints' lives will be fruitless unless the sincerity of the mediaeval writer is acknowledged at the outset.

There is one difference immediate and arresting between the mediaeval conception of biography and our own. We consider the biographer not as one who generalizes, but as one who individualizes. *Il ne classe pas; il déclasse.* He seeks, and has sought since Boswell, not the ideal, but the characteristic. This eagerness for particulars would not have been easily understood by the early biographers. During the Middle Ages the office or position, rather than the individual, frequently attracts the biographer, so that Bede writes his *Historia Abbatum*, or Matthew Paris his *Vitae Viginti trium Abbatum S. Albani*, or Gervase of Canterbury his *Actus Pontificum Cantuariensis Ecclesiae.* The tendency toward generalized biography is most marked in the development of saints' lives. In this particular literary type, the standard becomes strictly formalized. In the common popular biographies the saints lose their individual characters and tend to merge in a single ideal figure.

The typical life is reducible to a pattern. Direct characterization is slight and is usually formal. The figure of the saint is drawn by means of a mosaic of small anecdotes of action. For this reason, *Acta Sanctorum* becomes a fitting title for the collections. The life of a saint, to the orthodox mediaeval writer, could not be described by presenting his personal appearance, his thoughts, his peculiar bent of mind, the development of his opinions, his debt to society or his influence upon history. The life of a saint was a collection of his deeds.

Too much stress can scarcely be laid upon the fact that a saint's biography is a work for edification. The

incidents are chosen, the anecdotes amplified or cur-
tailed, with the sole purpose of encouraging the reader
to seek good and shun evil. Each history is a series of
sermons centred upon a single figure and affording, in
the phrase of John of Tynemouth, *vivendi efficacissima
exempla*. The prologue to the *Nova Legenda Angliae*, the
Golden Legend of the English saints, breaks out in such
glowing phrases as these: [1]

"O quam suavis est vita istorum sanctorum, qui duxerunt
vitas tam gloriose hic in terra! O homo, lege; et quod legeris
memento, quia (ut verum fatear) rem pulchriorem non scis
facere."

The anonymous early ninth century life of Alcuin takes
each one of its scanty incidents as a text for a disquisi-
tion on morality. Alcuin himself, in narrating the life of
Willibrord, lets slip no opportunity to drive home his
lessons. So, when he tells of the death of the unhappy
man who stole Willibrord's golden cross, he suddenly
turns to the brothers addressed throughout the biography and exclaims, "Videtis, fratres, quam terribili
damnatus iudicio, qui sancti Dei ecclesiam furtu vio-
lasse non timuit." [2] "It is permitted," he says elsewhere, "to all Christian people to celebrate the feasts of
the saints, to praise their victories, to imitate their
lives." And his enthusiastic and sustained closing chapters, with their panegyric of saintly glory, give perhaps
more clearly than any similar mediaeval writings the
purpose of the creator of such a biography. They may
be epitomized in his own phrase: "Videte, fratres karissimi, quanta gloria est Deum sequi." [3]

1. Ed. C. Horstmann, 1901, p. 7.
2. *Monumenta Alcuiniana*, 1873, p. 59.
3. *Monumenta Alcuiniana*, pp. 61–64.

Regarded as a type of literary biography, then, the saint's life has the merits of the exclusion of irrelevant materials, of concentrated unity in a central figure, and of a definite purpose. Its artistic defects, if less important than its qualities, are more numerous. The saint is not individualized. He is rarely a breathing creature. The necessary centring upon his holiness, which gives these lives admirable unity, makes characterization impossible. The result is generalized biography. Because of the limitations of its theme, duplication or reiteration of anecdotes is inevitable. In the early lives many incidents are transferred from the acts of the prophets, the apostles, and the Saviour.[4] In succeeding biographies earlier miracles are borrowed wholesale, until in the collections of the twelfth, the thirteenth, and later centuries, when conscientious hagiography was rapidly falling into decay, the memorial to a local saint is often a perfunctory patchwork of *mirabilia* plagiarized from a dozen sources.[5]

To this point saints' lives have been considered only as a type, a conventionalized form with a clear and single devotional object and a range so limited as to render sterile either creative imagination or detailed accuracy.

4. So in Bede's *Saint Cuthbert* occur parallels to the birds feeding Elijah, Moses bringing forth water from the rock, Christ calming the tempest or changing water into wine. Bede is at all times aware of his prototypes, and cites them upon occasions as additional authority for the truth of his own narrative. Thus he justifies the appearance of an angel on horseback to cure the young Cuthbert's tumor by the parallel of Raphael restoring sight to Tobias and that of the angels who came on horseback to the defence of Judas Maccabaeus and the temple of God.

5. The Bollandist, M. Hippolyte Delehaye, in *Les Légendes Hagiographiques* (1905), shows to an astonishing degree the poverty of invention among the ranks of hagiographers, the small number of stock incidents which are continually repeated because of the dearth of original materials, the borrowings from other lives, pagan parallels and survivals, adapted popular legends, and the accumulation of incidents about a single well-known figure.

It is in the exceptions to this type that the masterpieces
may be found. The great English hagiographers —
Eddius, Bede, Eadmer, Adam of Eynsham [6] — broke
away from this form, so that in their finest chapters the
saint is absorbed in the man.

The best pieces in native English hagiology before the
Norman Conquest fall within a period of less than fifty
years, between 690 and 730. The portraits of the saints
of the seventh and eighth centuries drawn so compe-
tently in contemporary biographies show the church
aggressive and expanding under the guidance of distinctive and varied leaders. The period in English ecclesiastical history is one of magnificent prelates, of bold
missionaries and revered anchorites.

Saint Columba is its precursor, and Adamnan, Abbot
of Iona, in writing the *Vita Columbae* at the close of the
seventh century, has produced not only one of the
earliest, but one of the most attractive biographies in
mediaeval literature. The work is full of the poetry of
Ireland, the delicate and resourceful imagination which
is most abundantly illustrated in the *Tripartite Life of
Saint Patrick*.[7] The division into three books bears witness only to Columba's qualities as a saint, and treats of
(1) prophetic revelations, (2) divine miracles, and (3)
angelic apparitions. Adamnan's pious credulity knows
no limits, and the miracles range from grandiose effects
in the Old Testament tradition to local wonders, such as
casting devils out of milk pails. Yet amid a diversity of
supernatural incidents, the figure of Columba stands
forth as a living man. Partly this illusion of reality rises

6. It is noteworthy that these biographers were either close friends and
disciples of the church dignitaries they commemorate, or were almost contemporaries, receiving their information as vivid recollections at first hand.

7. Rolls Series, 1887, 2 vols.

from the abundant detail, for each anecdote is carefully authenticated, and the names of places, actors, and narrators are given. Partly it springs from the contrasting largeness of the stage. Against a dark background of unfriendly elements and mysterious pagan priests whom Columba must blast, the saint is portrayed with sympathy and reverence. Across more than twelve centuries the beautiful and detailed account of his last days on earth is still fresh: Columba's farewell to the old white horse, the last journey to the hilltops of Iona, the relinquishing of the transcription of the Psalter after the lines, "Inquirentes autem Dominum non deficient omni bono," the death before the altar at midnight, which, in vivid simplicity, has rarely been surpassed:[8]

"Diormitius ergo, ecclesiam ingrediens, flebili ingeminat voce, 'Ubi es, Pater?' Et, necdum allatis fratrum lucernis, per tenebras palpans, Sanctum ante altarium recubantem invenit: quam paululum erigens, et iuxta sedens, sanctum in suo gremio posuit caput."

The sincerity and emotion of the entire biography, as well as its picturesque backgrounds, justify Montalembert in his estimate of the life of Saint Columba as "un des monuments les plus vivants, les plus attrayants, et les plus authentiques de l'histoire chrétienne."[9]

In form and in manner of treatment Bede's *Saint Cuthbert* is akin to Adamnan's *Columba*. Both are largely composed of a multitude of unconnected miracles. Each writer has been painstaking in his verification of his incidents. Both Bede and Adamnan were conscientious and careful. Yet, of the two, Bede was the more cautious. We do not find so frequently in his work

8. Ed. J. T. Fowler, 1894, p. 159.
9. *Les Moines d'Occident*, 1860–77.

such miracles as that recorded in Adamnan's third book, where he narrates how a brother falling from a housetop is caught up by angels before he strikes the ground. Bede's miracles are more homely. Many of them can be explained by natural causes. So, for example, Cuthbert learns that he is to become a bishop when the Lord speaks through the mouth of a child: a conceivable happening. He heals a damsel of a pain in her side by anointing her with oil: common medical practice. He is fed on a journey when his horse pulls down from a thatched roof a napkin containing bread: possibly irritating to the peasant who placed it there. He digs a well and water fills it: proof of God's bounty. He changes water into wine by taste only: this may show no more than the taster's will to believe. The unusual predominance of such "natural miracles" is in itself a tribute to Bede's accurate observation and historical sense, doubly important because of his faith in *all* miracles. For this reason, even in a *vita* surcharged with the supernatural, Bede may be considered, relative to his contemporaries, an accurate transcriber of the incidents of a life, with little attempt at imaginative embellishment.

In one chapter,[10] which includes the account of Cuthbert's patience in controlling the Lindisfarne monks, Bede presents a sustained attempt at pure character drawing. Yet the personality of Cuthbert seems to escape him, and it is only at rare intervals (as in the farewell of Benedict and Sigfrid in the *Historia Abbatum*, which is like the frescoes of Giotto in its quality of serene seriousness) that this master of historical panorama approaches Adamnan in enthusiastic and sympathetic characterization.

10. Chap. 16.

Bede's sense of biographical values is demonstrated in his condensation of Cuthbert's life to fit the perspective of his *Ecclesiastical History*.[11] In this briefer account the historian omits the commonplace and trivial miracles. Two, however, are added — the cures of paralysis and of an ocular tumor by means of the saint's relics. Evidently they occurred after the life of Cuthbert had been written, and seemed to Bede important enough to be included in this later work. In the main these short chapters in the *History* are confined to the historical events of Cuthbert's life. The account of his itinerant preaching around Melrose, the simultaneous deaths of the saint and his disciple Herebyrht, the disinterment of the body undecayed eleven years after burial — such incidents are transcribed from the earlier, fuller life with changes of only a few words and with little condensation. The impression remains that Bede did not distinguish in his mind between history and biography, as did Eadmer, for example, four centuries later. For Bede, the individual was a part of the historical scene, and history was composed of a series of interrelated life narratives. Bede the biographer follows the art of Bede the historian.[12]

After the sudden flowering of English hagiology in the early years of the eighth century, nothing of importance in the development of the saint's life as a literary form occurred before the Norman Conquest. Worthy works are written — Willibald's *Boniface* (ca. 755-786), Alcuin's *Willibrord* (ca. 782-789, ante 793), the anonymous *Vita Oswaldi* (995-1005), certain of the lives of Dunstan. They may be considered, in Bishop Stubbs'

11. Plummer, *Baedae Opera Historica*, vol. i (1896), chaps. 27-32.
12. For other outstanding biographies of this period, see Eddius' *Life of Wilfred*, the anonymous first life of Gregory the Great (ca. 713), and Felix of Crowland's *Life of Guthlac*.

phrase,[13] as "the memorials of the best men of the time written by the best scholars of the time," but they follow the old models and rarely display originality.

The coming of the Normans introduces a new attitude toward the writing of saints' lives. Style is still diligently cultivated, as it was — usually with less felicity — even among the first English hagiologists. The old gravity and mystery is supplanted by a spirit curious, practical, and vivacious. The saints are transformed into men of the world, astute politicians. Character drawing becomes an art. The great biographers of the twelfth and thirteenth centuries — William of Malmesbury, Eadmer, Adam of Eynsham — made the writing of lives something more than accidental; they endeavored deliberately to compass the full portrait of a man, and give to it depth through the use of shadow. They delighted in fine nuances of character that would not have appealed to their downright precursors. Biography as the conscious and unified record of a life became for the first time a literary form, and Giraldus Cambrensis, Eadmer, and Adam of Eynsham may be considered as early masters of a new type of anecdotal biography.

Eadmer (1060–1143?) is particularly fortunate not only because he has the receptive temperament of a good biographer, but also because in Anselm, with whom he had the privilege of close association through many years, he found a figure worthy of his powers. His *De Vita et Conversatione Anselmi Archiepiscopi Cantuariensis* comes nearer to the Boswellian type of biography than does any similar piece of work in the whole Middle Ages. "Not only," he says in the preface, "will I record

13. *Memorials of St. Dunstan*, 1874, Rolls Series.

the events of his life, but also whatever it contains which
seems of importance regarding his private conversation,
his own distinctive traits, or the display of his miracles." [14] These conversations of Archbishop Anselm's
are not, in the main, such records of public disputes as
Eddius in the eighth century recorded for Bishop Wilfred, but seek rather to reconstruct the reflections, the
table-talk, of one of the most brilliant conversationalists
and subtle thinkers of that age. They treat of such
themes as the education of the young without corporal
punishment, or of Anselm's preference for the company
of youths rather than of old men or children, since
their minds are capable of receiving impressions like
wax which is neither too soft nor too hard. The work
abounds in "minute and telling details of vivid personality." [15] Only from intimate acquaintance could
Eadmer have learned that as a child Anselm had believed that heaven rested upon the mountains above
Aosta. Through such simple personal touches, and
through the varied conversations, Eadmer brings out
the fineness of his patron and hero, this "mitissimus
hominum sui temporis qui habitabant in terra." But
the author excels in large dramatic incidents as well as in
minute observation. Outside the lives of Becket, there
are few scenes in early biography as vivid as the encounter in 1093 between William Rufus, who considered
himself to be on his deathbed, and Anselm, already
advanced in years and now to be created an archbishop
by a monarch inconveniently repentant. The contrast
between the blustering king, plagued by counsellors,

14. ". . . adeo quicquam in se contineat quod ad privatam conversationem,
vel ad morum ipsius Anselmi qualitatem . . . pertinere videatur." Ed. Rolls
Series, 1884, p. 313.
15. Rolls Series, 1884, ed. Martin Rule, Preface.

fitfully stubborn or frightened, and the tall, pale nobility of the priest, forcibly dragged off to be consecrated in an unwelcome office, is sketched with admirable craftsmanship. Even the favorite oath of William
the Red is not omitted.[16]

Most important to our study is the proof that Eadmer
produced such a notable work with deliberate artistic
purpose, and with a consciousness of the difference between history and biography. His *Historia Novorum in
Anglia*, extending from the death of William the Conqueror to 1122, is in fact little more than an account of
the political events of his own time as they affected
Anselm or were affected by him. It is an *Acta Anselmi*,
a life-and-times history, containing many of the incidents included in the *De Vita et Conversatione*. The
ordinary mediaeval historian would have considered it
thoroughly adequate as a *vita*. To Eadmer it was not
enough, and he wrote in addition a distinctive and separate work. He determined to create a memorial to
Anselm as he knew him, a more intimate record which
was to include the *privatam conversationem*, the *morum
ipsius Anselmi qualitatem*. The result entitles Eadmer
to the distinction of being considered as the first English
biographer in the modern spirit.

In his *Life of Geoffrey, Archbishop of York*, written
early in the thirteenth century, that master of entertaining histories, Giraldus Cambrensis, produced a
study of brotherly quarrels and church strife which de-
parts from the well-trodden paths of saintly life-writing
and approaches the type of royal biography. In a

16. That such details appealed to the Norman mind may be deduced from
the inclusion of the same incident and the same oath — *per sanctum vultum de
Luca* — in William of Malmesbury's adaptation of the life.

slighter degree this tendency is observable in all the best
original lives of the ecclesiastics of the period, where the
leader in the church was so frequently a leader in the
state. Giraldus narrates the career of this natural son of
Henry II without exaggerated praise. Thus, while he
will extol Geoffrey's loyalty in remaining with his dying
father while his retainers deserted the king and fled, he
will not hesitate to indicate Geoffrey's truculence and
overbearing pride, when, in disgrace with fortune, he
persists in having the archbishop's cross carried before
him, even though it necessitates travel along unfre-
quented lanes in order to avoid his opponents. Gerald
is at all times a conscious artist, and points out in his
preface that the ensuing work will show how virtue often
passes without reward. "I see," he says, "the evil and
the ill-deserving suddenly raised to the heights." This
air of the philosophic spectator he maintains throughout
the work, thus anticipating Boccaccio and Lydgate and
the sixteenth-century verse biographers in their view
of the life of the great as a tragedy of fortune.[17]

In its details Gerald's *Life of Geoffrey* is also original.
Many of the saintly biographies had contained character sketches of unstinted praise. In this life, with
his usual exuberance, the author has employed his vo-
cabulary of vituperation in the portrait of Geoffrey's
enemy, William Longchamp, Bishop of Ely, and has
created a personage who combines the traits of a Sue-
tonian emperor and a cathedral gargoyle. The descrip-

17. "Ubi & frangi superbum omne proclivique ab alto ruina descendere,
neque prosperitatem stabilem, nec aerumnam in tempore pertinacem esse
comperietur. Sic etenim nihil hic stabile, nihil hic permanens plasmavit con-
ditor ille; ut & eo vanitatis indicio mentes hominum, quoniam varium &
mutabile quicquid cernimus, ad vera perpetuaque bona efficacius provocet &
invitet." Prologus, lib. II, ed. Wharton, *Anglia Sacra*, 1691, p. 389.

tion verges upon caricature, and as an early example of a
hostile and bitter character sketch, the entire paragraph
is so unusual as to merit quotation: [18]

"Erat itaque statura exigua despectaque, et clune claudus
utroque; capite grosso, et tanquam simiam simulans usque ad
cilia fere fronte pilosa; colore nigerrimus, nigris ocellis et
confossis, naribus simis, facie canina, barba comaque infra
supraque lumine tenus hispida tota; mento reflexo, simula-
toque risui et ficto continuoque fere oris rictui, quem in dolo
praeferebat, valde accommodo; collo contracto, pectore gib-
boso, ventre praeambulo, renibus retrogradis, tibiis tortis, et
in modico corpore pes immensus. Quid plura?"

The description of the mental vices of Longchamp is
even more extended and equally savage. It draws on
Gerald's reserves of classical knowledge, quotes Seneca,
and contains this summary after the manner of Livy: [19]

"Ad haec etiam nullum ei jusjurandum, nulla fides, nulla
religio: puta cui falsitatibus atque fallaciis funditus addicto,
nihil minus menti quam non mentiri, nihil fas nisi nefas, nihil
aequum praeter iniquum videbatur."

Shortly after the close of the twelfth century the
Magna Vita Sancti Hugonis was written, probably by
Adam, Bishop of Eynsham from 1212 to 1225. This is
one of the longest of mediaeval biographies.[20] Like the
majority of saints' lives, it was written at ecclesiastical
command, in this case at the request of the monks of
Witham. In spite of the length, the writer confesses
that his work is not a complete life, for he has omitted
what others have already recorded. Moreover, who
could write the whole life of such a worthy? Who could

18. Ed. J. S. Brewer, iv, 420, Rolls Series, 1861–77.
19. Vol. iv, 423–424.
20. Its text occupies 378 pages in the Rolls Series.

even comprehend it? How could one do justice to the "vitae illius et morum sinceritatem, seu suavitatem, seu sanctitatem, seu singularem in tot gratiae spiritualibus charismatibus eminentiam quam talibus"?

The narrative is rich in picturesque and vivid incidents, most of which are derived from the author's own knowledge of Bishop Hugh.[21] The prologue to Book III shows the growing regard for thoughts and opinions as parts of a life, for it proposes to treat "praecipua gestorum ejus atque verborum" and is composed "ex ejusdem actibus et memorabilibus dictis." Chapter thirteen of this book is in effect a seventeenth-century "character" written in Latin some four hundred years before its time. No foible or peculiar trait is too insignificant to escape the eye of the biographer, who describes Hugh's hilarity at table, his love of children, his penchant for burials even while royalty waits, his firm friendship with Henry II, his conversations on journeys, his failing eyesight, his disapproval of too much fasting, his sense of obligation toward his parishes. We even learn of Hugh's delight in washing the kitchen scuttles.[22] His bluffness and bluntness and integrity are at all times apparent, and the scene of his reconciliation with King Richard in the church at La Roche d'Andeli, where he insists upon a royal kiss, is dramatically told. His was an independent spirit, and when on Hugh's sickbed Archbishop Hubert suggests that he ask pardon for provoking his senior, Hugh declares his intention of giving even more frequent cause for provocation in the future,

21. The preface to Book II assures us that for three years and five days before the Bishop's death "nunquam nisi per unam solam noctem abfui comitatu" and goes on to state that what the book contains "aut propriis vidi oculis, aut a sanctis ipsius labiis audivi."

22. Book IV, chap. 10.

if his life is spared. Adam's hero is a man *integer vitae*, of complete candor and independence. His biographer has portrayed him faithfully. In title the work is a saint's life, but in fact it is neither a life of a saint or a bishop as such, but the life of an individual. The man, not his perfection, is the focal centre of this biography. The miraculous element almost disappears. Hugh himself professed a scorn for miracles: "cum illi sola esset sanctorum sanctitas pro miraculo, sola sufficeret pro exemplo." With this phrase, written at the beginning of the thirteenth century, this study of Latin saints' lives as conscious and serious attempts at biography may well close, for it indicates a change in attitude, and a step forward toward the biographical ideal of the Renaissance.

The hagiographies that have thus far received specific mention have been included for two reasons: either they are notable for their actual biographical contents, or they show conscious principles on which certain biographers built their work. Saints' lives that more faithfully represent the whole mediaeval hagiographical tradition[23] have been passed over because of their slight interest as pure biographies. The emphasis in the typical Latin saint's life is upon *mirabilia* rather than *memorabilia*. This emphasis is even more pronounced in the hagiographies written in the vernacular, largely because they were addressed to a popular audience.[24] As far back as

23. Such as Felix of Crowland's *Guthlac* or Osbern's *Dunstan*. In a longer survey certain of these lives might well be studied in relation to mediaeval attempts at describing mental conflicts and psychological crises by means of concrete symbols — miracles and dreams, angels and demons.

24. This might be deduced from the fact that they are translated from a learned into a vulgar tongue. That this translation was at times done unwillingly, or at least with some misgivings and only after repeated urgings,

the middle of the ninth century may be found a Martyrology in Old English, drawn from Bede, Gregory of Tours, and the Roman Martyrology,[25] and from the days of Cynewulf and Aelfric until hagiography as a fine art had faded, there was no dearth of saints' legends in English.

Yet the increase in vernacular legends was by no means steady. At the opening of the eleventh century such a scholar as Aelfric condescends to write saints' lives in Old English,[26] but in the two centuries following the Conquest the tide flows noticeably the other way, and the translations are generally from English into Latin rather than from Latin into English.[27] From this

---

may be argued from the Latin preface to Aelfric's *Homilies*, whose thirty-nine chapters include the lives of several English saints:

"Non mihi inputetur quod divinam scripturam nostrae lingue infero, quia arguet me praecatus multorum fidelium et maxime aethelwerdi ducis et aethelmeri nostri, qui ardentissime nostras interpretationes amplectuntur lectitando." Ed. Skeat, E. E. T. S., Orig. Ser. lxxvi, 1881, p. 4.

Aelfric is not the only writer who performed such translation at the request of others rather than spontaneously. Lydgate's attempt in verse "to wryte the perfytenes of the holy martyr" Saint Alban followed the solicitations of a patron uncle.

25. E. E. T. S., Orig. Ser. vol. cxvi.

26. Ed. Skeat, E. E. T. S., Orig. Ser. lxxvi, 1881.

27. William of Malmesbury in his *Life of Wulfstan* draws attention to his vernacular source: "Is erit Colemannus Monachus vester; vir nec scientia imperitus, nec sermone patrio infacetus. Scripsit enim Anglice, ne gestorum avolaret memoria, Vitam ejusdem Patris." Wharton, *Anglia Sacra*, ii, 242.

Thomas of Ely, writing after 1175, states that his Latin life of Etheldreda is translated from an Anglo-Saxon biography.

The prevalence of Old English lives before the Conquest and the current practice of translating them back into Latin is indicated by Osbern in the prologue to his *Vita Sancti Dunstani*, wherein he alludes to a fire, about the year 1070, in the church at Canterbury, from which few manuscript lives were saved: "Sed ab his, inquiunt, aliqua in patrium, id est, in Anglicum sermonem translata supersunt; ex quibus id quod petimus elicere; & in Latinam denuo poteris linguam Deo suffragante transferre." *Ang. Sac.*, ii, 89.

Eadmer drew from the same English original in his own Latin life of Dunstan.

burial of the older English in the ignorance and indifference of the Anglo-Norman period, from two centuries of Latin writings, rise the great Northern and
Southern Legendaries at the close of the thirteenth century, written almost in another language. The purpose
of the saints' lives, as well as the language, had changed
by this time. Popular saints' lives ceased gradually to
be biographies and became diverting histories. Hagiography, one of the main currents of mediaeval literature,
mingled with other currents, blended with the romances
and the chronicles,[28] and introduced material drawn
from the Northern sagas, the fabliaux, and the literature
of the Mediterranean.[29] The demand for large miscellaneous collections of saints' lives in the vulgar tongue
did not flag. Caxton's *Golden Legend* (1483) was among
the first books from his press. In 1516 Pynson published a translation in English of the Latin *Nova Legenda
Angliae* attributed to Capgrave.

Beside the extended collections between the Norman
Conquest and the Renaissance, single saints' lives were
composed in the vernacular, usually in verse, by such
authors as John Barbour, Chaucer, Lydgate, Osbern
Bokenam, and John Capgrave.[30] These lives, written by
some of the foremost literary figures of the period, show
a dead level of uniformity. Their heroes are not con-
ceived as individuals, and the stock anecdotes, of Ursula

28. Cf. the various lives of Edward the Confessor or the martyred King
Edmund. Also C. Horstmann's *Sammlung altenglischer Legenden*, 1875; *Life
and Miracles of Saint William of Norwich*, ed. A. Jessopp and M. R. James,
1896; *Symeon of Durham*, Rolls Series, vol. i, Appendix II.

29. Cf. H. Delehaye, *Les Légendes Hagiographiques*, 1905.

30. Lydgate's *Albon and Amphabel*, his *Margaret*, and his *Edmund and
Fremund*, Capgrave's *St. Katherine of Alexandria*, and Osbern Bokenam's
Lyvys of Seyntys represent the best work in this *genre*, and are followed as
late as 1513 by Henry Bradshaw's *St. Werburge of Chester*.

or Cuthbert or Edmund, have little biographical value. Miraculous or romantic incidents are dominant throughout. Yet Chaucer considered his life of Saint Cecilia of sufficient merit to mention it specifically in his list of his own writings, and it may be regarded as typical of the saints' lives of the period, a late example in a biographical form which had undergone only slight modifications since the days of the Conquest. However charming the saints' lives of the fourteenth and fifteenth centuries may be as imaginative narratives, they add little to the history of English biography.[31] The older hagiographies lose their cumulative anecdotes of sanctity in Lydgate's verse, and the fragrant poetry of Chaucer's Christian choir-boy in the Jewry may also be found in such a graceful piece as Lydgate's *Legend of Dan Joos*,[32] who daily prayed five Latin Psalms to Mary, forsook the world, died, and was found in a convent with five roses growing from his mouth, eyes, and ears, roses lettered in gold with the name of Maria.

These examples from the almost untravelled, and at times the very flat, field of mediaeval English hagiology are cited as indices to show that the development of lives in Latin was accompanied by a like development in English, and that, in the centuries after the battle of Hastings, saints' lives became common property [33] and

31. Bede's sober spirit of truthfulness, even when narrating astounding miracles, is not to be found in the variations on the life of Saint Cuthbert which occur in English verse. For three versions, written respectively about 1285–95, about 1450, and in the fifteenth centuty, see *The Life of St. Cuthbert in English Verse*, ed. J. T. Fowler for the Surtees Society, 1891.

32. Cf. Lydgate's *Minor Poems*, ed. H. N. MacCracken, E. E. T. S., 1911, Ex. Ser., vol, cvii.

33. That the demand for such biographies was widespread is evident from the study of any single legend, such as Bertha E. Lovewell has made of Saint Cecilia. In various versions it is preserved in ten Middle English manuscripts, dating from 1300 to the fifteenth century. "It is also found in

formed an important part of the writings of mediaeval England.

But as the lives increased in popularity they decreased in value as biographies. The attempt to portray character was almost forgotten; even the didactic purpose was made subordinate to the desire to tell an astonishing story. With Robert of Gloucester, Bokenam, Lydgate, and the translators of John of Tynemouth, Capgrave, Jacobo da Voragine, and Gregory of Tours, the saints' lives became a religious Arabian Nights Entertainment for every day of the year, popular *novelle* with a moralizing bias. As types of serious biography they ceased to exist.

Contemporaneous with the numerous hagiographies in mediaeval England, rose another great group of writings from which modern biography springs. This group is contained in the chronicles. Just as the devotional spirit showed itself in the lives of the saints, the historical spirit took biographical form in the lives of the kings. One difference, however, may be noted. Although among the saints' lives several are of worth as biography and as literature, among the mediaeval royal lives there is none. As biographers Asser and Capgrave cannot stand in the same rank with Adamnan, Eadmer, and Adam of Eynsham.

In spite of the relatively great importance of biography in the Anglo-Saxon period, the lives of kings are

the Early English of Alfred's *Book of Martyrs*, in Aelfric, *Saints' Lives* Ms Cott(on) Jul(ius) E VII, in the *Second Nonnes Tale* of Chaucer, 1373, in Osbern Bokenam's *Lives of Saints*, Ms. Arundel 327, 1443–6, and in Caxton's *Golden Legend*, 1483." (*The Life of St. Cecilia*, 1898.) All these versions exist for the life of one saint, about whom no particularly popular cult had arisen. When we consider that one of the manuscripts in which the Cecilia history occurs contains 135 legends, another 94, and a third 50, it is plain that the Middle Ages did not lack popular biographies.

few in number apart from the hagiographies; and the heroes remain almost invariably churchmen rather than rulers.[34] The great and almost the sole exemplar of early English royal lives is Asser's *Alfred*. Written in Latin about the year 893, it is the first instance extant in England of the life of a layman.[35] In many respects the life of Alfred is unnecessarily clumsy, even for a period which lacked models for the biography of kings. Its construction indicates the close connection which existed throughout the Middle Ages between the chronicle and the royal biography. It is in great part a mere patchwork of events translated from the Anglo-Saxon Chronicle, beginning with the year 851, "which was the third of King Alfred's life." Much in these annals is irrelevant, and long digressions confirm the impression that structural skill is lacking and that Asser cannot be considered even a passable architect in biography. Furthermore, in

34. The complete ascendance of saints' lives during the early period determines the subjects for the first royal biographies. Thus there exists, in manuscripts in the Cottonian and Bodleian libraries, a separate life of Saint Edwin, King and Martyr, largely extracted from Bede. (Printed in Capgrave's *Nov. Leg. Angl.*) This legend became popular in various forms, and Edwin's piety, his conversion to Christianity under the influence of his wife Aethelburh, and the miracles performed at his shrine soon became common property. But he is more than a saint; he is also king of Northumbria; and though canonized, his death occurred in a battle against the Mercians and the Welsh. The same delight in hagiology influenced the popularity of all the kings before the Conquest, so that lives of Edward the Martyr (963?–78) and of Edward the Confessor will greatly outnumber the biographies of a more important king, such as Alfred.

35. The biographer, however, was a churchman. In the *Annales Cambriae* for 908 Asser is mentioned as Bishop of Sherborne, and that he was an esteemed companion of Alfred's, as well as a coworker with him in his educational projects, may be deduced not only from the life itself but from the preface to Alfred's translation of the *Pastoral Care*, which refers to Asser as "minum biscepe." The authenticity of the work has been called in question, but its most recent editor, W. H. Stevenson, considers it probably genuine. Unfortunately the single manuscript in which it had been preserved was destroyed in 1731 and cannot be of assistance in refuting the suspicion that the work is spurious.

those parts which are pertinent and personal, Asser repeats himself. Thus Alfred's inherent physical infirmity and his love of learning are reiterated without much purpose and almost in the same phrases.

Asser begins ambitiously with his king's genealogy from the time of Adam, and follows it with excerpts from the Chronicle. When at last, in Chapter 22, he considers Alfred as an individual rather than as an animate calendar under whom certain events took place, his work becomes of importance and originality. In addition to the conventional encomium, he dwells upon such characteristic qualities as Alfred's love of wisdom, his attraction toward native poetry, and his pleasure in hunting. He narrates an anecdote of the king's childhood, Alfred's memorizing a book of old English poems. His bravery and skill in war are given their due place. The piety of the monarch is exemplified by mention of the Book of Hours he carried in his bosom. The religious and moralizing note is not absent from this biography by the Bishop of Sherborne. Alfred's unknown and painful diseases are accordingly treated as afflictions sent by God for the preservation of his chastity and humility.

The history is full of faults. It does not consistently hold to its expressed aim of narrating the life, manners, and conversation, as well as the acts of its hero.[36] A great portion of it is an extraneous and copied chronicle; relevant sections are told and retold; the style, when it attempts formality, assumes a turgid Welsh exuberance, as in Asser's simile of the bee.[37] Yet the originality of

36. Chap. 73, p. 54, ed. W. H. Stevenson, Oxford, 1904.

37. In chap. 76, Asser describes Alfred seeking thirstily after wisdom and wise men, "velut apis prudentissima, quae primo mane caris e cellulis consurgens aestivo tempore, per incerta aeris itinera cursum veloci volatu diri-

the life outweighs its defects. Because it is a pioneer attempt to picture a brave and wise ruler, "eager in the investigation of unknown things," and because it succeeds in portraying his versatility as a warrior, a judge, a patron of learning, and a founder of monasteries, Asser's *Life of Alfred* honorably assumes its place as the first of the biographies of the English kings and queens.[38]

After the Norman Conquest, chronicles and histories increased in number and importance, and with them royal lives. Growing interest in secular and political affairs, the practical sense of the Normans, the rise of large religious foundations,[39] encouraged local and national historians. The numerous histories, copied and abridged and amended, ranged from bare annals and brief chronicles of dates to the imaginative fabric of Geoffrey of Monmouth, the comprehensive surveys of Matthew Paris, or the detailed partizan accounts of the Becket biographers.

Yet, in spite of the great number of histories written between the Norman Conquest and the sixteenth century, England produced no royal biography of major importance. It was the age of the chronicle, and the chronicler's method of narrating history in a series of minute incidents unrelated except in point of time, the chronicler's disregard for literary and logical form, the chronicler's provincialism and near-sightedness, vitiate

gens, super multiplices ac diversos herbarum, holerum, fruticum flosculos descendit, probatque quid maxime placuerit atque domum reportat. . . ."

38. See also Aelfric's Old English lives (ca. 997) of Saint Oswald, king of the Northumbrians, and Saint Edmund, martyred king of the East Angles. Abbo of Fleury had also written a life of Edmund in Latin (986).

39. At Saint Alban's a school of history flourished without interruption and maintained official historiographers.

to some extent the writings of even the best historians of the period, such as Matthew Paris or William of Malmesbury. In the approximations to royal biography, the monarch was reduced at best to a position as leader or arbiter in factional disputes; at worst he was used, as the Roman consuls were used, as a convenient means for distinguishing chronologically the occurrences in his realm. The life of a king was written as the diary of his kingdom, an almanac of observations on the weather, local politics, and warfare, marshalled according to the years of his reign. The Middle Ages had no standard for royal biography. Their substitute, the chronicle, lacked the unity which is secured in histories dominated by a spirit of intense partizanship, by a philosophy, or by a central and absorbing figure.

The material of the chronicles may at times be selected and rewritten as a biography, but the changes are seldom made in accordance with a definite plan, and the treatment remains that of the annalist. Such lives as the *Vitae duorum Offarum* of Matthew Paris, the anonymous twelfth-century *Gesta Stephani*, or the *Vita et Mors Edwardi II* attributed to Thomas de la Moore fall far short of adequate biography.[40]

The item in mediaeval royal biography which possesses the highest literary value is Lydgate's *Fall of*

40. Occasionally the royal memory will be preserved in an unusual form: in a funeral elegy such as that by John of London on Edward I; in Latin or Norman-French verse, as in some of the lives of Edward the Confessor; in the romantic and anonymous *Vita Haroldi* (ca. 1200); or in Blakman's extended character sketch of Henry VI (ca. 1436–48). At times these unusual contributions approach biography. The contemporary, anonymous *Versus Rhythmici de Henrico Quinto* is unified and well-rounded, while occasional longer histories, such as the *Gesta Regum Anglorum* by William of Malmesbury (d. 1143) and the *Historia Rerum Anglicarum* of William of Newbury, proceed almost as a series of connected biographies.

Princes. The voluminous works of this monk of St. Edmund's again illustrate the close connection between the royal chronicles and the saints' lives. In form and in manner of treatment, there is no great gap between Lydgate's *Glorious Lyfe and Passion of Saint Albon* and his *Fall of Princes.* His source for the latter is in prose; yet he translates it in the style of common verse lives, a style developed through metrical translations of the *Acta Sanctorum.* The lives of the saints had emphasized an ethical note, and Lydgate's lives of tyrants and emperors do not abandon it. The moral, however, must be changed, in substituting the great ones of the earth for the Christian martyrs. The central philosophy around which these lives cluster is essentially mediaeval; yet it continues to inspire and dominate the verse lives of the entire sixteenth century, and, in Cavendish's life of Wolsey, passes into English prose and modern biography.

This dominant idea is the uncertainty of worldly riches and worldly power. Ostensibly *The Fall of Princes* teaches resignation and the conquering of pride. Its philosophy is fatalism; its motto *Vanitas vanitatum.* Lydgate does not originate the conception,[41] though the uniform melancholy of his nature and his dignified and unobtrusive disregard for the world tinge this endless poem with his own personality. Lydgate is certain of the scope of his work:[42]

41. He draws from Laurence de Premierfait's French prose translation, completed by 1400, of Boccaccio's *De Casibus Virorum Illustrium* (1355–60), and it is therefore in Boccaccio that the idea finds its first literary expression in this form, though the general conception is as old as Boethius. For example, a parallel to the spirit of *The Fall of Princes* has already been pointed out in the *Life of Geoffrey of York* by Giraldus Cambrensis.

42. Book IX, lines 3450–56. Ed. H. Bergen, E. E. T. S., Ex. Ser. 1924.

"This book remembryng of the sodeyn fallys
Off famous prynces and surquedous pryncessys,
That wer unwarly cast from ther royal stallys,
Which wer in erthe worshepyd as goddessys,
Ynde stonys upon ther goldene tressys, —
What was ther ende?   Rede Bochas, ye shall se,
By fatal spynnyng of Parchas sustryn thre."

and of its didactic lessons (lines 3485–98):

"Dysdeyneth nat to have in remembraunce,
Ye be no goddys, ye be but men mortal;
Stonde undir daungeer of Fortunys chaunce,
More lyk to towmble and more neer to fal,
Than doth a beggere in this lyff mortal:
Off vertuous poore the fal is nat unsoffte;
Moost grevous fal, of them that sitte aloffte.

"Ye Princes quake, stond not in suyche caas;
Yit when deth comyth, ye can no bet socour
Than can the pore, record of Iohn Bochas;
Hath mynde heron and make yow a merour
Off suych as regnyd in glorye and (gret) honour
As ryche Cyrus and Sardanapalle,
How fro the wheel of Fortune they wer falle."

The idea of Fortune and her wheel, which the Middle
Ages found so fascinating that they endeavored to reconcile the goddess with Christian theology, will persist
in succeeding centuries. One of the striking illustrations
of the continuity of the biographical tradition is the
tenacity of this mournful and fatalistic mediaeval principle in the literary lives of the Renaissance, so that the
ideas of Lydgate, of Boccaccio, of Boethius, will inform
the work of Cavendish (ca. 1557), of Storer (1599), and
of Drayton (1607).

As a unique literary memorial among the royal lives
of the Middle Ages, John Capgrave's *Liber de Illustribus*

Henricis [43] is of first importance. In form it stands almost by itself, being a collection of the lives of famous individuals whose Christian name chanced to be Henry. This method of arrangement makes the collection even more fortuitous than those lives of successive abbots or archbishops of a particular foundation, which were frequent among mediaeval historians. The only connecting links between the characters of the book are their surname and their common goodness. Capgrave wrote the work as an encomium, composed it between 1446 and 1453 during the reign of Henry VI, and dedicated it to Henry VII. The subjects chosen for the lives show in striking fashion the mediaeval belief that only those of royal lineage or ecclesiastical dignity deserve an ambitious memorial. The book is divided into three parts. The first treats six emperors of the Holy Roman Empire; the second, an equal number of English kings; the third, twelve miscellaneous Henrys. Yet in this last collection of assorted dignitaries, six are royal and the others include a royal adventurer, an earl, a warlike bishop, an archdeacon, an Augustinian hermit, and a schoolman, Henry of Ghent, inserted, Capgrave states, in order "that the name of his king might be exalted by the learning of the clergy who have borne it, as well as by the renown of imperial, royal, and military Henrys."

The note of untempered praise is marked throughout, and is joined to an ever-present piety, which makes all of the Henrys good Christians during their lives or penitents before their deaths. Capgrave's belief in the inexpugnable virtues of his heroes becomes here and there strained. So, immediately after describing in detail Oldcastle's death — "primo tractus et suspensus, deinde in

43. Rolls Series, 1858.

partes divisus et evisceratus, ac postremo flammis ex-
cineratus est" — he continues without pause, "Haec
sunt acta hujus incliti, et generosi, ac Christianissimi
regis, Henrici Quinto." As the biography of a contemporary, the chapter on Henry VI is disappointing, and
contains little of interest apart from Capgrave's plea for
a navy and a few facts in his own life.

As a whole, the *Book of the Illustrious Henrys* is significant because it treats, within the confines of state and
church, a variety of men, and treats them as subsidiary
to Capgrave's governing idea: to glorify the king in the
stories of great men who had borne his name.

Capgrave made royal biography a vehicle for presenting virtuous precepts. At the beginning of the sixteenth
century the form became also a guide in statecraft and
policy. The anonymous English life of King Henry V
(1513) is more than mere eulogy. It contains "a deliberate design to apply the political lesson of the life
of Henry V to the times of Henry VIII."[44] The life,
which was evidently without effect, suggests to Henry
VIII the virtues of justice, continence, and humility.
The author draws largely from Titus Livius, yet he
adds his own moralizing in an attempt to make it useful
to his prince. His method of deriving lessons from every
incident may be illustrated by a quotation (p. 19):

'. . . amongest the first actes of his Coronacian [he] called
unto him all those younge Lordes and gentlemen that were
the followers of his younge acts, and had tofore bin most
familier with him, to everie of whome severally he gave right
rich and bounteous giftes, whereby they were all right greatly
inhaunced in substaunce. And then he commaunded them

44. C. L. Kingsford, "The First English Life of King Henry the Fifth
written in 1513 by an anonymous Author known commonly as The Translator of Livius," Oxford, 1911, Introduction, p. xlii.

that they that woulde change theire life and conversacion in like manner as he intended to doe shoulde abide with him and continewe in his Court. And to all them that woulde persever in their former light conversacion he gave expresse commaundement uppon paine of theire heads never after that daye to come to his presence. And in that he leaveth an excellent example to all Princes, as well to them that be present as to them that be comminge, to eschewe and avoide all companie that is susspect of vice."

Yet royal lives written in such exemplary fashion as Lydgate's *Fall of Princes*, Capgrave's *Henrys*, and this *Life of Henry V* are exceptional and late developments. In spite of their artistic inferiority to the saints' lives, the typical mediaeval royal lives are the true forerunners of the modern biography in their emphasis upon straight narration rather than upon moral purpose. Their aim was simple: to present events ordered and unadorned. The chronicles of kings might vary in spirit and credibility from the exuberant imagination of Geoffrey of Monmouth to the dry entries of the Anglo-Saxon Chronicle, yet the interest remained consistently in the narration rather than in any moral lesson. This concentration upon bald narrative, with little attempt at interpreting events or describing individual characters, affected royal biography deeply. To the mediaeval historian, the king was only conceivable in his capacity as ruler. His life might be adequately told by narrating the history of the kingdom during his reign. His private relations, his personality, his career before ascending the throne, were matters of little moment. In consequence, individualization in mediaeval royal biography is negligible. All the kings are alike. In Holinshed's *Chronicles* (1578) a small number of woodcuts, used time after time in rotation, suffices to give the portraits of all England's monarchs from legendary times to the sixteenth century. Such failure to differentiate between the kings is characteristic of the mediaeval sources upon which this history rests. The monarchs are interchangeable. Only a few historians — Giraldus, Malmesbury, Eadmer, Paris — knew how to draw individuals rather than generalized likenesses.

The native chronicle style in writing royal biographies survived strongly in the Renaissance and influenced even such classically schooled historians as Bacon and Hayward. The straightforward narration of the mediaeval royal biographers, as well as their lack of a didactic tone, exerted fortunate influences upon the development of biography. But the personalities of the royal heroes were presented hazily or not at all, and without individual character portrayal no form of biography can be satisfactory.

In the same year (1513) that the anonymous author of the *Life of Henry V* was composing his work, Thomas More, then under-sheriff of London, was writing his *History of Richard III*. With this brilliant study in personality, the mediaeval chronicles of kings close, and the royal biography of the Renaissance begins.

II

THE RENAISSANCE
1500–1600

Ther can be nothynge more meete for gentlemen then the readyng of histories. . . . By them we lerne to knowe howe princes and rulers of thys worlde have passed their lives.

The Institucion of a Gentleman, 1568

THE Renaissance has been described as the re-awakening of interest in the individual. Such a conception suggests its importance in the history of biography, which is the record of particular men's lives. The beginnings of English biography as we now know it, may be traced back to the varied new currents of thought introduced into England during the sixteenth century. Between the conventional saint's legend and Walton's intimate lives, between Capgrave's *Illustrious Henrys* and Bacon's *Henry VII*, between the generalized heroic portraits of Lydgate and the minute personal life-histories recorded by John Aubrey and Anthony Wood, the line of cleavage is distinct and wide.

Because it effected subtle and profound changes, the English Renaissance may be considered as an important period of transition in the history of English biography. The innovations in mode of treatment, in style, thought, and purpose, were not compassed in a few years; the entire sixteenth century, in a series of original essays in the biographical mold, introduced a new attitude and a new form, and prepared the way for the variety and complexity of lives in the seventeenth century.

The English Renaissance is a period of pioneering in the art of life-writing. The number of successful sixteenth-century biographies is small; but the number of first attempts in biographical forms later to prove most fruitful, is large. The century witnesses the translation of the principal classical biographies, with the resultant influence of classical models on expression and thought; it witnesses also the enrichment of native biography from contemporary continental sources; the growth of a national consciousness, with the accompanying searches of the antiquaries and their eager curiosity for all ascertainable facts in the lives of their countrymen; the rise of an independent and protestant religion which heralded the rich school of ecclesiastical biography in England; the increasing interest in the lives of authors, which brought about the significant use of biographies as prefaces; the new desire for written memorials to the dead, which, beginning with the printed epitaphs and poems, the funeral and university orations of the sixteenth century, expanded into the numerous and detailed seventeenth-century memoirs.

These new biographical forms are all alike manifestations of the change in spirit which has received the name of the English Renaissance. They are diverse and important. Their joint effect upon the development of English biography is the introduction of the particular. Moment, place, and person begin to be consciously differentiated; local color and the minute details of personality assume an importance unknown in mediaeval biography, wherein had been narrated, in the life of one individual, those elements which were applicable to all.

The change that overtakes biography during the Renaissance is comparable to that which takes place in portrait painting. The coldly formal Byzantine artists, the conventional mediaeval portrait painters, gave way before new generations of artists whose interest lay in the capture of exact and unmistakable likenesses. What Filippo Lippi and the Van Eycks had done, what Raphael and Dürer were doing, Hans Holbein learned to do, and introduced into England his passion for realistic portraiture. Holbein's sketches achieve concretely what the best biographers of the English Renaissance were working towards: the recording of significant and telling details which reveal personality. His drawings of the English courtiers, of Henry VIII, of Sir Thomas More and his family, come as a welcome contrast after the gloomy woodenness of mediaeval portraits.

The radical nature of the changes introduced into English biography by the Renaissance may best be studied in the work of a single figure at the beginning of the sixteenth century, Sir Thomas More, Holbein's friend and host. More's *Richard III* and *Pico della Mirandola* are both of major importance in the history of biography. Each of these works is without prototype in England, and their novel treatment cannot be understood apart from the classical culture which filled with enthusiasm Thomas More and his circle of humanists.

The Lyfe of Johan Picus, Erle of Mirandula was printed as a black-letter quarto by Wynkyn de Worde about the year 1510. Although the work is without parallel during the century in England, it must not be supposed that Thomas More departed widely from his original, the life by Pico's nephew Giovanni Francesco, or that he freed himself or desired to free himself from the traditions of the saints' lives. The *Life of Pico* is a moralizing biography of few incidents, adulatory containing little genuine individualization in spite of its enumeration of many of Mirandola's traits, which More discusses in rubric divisions, in the manner of Suetonius. It is largely concerned with his career as a pious school-man, and concentrates upon his challenge to open de-bate on any of nine hundred questions, and the analysis of his answers to the thirteen charges of heresy pre-ferred against him. The questions themselves show the boundless curiosity of the new intellectual movement.

The life is specific in giving the five reasons for Pico's enormous learning: his incredible wit, his memory, the facilities afforded him by wealth, his tirelessness, and his contempt for earthly things. "And so infatigable la-boure gave he to those studies: that yet a chylde and berdles he was bothe reputed and was in dede bothe a perfyte philosophre and a perfyte devyne." [1] Pico della Mirandola's self-imposed task was to reconcile these two ideals. Perhaps for this reason More was attracted by the kindred character of the young philosopher, im-petuous and humble, subtle and pious, loving liberty and authority, a follower equally of Plato and John the Evangelist. The biography is a strange new blend of the classical and the Christian. It narrates the attempt to graft a newly discovered Platonism on the established theology. As in a saint's life, Pico's birth is heralded by omens, just as a swarm of bees marked the birth of Saint Ambrose (p. 7): "We have oftyntymes red that suche unknowen and straunge tokens hathe gone before or foloweth the natyvytese of excellente wyse and ver-tuouse men." Yet the significance of the token is inter-preted by Platonic philosophy: "which apparence was

1. 1890, p. 9; reprinted from original edition.

peradventure a token that he whiche sholde that hour in
the companye of mortall men be borne in the perfeccion
of understandynge sholde be lyke the perfyte fygure of
that rounde cyrcle or garlande." The life is divided into
short titled chapters, not to be found in the Latin
original,[2] after the manner of the hagiographies, — "Of
the dispysynge of worldly glorye," — yet Horace is
quoted to uphold Christian virtues, and the biography
of this figure in the Italian revival of learning is rendered
into English by its distinguished translator with a purpose curiously combining classical philosophy with
Christian tenets, for it is dedicated to Joyce Leigh as a
spiritual New Year's gift, with the hope that it may be
found "profitable . . . to th'achyvynge of temperaunce
in prosperite, . . . to the purchasynge of pacience in ad-
versite . . . to the dyspysinge of worldly vanyte . . . to
the desyrynge of hevenly felycyte."

More's originality and his classical sympathies are
also evident in his life of Richard III, which is entirely
different from *Pico della Mirandola*, and even more important. *The history of King Richard the thirde* [3] affords
the finest instance of royal biography in English during
the sixteenth century. Almost alone among royal biographies, if we except the topical tracts occasioned by
the Civil Wars and the Revolution of 1688, the *Life of
Richard III* is hostile in spirit to its subject. More's
critical detachment that verges upon cool malice finds
parallels in Suetonius and Tacitus, but not among native

2. *Ioannis Pici Mirandulae Omnia Opera*, Venice, 1498.
3. Attributed to Sir Thomas More, written about the year 1513, and
published in the 1557 edition of his works in English. Along with Asser's
Life of Alfred and Cavendish's *Life of Wolsey*, its authorship has been ques-
tioned, but internal as well as external evidence returns it with a fair degree
of probability to More.

chroniclers. He may have derived his prejudice from association with John Morton, Archbishop of Canterbury, who was among Richard's adversaries and to whom the original Latin version of the life has been attributed.[4]

Throughout its length the *Life of Richard III* is more than an objective and impersonal chronicle. Philosophy and a subtle observation of mental states are for the first time consistently introduced into the art of royal biography.[5] At the very beginning, in speaking of Edward IV, the author shows himself a student of human nature: "hee was of youthe greatlye geven to fleshlye wantonnesse, from which healthe of bodye, in greate prosperitye and fortune, wythoute a specyall grace hardelye refrayneth." And again, Edward IV abandons obnoxious means of gathering revenues, for money "is the onelye thynge that withdraweth the heartes of Englyshmenne fro the Prynce."

More's homely knowledge of the reasoning of the common man is emphasized in the paragraph justifying the people's inaction after the perfunctory election of the king:[6]

"And in a stage play all the people know right wel, that he that playeth the sowdayne is percase a sowter [cobbler]. Yet

4. He may have secured a certain amount of material from the same source, a fact which is buttressed with circumstantial evidence by George Buck in his laudatory *History of Richard III* (1646, pp. 75–76). Buck mentions as a source for previous derogatory lives "Doctor Morton, who had taken his revenge that way, and written a Booke in latine against King Richard, which came afterward to the hands of Mr. Moore (sometime his servant). . . . Doctor Morton . . . made the Booke, and Master Moore . . . set it forth, amplifying and glossing it. . . . He began it 1513, when he was Undersheriffe." In the margin, regarding Morton's Latin life, Buck prints: "This Booke was lately in the hands of Mr. Roper, of Eltham, as Sir Edward Hoby who saw it told me." Roper was More's son-in-law.

5. Cf., later, *Eikon Basilike* or Henry Cary's *Edward II*.

6. 1557, fol. ed., p. 66.

if one should can so lyttle good, to shewe out of seasonne what acquaintance he hath with him, and calle him by his owne name whyle he standeth in his magestie, one of his tormentors might hap to breake his head, and worthy for marring of the play. And so they said that these matters bee Kynges games, as it were stage playes, and for the more part plaied upon scafoldes."

The paragraph just cited contains in the final lines a touch of that superior detachment and irony which distinguish the work as a whole and give it an individual piquancy in the midst of the mediocre chronicles and histories surrounding it. Specific instances in a work of this kind cannot easily be singled out for quotation, yet the entire sardonic scene of Richard's election should be noted, with its culmination in the forced speech by Buckingham begging Richard to take the crown (p. 66):

"If he woulde geve them a resolute aunswere to the contrarye, whyche they woulde bee lothe to heare, than muste they needes seke and shold not faile to fynd some other noble manne that woulde. These wordes muche moved the protectoure, which els as every manne may witte, would never of likelyhood have inclyned therunto."

Perhaps as effective as any single instance in More's terrible and sullen portrayal of the Lord Protector is the irony displayed in Richard's exaction of penance from Jane Shore (p. 56):

"And for thys cause (as a goodly continent prince clene & fautless of himself, sent oute of heaven into this vicious world for the amendement of mens maners) he caused the bishop of London to put her to open penance, going before the crosse in procession upon a sonday with a taper in her hand."

The history is unfolded with a delicacy of presentation without precedent in the thought or prose of the early sixteenth century. Shakespeare, through Holinshed, is indebted to More for the incident of the strawberries, an incident wherein Richard masks his thoughts and plans by a deft and irrelevant request for berries from the gardens of the Bishop ot Ely. This courteous and trivial conversation ushers in the tense scene of Lord Hastings' arrest as traitor. The treatment here, which demands a sense of statesmanship in the author as well as the dramatist's power to illumine a scene or a mind, is utterly foreign to the traditional lifeless narratives, and historically considered constitutes a *tour de force*, a transition from mediaeval simplicity to the complexity of the Renaissance. The maturity and surety of the writing point to classical models used with discrimination. To the little group of English scholars in which More moved, most of the Latin and Greek historians were familiar. Direct citations or quotations from Latin authors are not noticeable in the *History of Richard III*, but the characterization, the masterly handling of historical scenes and dramatic episodes, the shrewd, terse comments, point to Tacitus as a model.[7] As a final illustration of the dramatic and psychological skill of More's treatment, this paragraph may be given, dealing with the pursuit of Nemesis after the murder of the Princes in the Tower (p. 69):

"King Richarde himselfe as ye shal herafter here, slain in the fielde, hacked and hewed of his enemies handes, haryed on horsebacke dead, his here in despite torn and togged lyke a cur dogge . . . For I have heard by credible report of such as wer secrete with his chamberers, that after this abhominable deede done, he never hadde quiet in his minde, hee never

7. Perhaps the best example of More's skilful dramatic manipulation of complicated scenes may be found in his description of the London crowd after the speech by the Duke of Buckingham in favor of Richard.

thought himself sure. Where he went abrode, his eyen whirled about, his body privily fenced, his hand ever on his dager, his countenance and maner like one alway ready to strike againe, he toke ill rest a nightes, lay long wakyng and musing, sore weried with care & watch, rather slumbred then slept, troubled wyth fearefull dreames, sodeinly sommetyme sterte up, leape out of his bed & runne about the chamber, so was his restles herte continually tossed & tumbled with the tedious impression & stormy remembrance of his abominable dede."

The form of the biography is puzzling. The genuine section breaks off abruptly, and the rounded accounts of Richard in Holinshed and Stow are finished by other hands. Not only was it unfinished, but probably the extant form represents a rough draft without final revision. It is not concentrated as a unit upon Richard III, and may have been intended originally as a fragment of a longer history of the English kings beginning with Edward IV. The first half of the piece, which is inferior to the last, contains stretches of political narrative in the accepted historical manner, a long animadversion on the abuse of sanctuaries, and much of the traditional biographical paraphernalia, such as the oration of the dying Edward. Yet with the introduction of Richard as Lord Protector the interest of the writer focuses on the artistic problem of composing with mockery and brilliance the living portrait of a tyrant. From this point on, the presentation does not flag, and the beauty of its biographical unity is not dissipated by side excursions, except for the pathetic tribute to Jane Shore, included apologetically "amonge the remembraunces of great matters" as worthy of some poor memorial among the many "now famouse, only by the infamy of their il dedes."

Though the biography was not formally completed or approved, its language is in general vigorous and vivid, with balanced constructions and turns of speech that show its Latin ancestors and foreshadow *Euphues*. Because of the freedom gained by writing frankly and without the desire to conceal faults, because of the influence of classical models, notably Tacitus, and because of the abilities of the distinguished author himself, the *History of Richard III* sets a new standard in historical writing. The biography shows that More was not living in Asser's simple world, and for its polished and sophisticated spirit, as well as for its style, it deserves a higher place in English literature than it has generally received. Nowhere else in the history of English biography is there "so evill a tale so well tolde."

The two sketches of Colet and More written by Erasmus also mark the wide difference between the Middle Ages and the Renaissance. Where the mediaeval character sketch [8] enumerates superlative and generalized virtues, Erasmus seizes with discrimination the evanescent qualities that form the characters of his friends, and records his captured essences. This enthusiasm for the fine distinctions of personality resulted in the character sketches of the seventeenth century. They are portraits, as Erasmus himself calls them, written in the form of letters to his friend Hutten and containing subtle traits of character rather than events in chronological progression. With his own alert appreciation of literature and with two such distinguished subjects as the whimsical Catholic martyr and the founder of St. Paul's School, Erasmus presents the varied interests and qualities of his friends with brilliance and finesse.

8. A good example of a separate mediaeval character is Blakman's *Henry VI*, written about 1436–48 and printed by Copeland about the same time that Erasmus' brief biographies were published. Reprinted with a translation by M. R. James, Cambridge, 1919.

The second half of the sixteenth century witnessed the translation of the classical models which had given More's works maturity and sureness: [9] the art of life-writing in England was thereby given a definite stimulus. Golding's translation of Caesar appeared in 1565, North's Plutarch in 1579, and Holland's Suetonius in 1606. Of the two separate Latin lives which most deeply influenced English biography, Sir Henry Savile's translation of the *Agricola* of Tacitus was printed in 1591 and was frequently reissued, while the *Confessions* of Augustine first appeared in English in 1620. Augustine's autobiography became immediately popular; other editions appeared in 1631, 1638, and 1660. Between the years 1550 and 1600 such works as Curtius' *History of Alexander* (1553), Diodorus Siculus' *Successors of Alexander* (1569), and Justin's *Pompeius* (1563) were translated, as well as such historians as Herodotus (1584), Thucydides (1560), Livy (1544, 1570, 1596), and Sallust (1557, 1608).[10]

The influence of the Latin and Greek historians and biographers was widespread. The lives of the sixteenth and seventeenth centuries are studded with continual quotations in the original Greek and Latin or in translation. References to Plutarch, Suetonius, Tacitus, Livy, Diogenes Laertius, and Caesar are particularly common.

9. The same classical influences, less completely assimilated, are evident in Latin histories, such as Bernard André's *De Vita Henrici Septimi* (wr. 1500–21), a good example of a pretentious chronicle growing from the mediaeval tradition but heavily indebted to classical models. André was at least aware of the requirements for biography, since he refers to Plutarch's celebrated opinion that the distinguishing traits and manners of men rather than their actions are his proper study. The book is written as a work of art, in an oratorical style, with laments, prayers, and speeches interspersed. At times it breaks into verse.

10. For the dates of translations of minor biographies, see the admirable appendix to the *Cambridge History of English Literature*, vol. iv, chap. 1.

Three examples may here be cited to show how the classical lives in the time of the Renaissance were introduced into the current of English biography and remained there as an important influence. George Paule as early as 1612 models his life of John Whitgift on Plutarch's *Lives*, quotes Suetonius and Diogenes Laertius more than once, and admits in so many words that the *Annals* of Tacitus moved him to write the life of the archbishop. Peter Smith quotes in Greek from Plutarch's lives of Antony, Themistocles, and Agesilaus in his biography of Andrew Willet (1634). And, at the other end of the century, John Barnard in his *Life of Peter Heylyn* (1683) quotes Plutarch in Greek, and Sallust, Suetonius, and Tacitus, as well as Augustine, in Latin.

Not only the phrases, but also the forms of the classical historians were incorporated in English biography. It is difficult to judge precisely how much Tacitus colors More's *Richard III* with subtle irony, but it is not difficult to trace his influence when he is paraphrased directly, as in Heylyn's life of Charles the First (1658).[11] Nor is it difficult to see the influence of Suetonius in the repeated popular variations of the lives of the Roman emperors,[12] or Plutarch's influence in the parallel lives written in the seventeenth century,[13] or Caesar's influence, often acknowledged, in the military memoirs

11. "Quicquid ex Carolo amavimus, quicquid mirati sumus, manet mansurumque; est in animis hominum, in aeternitate temporum, fama rerum." Cf. close of the *Agricola*.

12. See the collections of Roman emperors by Richard Reynolds (1571), Edward Hellowes (1577), William Traheron (1604), Philemon Holland (1606), and Richard Braithwaite (1636), in Bibliography.

13. Such as *A Parallel betweene Cardinall Wolsey . . . and William Laud*, 1641, anonymous; or Sir Henry Wotton's *A Parallell betweene Robert late Earle of Essex, and George late Duke of Buckingham*, 1641.

that accompanied the Civil Wars.[14] The illustrations
given above furnish direct evidence of the influence of
the classics upon the development of English biography.
Their indirect influence in raising the standard of composition and freeing biography from its outworn traditions cannot so easily be calculated, although it is
even more important than the obvious imitations or borrowings.

By the end of the century the classical writers had become models for English biographers. They are of
particular note in the work of the historians Hayward
and Bacon, who, under the influence of ancient authors,
modified the practice of Elizabethan chroniclers and
established biography as an independent branch of
literature.

John Hayward, writing at the close of the sixteenth
century, is of importance in the history of biography not
only for his writings in themselves, but also because he
was the first Englishman to distinguish consciously between history and biography. He expressed, even
though inadequately, ideas which must have been hazily
present in the minds of his contemporaries. His conception of the historian's dual function as political inter-
preter and as biographer is most clearly offered in the
preface to *The Life and raigne of King Henrie the IIII*
(1599):

"Among all sortes of humane writers, there is none that
have done more profit, or deserved greater prayse, then they
who have committed to faithfull records of Histories, eyther
the government of mighty states, or the lives and actes of
famous men: for by describing the order and passages of these
two, and what events hath followed what counsailes they

14. See Chapter VI.

have set foorth unto us, not onely precepts, but lively patterns, both for private directions and for affayres of state."

The lives of the three Norman kings, William I, William II, and Henry I, demonstrate Hayward's artistic skill as a royal biographer. They are written in a smooth and resilient prose, adapted to Hayward's own ideal "that by pleasure in reading them, the profit in knowing them, myght more easily bee attayned." The author has shown taste and discretion in the selection of details, and in the exclusion of all matter not bearing upon the individual lives of his heroes.[15] This metamorphosis of history into biography is his own original contribution, for though he draws from William of Malmesbury and allied sources, the result is neither a chronicle nor a history, but the lives of kings. His *William the Conqueror* in particular avoids heaviness, and contains a number of vivid and diverting anecdotes, a just, unbiassed portrayal of character both by incident and description, a comprehensive battle of Hastings, and enough political exposition to set forth the life. There is a clarity, a buoyancy, and a lack of prejudice and pretence in his writings which is as delightful as it is unusual in the early history of royal biography.

Hayward's *William Rufus*, though it falls slightly below the level of his *William I*, is still in the first rank of royal lives, and contains occasional descriptive paragraphs such as this:[16]

15. The anecdote of Bacon's conversation with Queen Elizabeth regarding Hayward's thefts from Tacitus is too well known to be repeated here. To show, however, the strength of the native annalistic tradition even in a man of Hayward's classical training, it is interesting to note that Hayward includes as a necessary or desirable appendix to his *Life of William I* a chronicle of the accidental events of his rule, comprising such observations as "In the tenth yeere of his reigne the cold of Winter was exceeding memorable, both for sharpenesse and for continuance." 1613, pp. 129–139.

16. 1613, pp. 153–155.

"He was a man of meane stature, thicke and square bodied, his belly swelling somewhat round; his face was red, his haire deepely yealow, by reason whereof he was called Rufus; his forehead foure square like a window, his eyes spotted and not one like the other; his speech unpleasant and not easily uttered, especially when he was mooved with anger. . . . In publicke he composed his countenance to a stately terrour; his face sowerly swelling, his eyes truçulent, his voyce violent and fierce, scarce thinking himself Maiesticall in the glasse of his understanding, but when he flashed feare from his presence. And yet in private he was so affable and pleasant, that he approached neere the degree of levitie."

No less than Hayward, Francis Bacon was aware of the existence of biography as a distinct division in the field of human knowledge. Yet as the work of one who, in the *Advancement of Learning*, distinguishes with logic and a keen foresight the divisions of history,[17] Bacon's narrative of Henry VII is disappointing to the student of biography. It forms part of the history he contemplated some years before, "the storie of England that is to say, from the Uniting of the Roses, to the Uniting of the Kingdomes," which he considers, compared with a general history of England, "an excellent Periode of a much smaller compasse of time." [18] It is evident that Bacon intended this work to be a history rather than a life, that he modelled it on the *Annals* of Tacitus rather than the *Agricola*. It treats of Henry only as a monarch, begins with the battle of Bosworth Field and his accession, tells nothing of his early life, and throughout remains national in its scope. Thus, full accounts of such episodes as Perkin Warbeck's pretensions to the throne are given, together with discussions of the finances of the realm and versions of many Parliamentary and ambas-

17. See Chapter VII.   18. *Adv. of Learning*, 1605, p. 12vo, Bk. II.

sadorial speeches. The style of the annalist is followed throughout. Only at the conclusion does Bacon favor the reader with an extended and fairly adequate character of Henry VII. At last Bacon conducts his sovereign to the grave, where "hee dwelleth more richly Dead, in the Monument of his Tombe, then hee did Alive in Richmond, or any of his Palaces. I could wish he did the like, in this Monument of his Fame." [19] The stateliness and serious character of the history exclude all trivial anecdotes, and the few that are selected are narrated with something of the feeling of the classic historians for artistic and dramatic incident. As a whole this impressive and beautifully written work is of more significance as a monument in the history of English prose than in that of biography.

In this study, hardly less important than the *Henry VII* is Bacon's shorter sketch of Queen Elizabeth, "written by his Lordship in Latin only" and later translated and published in English by William Rawley (1657). "This Work," Rawley writes, "his Lordship so much affected, that he had ordained by his last will and testament, to have had it published." It is not difficult to understand why the author valued this piece; it is short and deep. Bacon lacked the skill to develop a personality by narrating the events of his life, as the *Henry VII* also illustrates; but the power of accurate observation necessary for a distinctive character sketch made him a master standing at the beginning of a century in which such ability was prized. Bacon realized that his *Queen Elizabeth* was not a life but an encomium when he said: [20]

19. *The Historie of the Raigne of King Henry the Seventh*, 1622, p. 248.
20. Ed. J. Devey, 1852, p. 492.

"But if I should enter upon her praises, whether moral or political, I must either fall into a common-place of virtues, which will be unworthy of so extraordinary a princess; or if I give them their proper grace and lustre, I must enter into a history of her life; which requires more leisure, and a richer vein than mine."

The "common-place of virtues" he eschews, and develops her character in more subtle fashion. The paragraph dealing with Elizabeth's handling of the religious issues is an appreciation of statesmanship written by a statesman, and the paragraph which succeeds it, touching upon a sensitive point in the Queen's disposition, — her dread of old age, — shows an intimacy and a personal knowledge rarely found in the biographers of royalty.

The permeating influence of a dignified classical tradition continues in the works of seventeenth-century royal historians, such as Stranguage, Buck, and Lord Herbert of Cherbury. Yet the Renaissance curiosity was not content with classical literature alone. Contemporary continental writers likewise furnished important biographical models. In 1596 appeared Thomas Danett's *History of Comines*, with its close scrutiny of the life of Louis XI.[21] This astonishing amalgam of political shrewdness and simple piety is faithfully rendered, and concludes with a chapter by Danett in the spirit of the times, showing "the miserie of mans life, by the examples of those Princes that lived in the authors time." "What goodlier examples," asks the translator, "can we find to teach us that man is but a shadow, that our life is miserable and short, and that we are nothing, neither great nor small?" [22]

21. Macchiavelli's *Florentine History*, 1575, is of some importance.
22. Tudor Trans., ii, 126 (1897).

Usually the European biographies translated were selected because of their bearing upon the course of the Reformation. One of the earliest and most deserving is Arthur Golding's translation from the Latin of *The Lyfe of Iasper Colignie Shatilion, sometyme great Admirall of Fraunce*, published in 1576. A political biography composed mainly of historical intrigues, with a character sketch appended, it contains occasional incidents of real dramatic force, as in the conversion of Coligny to the Huguenot faith (p. Bii):

"His wife Sharlot de Lavall a woman of a noble & auncient stocke, was wonderfully given to the following of godlinesse, (which he tooke too be a singular benefite of God) insomuch that she even incoraged hir husband too forsake superstition and the worshipping of Idolls, and to imbrace the christian religion with his whole hart. When the Admirall perceyved that she delt often and very earnestly with him in the matter, he himself also determined to deale earnestly with her at once. And therfore he told hir in many words, that in all his life he never sawe or hearde of any man eyther in Germanie or in Fraunce, but he was in daunger too be overwhelmed with great miseries and calamities, if he imbraced the religion any thing earnestly: and that the Lawes of King Frauncis the first, & of King Henrie the second, being looked to most streightly in all Courts of Justice, commaunded that all such as were condemned of that Religion, should be burned quicke in publike places, and all their goods be forfeyted to the King: and yet neverthelesse he trusted that his heart was so settled, as he should not refuze the comon cace of all the protestants, nor fayle of his dewtie. Shee answered that the cace of the protestants of that time, was none other then the cace of the true Christians of all ages had bin: nether dowted she but it should be the same still to the worlds end."

More's *Pico* had an Italian source, Golding's *Coligny* a French. Yet the originals of both were written in Latin.

Similarly, the most important biographical translation between More and Golding was made by John Roberts from a Latin life written by an Italian. *The lyfe of Hyldebrande, called Gregory the .vii. pope of that name: with the lyfe also of Henry the fourth, emperour of Rome and Almayne* was printed by Wynkyn de Worde in 1535. John Roberts, the translator, adds a great deal of his own to Benno's original, and in the controversy then waging between Henry VIII and the Papacy his bias in favor of the monarchy is unmistakable. His little work, therefore, presents an early example of biography used with a political or controversial end in view. The first part, dealing with Gregory, is designed to show that the pope can err, that Gregory himself was an Arian and immoral, and that schisms in the Roman Church were common. Roberts declares it to be "moche necessarye to be redde of all the kynges true subiectes." The second part comes nearer being a life, and treats Henry IV with sympathy and enthusiasm. The *proheme* constitutes a remarkable character sketch of Henry's emotional, humble, and pious nature, so that this section at least merits reprinting at the present day, as well for the freshness of the English prose as for the unique position this little-known work holds in the history of English biography.

The increasing nationalism exemplified in Roberts' *Henry IV* developed in the English Renaissance an ardent patriotism, a strong monarchy, and a national religion erected upon the ruins of feudalism and the church universal. The growing continental preoccupation with theories of kingship and aristocratic governance, which found expression in Guevara's *Dial of Princes*, Macchiavelli's *Prince*, and Castiglione's *Courtier*, met with a ready reception in England in translations or in such native works as Sir Thomas Elyot's *Boke called the Governour*. The interest in the rules of royalty and the conduct of kings finds ample biographical outlet in *The Mirror for Magistrates* and subsidiary verse lives. The patriotic ardor of this collection, which draws all its heroes from English history, is typical of the Renaissance. Yet the *Mirror* continues a mediaeval form of expression. The influence of Lydgate in the development of the numerous verse lives of the sixteenth century is of first importance. Lydgate, following Boccaccio, gives his histories dramatic and vivid possibilities by having his characters appear before him in a vision and narrate their lives in the first person. Here again he draws from the mediaeval store in adopting the dream frame for a narrative; and this convention is followed without deviation into the seventeenth century.

The Mirror for Magistrates is not a single work, but a miscellaneous collection, and includes, or inspires, the best of the verse lives during the second half of the sixteenth century. The first edition appeared in 1559, though part had been printed and suppressed as early as 1555, and the last volume of additions which assumed the name of the *Mirror* was published in 1610. The didactic note is betrayed even in the title, which shows also that it was calculated to serve as a text-book of *exempla* for those in a position of authority and influence. In his prefatory epistle, William Baldwin says: [23]

"For here as in a loking glas, you shal se (if any vice be in you) how the like hath bene punished in others heretofore, whereby admonished, I trust it wyl be a good occasion to

23. Haslewood, 1815, Preface to Part 3.

move to the sooner amendement. This is the chiefest ende, whye it is set forth, whych God graunt it may attayne."

This quotation provides a fresh angle from which the collection may be viewed: namely, as a complement to the saints' lives. Theoretically, the *Mirror* professes to reveal the consequences of evil, where the saints' biographies make clear the fruits of moral living. The single aim of teaching the good life by example is common to them both; but where the method of the saint's life is "the commendation of vertue," that of the *Mirror for Magistrates* is ordinarily "the detestation of vice." [24] Frequently, in choosing royal subjects, the contributors lose sight of a conscious moral aim and allow their sympathy or their dramatic sense to guide them; but even when no logical tragic fault is discoverable, death and the blows of fortune furnish convenient and unescapable substitutes to bring about the catastrophe. The saints' lives offer in individual biographies a series of divine comedies; obversely, *The Mirror for Magistrates* presents a gallery of gloomy portraits, a long line of royal tragedies.[25] Their dominant originality in subjective, dramatic treatment, and their broad philosophical outlook, coupled with singleness of tone and a focussing upon a central figure, influenced the development of almost all verse lives, and many prose biographies, as late

24. 1815, p. 8, note by John Higgins, one of the original contributors.

25. The individual lives are of relatively uniform worth, considering the number of poets who contributed. The general formation and some of the lives are the work of William Baldwin; John Higgins wrote many of the early lives; Thomas Blener-Hasset continued with the kings through Harold; George Ferrers did much to complete the original plan. Of particular value is Sir Thomas Sackville's *Buckingham*, which does not, however, attain the poetic level of the celebrated *Induction*. Thomas Churchyard's *Jane Shore*, which first appeared in 1563, is good, and treats with sympathy her character as intercessor for the poor with King Edward.

as 1628. The inclusion of Michael Drayton's *Cromwell* in the 1610 section of the *Mirror* illustrates the power the collection attained to attract to itself the best single verse lives of the time, as well as the series of lives contributed by its regular editors.[26]

The patriotism and Protestantism which together characterize the English Renaissance are clearly shown in the *Mirror for Magistrates* and Roberts' joint lives of Henry IV and Gregory VII. The same patriotism, the same Protestantism, often a combination of the two, furnish inspiration for a new class of biographical writers which flourished in the sixteenth century — the antiquaries. Such men as Leland, Bale, Foxe, and Parker, with their original pioneer collections, were the direct predecessors of seventeenth-century antiquaries like Pits, Fuller, Clark, and Wood, and inaugurated a tradition which culminates in the Dictionary of National Biography.

The desultory and uninspired short Latin lives written by the antiquaries of the sixteenth century contain the germ of modern biography. In spite of continued emphasis upon the church they broaden the legitimate field for the writing of lives by gathering together catalogues of writers and men of science as well as of states-

26. For other verse lives in the tradition of the *Mirror for Magistrates*, see particularly Thomas Storer's *Life of Wolsey*, 1599; Anthony Chute's *Jane Shore*, 1593; Christopher Middleton's *Humphrey of Gloucester*, 1600; and John Weever's *Sir John Oldcastle*, 1601. The best accessible volumes for a collection of such fugitive pieces are by Sir Egerton Brydges, *Restituta*, 1814–16, 4 vols.; *British Bibliographer*, 1810–14, 4 vols., and particularly *Censura Literaria*, 5 vols. in 2d ed. of 1815. Also J. P. Collier's *Bibliographical and Critical Account of the Rarest Books in the English Language*, 2 vols., 1865; and for titles, Joseph Ritson's *Bibliographia Poetica*, 1802.

Samuel Rowland's *John Leyden*, 1605, and *The Deplorable Life of Edward the Second* attributed to Francis Hubert show the waning of the form. Apart from the main current, William Forrest's *Grisild the Second* (Catharine of Aragon), 1558, and Charles Fitz-Geffrey's *Drake*, 1596, are notable.

men or clerics. They set a certain standard, even if it is inadequate, for determining who shall be remembered and what events in his life are worthy of record. The mere collecting of some hundreds of short biographies insures a uniformity in purpose and method which renders life-writing no longer sporadic and accidental, but deliberate and conscious. The antiquaries introduced a mass of information and traditions about the early writers of England which served as material for later biographers. Finally, they wrote not only to edify but to inform, thus supplanting the mediaeval conception of biography as an exercise in ethics by the modern conception of biography as a means of gratifying legitimate curiosity and contributing to knowledge.

Collections of lives are not unknown before the sixteenth century. The saints' lives were frequently gathered in this form, and such men as John of Tynemouth (ca. 1350) and John Boston of Bury (fl. 1410) anticipate the antiquarian zeal of the Renaissance in their collections of English saints and English ecclesiastical writers. But with Leland and Bale, the same curiosity and eagerness for knowledge which led to the revival of the classics brought about the discovery of English letters.

John Leland is commonly acknowledged the first and greatest of the sixteenth-century antiquaries. In 1534, in the official position of "king's antiquary," he began his travels throughout England in search of English antiquities. In this quest he found all things of interest, from existing topography to ancient coins; the records and registers of the old cathedrals and monasteries were the objects of his particular attention, and before his death in 1552 he had gathered a mass of biographical data to which all later collectors have been indebted.

For more than a century this part of his work was accessible only in manuscript. In 1709 Anthony Hall published an inaccurate transcript from Leland's autograph as *Commentarii de Scriptoribus Britannicis.* This consists of 593 short biographies. Although Leland's catalogue is not marred by such violent religious prejudices as obsess later antiquaries, it is nevertheless weakened by extreme credulity. In his desire to be complete, he has founded entire lives and lists of works on conjectures and local traditions, and the treatment of some of the earlier mythical creations belongs to the realm of imaginative romance. For the most part the commentaries deal with the writings of churchmen and Biblical commentators now obscure or forgotten. A certain number, however, treat of scientific writers, and even of literary figures. This is a significant step forward; it is noteworthy that whereas John Boston a century earlier had written a catalogue of the writers of the church, Leland widened the field to include all British writers. He also includes a short bibliography for each author. Furthermore, he considers it within his province to assess as well as to catalogue. He writes with some attempt at a pleasing style, and at times his appraisals of authors verge upon literary criticism.[27]

27. For example the following may be quoted from his paragraphs on Chaucer (1709, p. 421, Oxford):

"Bonis igitur avibus incepto operi incubuit, nunc libellos Gallica lingua compte, ornate, diserte scriptos in patrium sermonem transferens; nunc Latinos versus Anglicis, sed docte, sed apte, sed canore exprimens; nunc multa e suo capite nata, & Latinorum felicitatem aequantia, victuris chartis commendans; nunc lectori ut prodesset nervis omnibus contendens, & vicissim ut eundem delectaret sedulo curans: nec antea finem fecit, quam linguam nostram ad eam puritatem, ad eam eloquentiam, ad eam denique brevitatem ac gratiam perduxerat, ut inter expolitas gentium linguas posset recte quidem connumerari. Itaque in libris meorum *Epigrammaton* his versibus ejus gloriae assurgo:

Leland's work along biographical lines found a continuer. *The Laboryouse Journey and Serche of J. Leylande for Englande's Antiquities* was published in 1549 by John Bale, with copious comments, and concludes with Bale's *Regystre of the names of Englysh Wryters* from his own history of authors. The first version of this work was printed in 1548 at Ipswich with the title *Illustrium Majoris Britanniae Scriptorum Summarium in quinque centurias divisum*. It was enlarged, brought up to date, and the number of biographies almost trebled in the continental edition which followed after a lapse of ten years, when Bale was in exile during the reign of Queen Mary. The final edition of this painstaking work appeared at Basel with the date 1559 and the title *Scriptorum Illustrium maioris Brytanniae ... Catalogus*. The first part, of 742 pages, contains nine centuries, or nine hundred items; the second part of 250 pages has five hundred additional lives. Bale collects his materials from his own gleanings in ecclesiastical libraries at home and on the continent, from various continental writers, and from English bibliographers such as Boston and Leland, to whom he is heavily indebted.[28] Bale, like Leland, is not always careful as to

Praedicat Aligerum merito Florentia Dantem
Italia & numeros tota, Petrarche, tuos:
Anglia Chaucerum veneratur nostra poetam,
Cui veneres debet patria lingua suas."

Considering the age in which this was written, it is a discerning appreciation, and it may seem unfortunate that Leland did not try his hand at a complete single piece of biography. Tanner in his *Bibliotheca Britannica* records the existence of a *Life of Fulk Warren* by Leland, which at one time was in the possession of Humphrey Bourchier, father of the translator, and has since disappeared.

28. His notice of Leland, whom he styles "Antiquarius," is adulatory (1559, Cent. VIII, no. 81, p. 671): it was largely through Leland's intervention in 1537 that Thomas Cromwell shielded with his authority this out-

the actual existence of the authors or the works he describes, and Fuller in his *Worthies of England* [29] is not too severe when he speaks of the trash to be found in the first century of Bale under the names of such fictitious writers as Samothes Gigas, Magus Samotheus, Sarron Magius, and others. Bale adds to Leland's disregard for complete accuracy a rancor of his own which distorts his view of almost every churchman whom he includes. Restraint and impartiality fail him so wholly when he writes of religious differences that he has destroyed general confidence in his work, which remains nevertheless a monument of energy and an important contribution to the history of English letters. The fourteen hundred short lives he has gathered together often seek to gloss over ignorance by means of generalities and invented details; too many are argumentative and denunciatory rather than informing; yet as a whole they are capable; the biographical details and lists of works included suggest the indefatigability of the truculent Bishop of Ossory;[30] and a survey of the whole register, with its arrangement roughly chronological, gives a fair impression of the progress of English literature.

If Bale's gatherings illustrate the antiquarian curiosity as well as the religious fervor of his time, Foxe's

spoken and bitterly protestant controversialist. In drawing materials from Leland, Bale often carries over sections without change, as he does in the section on Chaucer, for example, or Gower. Sometimes, however, he paraphrases. Thus in the account of Caedmon, which both of the antiquaries found in Bede, Leland transcribes his authority almost direct, while Bale rewords the narrative to please his taste.

29. 1662, chap. 10, p. 26.

30. Bale's tireless pen and zealous Protestantism also produced two individual biographies of particular interest: a life of Sir John Oldcastle (1544), and Bale's own autobiography (1553). His *Pageant of Popes* (1574, Latin version included in 1559 edition of his catalogue) is an early instance of vituperative biography.

Actes and Monuments can only be considered as a product of ardent Anglican faith. It springs from the same zealous Protestantism which inspired Bale, and is contemporaneous, for the dedication of the Latin edition bears the same date (1559) as the final form of Bale's catalogue. The English version, amplified and corrected, first appeared in 1563. The industry of the great martyrologist was expended with the primary purpose of furnishing examples of Romish persecution of Protestants, rather than of affording detailed, accurate biographies. Foxe is deliberately writing a Protestant Calendar of Saints to supplant the Roman one. None of the lives in this collection is complete; few seek to unearth events and details further back than the beginnings of the religious controversies in which the martyrs are involved. The accounts of the trials of the sixteenth-century Protestants are full and dramatic, and for the most part accurate; their conduct in imprisonment, their progress toward the stake and flames is admirably narrated.

Antiquarian studies are carried on by Archbishop Matthew Parker in his *De Antiquitate Britannicae Ecclesiae* (1572), which includes seventy short lives of the archbishops of Canterbury.[31] The Anglican ardor of John Foxe and the antiquarian zeal of Matthew Parker, as shown in their large collections, instituted the fertile school of seventeenth-century ecclesiastical biography. The new spirit in the church also brought about some of the most important single translations. Like Roberts' *Henry IV* and Golding's *Coligny*, Theodore Beza's *His-*

31. This inspired, and served as a source for such later works as Francis Godwin's remarkable *Catalogue of the Bishops of England . . . together with a briefe History of their lives and memorable actions*, 1601.

torie of the life and death of Maister Iohn Calvin (1564) was translated because of the changing religious interests in England. Yet its importance does not lie wholly in its position as an early work among Protestant lives. It is of even greater interest as a first instance of a biography written as a preface. The English version, it is true, appeared separately, but the introduction states that "the purpose of the Auctor . . . was not to publishe it as an Hystorie, but onely for a Preface to the Commentaries of the saide Calvin uppon the Booke of Iosue." [32]

The prefatory life, destined to be so important a biographical form in later centuries, is again to be found in Speght's "Life of Geoffrey Chaucer" prefixed to an edition of his poems in 1598.[33] The life also shows the antiquarian spirit characteristic of the English Renaissance, and may best be summarized by reproducing its own picturesque and all-embracing summary. It contains:

"So much as we can find by Her- auldes, Chronicles, & Records, of his	{ Countrey. Parentage. Education. Mariage. Children, Revenues. Service. Reward. Friends. Bookes. Death."	With their	{ Mariage. Lands. Service. Reward. Issue. Death.

32. The growing need for prefatory lives may be seen in Foxe's *The Whole workes of W. Tyndall, John Frith, and Doct. Barnes*, 1573, and Camden's *Anglica, Normannica, Hibernica, Cambrica, a veteribus scripta*, 1603. Both contain brief lives of the writers included in the volumes, the first drawing from Foxe's *Book of Martyrs* and the second from Bale's catalogue.

33. For much of his material, Speght is indebted to John Stow, who edited Chaucer in 1561.

The biography is comprehensive, except that no attempt is made to determine Chaucer's character. Speght shows no imagination in his reconstruction of the poet's life. An attempt to give some idea of Chaucer's importance is, however, made in the memorials included after his death. Throughout, the method is painstaking. Accuracy is the watchword, and the result is not inconsiderable.

Finally, the Renaissance in England was characterized by a new desire that a man's memory might be preserved for posterity in some written memorial, and in consequence the sixteenth century produced first examples of many forms of pseudo-biographies which later became current. Funeral sermons printed as biographical memorials occur as early as 1509, when John Fisher published "a mornynge remembraunce . . . of the noble prynces Margarete countesse of Rychemonde & Darbye." His sermon on Henry VII was also printed. An extremely interesting example among memorial tributes is Thomas Wilson's *Vita et obitus duorum fratrum Suffolciensium, Henrici et Caroli Brandoni, prestanti virtute, et splendore nobilitatis ducum illustrissimorum, duabus epistolis explicata* (1559). Wilson mentions, without extensive quotations, classical and patristic writers; but the formlessness and uncertainty of the whole make it evident that the author is treading new ground. His desire to commemorate his patrons and friends produces a lament and a eulogy, followed by numerous *Epigrammata*. The most important section of the work is devoted to collected tributes written by the Oxford friends of the two Brandons.[34]

34. "Sequuntur Oxonienses Doctissimi, qui partim fama commoti, et existimatione tantorum Principum, partim sollicitati hortatione optimi viri,

This form of reverence to the dead in gatherings of verses, epitaphs, and elegies, usually written in the learned tongues, became one of the most popular biographical fashions between 1550 and 1650. Often such verses, prefaced to the works of an author, served the double purpose of panegyric and biography, although the biographical element was usually tenuous.[35] More worthy of consideration as lives are the extended verse epitaphs composed by George Whetstone between 1577 and 1587 and published immediately after the deaths of George Gascoigne, Sir Nicholas Bacon, Francis Earl of Bedford, Sir James Dyer, Thomas Earl of Sussex, and Sir Philip Sidney. Whetstone accepted seriously his office as historian of the dead, and called Plutarch, Seneca, and Ovid to his aid in order " that the Auncesters noble Monuments might be presedents of honour to their posteritie." [36] George Whetstone might reasonably be considered the first professional biographer in England.

Still another variant among the biographical memorials of the Renaissance is the published funeral oration.[37] This class was limited rather straitly to university men, but it afforded a precedent for, and easily merged with, the published funeral sermons popular in the seventeenth century.

Francisci Gavari, Hispani, & cognati Suffolciensibus: valde studiose in hanc partem elaboraverunt, ut nomen Brandonorum tam memorabile in immensum propagaretur."

35. A good example is the small memorial volume *Jonsonus Virbius*, published in 1637 shortly after the death of the dramatist and containing the collected tributes of the tribe of Ben.

36. *The life . . . of . . . Lorde Frauncis Earle of Bedford*, 1585.

37. Good examples are Edward Grant's *Roger Ascham*, 1576, and Degory Wheare's *William Camden*, 1623.

The sixteenth century, then, is a period of innovations, during which biographical tradition is far from single, and diverse unrelated forms exist side by side. The powerful current of mediaeval verse lives continues throughout the century in the *Mirror for Magistrates*, touched only lightly by the Renaissance. The tradition of the Middle Ages is strong, and two of the finest early English biographies, — Cavendish's *Cardinal Wolsey* and Roper's *More*, — although they are written in mid-century, remain closely allied with mediaeval royal biographies and saints' lives and show little evidence of the new influences around them.[38] But while the mature and settled tradition of the Middle Ages persists in such forms, the restlessness of the Renaissance is introducing a new leaven. The classical biographies are read and translated; the biographers of France, Italy, and Spain become known; past figures in English history are revived by the curiosity of the antiquaries; present figures are remembered in printed sermons and orations and characters and elegies; the lives of the leaders in the new religious divisions are diligently recorded. The untried forms are not always successful; few of the biographers had the comprehensive genius of Sir Thomas More. Experiments are many, achievements few. But this much at least the tentative lives of the English Renaissance accomplished: they destroyed the self-contained monotony of the mediaeval tradition, and by introducing classical and continental models and modes of thought, made possible the diversified and individualized biographies of the seventeenth century.

38. These two biographies are discussed in Chapter V.

III

ECCLESIASTICAL BIOGRAPHY [1]

His death is the last sermon, where, in the pulpit of his bed, he instructs
men to die by his example.

JOHN EARLE

THE beginnings of the new type of ecclesiastical
biography, which during the first half of the seventeenth century developed into a definite, conventional
form, are tentative and experimental. There are few
models to guide the writers. The whole corpus of
saints' legends affords one source from which they draw
patterns. Thus, the *Vita et Martyrium Edmundi Campiani* (1583) is in its tone and temper a saint's life of
this Jesuit leader; the *Florilegium Insulae Sanctorum
Seu Vitae et Acta Sanctorum Hiberniae* (1624) of Thomas
Messingham continues the old hagiological tradition
without a break and with no trace of a change in spirit.
The same may be said for Jerome Porter's *Flowers of the
Lives of the most Renowned Saincts of . . . England, Scotland, and Ireland* (1632).

Yet saints' lives, as these examples show, had a more
direct influence on the development of biography by
Catholics than on the lives written by members of the
Anglican Church.[2] The rupture with Rome under

1. Except for one or two unavoidable references, ecclesiastical biography
has been straitly interpreted in this chapter to include only the lives of English Christian ministers. Its influence in other fields, however, and particularly upon artless and intimate biographies, was great.

2. See, for example, John Fenne's *Catharine of Siena,* 1609; *Saint Wenefride,* 1635; Woodhead's *Life of the Holy Mother S. Teresa,* 1671; translations
of the saints' lives by Alfonso Villegas, 1621, and by Peter Ribadeneyra, 1659.

Henry VIII introduced a new ecclesiastical system into England. In consequence, the Anglican Church built up, largely independent of Catholic hagiography, its own new biographical forms. The Reformation, therefore, was the immediate cause of the rise of ecclesiastical biography. The numerous clerical lives in turn reflect the subsequent history of the Reformation in England — the Catholic persecution of the Protestants under Queen Mary, the strengthening of the Anglican Church, the rise of the Puritans, the exile and return of the royalist clergy, the growth of nonconformist sects.

The first independent ecclesiastical biography of importance in this new school,[3] Humfrey's *Ioannis Iuelli . . . vita & mors* (1573), is written in Latin. Laurence Humfrey, President of Magdalen and Dean successively of Gloucester and Winchester, was a friend and contem-

The number of saints' lives written under Catholic influence during the seventeenth century is apparent in the *Catalogus Bibliothecae Gualteri Rea Armigeri*, 1682, which on page 39 mentions lives of Becket, Philip Neri, St. Margaret of Scotland, Mary Magdalen, Gregory Lopez, Aloysius Gonzaga, Anthony of Padua, John Fisher, Elizabeth of Hungary, Jesuit leaders, and St. Genovesa Countess Palatine of Trevers. All of these biographies were written in English or translated, and published between the years 1619 and 1674.

These saintly lives furnished models for many of the biographies of women written during the century, particularly by the Catholics, and exemplified in Richard Smith's *Life of Lady Magdalen Viscountess Montague* (written in Latin, Eng. ed., 1627), Duncon's *Viscountess Letice*, 1627; *The Life of Jane Dormer, Duchess of Feria*, 1643; or R. Boreman's *Mirrour of Christianity, Or . . . The Life and Death of . . . Lady Alice, Dutchess Duddeley*, 1669. *The Holy Life of Mon^r De Renty*, translated from the French, 1658, is an exceptionally powerful biography in the straight hagiological tradition.

3. Cavendish's *Wolsey*, though dealing with a magnificent prelate, is in spirit not the biography of a cardinal but of a statesman, and is much more closely allied with the *Mirror for Magistrates* group and with royal biography than with the school of ecclesiastical life-writing. It narrates the fall of a prince, not the godly end of a pious spirit. Richard Hall's *Life of Fisher* (written about 1559) and John Josselin's fresh and original *Life of Archbishop Parker* (Eng. ed., 1574) are also omitted from this chapter because they are alien to the current of seventeenth-century biography. They are discussed in Chapter V.

porary of John Jewel, and his long work on the life of this bishop of Salisbury, who has been called "the official champion of Anglicanism," was published two years after Jewel's death with the sanction of Matthew Parker, Archbishop of Canterbury. The work tends to be pompous. That Humfrey labored virtually as a pioneer is evident in his choice of precedents for the production of such a life. He cites Homer, Hesiod, and Bale, a selection which proves him catholic rather than discriminating.[4] Jewel's life, he says (p. 13), may be considered as a tragi-comedy, as all lives truly are, and this tragi-comedy may be divided into five acts: his childhood, his academic career, his exile during the Catholic ascendancy, his elevation to the bishopric of Salisbury on his return, and, as a redundant fifth act, his death and the last catastrophe of life. The biography is developed in leisurely and elegant fashion, and contains many incidents of church strife during Jewel's career at Oxford, his escape from Bishop Bonner, his relations with Peter Martyr and the continental reformers, and, upon Elizabeth's accession, his actions as a leader of the Church of England. Incidents such as his public admission of cowardice at Frankfort in signing Catholic articles (1554) are not glossed over; but as a whole the biography is an enumeration of virtues and a glorification of Jewel's devout life.

The work was translated and abridged by Daniel Featley as a preface to Jewel's works (1609), and this

---

4. *Epistola Nunpcuatoria*, 1573: "Cum Homerus suum Achillem & Ulyssem praedicarit, Hesiodus Deorum suorum genealogias descripserit, Balaeus noster illustrium scriptorum in Britannia Centurias ediderit, aliique alios summis laudibus extulerint, cur nomen Iuelli nostra culpa in hoc albo non recensebitur, cuius scripta causa communi plurimum ponderis et splendoris addiderunt, & qui Ecclesiae nostrae decus & ornamentum extitit?"

English version was again included in Fuller's *Abel Redevivus* (1650). The whole purpose of such a life — and here may be felt the influence of hagiological tradition — is to allow the hero to die beautifully. Jewel does so: [5]

"Here, when one of those that stood by prayd with teares, That (if it might stand with Gods good pleasure) he would restore him to former health; Jewel overhearing him turned his eyes, as it were, offended, & spake to him in the words of S. Ambrose: *I have not lived so, that I am ashamed to live longer, neither doe I feare to die, because we have a mercifull Lord.*"

The prose of Featley's translation is clear and measured. It may not be out of place to point out that this translation preceded the publication of the King James Version of the Bible by only two years.

Ecclesiastical biography in English was not established in the form peculiar to the whole seventeenth century until the appearance in 1612 of *The Life of . . . John Whitgift, Archbishop of Canterburie* by George Paule. As a pioneer work this life is of singular maturity. Paule had profited by his readings in Plutarch, Tacitus, and Suetonius, and wrote a biography admirable for its restraint. Whitgift's life as archbishop involved him in the suppression of the Marprelate Press and various controversies, yet in treating all such delicate issues Paule attempts moderation: [6]

"Wherein yet, as farre as the importance and necessity of the cause will suffer, I have so warily tempered the sharpnesse of my penne, that I hope none of moderate humour himselfe, will justly charge me of being immoderate herein. . . . Neither is it my purpose to have the ashes of the dead raked up againe."

5. Paragraph 36, Featley's trans., 1609.
6. "To the Reader," in 1612 ed.

Elsewhere he exercises the same moderation in his estimate of the archbishop's character, and is temperate in his praise (p. 81):

"You see now of what an excellent nature this Archbishop was. . . . Yet was he not voide (as no man is) of infirmities . . . so may it be confessed of this Archbishop, that the greatest, or rather onely fault knowne in him was choler."

Dates and references are given in the margins, and the biography contains many important original documents which are quoted without paraphrase. George Paule does not write this life with vivacity or intimacy, but he produces a work, which, as the first example in English of a new class, is remarkable for its fidelity, its temperance, and its mature competence.

In 1628 appeared the *Vita Bernardi Gilpini* by George Carleton, which almost immediately (1629) was published in an English translation. The date of composition may be fixed as considerably earlier, since in the epistle dedicatory Carleton says that for "many yeeres" the writing had "lyne by me from the common view." It is written as the majority of such lives were written, for purposes of edification: "I conceive that such a patterne, would kindle the zeale of many good men, to walke in so faire a way, though happily they were not able to attaine to the perfection thereof." [7] Yet it is by no means a trite and conventional panegyric, and among the ecclesiastical biographies of the century it stands forth as a remarkable and successful achievement. Carleton, who became Bishop of Chichester in 1619, was educated in his boyhood under the supervision of Gilpin, and therefore writes the biography from

7. "Epistle Dedicatory," in 1629 ed.

the standpoint of *protégé* and admirer. The account of Gilpin's Oxford career brings out, almost subjectively, his early Catholic tendencies, the influence upon him of Peter Martyr, who then held the Divinity Lectureship at the University, and his slow "conversion from the Romane superstition to the light of the Gospell" (p. 32). At no point in the biography is there the customary inventory of virtues. Carleton chooses the more difficult and more convincing method of character portrayal by incident, and the book abounds in apposite anecdotes from which the reader may draw his own conclusions. Gilpin's integrity, for example, appears in his refusal to accept from Bishop Tunstall a living without residence, or in his reprimand from the pulpit, of his superior, Bishop Richard Barnes of Durham, for the conduct of the diocese, an admonition of such frankness and sincerity as to persuade Barnes to apologize, who before had planned to deprive Gilpin of his rectory (p. 57). His charity may be surmised from his generous foundation of a grammar school, his education of numerous young men, his well-spread tables from which none in the parish was barred, the gift of his own horse to a poor plowman whose plug had fallen dead in the field. Even the theological discussions which formed a large and important part of his life add to the conception of his erudition and earnestness. The following is characteristic as the vivid and concrete end of a discussion wherein Gilpin confutes two of Bishop Tunstall's chaplains who defend transubstantiation (p. 18):

"While they were houlding this disputation without speakeing aloud, because they were close at the Bishops backe, who at that time sate before the fire, for it was in the winter season: the Bishop leaned his chaire somewhat backwards, and harkened what they said. And when they had done speaking, the Bishop turning to his Chaplaines, useth these words, Fathers soule, let him alone, for he hath more learning then you all."

If his life in the ample, far-stretching rectory at Houghton is full of truth and charm, his annual journeys to preach in outlying districts are no less replete with adventure. These itinerant pilgrimages among "that halfe barbarous and rustick people" of Ridsdale and Tindale justify his name, "The Apostle of the North," and recall the lives of the great eighth-century missionaries. There is dramatic tension in the scene wherein he plucks from the rafters of a country church a glove hung as a challenge, and uses it as a text on forgiveness before his rude congregation. As an example of Gilpin's influence over the semi-civilized bordermen, and also as an illustration of the wide range of incidents and treatment possible in writing the lives of clerics, the subjoined account relative to his quelling a feud is given in full (p. 27):

"Uppon a time when Mr. Gilpin was in these parts at a towne called Rothbury, there was a pestilent faction amongst some of them who were wont to resort to that Church. The men being bloodily minded practised a bloody manner of revenge, termed by them Deadly-feod. If the faction on the one side did perhaps come to the Church, the other side kept away because they were not accustomed to meet together without bloodshed. Now so it was that when Mr. Gilpin was in the pulpit in that Church, both parties came to Church in the presence of Mr. Gilpin; and both of them stood, the one of them in the upper part of the Church, or Chancell, the other in the body thereof armed with swords and javelins in their hands. Mr. Gilpin somewhat moved with this unaccustomed spectacle goeth on neverthelesse in his Sermon: and now a second time their weapons make a clashing sound, and the one side drew neerer to the other, so that they were in danger to fall to blowes in the middest of the Church. Hereupon Mr. Gilpin commeth downe from the pulpit, and stepping to the ring-leaders of either faction, first of all he appeased the tumult. Next, he labowreth to establishe peace betwixt them, but he could not prevaile in that: onely they promised to keepe the peace unbroken so long as Mr. Gilpin should remaine in the Church. Mr. Gilpin seeing he could not utterly extinguish the hatred which was now inveterate betwixt them, desired them that yet they would forbeare hostility so long as he should remaine in those quarters: and this they consented unto. Mr. Gilpin thereupon goeth up into the pulpit againe (for he had not made an end of his Sermon) and spent the rest of the allotted time which remained in disgracing that barbarous and bloody custome of theirs, and (if it were possible) in the utter banishing of it forever. So often as Mr. Gilpin came into those parts afterwardes, if any man amongst them stood in feare of a deadly foe, he resorted usually where Mr. Gilpin was, supposing himselfe more safe in his company, then if he went with a guard."

Bishop Carleton made a valuable contribution to English biography in the introduction of Gilpin's personal letters. These he had sought for diligently and had justly valued and interpreted. They are included in such a fashion as not to break the continuity of the narrative, and often, as with the communication to his brother George in 1575 (pp. 32–41), which explains the development of his religious beliefs, the letters reveal the inner life of the rector more clearly than could be done by any other means.

The actions of Nicholas Ferrar (1592–1637) are as original as those of Bernard Gilpin, and his picturesque figure stands out among the numerous conventional churchmen in two biographies written some time after his death. John Ferrar, brother of this unusual character, wrote the earlier version about the year 1655. The more complete biography Mr. J. E. B. Mayor, on the authority of the manuscript heading, attributes to Dr. Jebb, who did little more than amplify and formalize the earlier life.[8] John Ferrar's work consists of a fragmentary collection of good anecdotes and letters developing the personality of his brother, who, after extensive continental travels, renounced an influential position in the Virginia Company, a seat in Parliament, and an heiress as wife in order to take deacon's orders and live in retirement in the barren colony of Little Gidding. The family life of this "Protestant nunnery," pious Mother Ferrar who after a fatiguing journey to the desolate settlement would not rest until the desecrating strawstacks and fodder had been removed from the family chapel, the female relatives and their domestic occupations — all these elements combine to produce an atmosphere not unlike that of *The Vicar of Wakefield*. Through each of these biographies runs a spirit of asceticism and deep-rooted faith which make the narrative "a story of a protestant family that outdid the severest monastics abroad." [9]

John Ferrar's ingenuous lack of method results in a life of the Walton type of pleasant piety. Sometimes Ferrar's character is portrayed through description (p. 68):

"Nicholas Ferrar's posture in his study was either walking or standing at a desk, to write or read at, seldom sitting at study or writing, and some things that he writ were upon a low desk, he all the time kneeling upon his knees."

Sometimes it is brought out by incidents (p. 54):

". . . he [Ferrar] went on saying. . . . When you have measured out the place for my grave, then go and take out of my

8. *Two Lives of Nicholas Ferrar*, 1855.   9. Dr. Jebb, p. 253.

study those three great hampers of books, that have stood there locked up these many years. (They were not many scores, but many hundreds, in all kinds of languages, which he had in all places gotten with great search, and some cost; they were comedies, tragedies, love hymns, heroical poems, and such like.) Carry, said he, those hampers to the place of my grave, and upon it see you burn them all: and this he spake with some vehemency and passion of indignation. . . . So it was performed, and a great smoke, bonfire, and flame they made."

The biography represents an original study of a man whose life was so exceptional in its rule of austere piety as to merit record. For success in painting a portrait without conscious art, it may be classed with Roper's life of More.

The religious controversies that preceded the Civil Wars touch the solitary life of Ferrar lightly. Yet they were important in determining the trend of ecclesiastical biography, as may be seen in the lives that concern the leader of the Anglican party, Archbishop Laud. It is not strange that such a reactionary and positive figure in the history of the Church of England should have found only partizan biographers, and most of the tracts that centre about his character are rabid in antagonism or unstinted in praise. His arrest and imprisonment by Parliament in 1641 brought forth the pamphlet, "A Parallel betweene Cardinall Wolsey and William Laud," and, indeed, occasioned the publication of Cavendish's biography of the Cardinal. In the same year, while the fate of Laud, imprisoned, was still in doubt, there appeared another topical tract entitled "Rome for Canterbury; Or, a true Relation of the Birth and Life of William Laud, Archbishop of Canterbury," whose thesis is: "Greatness and Goodness are two several blessed Attributes conferred upon Man; but seldom meet in one Person." As to Laud, "Here was Grace, which, had it been celestially inspired, as it was but temporally disposed, might to that Greatness have so combined Goodness, as, from thence, could have grown no such Tribulation." It is principally concerned in demonstrating, in paragraphs chiefly remarkable for their alliteration, this prelate's partiality for Popery.

When the pendulum swings to the other extreme, the royalist biographers are no less sedulous in using the Archbishop's life for their own purposes, and in the collections of royalist lives by Winstanley (1665) and Lloyd (1668), Laud occupies a place as leader of the clergy much as King Charles stands at the head of the nobility. The most pretentious of these biographies, more than five hundred pages in length, was published by Peter Heylyn in 1668 under the title, *Cyprianus Anglicus; Or, The History of the Life and Death of . . . William . . . Lord Archbishop of Canterbury.* This is distinctly a life-and-times piece, wherein Laud appears merely as the central figure in an involved and detailed history of the church. That it can hardly be considered a pure biography may be deduced from the fact that it begins with a forty-one-page "Necessary Introduction to the following History," outlining the tenets of the Anglican Church and the points that brought about the episcopalian controversy. The life, as Heylyn doubtless considered appropriate with so public a figure, rarely becomes intimate. The number of personages in church and state that are introduced renders the whole, in scope and scale, a history, and justifies the sub-title, "Containing also The Ecclesiastical History of the Three Kingdoms of England, Scotland and Ireland from His first rising till His Death." Even when Heylyn turns his attention on the final page to a personal sketch of the Archbishop, he does not become an ideal biographer. He confesses that his attempt has produced a "weak Character," and with this admission few will disagree.

One of the best ecclesiastical lives following the Restoration, and indeed one of the most finished biographies of the century, is *The Life of . . . Dr. H. Hammond* (1661) by John Fell. Dr. Fell knew Henry Hammond intimately, and spared no pains in writing a biography in a clear and classic style. It is full in detail from Hammond's birth in 1605 to his death in 1660, and includes his career at Magdalen, at the rectory of Pensehurst, as sub-dean of Christ Church, and as chaplain to Charles I. His voluminous writings are handled with unusual understanding, and in the analysis of Hammond's character Dr. Fell attains a subtle surety rarely met with in ecclesiastical biographers. Each quality is developed and individualized by numerous anecdotes, with particular stress on Hammond's friendships, — important in a personal history and usually neglected, — on his charity, and on his energetic industry. His abstention from food proves a pleasure on account of his myriad occupations, "so that his self-denials were quite contrary to the usual ones; for considering the time lost in Eating, and the vacancy succeeding it, his meals were the greatest pressure, and his fasting-day the most sensual part of his Week" (p. 105).

The work is an appreciation in which enthusiasm is tempered and reasonable; it is written on so full a scale and so high a level of prose that its peroration does not seem out of keeping (pp. 232–233):

"His Worth is not to be describ'd by any Words besides his own, nor can any thing beseem his Memory but what is Sacred and Eternal as those Writings are. May his just Fame from them and from his Vertue be precious to succeeding times, grow up and flourish still: and when that characters engrav'd in Brass shall disappear, as if they had been writ in Water, when Elogies committed to the trust of Marble shall be illegible as whisper'd accents, when Pyramids dissolv'd in dust shall want themselves a monument to evidence that they were once so much as ruine; let that remain a known and classick History describing him in his full pourtraiture among the best of Subjects, of Friends, of Scholars, and of men."

Fell is a distinguished contributor to biography not only for the lucidity of his expression but for his sense of form. The *Life of Hammond* is long and complete,[10] but its author never loses grasp of his material in awkward digressions, unwieldly political or theological papers, or extraneous incidents. Throughout, the focus is neither national nor trivial; it is personal, and Fell gains a rare victory in reproducing the life of an individual not only with intimacy and fullness but with dignity and literary grace as well.[11]

Richard Mayo's *Life and Death of Edmund Staunton* (1673) merits special notice as a charming little biography possessing savor and individuality. It is written with the definite purpose of benefiting Mayo's dearly beloved flock at Kingston-upon-Thames, where Staunton was his predecessor. It includes much from Staunton's diaries that is subjective, such as his youth-

10. 245 pp. octavo.
11. A biography by Fell similar in style and conception, but on a smaller scale, was published in 1684 as a preface to *Forty Sermons . . . By Richard Allestree.* It is notable as containing one of the first clear and complete statements of the purpose for which lives prefatory to other works should be written. Cf. Chapter VII.

ful pride, his conversion, and his student fear of dark devils in the bedroom which he "remembers well" in Corpus Christi, Oxford, a college of which he was later to become president. Unconscious humor is not lacking in some of the tiny incidents narrated, as in his falling from a swing in his father's kitchen at Birchmore, or in extracts from his diary (p. 34): "'When I was Minister of Kingston, I drank Ink one morning instead of Muscadine, yet I had no hurt.'" The whole story is told with a *naïveté* which is delightful.

The pious panegyrics of mid-century, the numerous nonconformist lives such as those sponsored by Richard Baxter,[12] and, indirectly, ecclesiastical biography as a type, are ridiculed in the anonymous *Life of Stephen Marshal* (1680), whose subtitle is an ironical trap to the unwary reader: "The Godly Man's Legacy To the Saints upon Earth [the presbyterians], Exhibited In the Life of that Great and Able Divine, and Painful Labourer in the Word, Mr. Stephen Marshal." Using, therefore, the exact forms of the lives of the churchmen, from a satirically pious title to an equally pious character sketch, the author secures his effect by making a mockery of the type. The life is lacking in taste and point, but its caricature of the usual sketch of virtues is worth quoting in part, since a literary form must be well known and widely accepted before it can be parodied with such assurance (p. 21):

"I come now to describe his Virtues.

"His Charity in giving, was as little as his Charity in forgiving; never so much as bestowing a penny, or piece of Bread at his Door the year throughout. . . .

"And tho' men say, the Puritan will not swear, but will lye damnably. This Impostor both swore and ly'd. . . .

12. See Bibliography.

"And here he tells the People strange Stories of the Fight (but not a word how valiantly like Peter the Hermit he ran away) and that to his knowledge (tho' he was in too much haste to tell the Slain) the King's Party lost five to one of the Parliament. . . .

"I am now enquiring after his Humility, if I could find it. . . . His Deportment was clownish, like his Breeding; his Garb slovenly (sometimes preaching without his Cloak) his Gate shackling, and the Furniture within not unlike the outside."

In contrast with the simple and pious life stories with their Puritan sympathies which are here parodied, is the type of biography in popular demand at the end of the century: such ample, formal lives, consciously ornamented or deliberately encyclopedic, as Thomas Plume's *John Hacket*, 1675; John Barnard's *Peter Heylyn*, 1683; Parr's *Usher*, 1686; John Hacket's *Scrinia Reserata*, published in 1693; *The History of . . . William Laud*, 1695; and Strype's ecclesiastical histories (1694–1718).

The Life of . . . James Usher, Late Lord Arch-Bishop of Armagh (1686) by Richard Parr is a faithful exemplar of the heavier type of ecclesiastical biography. It appreciates Usher's position as an antiquary, dwells on his published works, and is of special significance because it includes three hundred of Usher's letters. Parr, however, does not use these letters to interpret Usher's life; it would be more accurate to consider the biography as an introduction to a collection of letters.

The explanatory title to John Hacket's *Scrinia Reserata* is "A Memorial Offer'd to . . . John Williams . . . Containing a Series of the Most Remarkable Occurrences and Transactions of his Life in Relation both to Church and State." This large volume, completed as early as February, 1657, contains almost five hundred pages in folio; Hacket apologizes for the length of the work by recalling Williams' importance as judge and counsellor, as Lord Keeper of the Great Seal, Bishop of Lincoln, and Archbishop of York. Hacket was in an exceptionally favorable position to write a complete life, and fully realized the importance of his own undertaking. Yet *Scrinia Reserata* is disappointing as pure biography. The circumlocutory style is vexing (p. 8):

> "I have not added a Grain to the just weight of Truth, that his Sails were filled with prosperous Winds, which blew from the Cape of Nature, yet that he plied the Oar with main might to make a gaining Voyage."

The narrative is continually interrupted by quotations from Latin and Greek literature, the Greek Fathers, and the Bible, often inappropriate. The emphasis, as he admits, is not on the life (II, p. 229):

> "I need not admonish my Readers, for they find it all the way, that my Scope is not so much to insist upon the memorable things of one Man's Life; as to furnish them with reading out of my small store, that are well-willers to Learning, in Theological, Political, and Moral Knowledge. Yet in those Observations I have not set down a Cyrus, a feigned Subject, but wrought them into the true Image of this Prelate. So Nazianzen informs us, that when Athanasius drew out the life of Anthony the Hermite. . . . He drew out the Instructions of a Rural Hermetical Life in his Behaviour."

Hacket is not the first to present an odd mixture of universal history and universal knowledge as the life of a single individual; nor is he the last. In succeeding centuries, lives tend to increase in bulk, until the modern biographical fault is not so much undue panegyric as failure to exercise due selection. At the close of the seventeenth century John Strype published his *Memo-*

rials of . . . Thomas Cranmer (1694), a final example of the laborious and learned biographies wherein all artistic form is buried under the accumulated weight of details. "The Collections I have here made," Strype says,[13] "and do publish to the world, are chiefly from Manuscript Records, Registers, Letters, Orders of Council, Original and Authentick." He specifies the libraries of Cotton and Parker, a manuscript by Cranmer's secretary, papers of John Foxe, material from Lord Burleigh's secretary, the Registers and Records of the Cathedral Church of Canterbury, the Tower Records, four learned friends, and the manuscript library at Lambeth. He continually breaks the flow of his narrative by direct and clumsy quotations. The result is a patchwork study in the origins of the Anglican Church, occupying 467 folio pages with a 271-page appendix. Strype's importance in a history of biography must lie in the example he sets of how far into error biographers may stray. He continued these unwieldy, leviathan-like histories into the next century, with the lives of the archbishops Grindal in 1710, Parker in 1711, and Whitgift in 1718.

Some of the most beautiful and important lives of ministers of the Gospel, such as the writings of John Bunyan, of the Puritan Henry Burton, of the Baptist evangelist Vavasor Powell, of John Foxe and Richard Baxter, have been reserved for consideration as autobiographies, but should not be neglected in any complete survey of the type. The lives by Izaak Walton, which carry ecclesiastical biography to its highest development, are important enough to be treated in a separate chapter.

The typical ecclesiastical biography of the century

13. Preface, p. vii.

may also be studied in the collections of the lives of divines made by such writers as Henry Holland, Donald Lupton, Barksdale, Fuller, Lloyd, Winstanley, and Samuel Clark.

Henry Holland's *Heroologia Anglica* (1620) is not confined to the church, but includes statesmen and soldiers of the sixteenth century. His Protestant bias is furthered by the use of Bale as an authority, and all the principal lights of the church, such men as Wolsey, Tyndall, Latimer, Ridley, Cranmer, Pole, Jewel, and Parker, are included in Holland's gallery of portraits. The accounts are short and much in the style of the antiquarian compendiums.

This collection served as a foundation for a translation by Donald Lupton, published in 1637 under the title of "The History of the Moderne Protestant Divines, Containing their Parents, Countries, Education, Studies, Lives, and the yeare of our Lorde in which they dyed." The title is sufficient to show the prevailing conception of what should constitute the history of an individual. As a specimen of the execution of the programme announced on the title-page, the "Life of John Foxe," beneath a fine engraving of the martyrologist, may be quoted in full (pp. 276–282):

"*John Foxe.* Behold this Man, and thou canst not choose but wonder at his extraordinary labour and travaile, to gather together so many of Gods servants in a bundle: hee was borne in the County of Lancaster, his young yeeres shewed that he was layd out for a Scholler, and so he had education accordingly in a famous School. After being ripe, he was sent to Oxford, and was admitted into Magdalen Colledge, where hee gave himselfe strictly to study, and then profest Divinity: hee attained to an excellent skill in the Latine, Greek and Hebrew Tongues in King Edward 6. his Reigne, and for his better

safety and security, left this Kingdome in Queene Maries
dayes, and lived in the Low-countries. But when the Date of
that Queenes dayes were expired, he came backe into England, and proved a famous Divine. Hee had an excellent
faculty in preaching, and added to painefulnesse constancy
and willingnesse; but that worke of his called The History of
the Martyrs, made his name famous in this Kingdome, and
else where, and will for ever speake his praise. He was a man
of an humble spirit, and had truely learn'd that Doctrine of
St. Paul, *In what estate soever he was in, therewithall to be content.* Hee was one that had, as it seem'd, crucified himselfe to
the world, and its vanities, as it may appeare in a kind and
fatherly reprehension of his eldest sonne, who having a great
mind to travel into forraigne parts, which when hee had performed, he came to his Father in Oxford, then being old, and
he being attired in a loose out-landish fashion, who are you
said his Father not knowing him? To whom his sonne replyed, I am your sonne: to whom this Master Foxe answered,
Oh what enemy of thine hath taught thee so much vanity?
which speech of his shewed, that his minde was weaned from
the love of the world. And indeed, I cannot conceive how hee
could have any liberty to addict himselfe to follow delights
and pleasures, doing so exquisitely such rare pieces of Schol-
lership, which tooke up all his time: nay, it is rather to be
wondred, how he performed so great labours in so short a
time; which he could not have done without long and tedious
watchings, and fastings; which three, study, fasting, and
watching, will subject the flesh to the Spirit; and this course
tooke hee.

"This man never sought after greedily any promotions or
preferments, but held and approved of that estate in which he
dyed: He departed this life in London, and lyes buried in the
Church of Saint Giles without Cripple-gate, upon whose
Marble Monument his Sonne Samuel Foxe hath caused to bee
ingraven this Inscription,

"Christo, S.S.

"To John Foxe, his honoured Father, the faithfull Mar-
tyrologian of our English Church, a most disert searcher into

the Antiquities of Histories, a most stiffe Bulwarke, and fighter for the Evangelicall Truth, which hath revived the Martyrs as so many Phoenixes, from the dust of Oblivion, is this Monument made: He dyed 18. of Aprill, 1587. and of his age 70.

"He writ and set forth these things that follow . . ."

This brief life has been given here in its entirety because it represents the ecclesiastical biographies usually found in the collections. The royalist gatherings by William Winstanley (1665) and David Lloyd (1668) add little. Winstanley in his *Loyal Martyrology* hides his lack of knowledge under indiscriminate praise or abuse. Lloyd is an eclectic, and culls his materials from separate biographies, from funeral sermons, or from the accounts of relatives and friends to whom he applied. His *Church Worthies*, therefore, is anomalous, partly a catalogue digested and rewritten, partly a collection of individual lives composed by others.

Lloyd thus offers a convenient transition from the catalogues of Holland and Lupton to the groups of biographies published under the supervision of a general editor, like Thomas Fuller, Clement Barksdale, or Samuel Clark. Fuller, in his *Abel Redevivus or The dead yet speaking. . . . The Lives and Deaths of the Moderne Divines* (1651), establishes definitely the authorship of the various items which he includes.[14] The lives are ample, and are gathered or translated, often with only slight omissions, from longer separate biographies. A collector who, like Fuller, does not attempt to do justice to an entire class is usually less careless of the single life.

14. Daniel Featley, Thomas Gataker, and Fuller himself are each responsible for more than one biography; several are drawn from Holland's *Heroologia*, and separate lives are revised and included, such as Smith's *Andrew Willet*, Isaacson's *Lancelot Andrews*, and a few lives of continental churchmen.

This collection, therefore, may be considered the first gathering of lives in English that presents serious claims to literary form. Such collections show a growing consciousness of biography as a distinct branch of literature, a consciousness which Fuller did much to foster in his distinctive and voluminous productions. Moreover, such gatherings demonstrate increasing public curiosity as to the lives of the illustrious dead.

This curiosity was fed in the decade following the Restoration by Clement Barksdale, who published or reprinted in successive works no less than fifty biographies, wherein clerics played almost all the rôles. The same method of grouping and reprinting separate lives is characteristic of the numerous productions by Samuel Clark between 1646 and 1683. Clark justifies his collecting on the grounds that scattered and fugitive pieces are soon forgotten, and apologizes for his contractions by assuring the reader that nothing important is omitted. He does not confine his attention exclusively to churchmen. Biographies appealed to him indiscriminately, and in the same volume he will follow "A Collection of the Lives of Ten Eminent Divines" (1662) by the "Life of Gustavus of Sweden," and after Gustavus will descend from the sublime by adding a biography of Mistress Margaret Ducke. Such voluminous collections, from Holland to Clark, testify to the importance of ecclesiastical biography in the seventeenth century. Their contributions to the biographical form are negligible. In a history of biography their quantity rather than their quality is impressive.

Throughout the century classical biographies were well known to ecclesiastical biographers and frequently used by them.[15] But even more important in furnishing models for the seventeenth century school are the writings of the early church fathers, to which clerical writers turned with especial zeal after the break with Rome. Much of the material was made available in English translation.[16] References to, and quotations from, biographical or pseudo-biographical pieces by Dorotheus, Jerome, Gennadius, Epiphanius, Augustine, Eusebius, Ambrose, Paulinus, Posidonius, Gregory Nazianzen, and Chrysostom are frequent,[17] and two of these writers, at least, — Jerome and Augustine, — exercised an undoubted influence upon the development of ecclesiastical biography.

The influence of the Bible upon ecclesiastical biography is also profound, not so much in determining its shape and scope as in moulding its style. The slightest parallel between Scriptural history and incidents in the life of the subject will inspire many an author to copious Biblical quotation,[18] with chapter and verse in the margin. As an example, consider Edmund Vaughan's account of an accident to Dr. Thomas Jackson, once

15. See Paule's *Whitgift*, 1612; Humfrey's *Jewel*, 1573; Smith's *Willet*, 1634; Barnard's *Heylyn*, 1683; Hacket's *Williams*, 1693, as examples.

16. Henry Hawkins translated certain of Jerome's lives of the hermits in 1630; Wye Saltonstall published in 1637 his translation of *Eusebius His Life of Constantine*, and in 1659 appeared Edward Larkin's *Speculum Patrum*, a translated collection of the lives of early church fathers. William Cave published in 1675 and 1677 the lives of the apostles and of the primitive fathers to 300 A.D. His two volumes are based on wide knowledge of early church history and on a firm control of sources. Moreover, each individual is given a separate life, and the whole is not told as a history.

17. For striking cases of such influence, see Manton's *Jurdain*, 1655; Smith's *Lady Magdalen*, 1627; Bernard's *Usher*, 1656; Staunton's *Elizabeth Wilkinson*, 1659; Barwick's *Morton*, 1660; Plume's *Hacket*, 1675, and Barnard's *Heylyn*, 1683.

18. Cf. Clogie's *Bedell*, Paule's *Whitgift*, Barwick's *Morton*, Hacket's *Williams*, or Sikes' *Vane*.

President of Corpus Christi in Oxford, who in his youth narrowly escaped death while bathing: [19]

"He was in imminent peril of being drowned. The Depth closed him round about, the Weeds were wrapt about his head. He went down to the bottom of the Mountains, the Earth with her bars was about him for ever, yet God brought his soul from Corruption (Jonah 2.5, 6)."

In Izaak Walton Biblical quotations are frequent, and engross his thoughts to such an extent that he speaks of Jesus' promise to Mary Magdalen, that her memory will be preserved in his Gospels, as the precedent which led him to write his life of Donne and, again, his life of Sanderson — surely not a close or obvious parallel. Comparisons with Biblical figures are continually being drawn; Barnabas Oley likens George Herbert to David and Saint John; John Barwick calls his life of Bishop Thomas Morton *Hieronikes, Or The Fight, Victory and Triumph of S. Paul* (1660). The influence of the Bible on the writing of Christian biography is most strikingly seen in "The Life of a Christian" (1695) extracted from John Kettlewell's *Measure of Obedience,* in which the virtues usually ascribed to the English clerics — sobriety, humility, piety, charity, peacefulness, and obedience — are derived from the "commanding laws" of cited Scripture.[20]

19. *The Works of . . . Thomas Jackson . . . With the Life of the Author,* 1653, Preface, p. a2.

20. Occasionally the Bible furnished materials or inspiration for a biography in English. Even in Middle English this was true, as in the delightful *þe lyff of Adam and Eve* in the Vernon MS, or Lydgate's *Life of Our Lady* (Caxton, 1484). John Marbecke uses the Bible as a basis for his biographical dictionary, *The lyves of holy Sainctes, Prophetes, Patriarches, and others, contayned in holye Scripture,* 1574. Specimens in the seventeenth century are Anthony Stafford's *Female Glory: Or, The Life . . . of . . . the holy Virgin*

With such revered models in Biblical and patristic writings, with unusually frequent borrowings, quotations, and interrelations among the English clerical lives themselves,[21] it is not surprising that ecclesiastical biography formed a strong school and produced by the middle of the century a definite type. "God's Graces are much the same in all his holy ones," said Richard Baxter.[22] "When we describe their Humility, Piety, Soundness of Judgment, Fidelity, Peaceableness, Concord, secret and open Holiness, Sobriety, &c. we must speak over the same things of all."

One reason for the extraordinary flourishing of ecclesiastical biography in the seventeenth century lies in the increasing use of lives written to serve as prefaces to editions of theological works. The growing number of volumes of ecclesiastical history and controversy, therefore, is directly responsible for many lives of the clerics.[23]

Still another reason for the growth of devout biographies may be found in the custom of publishing funeral

Mary, 1635; the verse lives of Old Testament figures by Francis Quarles and Abraham Cowley; Jeremy Taylor's *Life and Death of . . . Jesus Christ*, 1649; and Samuel Wesley's *Life of . . . Jesus Christ. An Heroic Poem*, 1693.

The Bible also supplied convenient mottoes for ecclesiastical biographies, the most popular being "The memory of the just is blessed" (Proverbs, 10:7) and "Let us now praise famous men, and our fathers that begat us" (Ecclesiasticus, 44:1).

21. For example, successive, dependent lives of Bedell were written by Bedell, Clogie, and Burnet; of Ferrar, by Ferrar and Jebb; of Morton, by Baddily, Naylor, and Barwick; of Usher, by Parr and Bernard; of Heylyn, by Vernon and Barnard. Two of Walton's lives, the *Hooker* and the *Herbert*, had predecessors with which he was familiar.

22. Preface to Samuel Clark's *Sundry Eminent Persons*, 1683.

23. To cite illustrations, Thomas James' short *Wickliffe*, 1608; Featley's translation of Humfrey's *Jewel*, 1609; John Harris's *Arthur Lake*, 1629; Bagshaw's *Bolton*, 1633; Smith's *Willet*, 1634; Buchanan's *Knox*, 1644; Oley's *Herbert*, 1652; Vaughan's *Jackson*, 1653; Duppa's *Spotswood*, 1655, and Plume's *Hacket*, 1675, are all prefaces to works by the subjects of the biographies.

sermons followed by a brief life of the deceased.[24] The
tendency of all such writings, offering incense to the
dead, is to introduce indiscriminate eulogy. Ecclesiastical biographers were constantly tempted to write in the
de mortuis manner of funeral sermons. Too much stress
can hardly be placed upon the eulogistic tone that pervades the majority of these lives and deprives them of
significance and individuality. A biography becomes
little more than a religious homily when the first paragraph begins, "The venerable and sacred commemoration of the renowned lives and deaths of holy men, as it
is profitable to posteritie, so it is likewise acceptable and
pleasing unto God; who in their fame is chiefly honoured." [25] Harris sums up his *Bishop Arthur Lake*
(1629) under almost as many heads as Polonius used for
the drama. Lake is "a man rare and eminent for all
kinds of vertue, naturall, morall, theologicall, personall,
pastorall; and indeed one of the examples of his time."
Henry Isaacson, writing in 1650, entitles his contribution to this *genre*: *The Life and Death of . . . Lancelot
Andrewes, Late Bishop of Winchester, Which may serve as
a Pattern of Piety and Charity to all Godly disposed
Christians*. This biography is hardly a life at all, and
little more than an extended and edifying character
sketch, the portrayal of an incredible mixture of virtues
which include, sometimes redundantly, zeal and piety,
charity and compassion, fidelity and integrity, gratitude
and thankfulness, munificence and bounty, hospitality,

24. This may be studied in such pieces as William Walker's funeral sermon on William Lord Russell, 1614; Ashe's *Thomas Gataker*, 1655; Bernard's
Usher, 1656; Staunton's *Mrs. Wilkinson*, 1659; Barwick's *Morton*, 1660;
Gauden's *Brounrig*, 1660; or Tully's *Edward Rainbow*, 1688. William Bates
includes in his *Vitae selectorum aliquot Virorum*, 1681, four or five funeral
sermons without differentiating them from the other lives.

25. Peter Smith, *Life of Andrew Willet*, 1634, p. 1.

humanity, affability, modesty, indefatigability in study, profundity in learning, wit, judgment, gravity, humility, and a detestation of usury, simony, and sacrilege. Featley's "Life of Robert Abbot, Bishop of Salisbury," [26] closes with this peroration:

"For so soon as the Author had finished the piece, & brought it to this light, he himself passed to the light coelestiall: Having fitted his labour for the benefit of the Church Militant, he was called to the Church Triumphant; and caught up immediately from his defence of divine grace, to the fruition of divine glory."

In such biographies it would appear that the rediscovery of the individual in the Renaissance had been in vain. The authors have returned to the spirit of the saints' legends, and are magnifying God in the death of his servants. The biographies exemplify, with less of the brevity of wit, "The Character of a Grave Divine" which Earle draws in his *Microcosmographie* (1628): "His death is the last sermon, where, in the pulpit of his bed, he instructs men to die by his example." Through undue eulogy the biographers fell short of justice; and in their attempts to sanctify the life of their hero they made him a shadowy and indeterminate figure of ethereal merit, a ghost walking upon the face of the earth.

They damned with great praise.

Yet this very fault must be forgiven them, for it is an amiable weakness. The tendency to portray a character in the most favorable light is emphasized by the purpose for which most ecclesiastical lives were written: the desire to set an example for the living. Thus the Reverend William Hinde adds as an explanatory title to his puritanical *Life of John Bruen* (1641), "principally in-

26. *Abel Redevivus*, 1651, p. 555.

tended as a Path and President of Piety and Charity for the Inhabitants of the Famous County Palatine of Chester." Or Bernard's *Usher* begins: [27]

"The writing of the lives of Holy and Eminent Men departed, are for us surviving (as a Father sayeth) . . . as a Glasse to trimme our lives by, a Copy to improve our hands, a Sauce to sharpen our tastes of the heavenly Gift in them."

This eagerness to furnish shining patterns becomes fervent in Mayo's *Life of Staunton*: [28]

"To conclude, my heart's desire and earnest prayer is this, That God would use this Narrative for the doing some good in the World, that those who wont be guided by Rules and Precepts, may be a little mov'd by this holy man's example and practice."

And nowhere has the ideal of the ecclesiastical biography of the seventeenth century been more beautifully expressed than by Richard Baxter in his preface to the *Life of John Janeway* (1673):

"To teach me better how to live and die, in Faith, Hope and Love, is that for which I read this narrative; and that thou maist learn the same is the end of my commending it to thee!"

With this simple expression of the aspirations of ecclesiastical biography, this chapter may well close.

Among the extremely abundant lives of the clerics there is much dross, and the type as a whole is not particularly attractive to modern taste. Yet a class which can produce individual lives as intimate as Carleton's *Gilpin*, as faithful and dignified as Fell's *Hammond*, as vivid as the lives of Bunyan, Burton, and Baxter, and as charming as Walton's biographies, merits our appreciation and our love.

27. "To the Reader," in 1656 ed.   28. 1673, p. 57.

IV

IZAAK WALTON

Here's harmony, and wit, and art,
To raise thy thoughts and cheer thy heart.
IZAAK WALTON*

A STUDY of the ecclesiastical lives of the seventeenth century is a necessary preliminary in estimating the place of Izaak Walton among English biographers. He is a product of his forebears and his surroundings. If there had been no saints' lives, no contemporary ecclesiastical biography, no civil wars, and no church strife, his lives as we know them could not have been written. His susceptibility to the influences of his models and his environment is marked. Walton is important in the history of biography because he reflects in himself so many tendencies, and combines them with his own distinctive, gentle personality.

It is not as a disciple of the classical tradition that Walton is of primary importance, although he was not a stranger to it. His work represents, rather, the culmination of the saints' lives in that particular form which they assumed in the seventeenth century. In this respect Walton's lives furnish major examples of the solidarity of the biographical tradition and the continuation in modern times of forms developed in mediaeval England, and, at an earlier date, in the patristic writings of the church.

Walton, the Fleet Street draper, chose churchmen as the subjects for his biographies. The five lives of Donne,

* Dedication to Alexander Brome's *Songs and Poems.*

Wotton, Hooker, Herbert, and Sanderson which were published during Walton's long lifetime treat of men in holy orders.[1] Not only are all Walton's heroes notable for their piety; they are also distinguished as literary figures. The works of John Donne, Richard Hooker, and George Herbert have recognized places in English litera- ture. Wotton's pieces collected in the *Reliquiae Wot- tonianae* show a feeling for history and diplomacy and an appreciation of classic models comparable to Francis Bacon's; and Robert Sanderson in his published *Logic* and *Cases of Conscience* enjoyed a contemporary popu- larity which extended even to King Charles I.

This dual character of all Walton's heroes — their piety and their literary ability — cannot be dismissed as accidental. Walton's models reflect his own mind. He writes of pious artists because he is himself a pious artist. The inspiration for Waltonian biography is always a feeling of sympathy and admiration, and it is therefore natural that he should choose characters consonant with his temperament. The lives of Donne, Wotton, and Herbert are tributes written by a friend and an admirer.

Walton began his career as a biographer by the merest chance, and several of his lives of great freshness and charm were written originally in haste and almost under compulsion.[2] The circumstances which led to Walton's writing his first biography he himself tells us in the pref- ace to the 1640 edition of Donne's sermons. Walton's friend, Sir Henry Wotton, had produced several short

1. Sir Henry Wotton, though not primarily a churchman, took a preb- endary's orders in his later years when he assumed the provostship of Eton.

2. E.g., *Life of Wotton*, 1651, Preface. "If there shal be found some small Incongruities, either in time, or expression, in the Life of Sir Henry Wotton; The Reader is requested to afford him a gentle Censure, because it was by the Printer fetch'd so fast by pieces from the Relatour; that he never saw what he had writ all together, till 'twas past the Presse."

biographical pieces on the model of Plutarch.[3] He intended also to write a life of his friend the Dean of Saint Paul's, and to this end commissioned Walton to gather materials. Unfortunately Sir Henry Wotton died before "his powerfull pen," in Walton's phrase, had traced Donne's life. In the following year (1640), when an edition of eighty of Donne's sermons was about to appear, "indignation or griefe (I know not whether)," compelled modest Mr. Walton to take up his less powerful pen and give to the world some account of the author of such edifying and original discourses. The result is "The Life and Death of Dr. Donne, Late Deane of St. Paul's London," which fills seventeen folio pages as an introduction to the sermons, "the first edition of which," says Anthony Wood,[4] "coming into the hands of the best critick of the last age, I mean Jo. Hales of Eaton, he affirmed to his friends, that he had not seen a life written with more advantage to the Subject, or more reputation to the writer, than it."

The death of the Provost of Eton not only caused Izaak Walton to write the life of Donne, but also to compose the life of Wotton himself, the friend with whom he had so often angled on the banks of placid streams. This, too, is published as a preface to the subject's collected writings, and appeared in the year 1651. Walton's third essay, his life of Richard Hooker, issued separately in 1665, was reprinted with an edition of Hooker's works in the following year. It was written at episcopal request, largely to correct the careless and in-

3. Later included in *Reliquiae Wottonianae* and comprising the "Life and Death of Geo. Villiers, Duke of Buckingham," 1642; a parallel between the Earl of Essex and Buckingham, 1641; a panegyric of Charles I; and characters of Doge Giovanni Bembo and Ferdinando di Medici.

4. *Athenae Oxon.*, 1691, i, 475.

accurate life of Hooker by Bishop Gauden which had been published in 1662. Walton's life of George Herbert (1670), on the other hand, is a pure labor of love: he calls it "a Free-will offering, and writ, chiefly to please my self." It is the first of the lives which originally was intended as an independent piece rather than as an introduction. Last of all, in his old age Walton finished his life of Dr. Sanderson (1678), again written at the request of others, dedicated to George Morley, Bishop of Winchester, and followed by some of Sanderson's tracts which fill more than half the volume.

It appears, therefore, that in their original form, Walton did not intend these lives as literary works which were to stand alone, but as introductions and interpretations — as prefaces. This original conception he soon modified, not only by continually revising and extending his works, but by publishing as early as 1670 a collection of the four lives that had then been composed. A second edition appeared in the year 1674 [5] with minor changes and some expansion. Because of repeated subsequent publication apart from the works of their subjects, the lives may be considered as independent and sufficient in themselves.

At no point in his writings does Walton formally state his theories of the function and method of a biographer. These must be reconstructed from the lives themselves. As a starting point, the introduction to his life of Hooker (1666 edition) may be quoted in full, as it shows in some detail his own attitude as a biographer. The first para-

5. This is called in the title-page the fourth edition, probably because the lives of Donne and Wotton, which had appeared separately, were here reprinted for the fourth time.

graph explains his reasons for writing the life, to which
Walton might have added the importunity of Gilbert
Sheldon, later Archbishop of Canterbury:

"I think it necessary to inform my Reader that Doctor
Gauden (the late Bishop of Worcester) hath also lately wrote
and publisht the Life of Master Hooker; and though this be
not writ by design to oppose what he hath truly written; yet,
I am put upon a necessity to say, That in it there be many
Material Mistakes, and more Omissions. I conceive some of
his Mistakes did proceed from a Belief in Master Thomas
Fuller, who had too hastily published what he hath since
most ingenuously retracted. And for the Bishops Omissions,
I suppose his most weighty Business and Want of Time, made
him pass over many things without that due Examination,
which my better Leisure, my Diligence, and my accidental
Advantages, have made known unto me."

The accidental advantages to which he alludes sprang
from the wide circle of his acquaintances and friends
among the clergy of the Church of England. The diligence and leisure which Walton ascribes to himself have
a marked effect upon his biographical method. His
lives grow out of meditation. As early as 1670, in his
preface to the four collected lives, he suggests Dr. Sanderson and Dr. Richard Field as subjects worthy of the
biographer's attention. Yet eight years elapsed before
he published his life of Sanderson.[6] Walton's delibera-
tion and care further manifest themselves in his minute
attention to form. Throughout his life Walton is an in-

6. The mention of Dr. Field, whose life he never wrote, gives rise to speculation regarding the men who almost achieved immortality in Waltonian biographies. At least one other instance is on record: from the words of Dr.
King, Bishop of Chichester — that Walton "has done much for Sir Henry
Savile, the contemporary and friend of Mr. Richard Hooker" (Preface, *Life
of Hooker*) — it would seem that a manuscript biography of this distinguished
Warden of Merton may once have existed in addition to the slight mention of
him in the life of Hooker.

veterate reviser, both in minor phrasing and in the modification or addition of incidents. Five short biographies, together with *The Compleat Angler* and a few fugitive pieces, represent the entire production of this literary amateur during a period of forty years. Between the writing of the life of Wotton and that of Hooker, Walton as biographer confesses that he "lay quiet twenty years." [7] In the final form of the lives each sentence has been weighed, remolded and remodelled; the author is consciously meticulous. His style is dignified and supple, with a tendency to rhetorical balance and a fondness for coupled adjectives and alliteration. [8]

The second paragraph of his introduction to the life of Hooker hints at his attitude toward his sources and toward his readers; it also shows his conscious scheme of revision. With Walton a biography was never complete and finished; it was always to be improved:

"And now for my self, I can say, I hope, or rather know, there are no Material Mistakes in what I here present to you, that shall become my Reader. Little things that I have received by Tradition (to which there may be too much and too little Faith given) I will not at this distance of Time undertake to justifie; for, though I have used great Diligence, and compared Relations and Circumstances, and probable Results and Expressions: yet, I shall not impose my Belief upon my Reader; I shall rather leave him at liberty: But, if there shall appear any Material Omission, I desire every Lover of truth and the Memory of Master Hooker, that it may be made known unto me. And, to incline him to it, I here promise to acknowledge and rectifie any such Mistake in a second Impression, which the Printer says he hopes for; and by this means my weak (but faithful) Endeavours may become a bet-

7. "To the Reader," *Lives*, 1679.
8. E.g., *Donne*, 1670, p. 78: "Thus variable, thus vertuous was the Life, thus excellent, thus exemplary was the Death of this memorable man."

ter Monument, and in some degree more worthy the Memory of this Venerable man."

Walton's biographies rest largely on facts learned from friends and acquaintances, such information as he specifically solicits in the above paragraph.[9] He became increasingly indebted to original written sources, and says, for instance, regarding the dates of Sanderson's Oxford degrees, "the Reader is requested to believe that, if I be mistaken in the time, the Colledge Records have mis-informed me: But I hope they have not." Finally, Walton realized the importance of letters and documents, and profited by them. The biographies contain many of the private letters of their heroes, quotations from their poems, their sermons and their meditations, extracts from their wills. Those who hold that Walton as a biographer relied too much upon his own imagination and taste would do well to consider the importance he attached to such primary sources of information, and the large place they fill in his lives.

The third and last paragraph shows Walton's belief that biographies are important and should be more numerous; his modest belittling of his own powers is followed by the confession, which most biographers make sooner or later, that life-writing is a task exacting and difficult:

"I confess, that when I consider the great Learning and Vertue of Master Hooker, and what satisfaction and Advantages many Eminent Scholars and Admirers of him have had

9. Thus, some of his materials about Hooker are retailed afresh from a letter sent him by Dr. King (printed in 1670 edition of the lives), and other anecdotes, as he explains in his introduction, he received from William Cranmer, grandnephew of the archbishop, from Thomas Morton, and from Archbishop Usher. Many incidents in the life of Sanderson came to him in a letter from Dr. Thomas Barlow, Bishop of Lincoln (printed in Zouch's 1817 edition of the lives, ii, 332–338).

by his Labours: I do not a little wonder that in Sixty years no
man did undertake to tell Posterity of the Excellencies of his
Life and Learning, and the Accidents of both; and sometimes
wonder more at my self, that I have been perswaded to it;
and indeed I do not easily pronounce my own Pardon, nor
expect that my Reader shall, unless my Introduction shal!
prove my Apology, to which I refer him."

If, in all of Walton's writings, these three short paragraphs represent the fullest and most definite expression
of his conception of the biographer and his duties, it
seems necessary to turn to the lives themselves for a
clearer estimate of his methods and his importance in
the history of biography. A survey will show, moreover,
that even in a body of work as homogeneous as his own,
a development in his manner may be observed which
parallels roughly the development in the ecclesiastical
biographies of his time.

The *Life of Donne* is the most interesting of Walton's
biographies, largely because of the subject. From a
technical point of view, it is of first importance as showing the expansion of the narrative through various editions. The life first published is noticeably different
from the life in its final form. In the edition of 1658, reissued apart from the sermons, Walton declares the
work revised and improved, and sighs for the "pensil of
a Tytian or a Tentoret." The edition of 1670 contains
further changes, and that of 1674 inserts for the first
time important incidents. These additions and changes
assume varied forms. In 1640, Walton compares
Donne's humility in entering God's service to that of
Moses who said to the Lord, "Who am I?" In 1670 he
has thought of a further parallel, to Saint Paul: "Lord,
who is sufficient for these things?" — and he inserts it.

The account of Donne's clandestine marriage is amplified in later editions, and such philosophical notes as
follow are introduced: Love is "a passion that carries us
to commit Errors with as much ease as whirlwinds re-
move feathers," or "Love and Anger are so like Agues,
as to have hot and cold fits." The first draft does not
contain the anecdote of the Bishop of Durham's offer of
a large benefice to Donne if he will enter the church.
Donne refuses because of irregularities in his past life.
The offer and refusal are set forth at length in two
speeches full of elevated sentiments in the style of the
classic historians. Nor does the first form contain
copies of the two original letters that follow this incident
and show Donne's despair in the years of his sickness
and poverty. These are later inserted. In the first edition Walton praises Donne as a preacher. Later, upon
reflection, to demonstrate that this is not "an immoderate Commendation," he quotes a certain Mr. Chidley's
metrical eulogy.[10] This is a typical instance of Walton's
ingenuous proofs of his statements.

Many such insertions can be noted. Further subjective
passages are added, as in the description of Donne after
his wife's death.[11] Other imaginary conversations are
brought in, as in the dialogue between the Dean of Saint
Paul's and Dr. Henry King following Donne's sickness.
Political events cause Walton to modify his writings.
So in a later revision, written during the Civil Wars, he
will break off a discourse on the value of the old church
music and hymns with an elliptic and indignant, "But
now, oh Lord — 1656." [12]

The additions show that Walton tended to lay increasing emphasis on Donne's poems and letters as le-

10. 1670, p. 39. 11. 1670, pp. 41-42. 12. 1670, p. 56.

gitimate guides to his character. The noble deathbed hymn beginning

> "Since I am coming to that holy room
> Where, with thy quire of saints for ever more
> I shall be made thy musique . . ."

is not given in the first edition. Subsequent editions also quote from Donne's Latin records of the blessings of Providence toward him. The portrait of his character is also amplified. Further incidents of his charity are included in later revisions, and general spiritual virtues are introduced. Some of the most vivid incidents in the life of Donne are entirely absent in the original edition. As examples might be cited Donne's vision, while in France, of his wife who had just died in childbirth; or the painting of himself in his shroud, which, in his last days, the Dean of Saint Paul's ordered to be executed and placed in grim intimacy by his bedside.

Whether these incidents came to Walton at a later period or whether he ruled them out of his original efforts for reasons he later discarded is a question that cannot be answered with complete certainty. It seems obvious, however, that as Walton advanced in years he grew less concerned with rendering his narrative credible in all details. He became increasingly indifferent to that critical accuracy which would rigidly exclude, for instance, the dialogue between Donne and King, or the debated question of the apparition of Donne's wife. Such an incident, which at first was cautiously omitted, might well be brought forward at a time when he was detailing the dreams of Wotton's ancestors. Furthermore, it is consonant with his later theory expressed in the 1658 edition of the life of Donne:

"I either speak my own knowledge, or from the testimony of such as dare do any thing, rather than speak an untruth. And for that part of it which is my own observation or opinion, if I had a power I would not use it to force any mans assent, but leave him a liberty to dis-believe what his own reason inclines him to."

The changes in wording are frequent. Sometimes a phrase will be modified. So "while a gentle slumber seises him" in the 1640 edition becomes in the 1670 edition "whilst a gentle slumber gives rest to his spirits." Sometimes only a word will be changed. Thus the final word of Donne's life in the 1670 edition is "reanimated." In the 1640 edition Walton had used the coinage "re-inanimated."

Similar important and unimportant variants occur in his other lives, particularly in those which he had the opportunity to revise over a long period of years. In general, these additions to the original drafts, which have here been sketched in the mutations of the life of Donne, illustrate his conceptions of the functions and methods of a biographer. He continues to revise to the end of his life. He becomes increasingly aware of the value of original documents in illustrating a biography. His treatment of incident and detail is progressively more free and facile. The anecdotes are picturesque and intimate; the changes tend to make the biography more imaginative and more dramatic. Walton does not hesitate to express his hero's inmost thoughts at any period of his career. He will fashion complete dialogues and debates. At last, in the life of Dr. Sanderson he characteristically declares: "I desire to tell the Reader that in this Relation I have been so bold, as to paraphrase and say what I think he (whom I had the happiness to

know well) would have said upon the same occasions."
Finally, like Plutarch, he embraces the pleasant art of
digression, and includes more and more of his own philosophy and observations, side excursions which explain
in large measure the charm, the life, and the individuality of these biographies.

Before pointing out the particular traits that distinguish Walton's biographical method, we may take this
opportunity to consider the lives separately and determine to what degree they are individualized.

The *Life of Donne* gains much of its particular appeal
from the character of its hero and the intimate relations
existing between the biographer and his subject. Donne
even remembered Walton in his will. That a London
layman should undertake to write the life of this subtle
doctor of divinity is in itself remarkable. That the
biography should be successful is even more striking.
Incompatibility of temperament is no obstacle, because
Walton does not recognize its existence. Donne's intensity is mellowed by Walton's sweetness; the emotional fire and the scholastic imagination of the Dean of
Saint Paul's is hardly suggested by his biographer, who
sees in him "a preacher, always preaching to himself,
like an angel from a cloud," and who deliberately prefers to turn from his youthful poetry, the exercise of
"his sharp wit, and high fancy," to his "many Divine
Sonnets, and other high, holy, and harmonious Com-
posures." The life closes like a hymn, with a reverence
akin to prayer.

Of all Walton's biographies, the *Life of Sir Henry
Wotton* is the most objective, the most worldly and entertaining. Walton's pleasant wit is continually at work.

Wotton's warning James of Catholic plots against his life, a warning which he carries to Scotland under the guise of an Italian, Octavio Baldi, with the sequel embrace of the king and the bestowal of knighthood and an ambassadorship, is highly romantic. His epigram, "An Embassadour is an honest man sent to lie abroad for the good of his Countrey," rouses James's wrath in the unfortunate Latin rendering of "to lie" as "ad mentiendum." Wotton's wit and Walton's delight therein brighten the work frequently with apothegms and incidents, both in the picture of Venetian court life where the English embassy is a city of refuge in a brilliant world, and later in the account of Wotton's old age, when, after he "had for many years (like Siciphus) rolled the restless stone of a state imployment," he secures the provostship of Eton. Even in his death Wotton preferred to be remembered on his gravestone by an epigram rather than by name.[13] His retirement is compared to the "cloysterall life" of Charles V in his old age, and includes an account of Wotton's employment during his last years, "his innate pleasure of Angling," his quips against Papists, his broad-minded opinions, and his counsel to an ambitious diplomat always to speak truth, "for, sayes Sir Henry Wotton, you shall never be believ'd." The motto of his life, like that engraved on the rings given to his friends after death, might well be *Amor unit omnia*; and he is shown in this urbane little biography as a philosopher of tolerance, an angler of a brilliant wit, a gentleman of polish.

The *Life of Richard Hooker* marks the transition from the biographies written by Walton in his maturity to

13. "Hic iacet huius sententiae primus author. Disputandi pruritus ecclesiarum scabies. Nomen alias quaere."

those written in his old age. It is unique in that it deals with a figure not personally known to him. Walton, it is true, was also unacquainted with Herbert, but the circle of their common friends was large. The life of Hooker, however, is written sixty years after the death of the church historian it commemorates, and furnishes a glimpse of Walton working at a distance from his subject. Nevertheless, his method of collecting facts and setting them forth remains the same, and the informal tone of friendly admiration which he establishes in his earlier works is present in the life of this divine whom he had never known. The account of Hooker's life in the parsonage at Draiton Beauchamp is not surpassed in any of Walton's biographies, and it is remarkable that the following description could have been written more than sixty years after Hooker's death: [14]

"And in this condition he continued about a year; in which time his two Pupils, Edwin Sandys, and George Cranmer, were returned from Travel, and took a journey to Draiton to see their Tutor; where they found him with a Book in his hand (it was the Odes of Horace) he being then tending his small allotment of Sheep in a common Field; which he told his Pupils he was forced to do, for that his Servant was then gone home to Dine, and assist his Wife to do some necessary houshould business. When his Servant returned and released him, his two Pupils attended him unto his House, where their best entertainment was his quiet company, which was presently denied them; for, Richard was called to rock the Cradle."

The character sketch of Hooker is original and convincing, unexcelled in Walton's entire work (p. 22):

". . . the Innocency and sanctity of his Life became so remarkable, that many turn'd out of the road, and others

14. 1666, p. 8.

(Scholars especially) went purposely to see the Man, whose
Life and Learning were so much admired; and alas, as our
Saviour said of St. John Baptist, what went they out to see!
a Man Cloathed in Purple and fine Linen? no indeed; but an
obscure harmless Man; a Man in poor Clothes, his Loynes
usually girt in a course Gown or Canonical Coat; of a mean
Stature, and stooping, and yet more lowly in the thoughts of
his Soul; his body worn out, not with Age, but Study and
Holy Mortifications; his face full of Heat-Pimples, begot by
his unactivity and sedentary life. And to this true Character
of his Person, let me add this of his Disposition and behaviour; God and Nature blest him with so blessed a bash-
fulness, that as in his younger days, his Pupils might easily
look him out of countenance; so neither then, nor in his Age,
did he ever willingly look any Man in the face: and was of so
mild and humble a Nature, that his poor Parish Clark and he
did never talk but with both their Hats on, or both off at the
same time; and to this may be added, that though he was not
purblind; yet, he was short or weak-sighted; and where he
fixt his eyes at the beginning of his Sermon, there they continued till it was ended."

Yet the portrayal of a figure so far removed from his
own times compelled Walton to consider the scholarly
problems of the antiquary. Thus the life is followed by
an appendix in which he discusses such questions as the
disputed date of Hooker's death, the fate of his family,
and the authenticity of the last three books of the
Ecclesiastical Polity.

Furthermore, to explain the position of this divine in
his own particular age, Walton finds it necessary, as it
was not necessary with Donne, to enter into an extended
account of church history. Hooker's contemporaries
at Oxford, such men as Savile, Jackson, Reynolds, and
Jewel, are all mentioned in more than casual fashion.
When Hooker was admitted Master of the Temple in

London in 1585, his biographer pauses to give "a Character of the Times, and Temper of the people of this Nation." Walton's historical generalizations are always simple, sure of themselves, and by no means valueless. He has the knack of condensation; his mild convictions and explanations are plausible. He also sees fit to include a sketch of the life of Archbishop Whitgift.

The method of presenting an individual in relation to his surroundings Walton also uses in the life of Herbert and particularly in the life of Sanderson. This mode of treatment he first adopts in the life of Hooker, which therefore furnishes the most typical example of Waltonian biography, and shows all his narrative traits, from the humor and vividness of Hooker's bedraggled entrance into the Shunamite House, where he falls a victim to Mistress Churchman and her unmarriageable daughter Joan, to the sweet piety of his death.

The *Life of Mr. George Herbert* stands by itself. It is a holy poem, written entirely in the spirit of the beautiful introduction: "In a late Retreat from the business of this World, and those many little Cares with which I have too often incumbred myself, I fell into a Contemplation." Walton approaches his most angelic manner in the feminine portraits, — so rare in his work, — of Herbert's mother and his wife. The amity existing between Donne and Lady Herbert is compared to Chrysostom's affection for Olympias or Jerome's for Paula. Donne sent her hymns and songs in praise of her autumnal beauty. "These Hymns are now lost to us; but, doubtless they were such, as they two now sing in Heaven." Herbert's courtship and marriage and the portrait of his wife are no less idyllic. "And Mr. Danvers had . . . so much commended Mr. Herbert to her, that Jane became so much a Platonick, as to fall in love with Mr. Herbert unseen." Yet Herbert's character is sketched delicately, through phrases consonant with the devout cast of the biography, slight intimations regarding "his gentile humour for Cloaths," or carefully chosen incidents such as his first prayer before the lonely altar at Bemerton, or the alms tenderly bestowed upon an old woman of his parish.

The saintly character of this biography does not exclude realism. At times Walton combines the holy and the vivid in his poetic pastoral: "some of the meaner sort of his Parish did so love and reverence Mr. Herbert, that they would let their Plow rest when Mr. Herbert's Saints-Bell rung to Prayers, that they might also offer their devotions to God with him, and would then return back to their Plow." Or again, upon one of his journeys to Salisbury to hear and assist in the church music which was his delight, he helps a distressed traveller and his horse, but upon his arrival in the cathedral city apologetically dismisses the incident with a brusque, "And now let's tune our Instruments." His friendship with Nicholas Ferrar leads to an extended sketch of that pious man and the difficulty Ferrar had in securing the consent of the Vice Chancellor of Cambridge for publishing *The Temple* without deleting the couplet:

> "Religion stands a-tiptoe in the land
> Ready to pass to the American strand."

As a final quotation in this biography, Walton alters lines from a dirge by James Shirley:

> "All must to their cold graves,
> But the religious actions of the just
> Smell sweet in death, and blossom in the dust." [15]

15. The original, from Shirley's *Contention of Ajax and Ulysses*, may be quoted to show Walton's sensitive ear, his preference for slower and

Few biographers, in any literature, have done as much as Walton here does for Herbert, to make the actions of their heroes blossom sweetly in death.

At last, at the leisurely age of eighty-five, Walton published his final biography, *The Life of Dr. Sanderson* (1678). His gifts are such as do not appreciably decline with old age. His moralizing is more frequent, his rambles afield a trifle less cogent, but the familiar and friendly Izaak has not disappeared. We may feel that "this calm, this quiet and happy temper of mind" which Walton continually ascribes to Sanderson is in reality the reflection of his own temper. We may feel that Walton weakens this work by his partizan and extended arguments for all things Anglican against all things Puritan. We may feel that the chronicle style of gathering unrelated events about a date instead of around a personality shows a decrease in art as well as haste in writing.[16] But we cannot deny that the whole biography gives individuality to an elusive character, a man "timorous and bashful," a scholar who could produce a textbook on logic and yet was unable to preach a short sermon without trembling into forgetfulness, a divine troubled by afterthoughts, so that through continued revision and refinement he winnowed away his writings until they vanished. It is difficult to restrain a smile upon reading of Dr. Sanderson's decision to marry after meditating on "the sacred unutterable joys that

more sinuous rhythms, his continual and usually successful emendations. It runs:

> "Your heads must come
> To the cold tomb —
> Only the actions of the just
> Smell sweet and blossom in their dust."

16. At the conclusion, Walton's postscript states that the work was "hastned from me."

Children beget in Parents, and the mutual pleasures and contented trouble of their daily care and constant endeavours to bring up those little Images of themselves so as to make them as happy as those cares and endeavours can make them." [17] Yet nowhere has Walton surpassed in vigor the account of his own last meeting with the aged doctor — "accidentally in London in sadcoloured clothes, and God knows, far from being costly." The two "turn'd to stand in a corner under a Penthouse (for it began to rain)." To escape the downpour they retire to a nearby tavern where, over "Bread, Cheese, Ale & a Fire," Sanderson talks. Concerning these fireside confidences Walton says, "I shall relate a part of them, in hope they may also turn to the advantage of my Reader," and it is in such full-veined recitals as the one that follows that Walton anticipates by more than a century the table-talk of Boswell.

This incomplete survey of the separate lives shows, at least, distinct differences in treatment. The brilliance and the almost Elizabethan flavor of the *Life of Wotton* cannot be confused with the poetic piety of the *Life of Herbert*. The concentration on personal anecdotes in the *Life of Donne* is not the same as the diffusion, the large historical horizon, the Polonius meditations in the *Life of Sanderson*. This divergence is partly caused by differences in the characters portrayed. To some extent, also, it marks a development in biographical tradition. The fertile school of ecclesiastical biographers that flourished during and after the Civil Wars influenced Walton's methods, and it is difficult to imagine him writing in 1640 a life on as broad a scale, accompanied by such dis-

17. 1678, p. c7.

jointed documentation, as his *Life of Sanderson*.[18] In 1678 he was following the fashion of the decade. Last, the differences in the separate lives show a development in Walton himself. Almost forty years elapse between the life of Donne and that of Sanderson; it would be remarkable if in a period so extended Walton remained entirely unchanged. More and more in his later lives of Herbert and Sanderson, Walton uses his subject as a vehicle to express his own philosophy of religion and the teachings of the Church of England.

Yet in spite of these noticeable differences, Walton's work possesses an unmistakable unity in method, style, and temper. He himself considered his lives as linked to one another, since in a preface [19] he speaks of his friends Herbert and Wotton and Donne and says, "I judge it may not be unacceptable . . . to see this Conjunction of them after their deaths." One biography flows over into another, so that we will read of Donne not only in his own life but in the life of Wotton and the life of Herbert; and again, we will find both of these men — "your friend, Sir Henry Wotton" and the "holy Mr. Herbert" — in the life of Sanderson. Donne, Wotton, and Herbert are quoted in *The Compleat Angler*, and Wotton in Walton's tract "Love and Truth" (1680). It cannot

18. The Civil Wars affect to some degree all of Walton's later biographies, but it is in the *Life of Sanderson* that his indignation shows itself most fully in his description of the trials which fell upon England as the plague fell upon Athens, "this Nation, being then happy and in peace (though inwardly sick of being well)." Sanderson's prominent part in the troubled church councils of the early forties led Walton to a bitter denunciation of the "Reformers" and a long description of the terrors in England between 1648 and 1660. "For all corners of the Nation were fill'd with Covenanters, Confusion, Comittee-men and Soldiers, serving each other to their several ends, of revenge, or power, or profit."

19. *The Life of Herbert*, 1670.

be said that Walton never repeats. When an incident
moves him or seizes his imagination he does not hesitate to tell it again.[20]

His inquisitive, kindly temper occasionally brings
Walton close to garrulity and discursiveness. This
causes not only the repetition and multiplication of incidents, but the inclusion of numerous contemporary
portraits, short biographies of a single paragraph, historical surveys which fill a page, and brief discourses on
the tenets of the Anglican Church. The result is that
hardly an important figure or event in the history of the
church between the days of Hooker and those of Sanderson is omitted in his biographies. In the lives of his
friends, Izaak Walton has also written an informal ecclesiastical history. Of the character of Hooker's times,
Walton's patron, Bishop King, wrote: "you have given
us a more short and significant Account then I have received from any other Pen." [21]

Such consideration of the quintette of lives as an
historical pattern leads to the paradox that these biographies gain their joint unity from their common
tendency to digress. Walton's natural taste for rambling
anecdotes caused him to include many incidents entertaining rather than relevant. In his later biographies
Walton's digressions become more frequent, and do not
lose their effectiveness. Among these is the story of

20. In the life of Herbert he describes for a second time the rings John
Donne ordered to be given to his friends after his death, with their seal of
Christ crucified upon an anchor. The monastic retirement of the Emperor
Charles V is dwelt upon at some length in the lives of Wotton and Herbert.
Monica, mother of St. Augustine, is introduced as a parallel from early Christian history in the three successive lives of Donne, Wotton, and Hooker, while
the final two lives, of Herbert and of Sanderson, begin with twin prefaces
wherein Walton's meditations on Mary Magdalen are described as leading
him to write the ensuing biographies.

21. Letter printed in 1670 edition of the lives.

Hooker's old parish clerk who still survived in Cromwell's time, and seeing the church desecrated by Puritan
offices, said it was not thus in his master's days, quitted
his duties, and died broken-hearted. Again, Walton's
denunciation of the Scotch covenanting usurper who
cuts down a yew tree in the churchyard of Boothby
Pagnell has only the faintest relation to Sanderson's life,
yet it is a touch where stern excision would be regret-
table. As a further example might be cited the dream of
Nicholas Wotton which saved his nephew Thomas from
death at the time of Wyatt's rebellion, with which he
sympathized and in which he "thought he had not continued actually innocent, if his Uncle had not happily
dream'd him into a Prison." The anecdote is neatly
turned, but the connection with Sir Henry Wotton is
purely patronymic.

The last illustration naturally leads us to Walton's
wit. It is a quality peculiarly his, a quiet mirth which
will not bear detachment from the biographies themselves. In the smooth-flowing stream of his writings,
gleams and ripples appear unexpected and brief. Epigrams are common in the life of Wotton, and even in
his "Love and Truth," a pamphlet published in 1680,
Walton quotes his distinguished friend's warning to Englishmen not to believe that the further they went from
the Church of Rome, the nearer they were to heaven.
The sophisticated reader will occasionally find an added
pleasure in Walton's delicious humor through inability
to decide whether or not it is conscious. When Walton
says, "the Reader has a Liberty to believe that his
[Hooker's] Modesty and Dim sight were some of the
reasons why he trusted Mistris Churchman to choose a
Wife for him," the reader has the further liberty of de-

ciding whether Walton is in earnest. His appreciation
of a witty anecdote, a clever retort, or a keen turn of
phrasing is undeniable. This curious twinkling mirth
which enlivens Walton's biographies colors even the
most elevated passages: when he speaks in all reverence
of Bishop Jewel who "died in devout Meditation and
Prayer; and in both so zealously, that it became a Religious question, Whether his last Ejaculations, or his
Soul, did first enter into Heaven?" it would be a mistake to believe that Walton views this question with the
soberness of a mediaeval schoolman.

Walton has a gift for vivid presentation. His biographies are not made up of directly stated and generalized
qualities; they are composed of life-giving incidents. His
pictures are actual and warm — Donne preaching in his
pulpit like an angel from a cloud, Wotton whispering his
Venetian message in the ear of James, Hooker reading
the Odes of Horace in the fields or rocking the baby's
cradle while trying to entertain his friends, the passionate elopement of Donne, Hooker's pathetically droll
marriage, Herbert's Platonic courtship, Parliament's
soldiers tearing the prayer-book from the hands of the
old Dr. Sanderson.

Walton gains added vividness because of his subjective treatment. With the freedom and the effectiveness
of a classic historian he expresses in the first person his
heroes' thoughts as he imagines them to be. He creates
for them suitable meditations. He is a poet in biography. The conversation regarding his career between
Donne and Dr. Morton, Bishop of Durham, Wotton's
thoughts on revisiting Winchester School as an old man,
Whitgift's persuasive speech before Queen Elizabeth,
Sanderson's address on quitting the University Proctor-

ship, the marshalled theological opinions of Herbert and Sanderson — all are related with the surety, the omniscience, and the skill of a novelist.

One particular mode of treatment characteristic of all the biographies may be designated as "Waltonian suspense." Walton regards his subject as a precious museum piece on display; when it is necessary to fill in the historical background Walton takes leave of his hero in a formal manner and allows him to remain suspended between earth and heaven. The life of Donne [22] contains: "This sickness continued long, not onely weakning, but wearing him so much, that my desire is, he may now take some rest. And that thou judge it no impertinent digression (before I speake of his death) to looke backe with me upon some observations of his life, which (while a gentle slumber seises him) may (I hope fitly) exercise thy Consideration."

Again he will say in his life of Herbert: [23] "I have now brought him to his Parsonage of Bemerton, and to the Thirty sixth Year of his Age, and must now stop, and bespeak the Reader to prepare for an almost incredible story, of the great sanctity of the short remainder of his holy life."

Upon Hooker's admission as Master of the Temple in London in 1585, Walton formally announces that he will leave his hero and consider "a Character of the Times, and Temper of the People of this Nation."

In the life of Sanderson, Walton tells how the aged doctor was "forc'd to keep his bed. In which I desire he may rest, till I have given some account of his behaviour there, and immediately before it."

22. 1640, B3ᵛᵒ.   23. 1670, p. 60.

Occasionally this delight in laying aside or suddenly producing his hero leads to a curious objective attitude, as when he ends a digression in the same biography with:[24] "I should now return to Boothby Pannel where we left Dr. Hammond and Dr. Sanderson together, but neither can be found there." Thereupon he ingenuously explains that Dr. Hammond had retired, and that Sanderson had been imprisoned.

This Waltonian suspense, which is so marked in the lives, is not without significance. The mere fact that he considers it necessary to apologize when he abandons a direct consideration of his hero shows his concentration on an individual theme, his realization of the biographer's province. But there remains a corollary of even deeper import: through such treatment Walton betrays his belief in biography as an art. As he summons and dismisses his beloved puppets in these formal transitions, it becomes clear that his focus is literary rather than personal. He is master of his subjects, and they move only under his guidance. Here he is the antithesis of Boswell, in that Boswell's work is subordinate to his hero, whereas Walton's heroes are subordinate to his art. He is refining the lives of his friends and re-shaping them to fit a pattern of his own.

The introduction to the life of Hooker already quoted shows the time and care Walton spent on revisions of his own work; and a close scrutiny of the minute changes of phrasing in successive issues of his biographies con· vinces the student that Walton was a conscious artist in words and fine details. Walton's style has been justly characterized as "unique for apparent simplicity which

24. 1678, p. h5^{vo}.

is really elaborately studied art." [25] This careful clarity
in writing "hath inabled me," he says, "to make the
relation of these Lives passable in an eloquent and cap-
tious age." [26]

Walton as a literary artist was not preoccupied with
style alone. What is more important, he had also a
sense of form in viewing his task as a whole. Life itself
he saw as a work of art, a sacred and rounded whole,
and according to this ideal his heroes' lives are molded:

"Thus the Circle of his Life," he says of Sir Henry Wotton,
"(that Circle which began at Bocton, and in the Circumference thereof did first touch at Winchester School, then at
Oxford, and after upon so many remarkable parts and passages in Christendom) That Circle of his Life, was by his
Death clos'd up, and compleated in the seventy and second
year of his Age, at Eton Coledge (where according to his Will)
he now lies buried."

This is the haunting and funereal close of the life of
Donne: "To which place of his Burial some mournful
Friends repaired, and, as Alexander the Great did to the
grave of the famous Achilles, so they strewed his with
an abundance of curious and costly Flowers."

Walton attains high art and brings biography very
close to philosophy when he allows Sir Henry Wotton to
narrate how he revisited Winchester School in his old
age: [27]

"How usefull was that advise of a holy Monk, who perswaded his friend to perform his Customary devotions in a
constant place, because in that place we usually meet with
those thoughts which possess'd us at our last being there?

25. Dictionary of National Biography. Article based on notes by Andrew
Lang.
26. Dedication to Bishop George Morley, 1670 edition of the lives.
27. 1651, p. cii^{vo}.

And I find it thus far experimentally true, that at my being at
that Schoole, seeing that place where I sate when I was a boy,
occasioned me to remember those very thoughts of my youth
which then possess'd me; sweet thoughts indeed, that promised my growing years numerous pleasures, without mixture
of cares; and those to be enjoyed when time (which I therefore
thought slow pac'd) had chang'd my youth into manhood.
But age and experience have taught me, that those were but
empty hopes. . . . Nevertheless, I saw there a succession of
boyes using the same recreations, and questionless possess'd
with the same thoughts. Thus one generation succeeds another, both in their lives, recreations, hopes, fears, and
deaths."

Again, the finale to the life of Hooker is as inevitable
as it is beautiful: [28]

"And here I draw his Curtain, till with the most glorious
Company of the Patriarks and Apostles; the most humble
Army of Martyrs and Confessors, this most Learned, most
Humble, holy Man, shall also awake to receive an Eternal
Tranquillity, and with it a greater degree of Glory then com-
mon Christians shall be made partakers of. . . . And let the
Labors of his Life, his most excellent Writings be blest with
what he desired when he undertook them: Which was Glory
to thee, O God on high, Peace in thy Church, and good will to
mankinde. Amen, Amen."

This paragraph with its fervent and celestial music
might well be the close of a saint's legend; and an appraisal of Walton's place in biography may end most
aptly by considering him as the writer who raised to perfection the saint's life in English.

The books which most deeply influenced him con-
firmed his bent toward hagiography. The writings of the
early church fathers, and preëminently the Bible, color
all his work. It is difficult to open one of the lives at a

28. 1666, p. 26.

page which does not contain a Biblical reference or quotation. He bulwarks his biographies with holy parallels.[29] Yet Walton was as much a hagiographer by nature as by reading, and it is a curious coincidence that, without referring to the mediaeval Latin saints' lives and probably without having read them, Walton should so closely parallel their style and method. The very superlatives in the paragraph quoted from the life of Hooker have recurrent prototypes in the ideal Latin character sketches. Just as the saints' lives begin with accounts of the unusual holiness of their heroes in childhood, so Walton commences his life of Herbert with: [30] "the beauties of his pretty behaviour and wit, shin'd and became so eminent and lovely in this his innocent Age, that he seem'd to be marked out for piety, and to become the care of Heaven, and of a particular angel to guard and guide him." When George Herbert grows to manhood, Walton continues with the "almost incredible story, of the great sanctity of the short remainder of his holy life; a life so full of Charity, Humility, and of Christian vertues, that it deserves the eloquence of St. Chrysostom to commend and declare it." Walton shows Herbert before a Christian altar at Bemerton prostrate in prayer, just as Adamnan revealed the dying Saint Columba, more than a thousand years before, in the dark church on Iona.

29. He says, regarding Donne's ordination (1640, p. B2): "Now the English Church had gained a second S. Augustine, and I think none was so like him before his conversion; none so like S. Ambrose after it. And if his youth had the infirmities of the one Father, his age had the excellencies of the other, the learning and holinesse of both." Incidents from Augustine's *Confessions* he mentions frequently. Chrysostom and the biographies by Jerome are referred to, as are the works of many of the primitive fathers who were not biographers.

30. P. 18, 1670 separate ed.

To harmonize with this angelic mold Walton does not hesitate to interpret or to omit events in the lives of his heroes. Donne's early years are passed over in silence; his *Biothanatos*, which seeks to justify suicide under certain circumstances, enters Walton's biography as "A large and laborious Treatise concerning Selfe-murther . . . wherein all the Lawes violated by that act, are diligently survayed, and judiciously censured." The scandalous incident in Gauden's life of Hooker which principally caused the indignant Walton to write his counter-biography, is not outlined. It is not enough for him that the aspersions cast upon Hooker are false; he does not mention them even to refute them, for they would mar the harmony of his creation. Walton never undertook to write the life of a character he did not love or reverence. Friendship for him was sacred, and it is enshrined in his biographies. He even quotes from Sanderson's will to demonstrate his saintliness and Christian faith. Thus his personages proceed in a series of holy actions to their deaths, which are related with the pious exultation of the hagiographers. In the account of Hooker's last days,[31] "the Doctor . . . found him better in appearance, deep in contemplation, and not inclinable to discourse; which gave the Doctor occasion to require his present thoughts: To which he replied, That he was meditating the number and nature of Angels."

This, then, is the country Walton's heroes inhabit, a land where John Donne and Herbert's mother sing hymns in heaven, where Hooker wakes to an eternal tranquillity among "the most glorious Company of the Patriarks and Apostles, the most humble Army of Mar-

31. 1666, pp. 25–26.

tyrs and Confessors," where Walton himself, like the mediaeval hagiographers, closes his books with prayers for his own soul.

Wordsworth has written that

> ". . . the feather whence the pen
> Was shaped that traced the lives of these good men,
> Dropped from an angel's wing."

The moral purpose, the constant view of his heroes as patterns of virtue, links him closely to the old hagiologists, and a survey of his writings may well conclude with the quotation which ends his last work, the *Life of Sanderson*:

"Blessed is the man in whose spirit there is no guile."

V

INTIMATE BIOGRAPHY

The pageantry of life is taken away; you see the poor reasonable animal, as naked as ever nature made him; are made acquainted with his passions and his follies, and find the Demi-God a Man.

JOHN DRYDEN

THE two preceding chapters have treated ecclesiastical biography after the Renaissance. The secular lives remain to be surveyed. They constitute a group far more important, though less unified. During the Middle Ages, lives of laymen not of royal birth were virtually unknown. Yet this class of biography became the progenitor of modern life-writing as soon as the Renaissance had increased indefinitely the possibilities and the scope of biography by breaking the old molds and disregarding the old traditions. Secular biography came to include many of the most original and significant achievements among the lives of the sixteenth and seventeenth centuries, productions wherein for the first time in England the narration of a life became natural in its development, vivid in incident, unforced and simple in manner, and, above all, free from stiff pretensions and didactic overtones. The important writers discussed in this chapter, by delineating the private life, the modes of thought, the manners, and conversation of their subjects, contributed individually to the liberation of biography from its narrow confines and to its establishment as a supple literary form.

Yet the pioneers in the new type of intimate biography continued in certain respects the traditions of earlier ages. Roper's *Life of Sir Thomas More* is a direct descendant of the saints' lives; while Cavendish's *Life of Wolsey* is in its spirit a continuation of Lydgate's *Fall of Princes*, a variation in prose upon a theme which occupied metrical biographers during two centuries. These two works, written during the reign of Queen Mary, form a brilliant initial capital for this chapter.

George Cavendish was a gentleman usher in the magnificent household of Cardinal Wolsey. His position colors his writing, which throughout savors more of retiring rooms and dining halls than of libraries and council chambers. He views his lord the Cardinal from his own place as a faithful retainer, rather than as a confidant and friend. He was with his master until Wolsey's death (1530), after which he lived in comparative retirement, until, near the end of his life, he recorded in a well-ordered whole his memories of his old master.[1] "This was the George Cavendish," says Henry Morley,[2] "who, in the reign of Queen Mary, looking back upon what he had known thirty years before, with the reflec-

---

1. The religious disputes of the Civil Wars occasioned the first edition in 1641, although the work had previously had a wide circulation in manuscript. It was known to Stow and Holinshed, both of whom included large excerpts from it in their histories. Either in the original manuscript form or through some intermediate version such as Holinshed, Cavendish's incidents are used by Thomas Storer in his poem, *The Life and Death of . . . Wolsey* (1599). The familiarity of Shakespeare and Storer with Cavendish renders it at least possible, as Nicolson asserts in *The English Historical Library* (1714, 2d ed. p. 139), that a quarto edition was published in London in 1590. No such edition, however, is now known, and Nicolson's definite statement has been explained away by the ingenious argument of Joseph Hunter, that Cavendish's work has been confused with Storer's poem, first published in 1599. The life was edited by S. W. Singer in 1815 without the excisions and changes of the seventeenth-century editions, and in 1893 the Kelmscott Press issued a beautiful edition from the autograph manuscript, retaining the original spelling. Unless other references are specifically given, quotations will be drawn from the Kelmscott edition.

2. *Life of Wolsey*, 1885.

tions of ripe years to soften all, made of it one harmonious picture of the vanity of that ambition through
which, perhaps, he had himself partly learnt the blessed-
ness of being little."

Few biographers have possessed the visual imagination of this gentleman usher in the train of the Archbishop of York and Cardinal of England. Where other
writers are content with a bare narration of events,
Cavendish adds the description of those events in all
their picturesque details. He presents the life of Wolsey
as a narrative written by an eye-witness, by one to
whom the political or historical significance of the scenes
in which he participates is not as absorbing as their direct and concrete pageantry. He takes a naïve delight in
splendor for its own sake. Chapter five, for example, in
the 1641 edition — "Of the Orders and Offices of his
house and Chappell" — reads like the Arabian Nights
for imaginative munificence. The following passage
describing Wolsey's Sabbath progress through London,
illustrates the sumptuous paragraphs that constantly
recur: [3]

"Every Sunday hee would resort to the Court being then at
Greenwich, with his former rehearsed traine and Triumph,
taking his Barge at his owne staires, furnished with Yeomen
standing upon the sayles, and his Gentlemen within and
about, and landed at the three Cranes in the Vine-tree, and
from thence he rode upon his Mule with his Crosses, his Pil-
lars, his Hat, and his broad Seale carryed before him on horsebacke along Thames-street untill he came to Billingsgate, and
there hee tooke his Barge, and so went to Greenwich, where
hee was Nobly entertained of the Lords in the Kings house,
being there with staves in their hands, as the Treasurer,
Comptroller, with many others, and conveyed into the Kings
chamber, and so went home againe in the like Triumph."

3. 1641, chap. 7, p. 19.

Or the brilliant jewelry will flash out in sentences
(p. 21):

"Than had he ii great crossis of sylver . . . borne alwayes
byfore hyme whither so ever he went or rode, by two of the
most tallest & comlyest priests that he cowld gett within all
this realme."

The whole progress is played by one central figure in a
cardinal's robe against a background of "a great as-
semble of prelatts & lusty gallaunt gentilmen" (p. 20).
Here is Wolsey's farewell to his old servants after his disgrace (p. 160):

"& when they ware all there assembled, I assigned all the
gentilmen to stand on the right side of the chamber, and the
yomen on the lyft side. And at the last my lord came thether,
apparelled in a whyht rochett uppon a violett gown, of clothe,
lyke a bysshop's; who went strayt into the great window.
Standyng there awhyle, & his chapleyns abought hyme, be-
holdyng the nomber of his servaunts, devydyd in two parts,
cowld not speke unto them for tendernes of his hart; the
floode of teares that distilled frome his eyes declared no lesse:
the whiche perceyved by his servaunts, caused the fountayns
of water to gushe owt of ther faythfull harts down ther chekes,
in suche aboundaunce as it wold cause a cruell hart to lament.
At the last, after he had torned his face to the wall and wyped
his eyes with his handkercheffe, he spake to them after this
sort . . . "

Cavendish's own station in Wolsey's household might
be surmised from his interest in, and ability to describe,
the gorgeous liveries and banquets; and we cannot believe him when he disavows his own particular powers
and says that (p. 107) "to discrybe the disshes, the
subtylltes, the many straynge devysis, & order in the
same, I do bothe lake wytt in my grosse old hed, &
cunnyng in my bowells to declare the wonderfull and

curious imagynacions in the same inventyd and de-
vysed."

At no point does Cavendish endeavor to estimate the
Cardinal's character or his importance, except as it is
shown almost accidentally in the progress of the narrative. There is no laudatory or perfunctory character
sketch after the manner of the saints' lives, no attempt
to censure or praise the cardinal's actions, or even to interpret them. Cavendish is not a judge, but a witness,
and all critics have accordingly praised his marked impartiality.[4] This ability to "consider with an indifferent
eye" the progress of an admired master should be emphasized, for it is a quality rare among biographers.

Although his outlook is simple and direct, Cavendish
does not lack an artistic sense. Omens and premoni-
tions, preludes to the tragedy, are woven into the texture of the biography like bars of music anticipating a
final theme. The turn of the tide against Wolsey, when
Ann Boleyn is rising in the royal favor, is thus suggested (p. 39):

"Fortune . . . began to wexe some thyng wrothe with his
prosperous estate, thought she wold devyse a meane to abate
his hyghe port, wherfor she procured Venus, the insaciat god-
desse to be hir instrument."

And again, in the last days of his high estate, Wolsey's
silver cross, symbol of his papal titles, falls upon the
head of Doctor Bonner in the presence of the Cardinal
(p. 228):

4. For example, Cavendish estimates Wolsey as an administrator only in
one brief sentence, and his appraisal is cool and measured (D, iv): "In my
jugement I never sawe thys realme in better order, quietnes and obedyence,
than it was in the tyme of his auctoryte and rule, ne justice better mynestred
with indifferencye."

"Hath it, quod he, drawen any bloode? Yea forsothe my lord, quod I, as it semyth me. With that he cast down his hed, lokyng very soberly uppon me a good while with out any word spekyng. At the last, quod he, shakyng of hys hed, Malum omen; and therwith sayd grace and rose from the table, and went in to his bed chamber, there lamentyng, makyng his prayers."

Wolsey presages even his death, which seems thereby to become inevitable and doubly effective (p. 276):

". . . and incontynent the clocke strake viii., at which tyme he gave uppe the gost, and thus departed he this present lyfe. And callyng to our remembraunce his words the day byfore, howe he sayd that at viii of the cloke we shold lose our mayster, oon of us lokyng uppon an other, supposyng that he profecied of his departure."

Here, then, Cavendish is adopting an attitude toward life which derives from classical literatures. The career of his hero is of importance and of interest to the gods; it is ruled by the fates, and destiny is unescapable. Artistically this attitude is highly effective. Moreover, it is not difficult to find the sources for Cavendish's philosophy. The direct literary ancestors of *The Life of Wolsey* are Lydgate's *Fall of Princes* and Boccaccio's *De Casibus Illustrium Virorum*. During the same decade in which Cavendish wrote, appeared the first editions of the *Mirror for Magistrates*. The *Life of Wolsey* is in fact no more than a *Mirror for Magistrates* story told in prose. Dea Fortuna rules over all, and mournful meditation on her turning wheel, speculations on the fatality of man's "assendyng and dissendyng . . . from honorous estate," give a unity and progress to the biography. Cavendish does not trespass in the domain of history, and will even say regarding the ceremonies attendant

upon the accession of Henry VIII (p. 11): "I omyt &
leave the circumstances therof to hystorygraffers of
cronycles of prynces, the whiche is no part myn en-
tendement." Yet in the field of philosophy he occasionally walks, and he presents the exemplary career of
Wolsey with an appropriate admonition (p. 14):

> "... lett all men to whome fortune extendythe hir grace, not
> to trust to myche to hir fikkyll favor and plesaunt promysis,
> under colour wherof she cariethe venemous galle."

Again he breaks out reproachfully against the change-
fulness of the crowd which can turn against Wolsey so
easily in his defeat (p. 150):

> "O waveryng & newfangled multitude! Ys it not a wonder
> to consider the inconstant mutabilitie of this oncertyn world.
> The comen peple allwayes desiring alteracions and novelties
> of thyngs for the strayngenes of the case; which after tornyth
> them to small profett and commodytie."

The paragraph at the close of the manuscript aptly
sums up the effect of the biography and its tendency to
moralize on the unhappiness of the great:

> " ... this Lord Cardynall hathe felt bothe of the swette
> and the sower in eche degree; as fletyng from honors, losyng
> of riches, deposed frome dignytes, forsaken of frends, and the
> inconstantnes of prynces favour. Of all whiche thyngs he
> hathe had in this world the full felycyte as long as that for-
> tune smyled upon hyme: but whan she began to frown, how
> sone was he depryved of all these dremyng joyes & vayn
> pleasyrs; the which in xx yeres with great travell, study and
> paynnes opteyned, ware in oon yere and lesse, with hevynes,
> care, and sorowe lost and consumed. O madnes! O folyshe
> desier! O fond hope! O gredy desier of vayn honors, dignyties
> and ryches! O what inconstant trust and assuraunce is in
> rollyng fortune!"

The death of the Cardinal rouses Cavendish to the mournful majesty of a funeral oration (p. 276):

"Here is thend and fall of pryde and arrogauncye of suche men, exalted by fortune to honour and high dygnytes; for I assure you, in hys tyme of auctorytie and glory, he was the haultest man in all his procedyngs that than lyved, havyng more respect to the worldly honour of hys person than he had to his spirituall profession; wherin shold be all meknes, humylitie & charitie, the processe wherof I leave to theme that be learned and seen in the dyvyn lawes."

The wheel has come full circle, and the son of undistinguished parents, the "almosyner, clymming thus hastely uppe fortune's whele" (p. 15), the ambassador and papal legate, the all-powerful counsellor who was instrumental in banishing from royal favor the Queen of England and who was himself banished by the "gorgeous lady" (p. 51) who succeeded her, the Chancellor and Cardinal, has at last explored the end and fall of pride and is laid, with his honors, in the dust.

As in Shakespearean tragedy, this play does not terminate abruptly, but draws to a close in obvious and unruffled anecdote. Cavendish has never kept himself wholly out of the picture, and now, at the end, after he has performed the last duties of a loyal servant, his mind turns from the departed Cardinal to his own affairs, and the 1641 edition ends with a muffled curtain (p. 118):

"So I received tenne pounds of the Duke for my wages, and twenty pounds for my reward, and his Majestie gave me a Cart and six horses the best that I could chose out of my Lords horses to carry my goods and five marks for my charge homewards."

Cavendish's *Life of Wolsey* presents a unique pattern: a great figure of the Renaissance portrayed in the medi-

aeval manner, a story of ambition and subtlety used
to point the lesson of the vanity of worldly wishes,
a simple account of a ruler of England who found that
he was living in "a fooles paradice" (p. 262). In his
ripe years, the devoted servant, the observer who
neither praises nor blames, who is content with actions
and seeks not for causes, reviews the life of his magnificent master, delights in its splendors, sees them disappear like the pageant of *The Tempest*, and comforts
himself in his obscurity with the reflection which brings
his manuscript to a close (p. 286):

"Who lyste to rede and consider with an indifferent eye
this history, may beholde the wonderouse mutabilitie of vayn
honours, the bryttell assuraunce of haboundaunce, the on-
certynte of dignytes, the flateryng of fayned frends, and the
tykkyll trust to worldly princes."

If the life of Wolsey, containing "the originall of his
promotion, the continuance in his magnificence, his fall,
death, and buriall," is strongly influenced by the mediaeval conception of fortune's wheel, William Roper's
Life of Thomas More is no less guided by the exemplary holiness of the saints' lives. The first edition
(Paris, 1626) bears the title *The Mirrour of vertue in
worldly greatness*, and it becomes the biographer's pious
task, in all that he writes, to hold the mirror up to
virtue as exemplified in the life of his father-in-law, the
Lord Chancellor. Roper does not mention his idol as the
author of *Utopia*, but is careful to inform the reader of
the hair shirt Sir Thomas wore, his flagellations, and the
hours he spent in devotion; Erasmus and the brilliant
circle of humanists who were More's friends are referred
to only incidentally, but Roper is meticulous in commending the severe religious discipline which the Lord

Chancellor imposed both in his own family and in the nation at large. The life, therefore, rests upon the foundations of traditional hagiology. By accepting at the outset the devout Catholic cast in the biography of a figure soon known as "the blessed Sir Thomas More," the qualities which render Roper's work distinctive and fresh may be more easily ascertained.

Like Cavendish before him, like Walton, like Boswell after him, William Roper does not exclude his own personality from his work. He mentions three wishes of Sir Thomas More's: first, that the Christian world might be at peace; second, that it might be blessed with unity of doctrine; and third, that the question of King Henry's divorce might be amicably settled. Most biographers would have been content with mere enumeration. Roper, however, must make the wishes a vivid part of More's life by giving circumstances. In consequence, he shapes a clear-cut anecdote of an evening walk along the banks of the Thames, whose sweet waters, running softly, at last call forth More's confidences — almost a soliloquy spoken aloud — to his "son Roper." Even the charge of bigotry which forms the sole blot on More's reputation is unconsciously suggested, for they stroll along, in More's phrase, "treading heretics under our feet like ants." [5] The entire biography gives evidence of Roper's retentive and circumstantial memory, since it seems to have been written about 1558,[6] twenty years after the death of the Lord Chancellor. Roper prides himself that no man had equal opportunities to know Sir Thomas, "whom in sixteen years and more, being in his house conversant with him, I could never perceive as much as once in a fume."

5. 1626, p. 19.   6. Joseph Hunter suggests 1556.

The biography abounds in anecdotes to show the dry pungency of More's wit; again and again during his trial, chance remarks, vividly recorded, bring out the vigor and independence of his personality. The King walks with him in the garden, arm around his shoulder, but he is not deceived: [7]

"Howbeit, son Roper," he says, "I have no cause to be proud thereof, for if my head would win him a castle in France (for there was war between us), it should not fail to go."

The Court requests him to walk in the wedding procession of Ann Boleyn, an action which would tacitly condone Henry's marriage; More replies to the emissaries with the neat parable of the virgin (p. 32):

"Now, my Lords, quoth he, it lieth not in my power but that they may devour me, but God being my good Lord, I will so provide that they shall never deflower me."

He denies the king's conciliatory messengers, and Roper wonders how a man in such desperate condition may be merry (p. 38):

"In good faith I rejoiced, son, said he, that I had given the devil a foul fall, and that with those lords I had gone so far as without great shame I could never go back again."

His integrity cannot be shaken, and when in the tower he is threatened with torture and death (p. 37), "My lords, quoth he, these terrors be arguments for children, and not for me."

The members of his family are sketched in no less surely — "dearest Meg," who breaks through the crowd to throw her arms around her father's neck as he walks

7. 1902, p. 11.

to the Tower, Roper himself with his simple admiration and sharp eye, More's second wife, common and fretful, divided from her husband by a chasm which even imminent death cannot bridge. There are few scenes in literature as tragic as More's final interview with his wife in the Tower, not because an eternal separation is approaching, but because it is already at hand, and has always existed. Her husband's actions are in her mind pure folly, and the story of their entire married life is revealed in the fact that he does not try to explain his motives (p. 45):

"When Sir Thomas had continued a good while in the Tower, my lady, his wife, obtained license to see him. Who, at her first coming, like a simple ignorant woman, and somewhat worldly too, with this manner of salutation bluntly saluted him: 'What the good-yere, Master More,' quoth she, 'I marvel that you that have been always hitherto taken for so wise a man will now so play the fool to lie here in this close filthy prison, and be content thus to be shut up among mice and rats, when you might be abroad at your liberty, and with the favour and good will both of the king and his council if you would but do as all the bishops and best learned of this realm have done. And seeing you have at Chelsea a right fair house, your library, your gallery, your garden, your orchard, and all other necessaries so handsome about you, where you might in the company of me your wife, your children, and household, be merry, I muse what a God's name you mean here still thus fondly to tarry.' After he had a while quietly heard her, with a cheerful countenance he said unto her: 'I pray thee, good Mistress Alice, tell me one thing.' 'What is that?' quoth she. 'Is not this house,' quoth he, 'as nigh heaven as mine own?' To whom she after her accustomed homely fashion, not liking such talk, answered: 'Tylle valle, Tylle valle!' 'How say you, Mistress Alice, is it not so?' 'Bone Deus, bone Deus, man, will this gear never be left?' quoth she. 'Well then, Mistress Alice, if it be so,' quoth he, 'it is very well. For I see no great cause why I should much joy in my gay house, or in any thing thereunto belonging, when if I should but seven years lie buried under the ground and then arise and come thither again, I should not fail to find some therein that would bid me get out of doors, and tell me it were none of mine. What cause have I then to like such a house as would so soon forget his master?' So her persuasions moved him but a little."

In his living and faithful narrative, with no touch of pretentiousness, Roper has given a summary of More's early life which is well proportioned, and the story of his active years is not passed by without notice. But the larger portion of the biography forms the last act of a drama, the conduct of a great man in adversity, uncompromising and firm in his conviction that neither Parliament nor the King can pass a law that God is not God. In spite of Roper's apparent artlessness, few biographers have equalled him in rendering the last actions of their heroes with the same truth and completeness.

More, so important a figure in the English Renaissance, and standing at the head of new movements in biography with his *Richard III* and his translation of the *Life of Pico*, is himself the subject of a number of lives other than that by Roper. These should not pass unmentioned, since they deal with a figure who represents in many ways the Renaissance movement in England, which in its awakened interest in the individual is largely responsible for the rise of intimate biography.

The first extensive printed life of More, by Thomas Stapleton, appeared in 1588, where under the title of *Tres Thomae* the Chancellor is linked with the Apostle and Thomas Becket. This life of More, Stapleton says, is written to fulfill a popular demand, and the sources from which he draws are sufficiently extensive to show

this general interest.[8] Stapleton, unlike Roper, is interested in More's friends — Colet, Grocyn, Linacre,
Latimer, Elyot, Erasmus, and Croke. He also mentions
More's literary activities. More's Catholic piety is emphasized by an incident which Roper had diffidently
omitted: namely, More's conversion of his son-in-law to
the Catholic faith. A chapter of More's apothegms is included. The classic influence may be found in occasional
instances — for example, where Stapleton compares the
relation between the Chancellor and his gifted daughter
to that between Augustine and his disciple Adeodatus,
or where he draws a parallel between More and Livy's
Cato the Censor. Stapleton executes a well-planned,
conscientious, and thorough biography. The chapter
headings alone are illuminating. It becomes evident
that the biographer is walking completely around his
subject, viewing him from all positions, when, in a
biography of twenty-one chapters, he finds room for
separate sections with such diverse titles as "Adoles-
centiae mores, studia, actiones"; "De multiplici eius
eruditione & laboribus literariis"; "De doctis & claris
viris quos multiplex Tho. Mori eruditio familiares ei
fecit"; and "Doctorum virorum iudicia de nece Tho.
Mori." There is even a chapter devoted to More's
daughter.[9]

8. Although he is apparently unacquainted with Roper's work (he will,
for example, mention More's flagellations but omit his hair shirt), he cites as
authorities a Spanish Dominican biographer, Ludovicus Pacaeus, whose life
of More he had not seen, the letters of Erasmus and of Sir Thomas himself,
and, in More's own family circle, his wife, his secretary John Harris, Dr. John
Clemens, Margaret Roper, John Haywood, and his nephew William Rastell.

9. William Rastell and Nicholas Harpsfield are known to have written
early lives of More, and from such sources is drawn the anonymous life written toward the end of the reign of Queen Elizabeth by a zealous Catholic and
now accessible in Wordsworth's *Ecclesiastical Biography* (1818), ii, 57. But
the life which epitomizes all earlier work and marks the most pretentious

Written about the year 1559 and ascribed to Richard Hall,[10] is a *Life of Fisher* [11] in the manner of Cavendish and Roper. Many of the incidents, in fact, in the lives of More and Wolsey are here detailed minutely. The long divorce proceedings in which Bishop John Fisher played such a tragic rôle are fully given in the account of his trial, supplemented by papal bulls and letters cited in both Latin and English versions. The personal description, in contrast with the silence of Roper and Cavendish, is very full, and occasional incidents, such as the sordid death scene, are vivid. The life was written by an ardent Catholic, with erudite parallels and comparisons. Apart from these learned ornaments, Hall's style resembles that of other works of the period in its artlessness and lack of pretence; the author does not trouble himself with sentiment, undue eulogy, or rhetoric.

In 1574 appeared a small black-letter volume entitled *The life off the 70. Archbishopp off Canterbury presentlye Sittinge Englished and to be added to the 69. lately Sett forth in Latin.* It is a valuable and interesting little life of Archbishop Matthew Parker, remarkable as one of the earliest printed biographies in English prose. Although issued anonymously, it was almost certainly written in Latin by John Josselin, and translated by another hand.[12] The career of Archbishop Parker is

---

effort to portray the Chancellor is *The Life and Death of Sir Thomas Moore* by his great-grandson Cresacre More, published without date about the year 1631. It is an example of a class of life-writing which is to become more common in later years: the attempt to reconstruct the life of a personage at a great distance from the writer.

10. *D. N. B.*, article "Hall."   11. *E. E. T. S.*, cxvii (1921), Ex. Ser.

12. Strype conjectures that this translation was made by John Stubbs, and further considers that the mystifying notes printed in the margin are "foolish, scurrilous and malicious," probably inspired by Stubbs' antipathy to the Church of England.

given efficiently and briefly, so that the biographer is
never forced to fall back upon words and circumlocu-
tions to mask his ignorance. The *historiola*, as it is
called, deals first with the offices and benefices of this
first archbishop to be consecrated without the "olde
wives superstitions and unprofytable cerimonies off the
Romishe Pope" (p. 19), and then turns to the Archbishop's wider interests: his restoration of old buildings,
his thrift and his humility; the author next discusses his
coat of arms minutely, and studies his learning, his antiquarian interests, his editing the old historians Gildas,
Asser, Paris, and others, his corrections in the English
Bible, his mindfulness of death. Josselin, after the manner of the Elizabethans, is more interested in deeds than
in pious traits of mind, and it will be noted that his
nearest approach to a character sketch is confined to
actions rather than to qualities (pp. 9–10):

"But when he had once taken upon him this cheife cure
and charge off the Christian stocke, how wisely he behaved
him therin for those yeeres that are past, with generall allow-
ance, consent, and favour off all Good men, how discretly also
in so great diversitie and dissention off judgements, how up-
rightly and sincerely in other mens matters and controversies,
with how great gentilnes and patience in other mens wrath
and displeasure, with what forebearing and sufferaunce to-
wardes the evill that he might winne them, with what godli-
nes in reconciling the stomakes off gentilmen and determining
ther controversies, how lothe he was that contumeliously
they should drawe eche other into the law, lastly how often
his voice was hard to sound owt off the holy pulpittes, as well
off his cathedrall church as the churches off other meane
townes and villages, especially in this his old age, in his weak
and crazed state off bodie, in the middest off so great busines,
and in these contagious and pestilent times, all thes thinges I
will leave as matters untouched."

In its stress upon external incidents, its pride in outward show and general impersonal tone, the life resembles Cavendish to a marked degree. The dramatic
anecdotes of *The Life of Wolsey* are lacking, as well
as the pious character sketch which defaces the biographies of churchmen in the following century. The
description of the Archbishop's abundant tables is in the
tradition of Cavendish, and helps to give individuality
and charm to a little work born early and alone (pp. 14–
16):

"In the yeere off Christ 1565, which was the next yeere
after the restoringe off the hall, he prepared a feast very
magnifically and sumptuously, wher unto when they flocked
from every place in great companies, he placed them al at
diverse tables throughout the hall, which was garnished with
tapistery and other things very comely and beautifull,
brought out off flaunders and Holland . . . which feast howe
bountifull it was in daintie kates, how well and orderly all
thinges were served by the Archbishops howshold, how well
this his curtesie was accepted, how oftentymes the tables in
the hall were freshly furnished with new guestes the same day,
I, coveting to be short will not here declare. . . ."

A biography which has long escaped due recognition
and which is to-day not easily accessible is *The life
deedes and death of Sir John Perrott knight*,[13] written
during the last years of the reign of Elizabeth. This
sturdy Elizabethan memoir shows a marked influence of
the classics upon the unknown author. In a spirited defence of the utility of life-writing, he marvels [14]

"why the Historians of our later Times, especially those
of our Englishe Nation, have not taken the lyke Paynes [as
the Greeks and Romans], or used the lyke Diligence, in pub-

13. MS. title, published with a different t. p. in 1728.
14. 1728, Preface, p. viii.

lishing the general Accidents of theyr Contrie, and the particular prayse-worthy Actions of theyr Contriemen. . . . For I am persuaded, that even our latter Times have afforded Men of as great Magnanimitie, Corage, Wisdom and Experience, as ever the former florishing Ages of the World have afforded."

Sir John Perrot, Knight of the Bath, Lord Lieutenant of Ireland, furnishes his biographer with a stout example of the virtues he admires. Yet the author is just in his appraisals: his character sketch does not stop with Perrot's qualities, but mentions such faults as anger and prodigality. Moreover (p. 23), "he was high-mynded, and made no Accompt of any Man which he thought did not love hym; neither could his Heart be thoroughly humbled." "To conclude," the author says, "his Virtues were many, and his Faltes were not to be excused or silenced." Largely it is a biography of action, the history of a military leader. Incidents of privation and hardship in the field are placed beside lines from the Latin poets (pp. 59–60), and a stormy career as Lord Deputy of Ireland is graced with classical references. Plutarch and the Romans this writer had always with him; he begins the preface with a quotation from the *Life of Alexander;* Perrot's accession to power will suggest passages in the *Life of Antonius;* Perrot's "Pose and Majestie of Personage" is compared to Scipio's commanding presence. Yet the classical influence proves most powerful in determining the emphasis and the manner of treatment and does not mar the robust and vigorous English in which the piece is written. Sir John Perrot's coming to Ireland as Lord President of Munster reads like a whirlwind of battle; the trial by combat with the cunning rebel Fitz-Moris is breathless; and the tourney at the court of Elizabeth deserves quotation in full. Anecdotes and short dialogues are abundant, and the student of Plutarch had learned how to impart life to his characters (p. 36):

"The Queene [Mary] also did favour hym very well, and would say, That she did lyke exceeding well of him, and had a Hope he would prove a worthy Subject, but that (as hir Words were) he did smell of the Smoake, meaninge thereby his Religion."

This biography is unique inasmuch as it purposely omits the last years and the condemnation to death of its hero, exactly the years which for drama and a sense of impending disaster had figured so largely in Cavendish and Roper. But the *Life of Perrot* stops with his return from Ireland before the charge of treason was proffered against him and before, in 1592, he was condemned to death and executed. The author's reasons show him circumspect under the eye of a stern monarch (p. 290):

". . . to writte all that happned therin, may, perchaunce, breede Offence, and touch the Proceedings of Times past too much."

He continues with a covert reproach of Elizabeth which shows his sympathy with Perrot and his conception of life as an art from which much may be learned:

"Therfore for this time, there shall noe more be sayd of hym, but this, that his whole Life was lyke to a tragical Comedie, in the Beginnings prosperous and joyfull; in the Ende unfortunate and lamentable: At which let noe Man wonder, because he hath not had that Fortune alone; but rather make use of his Fall by making this Construction of his Fortunes, That Men of greatest Spirits are subject to greatest Perills; and that towards the Ende of Princes Raigne (especially in their declyninge Age) many Things happen otherwise than at other Times they did, or should doe."

The life concludes with an impartial appraisal of Perrot's career and presents the whole narrative to the reader as a useful example. Again, as with the *Life of Wolsey* and the *Life of More*, the purpose of this biography is didactic. The *Life of Perrot* is just and vivid, filled with stirring anecdotes and written in sturdy prose. With possible excisions of historical matter in the latter half, this biography merits reprinting, for it is in the class of Roper and Cavendish and has a subject in some ways as distinguished.[15]

As the last of the great portraits of the Renaissance stands Sir Fulke Greville's *Life of the Renowned Sir Philip Sidney*.[16] Considered as a systematic biography it is negligible; but as a memorial tribute written by a friend it has few equals in English literature. At the outset, Greville states sincerely his reason for writing (pp. 3–4):

"For my own part, I observed, honoured, and loved him so much; as with what caution soever I have passed through my dayes hitherto among the living, yet in him I challenge a kind of freedome even among the dead. So that, although with Socrates, I professe to know nothing for the present; yet with Nestor I am delighted in repeating old newes of the ages past; and will therefore stir up my drooping memory touching this man's worth, powers, wayes, and designes: to the end that in the tribute I owe him, our nation may see a Sea-mark, rais'd upon their native coast, above the levell of any private Pharos abroad: and so by a right Meridian line of their own, learn to sayl through the straits of true vertue, into a calm, and spacious Ocean of humane honour."

15. One further noteworthy biography written about 1600 and first printed in 1732 is *The Life of William Cecil, Lord Burghley*. For details, see Bibliography.

16. 1652 1st ed. written about 1610–12.

Partly, too, the life was written as a consolation for his own loss, a means for refining and making permanent his cherished memories, for Greville declares that he would "rather seek comfortable ease or imployment in the safe memory of dead men, than disquiet in a doubtfull conversation amongst the living." Greville's hero does not walk among ordinary mortals: "Sir Philip Sidney is none of this number; for the greatness which he affected was built upon true Worth; esteeming Fame more than Riches, and Noble actions far above Nobility it self." Sidney's worth is so matchless that his friend is conferring high honor upon the English nation, and even upon his sovereign, by preserving his memory from oblivion.

Yet the life is not solely laudatory, and Greville sees fit to include even such a painful incident as the quarrel on the tennis court with the Earl of Oxford, who called Sidney a "Puppy." In general it is a rambling tribute by an ardent admirer, reaching a climax in Sidney's chivalrous conduct at Zutphen, and in the account of his death, which is here quoted as an example of Greville's classically modelled and noble prose (pp. 159–160):

"The last scene of this Tragedy was the parting between the two brothers: the weaker shewing infinite strength in suppressing sorrow, and the stronger infinite weakness in expressing of it. So far did invaluable worthinesse, in the dying brother enforce the living to descend beneath his owne worth, and by abundance of childish tears, bewail the publique, in his particular loss. Yea so far was his true remission of minde transformed into ejulation, that Sir Philip, (in whom all earthly passion did even as it were flash, like lights ready to burn out) recals those spirits together with a strong vertue, but weak voice; mildly blaming him for relaxing the frail strengths left to support him, in his finall combate of separation at hand. And to stop this naturall torrent of affection in both, took his leave, with these admonishing words:

"Love my Memorie, cherish my Friends; their Faith to me
may assure you they are honest. But above all, govern your
Will, and Affections, by the Will and Word of your Creator;
in me, beholding the end of this World, with all her Vanities.

"And with this Fare-well, desired the company to lead him
away. Here this noble Gentleman ended, the too short Scene
his life; in which path, whosoever is not confident that he
walked the next way to eternall rest, will be found to judge
uncharitably."

Intimate biography may derive from other than the
noblest and most important figures of the period. The
growth of the mercantile classes in independence and
power brings a new class within the range of biography,
and the lives of the London and provincial burghers and
squires are interesting for their pious and conscious
pride.[17]

*London's Dove: or A Memoriall of the life and death
of Maister Robert Dove, Citizen and Marchant-Taylor
of London* (1612) was written the year of Dove's death
by Anthony Nyxon, with an edifying purpose which is
unique (p. A3):

"The chiefe and farthest point that my intention seekes to
arrive at in this, is but to leave to Posteritie a deserved Testi-
monie, and commemoration of his severall liberalities, to the
intent that the hand of Mercy which Heaven (in him) hath

---

17. To show the self-consciousness of the crafts and the growth of a reading public with new demands, it will be sufficient to quote the titles of a few
examples among the burgher pseudo-biographies: *The Honourable Prentice
. . . Shewed in the life and death of Sir John Hawkewood* (1616), Deloney's
*The Pleasant History of John Winchcomb . . . The famous and worthy Clothier
of England* (t. p. 13th ed. of 1672; 1st ed., 1596) and his *The Gentle Craft . . .
Shewing what famous men have been Shoomakers in time past in this Land*
(written 1597–1600, t. p. 1652 ed.), *The Honour of Merchant Taylors . . . Their
Honourable Loves, and Knightly Adventures* (1668) by William Winstanley,
and *The Honour of the Taylors: Or, The Famous and Renowned History of
Sir John Hawkwood* (1687).

stretcht forth over distressed people, being duly considered: Others (to whom God hath plentifully given his blessings) may be stirred up to trace him in the like steppes of true Charitie."

The biographer never swerves from his single aim of portraying the charity of a pious business man. The chapters will have such titles as "Of 13. aged men, to whom he gives yearely 20. nobles a peece, and at the end of every three years, to each man a gowne," "Of his Charitie to poore young beginners of the Company of Marchant-taylours," "Of his bountie to the Prisoners of Newgate, and his provision for the Tolling of the Bell, at S. Sepulchers, for condemn'd persons, which gifte is to continue for ever." The purposeful little black-letter tract closes: [18]

"Thus have you heard the vertuous life and Christian death of M. Dove; whose many deedes of Charitie, are more acceptable to God, and more memorable to men, in that they were done in his life time: God stirre up the hearts of Rich and Able men to follow his steppes, and give them grace to imitate his good example, That they may come to those unspeakable Joyes, wherein hee now resteth, through Christ our Lorde."

About the year 1626 the Reverend William Hinde wrote a biography published in 1641 with the astonishing title, "A Faithfull Remonstrance of the Holy Life and Happy Death, of John Bruen of Bruen-Stapleford, in the County of Chester, Esquire ... Exhibiting Variety of many Memorable and Exemplary passages of his Life, and at his Death, usefull for all sorts and sexes, but principally intended, as a Path and President of Piety and Charity for the Inhabitants of the Famous

18. P. D4^{vo}.

County Palatine of Chester." This is one of the most edifying of biographies, strongly puritanical. As a precedent of piety it tells the story of a gentleman of some means, a patron of religion, the husband of three wives, and the father of twenty-five children. In the detailed account of Bruen's adolescence, Hinde anticipates the Puritan autobiographers Henry Burton and John Bunyan. Bruen's youthful vices are not passed over in silence (p. 10):

"... by occasion of Musitians and a chest of Viols kept in the house, he was drawn by desire and delight into the Dancing-schoole, where he profited so well in that kinde of youthfull activity, that he did not only please himselfe too much, but his parents also much more than was meet, with those tricks of vanity. So he termeth those exercises himself, and yet (saith hee) they were held commendable in those dayes of ignorance."

His taste for religion is shown at an early age (p. 7):

"When he was about the age of six or seven yeares, his Father for some offence or fault, did rebuke him sharpely and correct him soundly, and being then in much griefe of heart for his Fathers displeasure, and desiring to see some meanes of comfort, and reliefe; tooke unto him a little prayer book, which at that time he had learned, and went apart into his Fathers Chappell, and there by reading and praying as wel as he could, was comforted with unexpressible joys. These be his own words."

Hinde often quotes Bruen direct, evidently from diaries or private meditations. There are sections that give life to minor characters, such as the chapter showing Bruen's compassion and care for Old Robert, his servant, or the paragraphs on the unlettered man who nevertheless knew the Bible by heart. The life contains

numerous Scriptural parallels and discussions; and
Hinde is fond of quoting Augustine, whose *Confessions*
influence the biography. The figure of John Bruen
stands out stern and strict in all his actions. He adopts
this frightening method of convincing his erring son-in-
law (p. 116):

"This master Done being young and youthly, yet very
tractable, could not very well away with the strict observation
of the Lords day, whereupon wee did all conspire to doe him
good, ten of my family speaking one after another, and my
self last, for the sanctifying of the Lords day. After which he
did very cheerfully yeeld himself, Blessed be God."

But Master Done was evidently not yet wholly re-
formed, and Bruen took stern measures:

"I comming once into his chamber, saith hee [Bruen], and
finding over the Mantletree a paire of new cards, nobody
being there, I opened them, and tooke out the foure knaves,
and burnt them, and so laid them together againe, and so for
want of such knaves, his gaming was marred, and never did
he play in my house, for ought that ever I heard any more."

Bruen glories in the castigation of the wicked (p. 143):

"Memorand. in Anno 1613, and in the Hey-Harvest, One
Richard Rogers, that dwelt in my farme at Wimble Strafford,
under Master Thomas Puleston my tenant there; seeing two
godly persons going in the way, said to one with him; Now
will I dance and swagger, and sweare to anger and make mad
yonder two Puritans. And did so, to the great grievance of
those two godly persons. And presently the revenging hand
of God was upon him; so that this wicked fellow fell so sick,
that he was carried home in a Cart, and within three dayes
died most fearefully. All glory to God."

There is something almost terrifying in the bigotry of
this character, which is not lessened by the even greater
harshness of his biographer. For in spite of the strict-

ness of Mr. Bruen's code of conduct, William Hinde is still more strict, and will thus censure the squire's propensities for hunting and hawking (pp. 28–29):

"I have not much to commend him for, in these matters, but rather thinke him blame-worthy for mispending so much precious time in such carnall pleasures, and wasting his estate upon base and brutish creatures to serve his lust, which might have been much better bestowed on his owne family, or on the poore members of Christ to do them good."

As a reward for Bruen's pious life, the Lord protects him and his. Instances of this special bounty are frequent, giving an illusion of reality to the narrative where more formal methods would fail (p. 143):

"Anno Domini 1602 and in July, 'My son John, being in Peaksmoore, took up a scith to see how he could mow, and the scith entered in at his stocking upon the shin bone, and followed his leg, shaving the haire, and came out at the backside of his leg; and toucht no flesh nor skinne. *Laus Deo.*'"

An interesting addition to the burgher biographies is *The Life and Death of Mr. Ignatius Jurdain, One of the Aldermen of the City of Exeter* by Ferdinand Nicolls.[19] Of particular value is the preface to the reader by Thomas Manton, which presents a lively and solid picture of the Mayor of Exeter through anecdote and quotation. As the antithesis of the generalizing and saintly methods, it deserves extended reproduction, which cannot here be given. Manton paints a stern, just, god-fearing burgher, in the plague, on the bench, as champion against ale houses and Sunday games. Nicolls' biography, though more formal and less convincing, contains countless enlivening touches such as the following:[20]

19. 1st ed., 1654; 2d ed., enlarged, 1655. 20. 1655, pp. 21, 49–50.

"He was a constant noter of Sermons, even when he was old, not for his own benefit alone, but for the good of his family, to whom he did constantly repeat the Sermons. And if he found himself overtaken with drowsinesse in hearing the Word (an infirmity incident to age,) his manner was to stand up, and to rowse up himself, that he might hear the more attentively."

"When he was Major, he did much reform the open profaning of the Sabbath, for whereas the hullers had wont to set their Mills going on the Sabbath, he put a stop upon them for that whole day, knowing that this day was wholly to be dedicated to God and his worship and service; and whereas it was usual to sell fruit and herbs, and other things on the Lords holy day, and Bowling and Cudgel-playing, and profane pastimes were then much used, by his zeal and vigilancy, and the care of good Officers under him, they were wholly removed, though not without much reluctancy and opposition, and danger at the first; for there were Commotions and Tumults, and great resistance, but by his constant zeal for God and his day, they were suppressed and quell'd."

The lives of the three strong Puritan citizens just discussed show the influence of ecclesiastical upon secular biography. An unusual variant among these pious offerings is to be found in John Duncon's *Holy Life and Death of the Lady Letice [Morrison], Vi-Countess Falkland.*[21] This biography, written by Lady Letice's chaplain, is in essence a character sketch developed by means of letters regarding her spiritual doubts, and a direct study in a single letter. Duncon's method as he explains it to the reader, is ingenious and imaginative:

"And after frequent Communication with this Lady, having learned all Her Objections against Her self; and having seen the chief sorrowes of Her heart, I composed them into these Letters, and annexed these Answers to them, and left them with Her.

21. T. p., 1653 ed.; 1st ed., 1648.

"And now they are the Figure of a Pious Soul, with its vicissitudes of Comfort, and Grief. . . . So it will appear that these Letters, and their Answers, are not a strict Relation, but a Representation: And in them I have taken the Liberty of a Representor, to expresse the height of Comfort, and the depth of Sorrow, suddenly succeeding one the other."

Her trials were not easy. Two years after the death of her husband — Clarendon's friend — and immediately after the death of Lorenzo, her youngest and most promising child, she cries out in despair,[22] "Oh, love me not, I pray, too much, and God grant I never love my friends too much hereafter; that hath cost me dear, and my heart hath smarted sore with grief for it already." The letters are an account of her rise from anguish where, she says (pp. 83–84), "I seem confined to a low vally, whence I cannot espy the least part of that Canaan; my sensitive, and my reasonable faculties, all of them, full of darkness, and dulness, and barrenness," to her joy in the Christian faith at the last. Her chaplain does little to individualize his lady or to give the accidents of her life, but as the record of a spiritual struggle the life ranks among the finest in seventeenth-century biography.

In the same notable family of the Falklands there exists a life of the mother-in-law of Lady Letice, written during the Civil Wars by "one of Lady Falkland's four daughters, a person of a strong and analytical mind, with much of the capacity of her mother, though with none of her graces of style." [23] Largely an account of a life shaped by religious conviction, the biography of Lady Elizabeth is a notable piece of individualization.

22. M. F. Howard ed., 1908, p. 19.
23. Introduction, 1861, when the life was first printed from a MS. in the Imperial Archives at Lille.

Its subtle appraisals and almost brazen analyses of motives are written with a certain dry intelligence that puts
to shame the effusive contemporary masculine biographers. The dramatic interest of the narrative lies in
Lady Elizabeth's decision to embrace the Catholic faith,
thereby breaking up her home, injuring her husband's
career, and separating herself from a large family of
children. The biographer possesses an unusual ability
to give life even to secondary characters, as she does in
the death of Lord Falkland, who (p. 46), "waiting on
the king . . . a-shooting in Tibald's Park, fell from
a stand and broke his leg, and instantly broke it in
a second and a third place with standing up upon it
at the King's coming to him." The leg is amputated
(pp. 47–48):

"Whilst they cut it off he never changed his countenance,
nor made any show of pain; no more he had not at the breaking of it (at which time he omitted not the least civility to any
one that spoke to him); nor all the time of the dressing of it;
only when they went to search how far it was gangrened, he
once frowned, and cried, 'Oh, softly!' . . .

"And a little after [he asked his wife] (still in French,
which he spoke ill enough) if her man were there — calling it
homme; which she took only for an ill phrase: but having told
him he that used to wait on her abroad was there, and that he
said he meant not him, she saw he meant her priest, and
called him so to distinguish him from a servant."

She advises him not to confess the Catholic faith on his
death bed because it would be prejudicial to his children's interests:

"And he being very near death, one of the surgeons desired
him to profess he died a Protestant or else (he said) his lady
being there and speaking much to him, it would be reported
he died a Papist. To this (which the man repeated three or

four times) he only still turned away his head without answering him; but, seeing he did not cease to bawl the same in his ears, he said to him at last, 'Pray do not interrupt my silent meditation;' which showed he could have said the other if he would."

The style is unfortunately Latinized with ungainly parentheses and participles, and the structure of the biography renders partial quotation unwise, but as a whole the life is distinctive and original, and succeeds in the highest aim of biography: the reconstruction of a personality in thought and actions.

The Civil Wars inevitably developed the biographies of the combatants.[24] In general these are not distinguished. One, however, stands apart from the rest by reason of its freshness: *Britannicae Virtutis Imago. Or, The Effigies of true Fortitude, Expressed to the life, in the famous actions of that incomparable Knight, Major Generall Smith* (1644). It was written by Smith's secretary, Edward Walsingham,[25] and is filled with incidents to bring out the central theme of the biography: soldierly courage. Concentrating on the impulsive chivalry and modest bravery of this young Royalist, Walsingham quotes Bacon's dictum regarding the scarcity of biography in England and expresses his hope that in writing this life he may "induce Historians those Goldsmiths of time in their elaborate rings the Chronicles and Relations of these daies, curiously to enchace this choicer Diamond to the delight and benefit of succeeding ages" (p. 28). At this late hour his wish

24. See Chapter VI.
25. Walsingham probably also wrote *Hector Britannicus or Sr John Digby*, first published in 1910, Camden Soc., 3d ser., vol. 18.

should be gratified, if in no other way than in reprinting the moving death of his hero after the clash and action of the battle of Bramden, a death which does not fall below the standard set by Cavendish and Roper and Greville (p. 19): [26]

". . . and though others were hardly induced to beleeve it, both now and before he expressed in a mild manner, that his life was neare a period: and conjured me by all the love and respect I ought him, to certifie his Deare Mother that he died with a quiet conscience, and a resigned mind, hoping likewise that she would not take his death with too much heavinesse, but rather rejoyce that she had a son to shed his bloud for his Soveraigne.

"He notwithstanding his deadly wounds, comes down staires on foote, & ascends the carriage with that stoutnesse, as hardly hath beene seene in a dying man: all the symptomes of paine you could perceive in him, was sometimes he would bite his nether lip, when his pangs with most extremity came upon him. When we drew neere Andover, he began to say (his senses being a little astonished) Good my lord let us charge up againe, let us charge them once againe, and the day is ours. As soone as we entred the towne he began to invoke the sacred name of Jesus, often repeating it with a soft voyce, as if he had taken a gust and sweetnesse in the divine vertue of it. Shortly after, over against the signe of the Angel, in a mild and sweet repose he expired: where it would have grieved the hardest heart to have seene him round enclosed with sundry Gentlemen, condoling with teares the untimely end of so Peerless a gentleman."

26. The same admiration for bravery is apparent in *The Loyall Sacrifice: Presented in the Lives and Deaths of those two Eminent-Heroick Patternes . . . Sir Charls Lucas, And Sir George Lisle* (1648). The execution of the royalist leader Lucas is stirring (p. 78): "And with a kinde of Religious indignation (for never was passion in such a spirit more sweetly subdued) pulling downe his Hat, setting his Armes a Kembow, (that was his posture) & tearing open his Doublet, he exposed his naked Brest (wherein such matchlesse Valour and Loyall Honour had been lodged) and crying out *Now rebels do your worst*, he was immediately dispatched."

Two contrasting figures in the Civil Wars, one the Royalist Duke of Newcastle, the other the Parliamentary Colonel John Hutchinson, found exceptional biographers in their wives. In his diary for March 18, 1668, Samuel Pepys mentions that he has been reading "the ridiculous history of my Lord Newcastle, wrote by his wife; which shows her to be a mad, conceited, ridiculous woman, and he an ass to suffer her to write what she writes to him and of him." Charles Lamb was more lenient, and spoke of her as "that princely woman, thrice noble Margaret of Newcastle" and of the life as "both good and rare," "a jewel." Perhaps more just than either is the inscription on her tombstone: "This Dutches was a wise, wittie, and Learned Lady, which her many Bookes do well testifie."

Her *Life of William Cavendishe* is remarkable in that it was written and published while he was yet alive (1667) and is in fact dedicated to him. The Duchess of Newcastle gives no account of her husband's youth, but is diligent in describing during the Civil Wars all the battles in the North wherein Newcastle was an important although ineffective leader. Then Lady Margaret herself comes into the story; there are incidents of the exile in France and Holland, odd references to "a famous Picture-drawer, Van Ruben," or to My Lord's horses, and a final restoration to a ruined estate. After the first two books, treating of Cavendish's career as a soldier and of his losses, the third book contains an extended character sketch which magnifies his qualities. "I may justly call him," says his wife, "the best Lyrick and Dramatick Poet of this Age" (p. 146). He becomes an epitome of virtue, since (p. 149) "I knew him not addicted to any vice, except that he has been a great lover and admirer of the Female Sex." After a personal description — "His Shape is neat. . . . His Behaviour . . . hath somthing in it of grandure, that causes an awful respect towards him" — she appends a fourth book containing "several Essays and Discources Gather'd from the Mouth of My noble Lord and Husband." These afford a more certain index to his character: [27]

"I have heard My Lord say, That those which command the Wealth of a Kingdom, command the hearts and hands of the People."

"That he had observed, That seldom any person did laugh, but it was at the follies or misfortunes of other men; by which we may judg of their good natures."

The biography is individual and follows no pattern. Its particular merit lies in its *naïveté,* for its exuberance and verbosity cannot be interpreted as power or completeness in portrayal. After her fanfare of prefaces, wherein mountains travail, the ensuing life of the Duke of Newcastle seems somewhat unworthy of its heralds.

Similar in character, but standing on a far different level of achievement, are the *Memoirs of the Life of Colonel Hutchinson* by his widow Lucy.[28] This, too, like a number of other seventeenth-century memoirs,[29] records the lives of two individuals. Biography combines with autobiography in a joint portrait of John and Lucy Hutchinson, a further addition to the Van Dycks in our gallery. Lucy Hutchinson does not slight her husband's career in the cause of Parliament, or his break

27. Pp. 162, 177.
28. Written about 1670; 1st ed., 1806; new ed., 1906.
29. Cf. life of Lady Elizabeth Falkland, *supra*; Margaret Cavendish's biography of her husband and her own autobiography; Lady Anne Fanshawe in Chapter VI.

with Cromwell. After the Restoration, without her husband's knowledge, his solicitous wife dares to pen a letter of "signal repentance" to the new Parliament and, although he was one of the judges of Charles I, he is allowed freedom and his estates. This action of love on the part of his wife Colonel Hutchinson regrets, and in later persecutions he does not defend himself. He is imprisoned in the Tower and later in a grisly country castle where in 1664 he dies. The biography is written by a woman of unusual intellect, who after her husband's death became increasingly Puritanical. The style is Latinized, with long circumstantial periods after the manner of Clarendon. The political sections are extended and form a great part of the narrative, since Mrs. Hutchinson considers it necessary to justify her husband's position. "But here," she says (p. 50), "I must make a short digression from our particular actions, to summe up the state of the kingdome at that time . . . but I shall only mention what is necessary to be remember'd, for the better carrying on of my purpose." This purpose — and the attraction of these memoirs lies herein — is to narrate in the lives of her cherished husband and herself the course of true love. She writes after his death to control her grief and to keep fresh his memory, and opens her introductory "To my Children" with a beautiful tribute in noble prose: [30]

"They who dote on mortall excellencies, when by the inevitable fate of all things fraile, their adored idolls are taken from them, may lett loose the winds of passion to bring in a flood of sorrow; . . . but I that am under a command not to grieve att the common rate of desolate woemen, while I am studying which way to moderate my woe, and if it were pos-

30. 1806, p. 19.

sible to augment my love, can for the present find out none more just to your deare father nor consolatory to myselfe then the preservation of his memory, which I need not guild with such flattring commendations as the hired preachers doe equally give to the truly and titulary honorable; a naked undrest narrative, speaking the simple truth of him, will deck him with more substantial glorie, then all the panegyricks the best pens could ever consecrate to the vertues of the best men."

The personal descriptions show an intense and loving study (pp. 6 and 17):

". . . there was somthing extraordinary and tending to vertue, beyond what I can describe, or can be gather'd from a bare dead description; there was a life of spiritt and power in him that is not to be found in any copie drawne from him."

"The heate of his youth a little enclin'd him to the passion of anger, and the goodnesse of his nature to those of love and griefe, but reason was never dethron'd by them, but continued governesse and moderator in his soul."

She lingers over the love story: Colonel Hutchinson first discovers a few odd Latin books and learns they belong to Mistress Apsley; he admires a song which was written by Mistress Apsley; he hears of Mistress Apsley's rumored engagement to be married, and before he had seen her "immediately turned pale as ashes, and felt a fainting to seize his spiritts. . . . Little did any of the company suspect the true cause of his sudden qualms" (pp. 41–42). They meet:

"She was not ugly, in a carelesse riding-habitt, she had a melancholly negligence both of herselfe and others, as if she neither affected to please others, nor tooke notice of anie thing before her; yet spite of all her indifferency, she was surpriz'd with some unusual liking in her soule, when she saw this gentleman, who had haire, eies, shape, and countenance enough to begett love in any one at the first, and these sett of with a gracefull and generous mine, which promis'd an extraordinary person."

Colonel Hutchinson gives high proof of his love (p. 45):

"That day that the friends on both sides met to conclude the marriage, she fell sick of the small pox, which was many wayes a greate triall upon him; first her life was allmost in desperate hazard, and then the disease, for the present, made her the most deformed person that could be seene, for a greate while after she recover'd; yett he was nothing troubled at it, but married her as soone as she was able to quitt the chamber, when the priest and all that saw her were affrighted to looke on her: but God recompenc'd his justice and constancy, by restoring her, though she was longer then ordinary before she recover'd, as well as before."

From these memories, from the repeated recollection of his silken brown hair, Lucy Hutchinson turns with a sigh of regret (p. 44):

"I shall passe by all the little amorous relations, which if I would take the paynes to relate, would make a true history of a more handsome management of love then the best romances describe: for these are to be forgotten as the vanities of youth, not worthy mention among the greater transactions of his life."

It had been a beautiful story, filled with that sincerity and emotion which so seldom are allowed to enter into what is called a life. The accounts of the Civil Wars go on, with actions evil or great or merely dull, and Colonel Hutchinson, because he will not permit his wife's love to save him at the sacrifice of his integrity, progresses to a lonely death in a castle prison. Then, with his injunction not to grieve fresh in her mind, his widow set herself the task of writing the life of the person with whom she was so closely identified (p. 12): "all that she was, was *him*, while he was here, and all that she is now at best but his pale shade."

In the last half of the seventeenth century the biographies of purely literary men increase. They were usually written, as Walton's lives were written, in the form of prefaces to published works; others may be found in the collections of Fuller, Langbaine, Aubrey, and Wood. One of the earliest of these biographies of authors is Davies' life of John Hall, prefixed to Hall's English translation of *Hierocles Upon the Golden Verses of Pythagoras* (1657), which gives a clear account of this brilliant young Cambridge scholar and of his works. The order of their composition, with dates, is recorded from Davies' personal knowledge, and is followed by a character sketch which distinguishes its subject (p. 16):

"Having thus viewed him in his works, it will not be amisse to consider him a little in his person. He was somewhat above the ordinary stature, but not proportionably strong; besides that the breaking of a leg in his youth made him somewhat weaker, whence it came that he avoided much walking. He had a severe and melancholly look, but awakened with any thing of discourse he put on much facetiousnesse and affability. In point of conversation he was another Alcibiades, contemned no man, shook hands with any, which made him guilty of a familiarity many times with persons below him. He was so impatient of solitude, that to avoid it he would often purchase even inferiour company: he was naturally very cholerick, being soon incensed, and as soon appeased."

John Davies, although he commends leniency in biographers, does not himself hesitate to note Hall's alleged atheism, and makes a brave attempt as a sympathizing friend to justify his subject's views. The ex-

tolling of virtues is common in biography, but a loyal
defence of what might be regarded as a moral flaw is almost unique in the annals of biography and will therefore be quoted in full (pp. 19–20):

> "But since there is one reproach lies heavier than all the
> rest, viz. That he was guilty of a certain neglect and dis-care
> of things sacred, which some ignorantly, some enviously,
> stretch to a kinde of Atheisme, I think my self, though the
> objection be sufficiently absurd, obliged to say something to
> it. It is a generall injustice in the greatest part of mankinde,
> where the matters of Religion are so abstruse, and remote
> from the disquisition of ordinary capacities, to be so petu-
> lantly censorious, as to measure all others by their own fan-
> tasticall apprehensions. Mr. Hall indeed (as a many more)
> had an esteem of the Ministery proportionable to their abili-
> ties and learning, animated by a piety void of great eye-brows
> and hypocrisie. But for those whom a necessitous confidence,
> and a liberality of insinuation and talk furnished the Pulpit
> with, he had a patience much like that of an experienced Phy-
> sician for the Declamations of a Mountebank. He thought it
> indeed no great devotion to hear a sort of people whose Tenets
> are as different as the laces of their caps, or the colours of the
> cushions they beat. If this be to have an indifference for Re-
> ligion, and the affairs of future felicity, I must acknowledge
> Mr. Hall was haply so unfortunate, as to make one of the
> many, I say, the many, who have a just contempt for a fawn-
> ing pragmaticall sanctimony."

The biography is written with intimacy and insight
based on (p. 24) "the great advantages I might have
made of his conversation, I may say, familiarity, for the
space almost of ten years." Though short, it attempts a
critical survey of Hall's writings. If the subject of the
life were more widely known, there is no doubt that
Davies' little biography would receive the recognition
which, intrinsically, it merits.

Thomas Sprat's biography of Cowley, which appeared in 1668 in both Latin and English versions as prefaces to Cowley's works, has been called the first independent life of an individual who was purely a man of letters.[31] Because of the numerous editions through which Cowley's collected poems ran [32] and Sprat's definite theories regarding biographical propriety, this life is of first importance in the history of biography. Sprat's great blow to the development of life-writing lay in his attitude toward the inclusion of private original sources, of intimate letters in particular.

"The truth is," he says (p. d1ro), "the Letters that pass between particular Friends, if they are written as they ought to be, can scarce even be fit to see the light. They should not consist of fulsom Complements, or tedious Politicks, or elaborate Elegancies, or general Fancies. But they should have a Native clearness and shortness, a Domestical plainness, and a peculiar kind of Familiarity; which can only affect the humour of those to whom they were intended. The very same passages, which make Writings of this Nature delightful amongst Friends, will loose all manner of taste, when they come to be read by those that are indifferent. In such Letters the Souls of Men should appear undress'd: And in that negligent habit, they may be fit to be seen by one or two in a Chamber, but not to go abroad into the Streets."

How, then, does Mr. Sprat propose to write a biography? He begins with a definite breaking from the high histories of the nominally great. This in itself is salutary, as is also his stress upon the interest and value of humbler lives. "I know it is the custom of the World," he says (p. e2vo), "to prefer the pompous Histories of

31. With such predecessors as Speght's *Chaucer* or Davies' *Hall* it is apparent that this statement cannot be admitted without qualification.
32. The seventh appeared in 1700.

great Men, before the greatest Virtues of others, whose
lives have been led in a course less illustrious. This indeed is the general humour. But I believe it to be an
errour in mens judgments. . . . It is from the practise of
men equal to our selves, that we are more naturally
taught how to command our Passions, to direct our
Knowledge, and to govern our Actions." This statement by itself is fearless and convincing. It opens untravelled regions to the biographer. Yet according to
Mr. Sprat's own dictum regarding private correspondence, those who are not the personal friends of a worthy
man should have no opportunity to become so vicari-
ously. They may be introduced to him in stiff full-dress,
but never in carpet slippers. Sprat's *Life of Cowley*
shows the flaws of his method. In barring the informal
and confiding letters which would have allowed Cowley
to reveal his own nature, Sprat has taken the first step in
rendering his biography innocuous.[33] He weakens it
further by selecting only Cowley's gentle virtues and ex-
tolling them at length. "Eminent goodness" is apparent on every page. Here are the opening sentences of
seven successive paragraphs (p. d2):

"He had indeed a perfect natural goodness, which neither
the uncertainties of his condition, nor the largeness of his wit
could pervert. . . .
"There was nothing affected or singular in his habit, or
person, or gesture. . . .
"His Conversation was certainly of the most excellent kind;
for it was such as was rather admired by his familiar Friends,
than by Strangers at first sight. . . .

33. Sprat's Latin life of Cowley (1668) gives diabetes as the cause of
Cowley's demise. In accordance with his principles of propriety, Sprat is
vague concerning Cowley's death in his English biography.

"In his Speech, neither the pleasantness excluded gravity, nor was the sobriety of it inconsistent with delight. . . .

"His Wit was so temper'd, that no man had ever reason to wish it had been less. . . .

"He never guided his life by the whispers, or opinions of the World. . . .

"He perform'd all his Natural and Civil Duties, with admirable tenderness."

Only once does Sprat disclose a trait in his hero which shows his abnegation and distinguishes him from the common run of authors: "he never willingly recited any of his Writings." Elsewhere, the sugary lack of character of Sprat's pleasant phrases does little to preserve the memory of Cowley. This biography, by displaying too much clemency, fails to attain justice; its smooth and sanctimonious style did not save it from exerting an unfortunate influence upon the development of frank biography.

One of the most satisfactory lives of literary men produced during the seventeenth century is Dryden's *Life of Plutarch* (1683), prefixed to the edition he himself supervised. Not only is it written in Dryden's dignified and masterly style, but the marshalling of scanty materials is clear and admirable. "We are forced to glean from Plutarch," Dryden says,[34] "what he has scattered in his writings concerning himself, and his original. Which (excepting that little memorial, that Suidas, and some few others, have left concerning him) is all that we can collect, relating to this great Philosopher and Historian." Yet Dryden manages to construct a life of considerable detail, followed by a discourse on the relation of biography to history, and a criticism of Plutarch's

34. 1758, p. xiv.

works. In the field of biography as in other departments
of literature, Dryden is not so much an innovator as a
perfecter. He profits by the mistakes and successes of
others, culls his materials from diverse sources, adds
some original criticism of his own, and shapes the whole
according to his own unimpeachable taste. The result
is a life of Plutarch which is in itself a model.

As a supplement to these prefatory biographies are the
lives of writers to be found in collections. Fuller's
Worthies of England (1662) contains numerous short
and scintillating life-sketches in the midst of his choro-
graphical excursions among the English counties. The
credulity of earlier antiquarians he deplores and dis-
trusts, replacing it with his own whimsical curiosity.
The lives of the worthies of each shire are generally too
brief to be considered as complete biographies in themselves, but Fuller's restless wit and inquiring spirit make
them delightful reading.

Other collected lives of authors may be found in
Edward Phillips' *Theatrum Poetarum* (1674), which includes cursory notices of both ancient and modern poets,
and in William Winstanley's *Lives of the most Famous
English Poets* (1687), which is more nearly a catalogue of
writings than a biographical dictionary, and is perfunctory and careless. Gerard Langbaine's *Account of the
English Dramatick Poets* (1691), on the other hand, is the
fruit of diligent investigation. In the preface, Langbaine definitely states what he proposes to perform:

"In the First place then I have given a succinct Account of
the Time in which most of the Ancient Poets liv'd; the place
of their Nativity, Quality, Death, Writings, &c. in a larger
manner than either Mr. Philips or Mr. Winstanley; and have
collected all the material Passages of their Lives, which I

found scattered in Doctor Fuller, Lloydd, à Wood, &c. into One Volume, for the greater Ease of the Reader, and Advantage to the Work."

Further, he gives an account of the title-pages of the authors' dramas. Last, he indulges one of his particular interests by reviewing the historical sources for the plays, as well as their sources in foreign literature and romance. His scholarly and relatively dependable accounts show him to be painstaking and thorough, but the collection, which grew out of his earlier *Catalogue of Plays*, remains primarily critical and not biographical.

At the end of the century, as a fitting culmination of the antiquarian tradition of Leland, Bale, Pits, and Fuller, appeared Anthony Wood's *Athenae Oxonienses, An Exact History of all the Writers and Bishops who have had their education in . . . Oxford from . . . 1500, to the end of the year 1690*.[35] The work is thorough; its general accuracy and completeness is evident in that it remains to-day an authority.[36] Wood's industry is remarkable; his search for the minutest details no less so.

"When this Work some years since was first undertaken," the preface states, "he not only consulted all the Registers relating to the University, but all other Writings and Records, MS. and printed, whether in the Tower, Exchequer, Paper Office, or elsewhere, that could give him any notice of these Authors, or let him into the true knowledge of their Lives, Performances, and Writings. The Registers of the ancient Churches and Cathedrals were diligently consulted; the Wills of the deceas'd persons were at the Prerogative Office examin'd; the Windows of Churches, Epitaphs and Inscriptions,

35. 2 vols., 1691–92.
36. Wood's enthusiasm for antiquities was roused by a perusal of Dugdale's *Antiquities of Warwickshire* (1656), and his study of his own university was encouraged by another distinguished Oxford biographer, Bishop John Fell, then Dean of Christ Church.

have been search'd; the Genealogy of the Authors at the Heralds Office hath been inquir'd into; and no method hath been unattempted which could contribute to a true History of these Writers, or ascertain the least date and circumstance of their lives."

In addition to his indefatigable quest for the *minutiae* of a career, and closely connected with it, is Wood's passion for truth, an instinct so highly developed in the antiquary of Merton Street that he frequently failed to distinguish truthfulness from truculence. His uncompromising judgments brought official censure from the authorities of the University for the glory of which he had undertaken the work. "All good Antiquaries," Wood had said, "have always been of the same Principle: They all equally sacrificed to Truth and Learning." When the offending pages of the *Athenae Oxonienses* were publicly burned, Wood's sacrifice was complete.

There is no attempt at pleasing presentation in Wood's history of Oxford writers. His information is given in terse, elliptical phrases, and the emphasis throughout is upon dates, facts, events. In his complete loyalty to the truth as he found it, in his assiduous search for the most humble details, Anthony Wood stands at the head of the antiquaries of the seventeenth century, as one of the fathers of scientific life-writing.

As a foil to Wood's dogged scholarship and precision stands John Aubrey, whose *Brief Lives* were collected between 1669 and 1696 at the suggestion of his Oxford friend, and were incorporated in large part in the *Athenae Oxonienses*. Wood, who quarrelled with Aubrey as he quarrelled with everyone, refers to him as a "roving, maggoty-pated man," and this uncharitable judgment has been too widely accepted. John Toland [37] speaks of him as "a very honest man, and most accurate in his accounts of matters of fact." And Malone, who did not neglect Aubrey in his Shakespearean studies, says: [38] "However fantastical Aubrey may have been on the subjects of chemistry and ghosts, his character for veracity has never been impeached, and as a very diligent antiquarian his testimony is worthy of attention."

Aubrey's *Brief Lives* were gathered over the dinner-table in English country-houses; and amusing, often irrelevant anecdotes absorbed his attention. His longest item, the life of his friend Thomas Hobbes, shows his power to collect a diversity of small facts and anecdotes, but also demonstrates his inability to organize them. His sharp eye and lively temper are more remarkable than his judgment. His work is a collection of jottings that reveal the writer, in their informal fragments, as a forerunner of Boswell. Yet because Aubrey's writings are unfinished notes and to a large extent formless, they are not of major importance in a study of the art of English biography.

Gilbert Burnet stands out as a historian who is also a biographer. In contrast to the short biographical notices in the collections of Fuller and Wood, he contributes single lives of his contemporaries. Between 1673 and 1685 Bishop Burnet issued four biographies separately printed. The range in subject is wide, but the lives are uniformly marked by restraint and an unusual dignity in narration. Their form and measure Burnet derives from Plutarch and Caesar; their documentation and fullness from continental historians.[39]

37. *History of the Druids*, 1814, p. 159.   38. *Shakespeare* (1821), ii, 694.
39. Such as Philippe de Commines, Guicciardine, and Davila, whom he knows and mentions, and particularly Jacques de Thou.

As intimate biographies, the two most interesting are the *Life of Rochester* (1680) and the *Life of Sir Matthew Hale* (1682). His study of John Wilmot, Earl of Rochester, is unique and dramatic. A large part is taken up with dialogues between Rochester and Burnet, wherein the Earl's arguments against Christianity are vividly set forth, with no attempt to belittle them, followed by Burnet's answers. Rochester in his last sickness called upon the Bishop and finally confessed his repentance, so that the biography is written not as a revelation of brilliant profligacy, but as an example to sinners. The account of Rochester's doubts and the steps in his conversion is given in detail, in conversations which set off Rochester's logical, scoffing mind more clearly than any analysis could do. The small anecdotes and arguments which indicate his beliefs and the Bishop's convictions, reach in subtlety the height of biographical art. And yet this complicated conflict between the skeptical courtier and the zealous churchman is narrated throughout in language which can become as simple and moving as this account of the death of Rochester (pp. 157-158):

"So on Saturday at Four of the Clock in the Morning I left him, being the twenty-fourth of July. But I durst not take leave of him; for he had expressed so great an unwillingness to part with me the day before, that if I had not presently yielded to one day's stay, it was like to have given him some trouble, therefore I thought it better to leave him without any Formality. Some hours after he asked for me, and when it was told him, I was gone, he seem'd to be troubled, and said, *Has my Friend left me, then I shall die shortly.* After that he spake but once or twice till he died: He lay much silent: Once they heard him praying very devoutly. And on Monday about Two of the Clock in the Morning, he died, without any Convulsion, or so much as a groan."

Two years later Bishop Burnet issued a further biographical study, the *Life of Sir Matthew Hale*. This work shows that Burnet had formulated conscious and definite theories of the biographer's function: incidents of doubtful authenticity must of course be omitted, but in addition Burnet wishes to exclude trifling accounts of childhood and education and of those domestic and private affairs "in which the world is little concerned" [40] — the same narrow and formal conception which was maintained by Bishop Sprat and Samuel Clark and which checked the growth of biography from the Restoration to the time of Boswell. Writing within the limitations he set for himself, Burnet produced a biography which, though it lacks movement and color, is not wanting in thought, style, or dignity. Sir Matthew Hale as portrayed by his biographer, resembles the earlier sketches of Sir Thomas More in his piety, unobtrusiveness, integrity, subtlety, his knowledge of the law, and the number of his distinguished friends. Burnet's stately life of the Lord Chief Justice lays particular stress upon Hale's character and his intellectual traits. It is supplemented by "Additional Notes" written by Richard Baxter, which give a sharp and detailed character study of Sir Matthew in his old age.

No less than Fuller and Burnet, Richard Baxter, the most fascinating and prolific among the nonconforming clerics, held definite theories regarding the art of biography, and was responsible for the publication of several lives. The best of these, issued the year of his wife's death (1681), is *A Breviate of the Life of Margaret Baxter*. Not only in the biography, but in the preface also, it is evident that this memorial to his wife is the

40. 1805, Preface, p. viii.

outpouring of a full heart (A1ᵛᵒ): "mine own Affections urged me to premise this Breviate of her own life: Written, I confess, under the power of melting Grief, and therefore perhaps with the less prudent judgment; but not with the less, but the more Truth: For passionate Weakness poureth out all, which greater Prudence may conceal." As in his own autobiography, Baxter is here subjective and personal: in the first chapters he uses letters and extracts from her private journals and meditations — "self-judging Papers" — to show her humility and her passionate sense of religion. In this respect he almost permits Margaret Baxter to write her own autobiography; yet his own estimates of her character are subtle and refined, marked by a rare combination of psychological penetration, sympathy, and observation over extended periods (p. 43):

"She had a natural reservedness, and secrecy, increased by thinking it necessary prudence not to be open; by which means she was oft misunderstood by her nearest friends, and consequently often crost and disappointed by those that would have pleased her. And as she could understand men much by their looks and hints, so she expected all should know her mind without her expressing it, Which bred her frustrations and discontents."

Again, in a chapter "Of her Mental Qualifications, and her Infirmities" he will begin one of the numbered lists of which he was so fond (p. 75):

"But 1. she was prone to over-love her Relations, and those good people (poor as much as rich) whom she thought most upright. The love was good, but the degree was too passionate.

"2. She over-earnestly desired their spiritual welfare. If these whom she over-loved, had not been as good, and done as well as she would have them, in innocent behaviour, in piety, and (if rich) in liberality, it over-troubled her, and she could not bear it."

Later he says (p. 79):

"One infirmity made her faulty in the omission of much of her duty: She was wont to say, that she had from her childhood Imprinted a deep fear and hatred of hypocrisie on her mind, that she could never do the outside of her duty, as to the speaking part, for fear of hypocrise; I scarce ever met with a person that was abler to speak long, for matter and good language, without repetitions, even about Religious things; and few that had more desire that it were well done; and yet she could not do it her self for fear of seeming to be guilty of ostentation."

At the end of his delicate and discriminating tribute, which draws moral lessons in abundance from the meek pilgrimage of his wife, Baxter listed twenty-one specific ways in which the narrative will be "useful . . . to considering men." With this end in view, Richard Baxter, upon the death of Margaret, set himself to write the story of his young wife, with whom he lived for nineteen years (p. 93) "in constant Love, and Peace, and Concord, except our differing Opinions about trivial occurrences, or our disputing or differing mode of talk." [41]

One further tender memorial merits our attention. Near the end of the century John Evelyn wrote the *Life of Mrs. Godolphin*.[42] Like Fulke Greville's *Sidney*, it is a monument to friendship, written with fervent

41. Such commemoration of Protestant women for their pious lives is common before Richard Baxter in such works as *A Christal Glasse for Christian Women* . . . *the Godly Life and Christian Death of Mistris Katherine Stubbes* (1592), *The Honour of Vertue. Or The Monument erected by the sorowfull Husband, and the Epitaphes annexed by learned and worthy men, to the immortall memory of that worthy Gentle-woman Mrs. Elizabeth Crashawe* (1620), or *The Life and Death of Mrs. Margaret Andrews* (1680).
42. Ed. S. Wilberforce, 1847.

and personal emotion; like Walton's lives it is a glorification of piety in graceful language. In form it is unique, inasmuch as it is addressed throughout to a single lady, Anne Howard, wife of Sir Gabriel Sylvius, at whose request Evelyn writes. The biography of a beautiful girl who died young,[43] it presents a dramatic contrast between her own purity and religious fervor, and the prevailing tone of the court in which she was placed at the age of twelve. As a biographer John Evelyn's opportunities were enviable. He was reluctant to meet her, "for," he says (p. 30), "I was the most unfitt person in the world for the entertainments of the Anti Chamber, and the little Spiritts that dwell in Fairy Land." Yet there soon grew up between this disparate pair [44] a complete understanding, and the scene in which they swear inviolable friendship Evelyn presents with such enthusiasm that at last he writes in dismay, "whither has this Indearing topic transported me?"

But Evelyn speaks from knowledge as well as sympathy. Each year Margaret Blagge sent him a brief narrative of her life. Furthermore, he had access to her diaries and meditations and made use of them in the biography; her letters, too, are singularly subjective and filled with a sweet piety, so that Evelyn vows that (p. 4) "it would become a steadier hand, and the penn of an Angells wing to describe the life of a Saint." The beginnings of her love for Sidney Godolphin she confided to Evelyn in a tender and circumspect relation (pp. 51–55). There followed a nine-year courtship during which Margaret was torn between two loves — her religion and her future husband.

43. Margaret Godolphin, 1652–78.
44. Evelyn was thirty-two years the senior of Mistress Blagge.

"I have really been touch'd in the deepest sence," says Evelyn (pp. 65–66), "to see the Conflicts this devout Creature underwent, betweene her love and her devotion; or shall I call them both her love; for soe they were: a thousand tymes has she told me she would abide as she was, and then her pitty for him who could not live in her absence, divided her afresh, and peirc'd her to the soule; and when she was in the deepest of this Concerne for him, nothing I have ever read in the Epistles of Seneca, had that excellent Stoick been indeed a Christian, appear d more divinely philosophicall then the Topics she would use to divert his passion, and reason him into an indifference for her, when (of all things in the world,) it was not indifferent to her that he should have lov'd her less."

They were secretly married, which hurt Margaret's friend, but led to a scene between them of great emotional beauty, of which Evelyn says, "I recount this passage to your Ladyshipp more minutely, as being the most passionate and most mysterious." Her happiness with her husband was short, for she died in her twenty-sixth year after giving birth to a son. As the final record of her life, Evelyn includes Margaret Godolphin's last letter to her husband (p. 152):

"My deare, not knowing how God Allmighty may deale with me, I think it my best course to settle my affaires, soe as that, in case I be to leave this world, noe earthly thing may take up my thoughts. In the first place, my dear, beleive me, that of all earthly things you were and are the most dear to me; and I am convinced that nobody ever had a better or halfe soe good a husband. I begg your pardon for all my Imperfections, which I am sencible were many. . . . Pray, my deare, be kind to that poore Child I leave behind, for my sake, who lov'd you soe well."

The entire little biography is a piece of art, and even minor events in the life of his heroine are colored by

Evelyn's poetry, as in the scene where he describes to the Lady Sylvius Margaret's departure from the court (p. 58):

"I leave you, Madam, to imagine how the rest of the Court mourn'd this Recess, and how dim the tapers burnt as she pass'd the anti-chamber. 'Is Mrs. Blagge goeing,' sayes a faire creature; 'why stay I here any longer?' others, 'that the Court had never such a Starr in all its hemispheere.' . . . She took her leave of the mother of the Maids as became her; butt she could not weepe till your Ladyshipps sister, whome she was still to leave in Captivitye fell on her neck, and then there fell mutuall tears, that trickled downe her Cheeks like the dew of Flowers, and made a lovely griefe."

At times, contemplating her purity, Evelyn breaks out in rhapsodies, which he hopes Madam will not imagine "a Romantick folly, or the transport of some lover." The account of her spiritual conflicts is with Evelyn of primary and absorbing interest, so that he will declare his portrait "reaches the profill onely, and wants a world of finishing" (p. 162). Yet her daily rounds, her life in the court, her mindfulness of the poor, her charity, her reading, her household management, are not forgotten. He delights in emphasizing the contrast between his heroine and the court, and nowhere is this more striking than in the masque wherein she wore jewels worth twenty thousand pounds and played the most illustrious part. Yet "amidst all this pomp and serious impertinence, whilst the rest were acting, and that her part was sometymes to goe off, as the scenes required, into the tireing roome, where severall Ladyes her companions were railing with the Gallants trifleingly enough till they were called to reenter, she, under pretence of conning her next part, was retired into a Corner, reading a booke of devotion, without att all concerning herselfe or mingling with the young Company" (pp. 97–98).

It is often apparent that this sweet saint was also very human and very young. One evening she loses three pounds at cards, and "with what remorse, with what discretion" enters the following resolution in her secret diary (p. 215): "June the 2d. I will never play this halfe year butt att 3 penny omber, and then with one att halves. I will not; I doe not vow, but I will not doe it, — what, loose mony at Cards, yett not give the poore? 'Tis robbing God, misspending tyme, and missimploying my Talent: three great Sinns. Three pounds would have kept three people from starveing a month: well, I will not play."

The life fittingly ends with a dirge, for it is one of the most poetic of biographies, both in its flowing style and in its sentiment. Evelyn himself has epitomized the *Life of Margaret Godolphin* in the device which introduces his manuscript: a five-pointed star, symbol of eternal friendship, flanked on opposite sides by the words "un dieu" and "un ami."

Freed alike from the sanctifying purpose of ecclesiastical biography and from the formal panegyrics of the royal lives, the secular lives added much of permanent value to the art of biography. In the hands of such writers as Anthony Wood, the collecting of the facts and measurements of a life, the assiduous treasuring of dates and little details, transformed biography almost into a science. But accuracy and knowledge is not enough. The best secular biographers of the sixteenth and seventeenth century added something more: they succeeded in introducing a sense of sympathy and intimacy rarely found in earlier writings. The figures of More, Wolsey, and Sidney, of Major General Smith and Colonel Hutchinson, of Mrs. Baxter and Margaret Godolphin, do not stand forth vividly in their biographies because of any common quality in their own persons. They are united and rendered unforgettable because of the understanding and enthusiasm of their biographers. Their own unique virtues have not insured their immortality; they live because of the respect of Son Roper, the faithfulness of a Gentleman Usher, the noble friendship of Fulke Greville, Secretary Walsingham's admiration for courage, the love of Lucy Hutchinson, the grief of Richard Baxter, the adoration of John Evelyn.

Biography is not made convincing and complete solely by the good intentions of the saints' lives, or by the dignity in form of the versifiers, or by the grandeur of royal chronicles, or by the knowledge of the antiquaries. A further quality is needed to render a character human and vital, and that quality — the element of intimate sympathy — gives to the best secular lives of the seventeenth century a distinctive warmth and interest rarely found in earlier English biography.

VI

THE AUTOBIOGRAPHY

The writer of his own life has at least the first qualification of an historian, the knowledge of truth.   SAMUEL JOHNSON

THE distinction between biography and autobiography before 1700 is slight. A greater difference exists between early life-writing (including autobiography) and modern life-writing, than between biography in general and autobiography in general. During the period here studied, biographers based their works upon the seldom-questioned assumption that the life of an individual might be expressed as the sum of his separate acts. With such models in sixteenth- and seventeenth-century life-writing before them, the autobiographers themselves also produced objective accounts — impersonal annals and chronicles of *res gestae*. The ideal of the two forms was the same: to represent faithfully the life of an individual. In general the raw materials, the methods of treatment, the difficulties and the successes were shared alike by biography and autobiography. One of the characteristics, therefore, which this chapter will illustrate, is the objective quality of early autobiographers, their unconscious neglect of those opportunities for self-analysis which ordinarily lend a fascination to this branch of literature.[1] The only other generalization which may fairly be drawn is that the school of autobiography is much looser than the school of biography.

1. To the rule of impersonality in early autobiography, important exceptions may, of course, be discovered, and these will be noted.

Interrelations and derivations are less frequent, not because of greater originality and independence among the writers, but because autobiographies were published at rarer intervals than biographies, and remained isolated phenomena.[2]

Autobiography was not deliberately cultivated during the Middle Ages. Self-analysis, or the study of individuals except as pious examples, did not form a part of the mediaeval system. The infrequency of mediaeval self-chronicles shows that autobiography is essentially a modern form. Bede, it is true, closed his *Ecclesiastical History* with a brief, matter-of-fact paragraph about himself, a miniature account serving the same purpose as the *pinxit* on a mediaeval altarpiece, or the self-portrait of the artist in an Italian fresco. Or again, the fascinating Welshman, Gerald de Barri (1146?-1220?), left an extended self-study in mediaeval Latin, which originally contained a large collection of his sermons, his letters, and his interpretations of visions, but which is preserved to-day, regrettably, only in fragmentary form. Yet these are lonely examples.

With the English writers of the fifteenth century autobiographies become more frequent. The short little lives by Lydgate and Hoccleve follow the same form as Bede's brief notice of himself, and are added as identifying signatures to longer works.[3] Both Lydgate and

2. Where autobiographies became generally known to any class of readers, a tradition was formed. The Quaker autobiographies, for example, were widely circulated in the Society of Friends, with the result that most of them are written in an easily recognizable and formalized manner.

3. So Lydgate's *Life and death of Hector* contains the lines:

"I am a Monk by my profession
In Berry, call'd John Lydgate by my name,
And wear a habit of perfection;
(Altho my life agrees not with the same)."

Hoccleve, however, also produced longer separate autobiographical poems which are vivid retrospections. The
"Testament of John Lydgate" shows the author sincerely repentant after a wanton boyhood wherein he
preferred counting cherry stones to attendance at
church. The verses contrast poignantly his japing
youth and his withered eld, and reveal his faith, even in
the kalends of death, that his place "is bylded above the
sterres clere." Hoccleve's *Male Regle* is a versified account of his own spendthrift youth in the mire of London, among tavern maids and boatmen; from his *Complaint* one may infer the cowardice, the vanity, the fits
of madness, the repentance of this poor clerk in the office
of the Privy Seal.

The mediaeval current of rhymed lives does not break
off abruptly. Autobiographies in verse flourished in the
second half of the sixteenth century, among which the
most notable are George Gascoigne's mystical account
of his adventures in love, Thomas Tusser's cantering
doggerel describing his checkered career (1573), Thomas
Churchyard's *Tragicall Discourse* (1575), which ranges
from stirring martial stanzas to retrospective melancholy and closes with a testament in the mediaeval
tradition of François Villon, and Hugh Holland's life
prefatory to *Pancharis* (1603), rich in local allusions,
humor, and a broad philosophy of living.[4]

(Quoted from Fuller's *Worthies*, iii (1662), 69. "Berry" is St. Edmund's
Bury in Suffolk.) It is followed by a prayer for the reader's gentleness and
Lydgate's acknowledgement of Chaucer as his master. Hoccleve begins his
Regement of Princes with a dialogue between himself and an old beggar which
is self-revealing and personal.

4. Closely allied with these poetical and melancholy self-lives of literary
men are Robert Greene's *Mourning Garment* (1590) and *Groatsworth of Witte*
(1592) in prose. The first contains an interesting preface explaining why
Greene turned from his former evil ways, addressed to the students of the two
universities. The second begins as a *novella* having for a hero "Robertus."

It is to John Bale that we must turn for the first separately printed prose autobiography in English. *The Vocacyon of Iohan Bale to the Bishoprick of Ossorie in Ireland, his Persecucions in the same, and finall Delyveraunce* was published at Rome in 1553.[5] It is a detailed account of his life from his appointment as bishop in August, 1552, to his entrance into Germany in the following year. As such, it cannot be a complete life. Like his catalogue of writers, it is also bitter in anti-Catholic prejudices, and Bale upbraids the English church from abroad for having (p. 427) "brought fourth Ydolatrie, Blindenesse, Impenitencie, Frowardnesse, Crueltie, Pride, Fornication, Unclennesse, Covetousnesse, ingratefull Contempte of the Truthe, and Hate of the faithfull Preachers therof." Yet, in spite of its fragmentary character and its fanaticism, the *Vocacyon* remains a good account of the incidents of a year in Bale's career. It is written at times with a vigor and an imaginative comprehension which suggests Bale the playwright as well as the controversialist (p. 421):[6]

"Than sayde the forseid Downinges in great Displeasure, Gods Sowle, what do I here? This is but a dronken Matter, by the Masse; and so went his Waye in a Fume."

Sir James Melville's *Memoirs of his own life* furnish an early example[7] of a type of autobiography prevalent

Soon, however, Greene abandons the thin disguise and speaks in his own person, dispensing good advice and ending with a touching letter of repentance to his wife.

5. Reprinted in *Harleian Miscellany*, v. 6.
6. Included in his *Catalogue of Illustrious Writers* is a life of Bale by himself. His method is the same for biography and autobiography, except that the latter is written in the first person. He is conscientious and explicit. Similarly the antiquary Pits closes his catalogue with a section entitled *De Meipso*, written before his death in 1616 and included in the 1619 first edition under the heading *De Ioanne Pitsio*.
7. Melville b. 1549, d. 1593.

in the seventeenth century, the autobiography written for the instruction of relatives and descendants. Such writing usually springs from a sense of family pride, and almost without exception the authors are members of the gentry or nobility. Melville begins his account with this interesting statement of its genesis: [8]

"Sone, sen thou hes schauen thy self sa willing to satisfie my expectation of the, in folowing and observyng many of my formar preceptis during thy yong yeares, I grant now unto the thy requestis the mair glaidly, quhilk is to put in wret for thy better memorie sindrie thingis that thou had hard me rehers betymes, baith concernyng maneris, with some meit preceptis for thy barnely age; and also how to temper the rage of furious youth be the reule of godlynes and raisoun; . . . And now entring in rype age, to let the wit what tred of lyf I had led during my perigrination throw the maist part of Europe."

These memoirs are more important as the forerunner of an impressive class than for any merit of their own. Melville, a Scotchman of some distinction in court circles, confines himself to incidents of diplomacy. He does not appear as a man, always as a courtier or ambassador. His memoirs, consequently, are lacking in characterization and vitality.

In 1609, four years before his death, Sir Thomas Bodley wrote his own life which was published at Oxford in 1647. It narrates deliberately and completely the events in his career, and is written in a restrained and stately manner. In business-like and colorless phrases, Bodley seems to be pleading before the solemn tribunal of history and justifying his actions for eternity. Dates are given meticulously, with accurate accounts of his actions

8. 1827, p. 3.

at all periods of his life. After many years as ambassador at The Hague, he apologizes for withdrawing from
court and states his motives precisely. The account of
his determination to found the Bodleian Library is
worth quoting not only for its intrinsic interest but also
because it shows the nearest approach made in this sober
autobiography to analysis of motive: [9]

"Yet withall I was to think, that my duty towards God,
the expectation of the world, my naturall inclination, & very
morality, did require, that I should not wholly so hide those
little abilities that I had, but that in some measure, in one
kind or other, I should doe the true part of a profitable member in the State: whereupon examining exactly for the rest of
my life, what course I might take, and having sought (as I
thought, all the waies to the wood) to select the most proper,
I concluded at the last to set up my Staffe at the Library
doore in Oxford; being throughly perswaded that in my solitude and surcease from the Common-wealth affaires, I could
not busy my selfe to better purpose, then by reducing that
place (which then in every part lay ruined and wast) to the
publique use of Students. . . ."

Sir Thomas Bodley's work is the first full life in English
which preserves throughout the same efficient, formal
tone, a good example of impersonal autobiography.

In sharp contrast to the stiffness of Bodley's life is a
small group of memoirs filled with a reckless spirit and
written with an intimacy and freshness that link them
with Roper and Cavendish and the native English
tradition. First among them stands the *Memoirs of the
Life of Robert Cary . . . Earl of Monmouth.*[10] His frankness is evident in the first paragraph:

"I had the happinesse to be borne of good parents: I was
yongest of tenne sonnes; they brought mee up under tutors

9. 1647, p. 14.
10. 1759 orig. ed. Reprinted 1905. Written after 1623.

and governours, to give mee learning and knowledge, but I must acknowledge my own weakenesse, I had not ability to proffit much thereby."

He then plunges immediately into the story of his career abroad and his adventures in the wars in Holland. All events are seen with his own eye. There is no attempt at historical interpretation. The Armada is for him a personal fray (1759, p. 17):

"The next yeare the King of Spain's great Armado came upon our coast, thinking to devour us all. Upon the newes sent to court from Plimouth of their certain arrivall, my Lord Cumberland and myselfe tooke post horse, and rode streight to Portsmouth, where we found a frigot that carried us to sea."

Finally he becomes Warden of the West Marches in Scotland, where his boldness finds scope (p. 54):

"Thus after I had passed my best time in court, and got little, I betooke myself to the country, after I was past one and thirty years old, where I lived with great content: for wee had a stirring world."

His border adventures — the hanging of Giordie Bourne, the death of Sim of the Cathill, the battles with outlaws — flow easily from his pen. His interviews with Queen Elizabeth are dramatic:

"Shee grew yntoo a grate rage, begynnynge with Gods Wonds, that she wolde sett you by the feete." (Letter to his father.)

"Our first encounter was stormy and terrible, which I passed over with silence." (P. 74.)

In contrast, his last meeting with the dying Queen is vivid and moving (p. 136):

"I found her in one of her withdrawing chambers, sitting low upon her cushions. Shee called mee to her, I kist her hand, and told her it was my cheifest happinesse to see her in safety and in health, which I wished might long continue. Shee tooke mee by the hand, and rung it hard, and said, 'No, Robin, I am not well,' and then discoursed with mee of her indisposition, and that her heart had been sad and heavy for ten or twelve dayes, and in her descriptions she fetched not so few as forty or fifty great sighes. I was grieved at the first to see her in this plight; for in all my lifetime before I never knew her fetch a sigh, but when the Queene of Scottes was beheaded."

Cary was present in tears at her death, but immediately after rode posthaste to Edinburgh to gain James's favor by first bringing him the glad news. He managed also to keep in the good graces of Charles, and the account ends with his being created Earl of Monmouth in 1626. The romantic dash of the narrative endeared it to such men as Horace Walpole and Scott. Throughout it is delightful reading: the adventurous life of a man self-centred, frank, and unmeditative.

The curious researches of Walpole were also responsible for the publication in 1764 of the autobiography of Edward Lord Herbert of Cherbury, which is allied in spirit with Cary's memoirs. The life stops with Herbert's return from France in 1624, although Cary did not set it down until about the year 1643. His egotism is marked. The biography begins with his precocity and his first question, "Why was I born?" a question which the life does not attempt to solve. That Herbert was an original and serious thinker cannot be gleaned from his autobiography. He is ingenuously conscious of his own attractions, his beauty, and his bravery. His portrait, he mentions, was sought by great dames and "gave oc-

casion . . . of more discourse than I could have wished"
(p. 128). Once, upon entering Lady Ayres' chamber, he
says (p. 129), "I found it was my picture she looked
upon with more earnestness and passion than I could
have easily believed."

Lively anecdotes, repartee, and epigrams crowd his
pages; his continental career is largely composed of
challenges and duels, with a side-pilgrimage to a country
inn to see the daughter of the host, reputed the most
beautiful woman in Europe. She does not move him.
His diplomatic career in the Embassy at Paris is marked
by typical self-esteem (p. 198):

"When I came to Paris, the English and French were in
very ill intelligence with each other, insomuch that one
Buckly coming then to me, said he was assaulted and hurt
upon Pontneuf, only because he was an Englishman: nevertheless, after I had been in Paris about a month, all the English were so welcome thither, that no other nation was so
acceptable amongst them, insomuch, that my gentlemen
having a quarrel with some debauched French, who in their
drunkenness quarrelled with them, divers principal gentlemen of that nation offered themselves to assist my people
with their swords."

This entertaining and frivolous succession of anecdotes follows oddly upon the heels of his declaration:
"I have thought fit to relate to my posterity those passages of my life, which I conceive may best declare me,
and be most useful to them." Possibly Cherbury could
have fitted into this brave scheme his duels, and amours.
It is enough for us that such anecdotes sparkle, and that
his boastful pen does not grow weary.

Of this little group of informal and intimate memoirs,
the most interesting and original are the *Private Mem-*

oirs of Sir Kenelm Digby.[11] The motive for this autobiography is unique (p. 10): "I will set down in the
best manner that I can, the beginning, progress, and
consummation of that excellent love which only makes
me believe that our pilgrimage in this world is not indifferently laid upon all persons for a curse."

Elsewhere he says he is writing "only for my own
private content" (p. 326), and again, "to please myself
in looking back upon my past and sweet errors" (p.
327). The piece was never intended for publication:
"If these loose papers should have the fortune to fall
into any man's hands, to the which they were never designed, I desire that this last scrawl may be pardon for
the rest." The work, then, is written for his own pleasure, and this circumstance may account for its fanciful
intimacy.

In form it is an autobiographical novel intended to
justify in his own mind his indiscreet marriage with a
charming woman. Digby himself figures as Theagenes,
Venetia Stanley as Stelliana, and the private memoirs
form a love story which rises at times almost to poetry,
as in the description of Stelliana's beauty as it appears
to Digby through the enchantments of a Brahmin (pp.
146-148). Plato's influence is marked, and philosophical
dialogues abound.[12] But the memoirs are most striking
as a link between the sixteenth-century prose of the
Arcadia and *Euphues* and the sentimental novel of the
eighteenth century. Actual happenings are refined until
they might well fit into the mediaeval code of the court

11. First published from the original manuscript in 1827, but composed
before the year 1633 (Digby, 1603-65), since it was written before the death
of his wife, the lovely and notorious Venetia Stanley.

12. E. g., 1827, p. 233 or 239.

of love. Venetia as a young girl is thus addressed by a courtier (p. 23):

"One day Ursatius, a principal nobleman of the court, whose heart was set on fire with the radiant beams that sparkled from her eyes, took the confidence to speak unto her as he sat next to her at a masque, in this manner: 'Fair lady,' quoth he, 'I shall begin to endear myself to your knowledge by taxing you with that which I am confident you cannot excuse yourself of; for if by the exterior lineaments of the face, we may conjecture the frame and temper of the mind, certainly yours must be endowed with such perfections, that it is the greatest injustice and ingratitude that may be, for you to imprison your thoughts in silence, and to deny the happiness of your conversation to those whose very souls depend upon every motion that you make: and so to rob Him of the honour due to Him who is the Author of all good; and who in retribution expecteth that they unto whom he hath been most liberal of his favours, should by due communication of them most glorify him.'

"Stelliana, who was surprised by the unexpected discourse of one that she knew no otherwise but by name, and being disturbed from her pleasing thoughts, was some time before she could recollect herself: but after she had sate awhile as one amazed, civility called upon her to return some answer to him, that she knew was the person of most respect and note about the king; wherefore at length with a modest blush she thus replied to him: 'Sir . . .'"

Digby manifests an elegance of sentiment that eclipses Richardson (p. 48):

"'Alas!' replied Stelliana [alone in a room with Ursatius at her bedside], after a deep sigh, 'how ill your deeds and words sort together! you mention love, but perform the effects of extreme hatred! you sue to me for life, and in a treacherous manner have brought mine into your power; but, howsoever, at least I have this content remaining, that I shall find out sundry ways to death, if you attempt any thing upon my honour; the loss of which I am resolved never to outlive: and then my injured ghost shall be a perpetual terror to your guilty soul, which I will so pursue, that I will make you fly to hell to save you from my more tormenting vengeance.'"

Love takes away Digby's perspective, and when Venetia dances in a *corrente* (p. 26), he rhapsodizes on the pleasure he finds "to contemplate her motions, that were so composed of awful majesty and graceful agility, that all the beholders being ravished with delight, said, surely one of the Graces was descended from heaven to honour these nuptials."

Such passages in this ornate and imaginative narrative account for the hesitancy shown by this brilliant and extraordinary figure in destroying his work (p. 320):

"The remembrance of the original cause that hath drawn these lines from me, is so sweet that I cannot choose but nourish whatsoever refresheth it in me, which appeared in that I had not the power to sacrifice these trifles in the fire."

The group of adventurous anecdotal autobiographies of the first rank should also include the *Autobiography of Thomas Raymond*, first printed in 1917 by the Camdem Society from a manuscript in the Bodleian Library. Though fragmentary, it is vivid, and possesses an astonishing amount of humor and subtle psychology. In his boyhood Raymond was afraid of the dark, and the account of his searches under the bed, or of his cunning arrangement of a bell before an aperture where enemies might invade his bedroom, is skilfully told. He is not a believer in the suppression of youth or in corporal punishment (p. 20):

"Wee were four children three sonns and one daughter, of all which my selfe, being the second, was least beloved of him [his father], but upon all occasions (though I was not above twelve years old at his death) felt the effects of his cholor, which was of greate mischeife unto me, being of a softe and tymorous complexion. And indeed thus soon began the un-happy breaches made upon my spirit, which hath followed me in all the variations and course of my life, and proved a great obstacle to the advancement of my fortunes. So mischevous is the nipping the bud of a tender masculyne spiritte. . . . I dare avou many a gallant boyes spiritt hath beene abused and spoiled, which otherwise might have made a brave man."

His miniature character sketches strike home and are not lacking in malice, as in this description of his uncle's wife (p. 25):

"She was well advanced in yeres, well fietured all but hir face, an excellent voyce and well skild in songs, of disposition proud and dissembling and basely miserable."

After various irrelevant but entertaining anecdotes of travel in the Low Countries, he decides to take up arms (p. 35): "I had in this brave place a very unbrave life, and therefore resolved to change the scene. From the Court to the campe I went, and soe now *arma virumque cano*." The ensuing military memoirs are concrete, realistic, and never self-deluding (p. 38):

"At my first comeing before the towne my courage began somewhat to faile me, and, being younge and never being on such an employment, wrought the more upon me. I remem-ber I had an aurange tauny feather in my capp, and at first I thought that every gun that was discharged toward our quar-ter had been aymed at it, the Spaniards not enduring that colour. But within few dayes I tooke my selfe to be a very gallant fellow, and had noe more dread of danger then if I had been in a fayre."

Later the Venice he describes is a stirring place, and the

entire biography gives a portrait of a merry gentleman who is, above all, entertaining in his selection of anecdotes. In his frank criticism of family ties, his wit, and his subtle insight, Thomas Raymond, so lately rescued from oblivion, may stand comparison with such nineteenth-century mental analysts as Stendhal and Samuel Butler.

Without counterpart in the seventeenth century and forgotten in the twentieth, is "Fortune's Uncertainty, or Youth's Unconstancy. Wherein is contained A true and impartial Account of what hapned in the space of few Years to the Author, whom you will know in this ensuing Discourse by the name of Rodolphus" (1667). The autobiographer, Charles Croke, asks of the reader only a contented perusal, and does not seek to instruct. His mind is commonplace, but in telling his story he is unreserved and confidential. He narrates all the aimless adventures of a young blade to the time of his marriage to "a Gentlewoman, which the Heavens had decreed to be his." He grows weary of his aesthetic companions at Christ Church, Oxford, with "their long yaunings, nor false spittings, with their counterfeited smiles nor Crocodile tears," and runs away to London to see Cromwell's funeral. After finding the Army life is not to his taste, young Croke was shipped by his family to Virginia where he was "as fairly sold as any Slave." His liberty is purchased by a gentlewoman, a "generous soul," and the candid Rodolphus is at a loss to repay her.

"This unheard of generosity," he says (p. 51), "surprized our young Captive so much, that had he found the least correspondency either in Birth, Parts, or person with himself, or indeed had he found either Youth or Beauty in her, I am perswaded his soul was then so full of gratitude, that he would have thought of no other requital then himself to give her; but where all such invitations are wanting, and only the relicks of a rough Planter to be courted, he thought the return of her immense kindnesses could not be better acknowledged then by present thanks, and future profit, as he plentifully promised; for indeed had there been all that belongs to the accomplishment of a woman in this Virginian widow, his youthful Inclinations were already prepossest, and the entire Affections which he then owed to a young Lady in England, made him altogether uncapable of a second passion."

Therefore he escapes, and on his return to England is shipwrecked off the Bristol coast and received kindly by a distant relative. When she offers him a suit of her husband's clothes, however, Croke "gladly returned them with thanks," partly because they were far too large for him, and partly because "he had a real desire to see his own Relations in the conditions he was then in, believing to move some of them to a sorrow, especially those whom he thought the cause of this mechanick Voyage."

Through such ingenuous anecdotes the narrative progresses. His Portuguese travels are recounted, his loves and disappointments, his lukewarm study of the law to the time of his marriage. Charles Croke is not a brilliant or an important figure, but his autobiography gives a frank unforced reflection of his career, is entertaining throughout, and is well worth reprinting.

The Civil Wars gave new life to an autobiographical form as old as Caesar — namely, to military memoirs. For the most part they are not appealing to modern taste, but they cannot be dismissed without mention, for they are consonant with the impersonal autobiographical tradition of the century. They are written on much

the same plan and possess little individuality.[13] Most of
the incidents are similar to Sir James Turner's narration
of his argument with a German antagonist (p. 16): "I
accusd him of eleven points of treason; bot the con-
troversie betweene him and me was decided by a canon
bullet, which tooke away his heade." In Sir James Turner's memoirs, as in many of the others, there are vivid
anecdotes. But all of them are battle pictures, and the
story of this soldier who was imprisoned by the republi-
cans and ill requited by the royalists is told only through
skirmishes of horse.

The best-known and most justly celebrated autobiography of the type of political memoirs is *The Life
of Edward Earl of Clarendon, Lord High Chancellor of
England*.[14] This life is particularly interesting because
it treats practically the same period which Clarendon
covers in his *History of the Rebellion*. His procedure
should therefore illustrate the historian's conception of
the distinction between biography and history. Clarendon realized a difference. The focus is naturally nar-
rower and more concentrated in the autobiography.
Yet he was far from reducing his own life to strait limits;
and this work might be thought more a history than a
biography were it not for the persistent intrusion of
"Mr. Hyde" or "the Chancellor." Clarendon's unusual
procedure in using the third person for his whole narration illustrates an attempt toward that impersonality

13. As examples might be mentioned Bulstrode Whitelock's extended
Memorials, 1682; *The Memoirs of Edmund Ludlow . . . 1625-72*, 1698; *The
Memoirs of James Lord Audley Earl of Castlehaven, His Engagement and
Carriage in the Wars of Ireland, From the Year 1642 to the Year 1651*, 1680;
Memoirs of his own life and times By Sir James Turner. 1632-1670, 1829;
Short Memorials of Thomas Lord Fairfax, 1642-44, pub. 1699; *Military
Memoirs of Colonel Birch. 1642-45*, Camden Soc., 1873.

14. Written about 1668-72, first published 1759.

characteristic of this century, in which autobiographers chose to approximate the methods of biographers.[15] Clarendon's catalogue of his faults and his self-analysis also demonstrate his detachment. He is aware of his own ambition and of his Epicureanism, and he impartially deals out praise and blame in his self-scrutiny (pp. 63–64): "He had a fancy sharp and luxuriant; but so carefully cultivated and strictly guarded, that he never was heard to speak a loose or profane word"; "He was in his nature inclined to pride and passion, and to a humour between wrangling and disputing very troublesome."

Like many memoirs of the period, Clarendon's life was written for the perusal and benefit of his family, as he himself acknowledges. He begins one section (vol. i, p. 267): "Moulins, June 8, 1672. Reflections upon the most material passages which happened after the king's restoration to the time of the chancellor's banishment; out of which his children, for whose information they are collected, may add some important passages to his Life, as the true cause of his misfortunes."

The political events of his career, his interests and preoccupations, are well given; his domestic relations are omitted. The work extends from his birth in 1609 to the year 1668 after his exile in France. The drama of his life ends in a minor key with a banishment which he finds bitterly unjust. Exile affects his writings, so that he does what few autobiographers have the courage or ability to do: he estimates the value of life as he sees it and sets forth his conclusions (vol. ii, p. 594):

15. Only inadvertently does this mask of impersonality slip from him, as when he says (1857, p. 24), "The Archbishop desired him [Thomas Aylesbury] to send him [Clarendon] to him, for he heard well of him; and the next morning I attended him."

"These unavoidable reflections first made him discern how weak and foolish all his former imaginations had been, and how blind a surveyor he had been of the inclinations and affections of the heart of man; and it made him likewise conclude from thence, how uncomfortable and vain the dependence must be upon any thing in this world, where whatsoever is good and desirable suddenly perisheth, and nothing is lasting but the folly and wickedness of the inhabitants thereof."

In the characters of men, their thoughts and conversations, Clarendon took great delight. He was one of the first to realize how important a part in a man's life is played by his friends. He shows his unsurpassed skill at character portrayal in a series of sketches which begins with the acquaintances of his London youth — such men as Jonson, Selden, Cotton, and Digby — and includes almost all of the important state figures of the mid-seventeenth century. The result is a vast political portrait gallery painted in a noble and flowing style, wherein the actions of his friends, their inmost thoughts, almost the sound of their voices and the flash of their eyes, are presented in variety and abundance. And in the long progress from his brilliant, ambitious youth to his embittered old age, Clarendon also presents, in the midst of innumerable sallies and excursions, a full self-portrait of a royalist, an aristocrat, and a social being.

Autobiographies of churchmen never completely disappear from the current of English literature; in the period following the restoration they become plentiful. One of the most important is Richard Baxter's account of his own life, written "for the most part in 1664." The style is nervous and fluent, but the work as a whole suffers from lack of organization and correlation. Baxter follows de Thou's method of narrating national history from an individual viewpoint, a method increasingly popular in England during the latter part of the seventeenth century and culminating in Bishop Hacket's *Scrinia Reserata* and Bishop Burnet's *History of His Own Time*. Such blurring of the focus is unfortunate in its effects upon biography, and leaves Baxter's life of himself fragmentary and disjointed. Yet in spite of its lack of structure, the autobiography of this admirable nonconformist leader contains some of the best passages of the seventeenth century. At the beginning of his work, the account of his childhood teachers and the parish ministers is unparalleled. His conscientious scruples and the doubts which disturbed his early years are fully described. His power of analysis causes him to fall into the habit of numbering the reasons for events or for beliefs, and this method of division prevails throughout his writings. So he will give a summary of why he considers that the sickness which held him infirm and consumptive throughout life was nevertheless God's mercy: first, it weakened temptation; second, it gave him a greater contempt for the world; third, it made him realize the value of time; and last, it taught him compassion.[16] His energetic and lucid mind is thus busied through the entire work, and his logic, coupled with his fearlessness and integrity, go far to explain Dr. Johnson's rare compliment of unqualified approval of all Baxter's writings. The later sections of the *Reliquiae*, heavy with documents and controversy, are annals in their character; but the first part, in spite of its lack of form, remains a true autobiography. The concluding paragraphs (pp. 124–138) which he terms "the Alterations of my Soul since my younger years," are unsurpassed in English biography for subtle analysis of char-

16. 1695, p. 21.

acter. They show, with dignity and some pathos, his mellowing from fire and partizanship to a more tolerant attitude, and present, in the contrasting portraits of his youthful and mature self, a Plutarchian parallel of extreme delicacy. This final section is searching and without pattern except for Augustine's *Confessions* (p. 129): [17]

"Heretofore I knew much less than now; and yet was not half so much acquainted with my Ignorance: I had a great delight in the daily new Discoveries which I made, and of the Light which shined in upon me (like a Man that cometh into a Country where he never was before): But I little knew either how imperfectly I understood those very Points, whose discovery so much delighted me, nor how much might be said against them; nor how many things I was yet a stranger to: But now I find far greater Darkness upon all things, and perceive how very little it is that we know in comparison of that which we are ignorant of, and have far meaner thoughts of my own Understanding, though I must needs know that it is better furnished than it was then.

"Accordingly I had then a far greater opinion of Learned Persons and Books, than I have now. . . ."

Such a life of the spirit had hitherto passed almost unrecorded in the history of English biography. In the latter part of the seventeenth century, however, Baxter is not without companions. From his thoughtful narrative it is only a short step to the small group of Puritan autobiographies — notably those by Burton, Bunyan, and Powell — which are intensely personal and fervently devout. It is not remarkable that the sects which emphasized the importance of individual experience in

17. It is fortunate that Baxter's autobiography with judicious excisions has recently been made accessible in a popular edition, ed. J. M. Lloyd Thomas, Dent, 1925.

religion should embrace many of the important autobiographers of the century.

A Narration of the Life of Mr. Henry Burton is the
earliest of this subjective religious group, and was
actually in print by 1643. Its consideration has been
delayed to this point in order to include it in the group
with which it is so closely allied. It is the forerunner of
the school of Bunyan and Fox, and narrates the persecutions of a nonconformist. It reflects the motive for
writing common to most of the religious autobiographies: [18] "to give a just account to God's people of that
divine support and comfort, which it pleased the Lord
to uphold mee with, in all my tryalls." These trials
were not imaginary. Henry Burton, educated at St.
John's, Cambridge, tutor to Prince Henry and Charles,
entered the ministry at the age of thirty and began publishing Puritan tracts offensive to Laud. Summoned
before the Star Chamber for his sermons, he was condemned to have his ears clipped and to suffer imprisonment for life. The rest of the biography is an account of
prison hardships and spiritual comforts. "I may say,"
Burton writes, "as old Jacob, and no lesse truly, few
and evill have the dayes of the yeares of my pilgrimage
been."

He has a gift for incidents that have the breath of
life (p. 7):

"And another time, in the same place [London-house], the
Bishop in his Chaire was proudly insulting over me standing
at the other end of the Table, and a friend of mine standing
by, I (thinking thus with my selfe, What doe I standing here
to heare such language) did thereupon without replying, turn
my back, and goe towards the doore to be gone, and looking

18. 1643, Preface.

back for my friend to follow, the Bishop at that very instant changed his note, and began to speak me as faire, as possibly could be, whereupon I came towards him againe, saying within my selfe, that if he spake reason, I would heare him. Nor was I at any time before him, but methought I stood over him, as a School-master over his School-boy."

His Lancashire prison is described with full details (p. 15):

"And the room had one quality more, that I could not walk in it, for it was floored with thick planks that were round upward, and so distant one from another, that I could not set one step, but I must look to every footing."

The prison life culminates in this final horror:

"And, to adde to their cruelties, there was a dark roome under mine, where they put five witches, with one of their children, which made such a hellish noise night and day, that I seemed then to be in hell, or at least in some Popish Purgatory, the Region next above hell, as the Papists tell us."

The reader feels that he has stood with Burton in his prison room in the fourth story of Guernsey Castle, "the sea comming as neere the shore on that side, as that I might from my window throw an apple into it," and has seen with him the joyful omen of the rainbow lying flat on the surface of the water and moving off toward England from Guernsey — "no naturall and ordinary Rainbow, but supernaturall and miraculous . . . sent . . . to me for some speciall use." He believes in dreams and narrates them frequently: they were part of his life. He describes his comforts at Guernsey — reciting the Psalms and preaching to himself, reading in the Greek, French, Latin, and Hebrew Bibles, examining his conscience, mentally indicting all tyrannical prelates, medi-

tating upon Paul and comparing himself to that
apostle.

His faith supports him in affliction. This is the account of his learning of his daughter's death, while he
is still in prison (p. 29):

"In this interim, I heard of the good pleasure of God, in
taking away my deare and only daughter. It was a little before supper that Mr. Lieutenant began darkly to intimate the
same unto me, untill I prayed him to deale plainly with me,
which he did: whereupon craving pardon, I immediately retired to my lodging, and there on my knees gave the Lord
solemne thanks, that it had pleased him to translate my
daughter, now his alone, unto his Kingdome of glory. . . .
For a holy and sweet conditioned Maid she was ever from her
childhood."

His faith transmutes the pain of the pillory into an
ecstasy which almost transcends his words (p. 13):

"All the while I stood in the Pillary, I thought my selfe to
be in Heaven, and in a state of glory and triumph, if any such
state can possibly be on earth. . . . For my rejoycing and
glorying was so great all the while, without intermission, in
the Pillary, that I can no more expresse it, then Paul could
his ravishments in the third heaven."

He exhibits the infirmity of all good story-tellers —
garrulity. This anecdote, for example, is repeated elsewhere in almost the same form: [19]

" . . . a godly woman, going along in the troope neere
Charing Crosse, at my returne from banishment to London,
(which God was also pleased to cloth with so great glory) she
said to me, O Sir, this is a glorious wedding day; to whom I
replied, it is indeed, blessed be God; I, said she, but your
wedding day on the Pillary was much more glorious: I ad-
miring the womans speech, answerd, it is indeed most true,
good woman, blessed be our God."

19. Pp. 13–14; repeated pp. 42–43.

The biography ends triumphantly with a last sign of God's favor. An attorney-at-law maligns Burton and mysteriously the attorney's ear begins to bleed. Throughout, the style is Biblical, as devout and as robust as Bunyan's. It is an autobiography of faith, full-blooded and individual. Its genuine emotion and sturdiness entitle it to an important place among English autobiographies.

John Bunyan's *Grace Abounding to the Chief of Sinners* appeared in its first edition in 1666 and had reached the seventh edition by 1692. In its fashion it is as frank a document as Augustine's *Confessions*. Bunyan's complete simplicity, his natural conversational style, his clarity, the shrewdness of his reasoning, his imagination, give the book a character of its own. The famous passages — the church steeple that seems about to fall and crush him, his great shame when he is reproached for his godlessness by a woman herself loose and ungodly — remain in the mind because they are the stuff of life. There is here no formal or half-hearted warming up of dead events. Where can a passage be found to equal this for brutal analysis (1692, p. 10):

"Wherefore I found within me a great desire to take my fill of sin, still studying what sin was yet to be committed, that I might taste the sweetness of it; and I made as much haste as I could to fill my Belly with its Delicates, least I should dye before I had my Desire; for that I feared greatly. In these things, I protest before God, I lye not, neither do I feign this form of Speech; these were really, strongly and with all my heart, my desires: The good Lord, whose Mercy is unsearchable, forgive me my transgressions."

Or this for ingenuous realism (p. 22):

"Nay, one day, as I was betwixt Elstow and Bedford, the Temptation was hot upon me, to try if I had Faith, by doing

some Miracle; which Miracle, at that time, was this; I must
say to the Puddles that were in the Horse-pads, Be dry; and
to the dry places, Be you the Puddles: And truly, one time I
was going to say so indeed; but just as I was about to speak,
this thought came into my mind; But go under yonder
Hedge, and pray first, that God would make you able: But
when I had concluded to pray, this came hot upon me; That
if I prayed, and came again, and tried to do it, and yet did
nothing notwithstanding, then be sure I had no Faith, but
was a Cast-away and lost. Nay, thought I, if it be so, I will
not try yet, but will stay a little longer."

The intensity of his feelings blends with his power to
realize a scene in the fewest possible words. The effect is
unmistakably his own, even in such a short sentence as
his outdoor meditations on God's goodness (p. 40):

"I thought I could have spoken of his Love, and of his
Mercy to me, even to the very Crows that sat upon the plowed
Lands before me."

The unaffected power of his writing conveys his thought
on entering prison as if there were no intervening me-
dium of words, and Bunyan touches the heights to
which autobiography seldom attains (p. 149):

"But notwithstanding these helps, I found my self a Man
and compassed with Infirmities; the parting with my Wife
and Poor Children hath often been to me in this place, as the
pulling the Flesh from my Bones; and that not only because I
am somewhat too fond of these great Mercies, but also because I should have often brought to my mind the many
hardships, miseries and wants that my poor Family was like
to meet with, should I be taken from them, especially my
poor blind Child, who lay nearer my heart then all I had besides; O the thoughts of the hardship I thought my blind one
might go under, did break my heart to pieces.

"Poor child! Thought I, what sorrow art thou like to have
for thy Portion in this World? Thou must be beaten, must

beg, suffer hunger, cold, nakedness, and a thousand Calamities, though I cannot now endure the Wind should blow upon thee; But yet recalling my self, thought I, I must venture you all with God, though it goeth to the quick to leave you; O, I saw in this Condition I was as a Man who was pulling down his House upon the Head of his Wife and Children; yet thought I, I must do it, I must do it."

Grace Abounding is an account of protracted spiritual struggles and ill-quieted doubts (p. 156):

"I have sometimes seen more in a Line of the Bible, then I could well tell how to stand under, and yet at another time the whole Bible hath been to me as dry as a stick; or rather my Heart hath been so dead and dry unto it, that I could not conceive the least dram of Refreshment, tho' I have look't it all over."

It is dedicated by Bunyan "to those whom God hath counted him worthy to beget to Faith, by his Ministry in the Word." The autobiography is to serve as an example to believers, that they may take comfort in viewing Bunyan's troubled misgivings and final certitude (Preface): "I can remember my Fears, and Doubts, and sad Months, with Comfort; they are as the Head of Goliah in my Hand."

Grace Abounding is *Pilgrim's Progress* reduced from the general to the particular. If, in the gray domain of allegory, Bunyan can create illusions of such vitality, it is not strange that he should produce, in writing his own life, a work vibrant, vigorous and fervent, signal among the biographies of the seventeenth century.

Following the form of Bunyan's autobiography, and treating only of spiritual and religious experiences, is *The Life and Death of Mr. Vavasor Powell* (1671). Like Bunyan, this Welsh Baptist evangelist was converted after a sinful youth, and records the exact circumstances (p. 2):

"I had no esteem for the holy Scriptures, nor cared at all to look into them, but either Hystorical or Poetical Books, Romances and the like were all my delight, the Sabbath I much profaned by all sports, though God was pleased to magnifie his grace so much as to make that the occasion of my Conversion. For being one Lords day a stander by divers Games, being then my self a Reader of Common-Prayers, and in the habit of a foolish Shepheard, I was ashamed to play with them, yet took as much pleasure therein as if I had; whereupon a Godly grave Professour of Religion (one of those then called Puritans) seeing me there, came to me, and very soberly and mildly asked me, doth it become you Sir that are a Scholar and one that teacheth others, to break the Lords Sabbath thus? to whom I answered as those scoffers in Malachy, Wherein do I break it; you see me onely stand by but I do not play at all; to which he replyed, but you find your own pleasure herein by looking on, and this God forbids in his holy Word. . . . I was for the present silent, and took it so far into consideration, as to resolve never to transgress in the like kind again."

Later his conversion is strengthened in an unusual way (p. 4):

"At this time the Lord visited me with a very sore and great pain of the Tooth-ach . . . and by another good providence, I met with a little book of Mr. Perkins, and in that, with this expression, if the pains of one little bone, or tooth, be so grievous for a few days, what then will the pains of the whole body and soul be in hell for evermore? Upon this my terrour began in Conscience to that degree, that it made the other pain to seem somewhat more easie, and both together, put me upon crying out to God with greater sense then before, and between fear and pain, a troubled moody spirit of prayer began to spring up, and perceiving I had some help, I pumped harder, and so found at last my heart began to be in-

larged with confessions, and my sins were brought into remembrance."

Such revealing incidents are peculiar to autobiography
alone; biography is capable of exposing character only
deliberately. To Mr. Vavasor Powell, Satan was as
actual as he was to any mediaeval St. Anthony, and his
struggles with the devil are narrated (pp. 8–9):

> "At this time and long after, he also shewed me my sins,
> in their number, and nature, to be such, and so many as that
> there was no pardon for them, and therefore tempted me oft,
> and divers wayes to destroy myself: Sometimes by casting
> my self into a River to drown my self, whither he brought me,
> and whilst I reasoned the case with him, this was frequently
> his motive to me, the fewer sins I committed in this world,
> and the shorter time I lived in it, the less would be my tor-
> ment."

The subjective character of the narrative is further emphasized by detailed accounts of some of the Lord's
"providences" to him, such as escapes from death, his
cures and success as a preacher, and by a confession of
faith, choice sayings, and extracts from his diary, all of
which are concerned with the state of his soul. His own
emphasis on mental disquietude is the more remarkable
because his life was crowded with action, as is revealed
in its continuation, written by his wife and his friends.
From 1640 until his death in 1670 Powell spent most of
his time in prison or in controversies and trials.

From the life of Vavasor Powell, imprisoned and per-
secuted as a nonconformist, the transition to the autobiographies of the Quakers is natural. With no other
sect was religion so personal, and it is not surprising
therefore that the Quakers transformed autobiography
into a normal expression of devotion and an encourage-

ment to Friends in the same faith. Most of these self-records, which became even more common in the eighteenth century, are of little value as biographies. The writers relate in an unsatisfying manner their own mystical experiences; they centre constantly on the individual's relation to his Lord; they are redundant and blurred in their materials, imitative in their style.

The model for all later Quaker autobiographies is the journal of George Fox, written shortly after 1674–75. Fox adopted the unusual method of dictating his autobiography, or rather his journal, to an amanuensis.[20] His work is not so much an autobiography as it is a Quaker Odyssey, a narrative of strife and an account of itinerant preaching. Even the description of Fox's journey to America is included, where he preaches to "the Indian Emperour and his Kings," who come to him "with some of their Cockarooses." The account of his youth is the story of his spiritual struggles in which he finds the clergy powerless to help him and "like an Empty, hollow Cask." All of them give him advice which profits him little (p. 4): "After this, I went to another Ancient Priest at Mansetter in Warwick-shire, and reasoned with him about the Ground of Despair and Temptations; but he was ignorant of my Condition: And he bid me Take Tobacco, and Sing Psalms. Tobacco was a thing I did not love; and Psalms I was not in an Estate to Sing; I could not Sing." His younger days may be summarized in his own phrase (p. 30): "And as I traveled through Markets, Fairs and divers Places, I saw Death and Darkness in all People."

20. In the first edition of the journal (1694), the beginning of his life, and his death — "a valiant is fallen in Israell this day" — are cleverly added by his friends, and the whole is given a preface by William Penn.

After his conversion, the book contains but two types of incidents, the first internal [21] — "I felt ye power of darknesse 20 miles afterwards, as I was at sea"—; the other external [22] — "And they sseised upon mee with watch bills & pikes & stakes & halberts & garded mee backe againe to this Patrington about three miles." This latter type of incident is by far the more common. The journal also contains extracts from his sermons and meditations or letters, such as that to Margaret Fell (vol. ii, p. 211), but usually it is a simple narrative of action, set among fresh English countrysides (vol. i, p. 112):

"And when I came Into ye steeplehouse yarde I saw people comeinge as to a fayre: . . . & beinge very thirsty I walkt about a quarter of a mile to a brooke & gott a litle water & refresht my selfe."

In an account almost wholly objective, filled with "glouriaes" and "prescious" religious meetings, a clear picture is given of this prophet of the Friends — truthful, egotistic, strong, shrewd, simple, and devout.[23]

In contrast with the heartfelt innocence of autobiographies after the manner of the Puritans and Quakers, is Abraham Cowley's delicate and original essay, "Of Myself," first published with his works in 1668. If Thomas Sprat's life of Cowley, published in the same volume, is important in the development of biography, Cowley's self-study is no less important in the history of autobiography. It marks a significant advance in

21. Vol. ii (1911), p. 147.
22. Vol. i, p. 30.
23. Among the Quaker biographies, the *History of the Life of Thomas Ellwood, Written by his own Hand* deserves special mention. It extends from 1639 to 1683, shortly after which it was composed. First ed. 1714.

technique and a liberation from the colorless formality of the objective tradition.

Cowley immediately takes the reader into his confidence (p. 143):

"It is a hard and nice Subject for a man to write of himself, it grates his own heart to say any thing of disparagement, and the Readers Eares to hear any thing of praise for him. There is no danger from me of offending him in this kind; neither my mind, nor my Body, nor my Fortune, allow me any materials for that Vanity."

He continues his gentle retrospection in a manner as disarming in its openness as it is pleasant in its flow:

"As far as my Memory can return back into my past Life, before I knew, or was capable of guessing what the world, or glories, or business of it were, the natural affections of my soul gave me a secret bent or aversion from them, as some plants are said to turn away from others, by an Antipathy imperceptible to themselves, and inscrutable to mans understanding. Even when I was a very young Boy at School, instead of running about on Holy-daies and playing with my fellows; I was wont to steal from them, and walk into the fields, either alone with a Book, or with some one Companion, if I could find any of the same temper."

His account of the genesis of a poet furnishes a reminiscence life-like and exact to the most trivial detail. He has just quoted an ode written at the age of thirteen (p. 144):

"You may see by it, I was even then acquainted with the Poets (for the Conclusion is taken out of Horace;) and perhaps it was the immature and immoderate love of them which stampt first, or rather engraved these Characters in me: They were like Letters cut into the Bark of a young Tree, which with the Tree still grow proportionably. But, how this love came to be produced in me so early, is a hard question:

I believe I can tell the particular little chance that filled my head first with such chimes of Verse, as have never since left ringing there: For I remember when I began to read, and to take some pleasure in it, there was wont to lie in my Mothers Parlour (I know not by what accident, for there her self never in her life read any Book but of Devotion) but there was wont to lie Spensers Works; this I happened to fall upon, and was infinitely delighted with the Stories of the Knights, and Giants, and Monsters, and brave Houses, which I found every where there: (Though my understanding had little to do with all this) and by degrees with the tinckling of the Rhyme and Dance of the Numbers, so that I think I had read him all over before I was twelve years old, and was thus made a Poet as immediately as a Child is made an Eunuch."

Passages of such freshness and poetic truth are rare in any biography before this time, and Abraham Cowley's essay on himself, though short, is of major importance in biographical history. For intimacy and charm and whimsical sentiment it has no forebears. Like Walton, Cowley looked upon life as an art in itself and wrote this little essay to prove his belief that (p. 145):

> "Well then; I now do plainly see
> This busie World and I shall ne're agree."

Furthermore, he had the literary skill to select those incidents that might set forth his character in a small space. Cowley's diffident amateur approach, his casual confidences, his informality, make his "Of Myself" an attractive pioneer work among reminiscences and biographical essays.

In contrast with these masculine autobiographies of adventure, politics, or introspection, are the delicate self-portraits by women. The first of the feminine autobiographers is Margaret Cavendish. "A true Relation of my Birth, Breeding, and Life" appeared in 1656 in a volume bearing the ornamental title of *Natures pictures drawn by fancies Pencil . . . by . . . the Lady Marchioness of Newcastle*. It opens with a description of her family wherein "all the Brothers were Valiant and all the Sisters vertuous" (p. 372):

> "But to rehearse their Recreations. Their customes were in Winter time to go sometimes to Plays, or to ride in their Coaches about the Streets to see the concourse and recourse of People; and in the Spring time to visit the Spring-garden, Hide-park, and the like places; and sometimes they would have Musick, and sup in Barges upon the Water; these harmless recreations they would pass their time away with. . . ."

Against such colorful backgrounds she paints her own two years of court life at Oxford as maid-in-waiting, where she meets William Cavendish whose life she was later to record: [24]

> ". . . my Affections were fix'd on him, and he was the onely Person I ever was in love with: Neither was I ashamed to own it, but gloried therein, for it was not Amorous Love, I never was infected therewith, it is a Disease, or a Passion, or both, I onely know by relation, not by experience; neither could Title, Wealth, Power, or Person entice me to love; but my Love was honest and honourable, being placed upon Merit, which Affection joy'd at the fame of his Youth, pleas'd with delight in his Wit, proud of the respects he used to me, and triumphing in the affections he profest for me. . . ."

The autobiography is lacking in incidents and dramatic quality, but her analyses of men and women are always interesting and often show a lively observation. The summary of her own character is naïve and proud. Self character sketches at such length [25] are rare, and this

24. P. 375. See Chapter V.   25. Pp. 386–391 in folio.

one is worth extended quotation as a fully conscious attempt to convey the essentials and the accidentals of one's own mind:

". . . as for my Disposition, it is more inclining to be melancholy than merry, but not crabbed or peevishly melancholy, but soft melting solitary, and contemplating melancholy. . . . Likewise I am gratefull, for I never received a curtesie but I am impatient, and troubled untill I can return it, also I am Chast, both by Nature and Education, insomuch as I do abhorre an unchast thought: likewise I am seldom angry, as my servants may witness for me, for I rather chose to suffer some inconveniences, than disturbe my thoughts, which makes me winke many times at their faults; but when I am angry, I am very angry, but yet it is soon over, and I am easily pacified, if it be not such an injury as may create a hate; neither am I apt to be exceptious or jealous . . . likewise I am neither spitefull, envious, nor malicious, I repine not at the gifts that Nature, or Fortune bestows upon others, yet I am a great Emulator; for though I wish none worse than they are, nor fear any should be better than they are, yet it is lawfull for me to wish my self the best, and to do my honest endeavour thereunto, for I think it no crime to wish my self the exactest of Natures works, my thred of life the longest, my Chain of Destinie the strongest, my minde the peaceablest, my life the pleasantest, my death the easiest, and the greatest Saint in Heaven; also to do my endeavor, so far as honour and honesty doth allow of, to be the highest on Fortunes Wheele, and to hold the wheele from turning, if I can. . . . I am very ambitous, yet 'tis neither for Beauty, Wit, Titles, Wealth or Power, but as they are steps to raise me to Fames Tower, which is to live by remembrance in after-ages . . . if any of my neerest friends were in danger I . . . would willingly, nay cheerfully, resign my life for their sakes . . . but in a danger, where my Friends or my Honour is not concerned, or ingaged, but only my Life to be unprofitably lost, I am the veriest coward in Nature, as upon the Sea, or any dangerous places, or of Theeves or fire, or the like, Nay the shooting of a gun, although but a Pot-gun, will make me start, and stop my hearing, much less have I courage to discharge one . . ."

She concludes her extended survey of herself with a reason for writing it which seems somewhat inadequate (p. 391):

"I hope my Readers, will not think me vain for writing my life, since there have been many that have done the like, as Cesar, Ovid, and many more, both men and women, and I know no reason I may not do it as well as they . . . I write it for my own sake, not theirs; neither did I intend this piece for to delight, but to divulge, not to please the fancy, but to tell the truth, lest after-Ages should mistake, in not knowing I was the daughter to one Master Lucas of St. Johns neer Colchester in Essex, second Wife to the Lord Marquiss of Newcastle, for my Lord having had two wives, I might easily have been mistaken, especially if I should dye, and my Lord Marry again."

Thus it ends. For self-taught and original philosophy and for disarming and insistent egotism, the Marchioness of Newcastle is unique. As a supplement to this biography her *CCXI Sociable Letters* (1664) should be read. They are addressed to a female friend and are written formally on many philosophical subjects, always with a glance toward that "after-Fame" which with her is an enduring passion.

When Margaret Cavendish, "the mad duchess of Newcastle," painted her own portrait as a *précieuse ridicule* at large in England, she composed the first important piece in a series of autobiographies by women. As a class they are far more interesting and important than the autobiographies by men — more personal, informal, and lifelike. Where the men tend to digress on questions of history, or grow prolix in controversial accounts, the women remain self-centred and confidential, engrossed in the more enthralling problems of their own lives.

One of the best autobiographies by women is to be found in the memoirs of Anne Lady Fanshawe, transcribed under her own supervision in 1676 and disclosing a full picture of a noble man and a noble wife. There are few biographies which present a love as complete and as sympathetic as that between Sir Richard Fanshawe and Anne: [26]

"Glory be to God we never had but one mind throughout our lives, our souls were wrapped up in each other, our aims and designs one, our loves one, and our resentments one. We so studied one the other that we knew each other's mind by our looks; whatever was real happiness, God gave it me in him."

This love is expressed even unconsciously, as when she inserts an innocent adverb in this sentence (p. 13): "He was married at 35 years of age, and lived with me but 23 years and 29 days."

For her son's betterment she includes at the outset certain general precepts which her own experience had tested (p. 2):

"Endeavor to be innocent as a dove, but as wise as a serpent; and let this lesson direct you most in the greatest extremes of fortune. . . . Be civil and obliging to all, dutiful where God and nature command you; be friend to one — and that friendship keep sacred as the greatest tie upon earth. And be sure to ground it upon virtue, for no other is either happy or lasting."

The story progresses without effort, and the fortunes of the two principal figures are traced — the marriage at Wolvercote Church near Oxford, the vicissitudes of the Civil Wars, the travels of the Court to the Scilly Islands and Jersey, a last leave-taking from the king, war in

26. 1907, p. 5.

Ireland, and exile in France. She does not scruple to insert the most realistic details, and has decided opinions on such subjects as the Irish fleas or the "very bad cheese" of Nantes. Her anecdotes are sharply cut, as is the story of the ghost she saw while sleeping in a massive old pile in Ireland (p. 58):

"She spake loud, and in a tone I never heard, thrice 'Ahone'; and then with a sigh more like wind than breath she vanished, and to me her body looked more like a thick cloud than substance. I was so much affrighted that my hair stood on end and my night-clothes fell off."

Her love for her husband guides the course of the whole narrative. At times she is to be seen in man's garb, standing on deck to be near her husband when their ship, on its way to Spain, is threatened by a Turkish man-o'-war (p. 64). "But when your father saw it convenient to retreat, looking upon me he blessed himself, and snatched me up in his arms, saying, 'Good God, that love can make this change!'; and though he seemingly chid me, he did laugh at it as often as he remembered that voyage."

Again, with a dark lantern she steals at four o'clock in the morning towards Whitehall to comfort her imprisoned husband (p. 80): "And I would go under his window and softly call him. He that after the first time expected me never failed to put out his head at first call. Thus we talked together; and sometimes I was so wet with rain that it went in at my neck and out at my heels." She never flatters herself. When she escapes to France in 1658 by feigning to be a common woman, she leaves her maid at the gate, "who," she says, "was much a finer gentlewoman than myself." Again she returns a young lion given her as a present by a Spanish official (p. 140), "but I desired his Excellency's pardon that I did not accept of it, saying I was of so cowardly a make I durst not keep company with it."

The last half of the autobiography describes Lady Fanshawe's life after the Restoration, in the Embassy at Madrid. In recording "the customs and principles and country" of Spain she is graphic. After these years of splendor as a great lady, she must also record the death of her husband, and, beautifully, she quotes from his own translation of one of Horace's odes, without comment: [27]

> "Lollio, thou art a man hast skill
> To fathom things; that being tried
> In either fortune, couldst abide
> In both upright; and Lollio still . . ."

The narrative does not survive his death, but breaks off abruptly. Although the biography is objective and anecdotal, Lady Anne and Sir Richard are solid figures; their mutual love colors the entire work and gives it steadiness and unity.

If the memoirs of Margaret Cavendish and Anne Fanshawe are characteristic of their century, the autobiography of Anne Lady Halkett [28] is a foreshadowing of later developments. In style it closely approaches a novel. It is intimate and full, not a mere diary or patchwork, but a relation of the important incidents in her life, principally of her three love affairs with Thomas Howard, Colonel Bampfield, and Sir James Halkett. Her self-analysis is always penetrating and is evidently impartial, since she can write (p. 17): "It was reported Mr. H. was in love with my lady E. M. and shee with

27. P. 194. From Book IV, 9.
28. Written about 1678. Published 1875.

him, att which some smiled and said itt might bee her witt had taken him butt certainly nott her beauty (for shee had as litle of that as my selfe)." Her dissection of motives, her power in disclosing the psychological roots of a situation, is remarkable at so early a date. This, for example, is a partial summary of the embarrassing position in which she finds herself in the family of the Howards, owing to the machinations and slanders of their chaplain, Mr. Nicholls (p. 43):

"I saw dayly my Lady H. grow now to that height of strangeness that when I spoke to her shee would give mee noe answeare, or if shee did, itt was with that slightnese that I could nott butt bee very sencible of itt. And that wch angred mee most was, that when ever Sr Ch. came where I was, hee was ten times more free in his converse then hee had beene before I had spoken to him. These two extreames with my owne presentt condittion was deplorable, having spentt all the mony I brought with mee, beeing in a strange place where I had neither friendship nor acquaintance with any. To London I durstt not goe, for feare of beeing secured upon the accountt of the Dukes escape [the Duke of York]; and besides, I knew I need not expect any thing butt unkindnese from my brother and sister; and how to send to C. B.[ampfield] to advise with him I knew nott. To stay where I was I had no manner of sattisfaction. And if I had known whither to goe, to leave that familly with such an odium as was laid upon mee, could nott butt make mee unwellcome any where. Thus, when I reflected upon my disconsolate condittion, I could find content in nothing butt in resorting to The hearer of prayer, who never leaves or forsakes those who trust in him."

The narrative is tinged with some piety and with very much more femininity. Occasionally in dramatic scenes Anne reveals her character almost unconsciously, as in the last meeting with Colonel Bampfield, to whom she at one time had considered herself almost engaged (p. 99):

"Hee said hee desired mee only to resolve him one question wch was whether or nott I was maried to Sr J. H. I asked why hee inquired. Hee said because if I was nott, hee would then propose something that hee thought might bee both for his advantage and mine; butt if I were, hee would wish mee joy, butt never trouble mee more. I said nothing a litle while, for I hated lying, and I saw there might bee some inconvenience to tell the truth, and (Lord pardon the equivocation!) I sayd I *am* (outt aloud, and secrettly said *nott.*) Hee imediately rose up and said, 'I wish you and him much hapinese together'; and, taking his leave, from that time to this I never saw him nor heard from him."

The autobiography comes to an end about the time of her marriage. It is an entertaining and subtle account of the woman herself. There is nothing extraneous. The search for the reasons governing her actions and emotions amuses Lady Halkett. In a later age she might have written novels; in her own time she did not produce a *Jane Eyre*, but her own fascinating autobiography.

A wide perusal of the diversified autobiographies of the period presents the seventeenth century to the reader in solidity and vigor. They may be said to vivify history. The general trend may be pointed out, but every phase of national life is represented by some individual autobiography. These range from the spacious Elizabethan anecdotes of Robert Cary's memoirs to the religious introspection of the Puritans, from the military journals of Bulstrode Whitelock to the analysis of spiritual development by Richard Baxter, from the business-like statement of Thomas Bodley to the complex self-study of Lady Anne Halkett or to Anthony Wood's interminable talk about himself.

The narratives written because of a sense of family pride form a long list, yet they are in themselves diverse and individual — Cherbury's and Lady Anne Fanshawe's might be cited as examples. This class of autobiography contrasts sharply with the various separate pieces which nearly approach romances. Such erratic autobiographies elude classification and have not here received much attention. Yet entertaining reading is to be found in such accounts as *The Relation of Sydnam Poyntz*,[29] the story of a soldier of fortune in the Thirty Years' War who spent his life having horses shot from under him and marrying rich wives; or in *The Autobiography of Dr. Simon Forman, the celebrated Astrologer, From 1552 to 1602*; or in that biography of another famous astrologer, *Mr. William Lilly's History of His Life and Times*,[30] with its odd anecdotes of scurrilous solemnity; or in the thrilling Latin autobiography of the Jesuit Father John Gerard,[31] with its extraordinary episodes of his life during the Catholic persecution; or in Adam Elliot's strange story of slavery and escape on the Barbary Coast.[32]

It is this very diversity which makes the study of autobiography of such interest. Each life is unique. There are no "schools" of autobiography, principally because the most striking and original lives were permitted to go unpublished until their discovery by the social historians of later centuries. A dearth of autobiography in mediaeval times, the growth of self-portraits among rhymesters and antiquaries, the pre-

29. Written 1636. Published 1908.
30. Published 1715. Lilly lived 1602–81.
31. Written about 1609; Eng. tr., 1886.
32. "A Narrative of My Travails . . ." in *A Modest Vindication of Titus Oates*, 1682.

dominance of family memoirs in the seventeenth century, the rise of military memorials at the time of the Civil Wars, the cultivation of autobiography by independent Protestants, the entrance of women writers into the field, and, in the main, an objective, impersonal style of narration, stand out signally in this survey. Further generalizations would be misleading, since one of the qualities of early autobiography is its variety.

As a whole the early autobiography does not attain the literary standard of the biography. Lack of classical and native models accounts in part for this deficiency, so that the same circumstances which diversify English autobiography tend to minimize the importance of literary form as an end in itself. Furthermore, many of the pieces are fragmentary or unfinished, and many more are rough drafts which were never subjected to revision. Yet in general these lives satisfactorily answer the question Henry Burton prefixes to the narrative of his life: "who fitter then a man's selfe [to set forth his history] as being best acquainted with, and most privy to the many passages of his life?" And in a few rare instances an autobiography may be discovered which fulfills the ideal of self-revelation and is written "as if no one in the world were to read it, yet with the purpose of being read." [33]

33. "... comme si personne au monde ne devait jamais la lire et en même temps avec l'intention d'être lue." Marie Bashkirtsev's *Journal*, Nelson ed., p. 12. Quoted from A. R. Burr, *The Autobiography*, 1909.

VII

A CRITICAL SURVEY

The biographical part of literature . . . is what I love most.

SAMUEL JOHNSON

THE historical survey of early English biography is
at this point completed. The main forms which
biographical writings assumed have been studied in their
isolated development; yet such divisions, though convenient, are arbitrary. There remains the task of gathering the separate threads together and determining
whether or not they make a pattern. This chapter will
therefore consider in succession: the limits of early biography as distinguished from other branches of literature;
definite theories and conceptions of biography as expressed by early writers; the practice of these theories,
with the general characteristics of early English biography; and last, the differences between early and modern English life-writing.

The confusion of *genres*, the blending of biographical
elements in diverse types of writing, was during the early
centuries more frequent than it is to-day. From such
confusion it may be inferred that the conception of biography was neither conscious nor clear-cut. The word
"biography" itself was not introduced into English until
a late date.[1] The Oxford New English Dictionary states:

1. A concept is rarely of general currency before there is a word to express
it. New words follow close on the heels of new ideas; they are the mechanical
and convenient indexes of changing thought. For this reason, the history of
the word *biography* is of importance, since it shows definitely when this form
of writing attained sufficient independence and individuality to demand for
itself a new descriptive term.

"... Βιογραφια is quoted from Damascius c. 500. Biographus, biographia, were used in modern Latin before any words of the group appeared in English, where *biographist* was used by Fuller 1662, *biography* by Dryden 1683, *biographer* by Addison 1715, *biographical* by Oldys 1738; all the others are later." [2]

The account in the New English Dictionary suggests a sudden introduction of the word into the English language by the ingenious Doctor Fuller, somewhat like a "sport" in the field of botanical experimentation. His delight in strange verbal coinage, borrowing authority from the classical tongues, is plain in such words as *fictious, docible*, and *omnividencie* which adorn the pages of *The Worthies of England*. The implication from the Dictionary's findings is that after Fuller in 1662 spoke casually of "the biographists of these Saints," introducing a word which was born obsolete, it remained for Dryden twenty-one years later and for Addison in the next century, to bring forward those forms which are now in common use.

This is not the case. Before the publication of *The Worthies of England* and preceding Dryden by more than twenty years, both "biography" and "biographer" were known. *The Works of Mr. Richard Hooker* was published in 1662 with a prefatory life by Bishop

2. Oxford University Press, *s. v. biography*.
The use of "Biographus" and "biographia" in Latin was not common during the Middle Ages, and seems not to have influenced English writers and translators. So, for example, as late as the seventeenth century, Henry Holland in his *Heroologia Anglica* will use a form of the word as a Greek expression in his Latin text (1620, p. 169), in referring to Bishop Jewel's prediction of his death in two letters sent to the Bishop of Norwich: "prout lucide apparet ex Βιολογια ejus a doctissimo Laurentio Humfredo nostro accuratissime descripto." Holland's use of the word *Biologia* where Humfrey had designated his own work as *vita* and where *biographia* is clearly more descriptive, shows that usage was not common enough to have become fixed.

Gauden. This life speaks of "Others (who warped from the Church of England) and have ventured to be (*Biogrrphers*) writers of the lives of some English Divines." This misprint tends to show the unfamiliarity and strangeness of the newly coined word, and Gauden's own explanatory phrase shows the term to be practically unknown. The anonymous *Life of . . . Dr. Thomas Fuller* (1661) [3] and the *Flagellum: Or The Life and Death . . . of O. Cromwell* (1663) [4] use the word *biography* in its usual modern sense, without an explanatory synonym. These examples indicate that shortly after 1660 the word *biography* and its allies appeared in more than isolated instances, and appeared suddenly.[5] The introduction of the word at such a late date is the more remarkable because the allied term *historiographer* had been in use in various forms since the end of the fifteenth century, and, in frequent instances, actually supplied the substitute for the word *biographer*.[6]

The fact that the same word was used to describe the writer of history and the writer of individual lives shows the confusion between the two forms and the prevailing lack of consciousness of biography as a definite and distinct branch. The mediaeval chronicler combined the rôles of historian and biographer, narrating the annals of the English nation as a family memorial, expounding

3. P. 105.
4. Epistle to the Reader.
5. It seems possible that the word was imported from France at the time of the Restoration. No satisfactory appeal may be made to French lexicons as to whether the word *biographie* was then in common use.
6. Cf. instances cited in the N. E. D., s. v. Specifically, André (1500–21) speaks of Plutarch as "Graecus historiographus" in his preface to the *De Vita Henrici Septimi*, where, moreover, he alludes to himself as the historiographer of the king. George Whetstone in his *The life, death, and devine vertues, of . . . Lorde Frauncis Earle of Bedford* (1585) alludes to "Historygraphers" in the sense of writers of individual lives.

the lives of its monarchs as a series of political and military exploits. The result is neither history nor biography as we understand the terms, but a combination of both. Little distinction may be drawn between the *Chronica Majora* of Matthew Paris, which includes the lives of various kings and church leaders, and his *Vitae . . . viginti trium Abbatum S. Albani*, which is more the history of a monastic foundation than the individual sketches of its abbots. The biographical writings of the Middle Ages are principally composed of actions and achievements. Asser writes his *Alfred* as *De Rebus Gestis Aelfredi*, Gervase of Canterbury writes not the *Vitae* but the *Actus Pontificum Ecclesiae Cantuariensis*, Peter Basset (d. 1430) narrates the life of his friend and master as *The Acts of Henry V*, and Edward Braynewood (d. 1556) publishes a series of biographies under the title of *Virorum illustrium res gestae*. Mediaeval lives, therefore, tend to remain histories in form and matter.

The Renaissance disclosed a line of cleavage between history and biography, and this distinction was first clearly stated by John Hayward and Francis Bacon.[7] Yet in spite of definite lines of separation, which are reiterated later in the century by such writers as Sir Henry Wotton, Thomas Stanley, Margaret Cavendish, Thomas Fuller and John Dryden, history and biography are repeatedly confused. Edward Lord Herbert of Cherbury calls his work on Henry VIII "The Life and Raigne" (1649) and does not differentiate between the two. Sanderson's *Lives and Reigns of Mary Queen of Scots and . . . James the Sixth* (1656) is pure patchwork

7. Their theories are discussed later in the chapter in the consideration of conceptions of biography.

history, and William Drummond's *Lives and Reigns of the Five James's* (1655) cannot be regarded as a series of biographies. Throughout the century, the life and reign of a monarch are not separated. Pageantry and politics are introduced to give amplitude to a monarch; they end by glorifying his position at the expense of his person. Particularly during the last half of the seventeenth century, the tendency was toward the expansion of the narrative, and the influence of continental and ecclesiastical historians contaminated the purity of the biographical tradition. This blurring of the focus, which produced a type of history viewed from a biographical or autobiographical standpoint, appealed to such practiced and distinguished English biographers as Clarendon, Burnet, and Baxter.[8] It was clumsily continued by John Strype in his *Memorials of . . . Thomas Cranmer* (1694) and his subsequent tomes on Cheke, Grindal, Parker, and Whitgift (1705-18). These are histories cluttered with uncoördinated documents, wherein, under the pretence of writing lives, the author has produced works which should have been relegated almost entirely to appendixes.

Before 1700, then, thoughtful biographers had recognized and repeatedly expressed the distinctions between history and biography. Yet strange hybrids continued to flourish; and at the end of the century, a powerful and prolific school tended to plunge life-writing once

8. See also *Ecclesiastical Biography*, later sections, under Hacket, Heylyn, Parr. The principal model for such writings was De Thou's *Historiarum sui Temporis . . . Libri CXXXVIII* (1543-1607; published 1620-28), which included his own *De vita sua* of 102 pages. De Thou, who is frequently cited by English writers, was an observer keenly alive to the modern spirit. So, in his notice to the reader before the history, he compares the simplicity of Livy's Roman world with its present complexity, a complexity which he proceeds to demonstrate in five volumes, each of about eight hundred pages.

again into the historical tradition from which it had emerged with so much difficulty during the days of the Tudors and the first Stuarts.

If biography is allied closely with history, its relations to other branches of literature — to poetry, the romance and the novel, to literary criticism and polemical writings — are no less complicated and close. A brief review of these relations, an attempt to fix the bounds of biography, will show the wide range touched upon in early English life-writing.

The poetical mood is not usually compatible with the biographical aim of reflecting a life truthfully and completely. The mechanical details which form the skeleton of all biographies prove singularly recalcitrant to metre; and the analysis of character, the explanation of complicated events and actions, the general unemotional attitude of candour and impartiality, do not lend themselves to song. But a study of verse lives shows that from the Conquest to the Renaissance biographies in English were almost entirely limited to rhyme, and that metrical lives continued to thrive into the seventeenth century. During the Middle Ages, verse was used, not because it was especially suited to the needs of biography, but because the first literary attempts in the new and growing language were metrical, and writers were not sufficiently aware of the requirements of biography and the limitations of metre, to create a more suitable form for their biographical productions. One branch of poetry — verse of epic pretensions — was discovered to have distinct possibilities in narrating in lofty strains the high heroic actions of the great. The subjects for these elevated verse lives are confined almost exclusively to kings or political and ecclesiastical dignitaries; in spirit they are mournful, and seek to teach a philosophic resignation to fortune; their style is ambitious and ornate; in the hands of a few writers — Sackville, Storer and Drayton — verse adds dignity and unity to the prevalent methods of writing biography. The verse lives of the school of *The Mirror for Magistrates* present the most highly developed and widely practiced biographical form of the sixteenth century, and afford a bridge, in the history of biography, between the Middle Ages and the Renaissance.[9]

The influence of biography in the transition of romance into the novel is of great importance. The mediaeval romance made slight pretence to realism in setting or incident, and characterization was rudimentary.[10] In the hands of the pamphleteers and professional writers at the close of the sixteenth century, the autobiographical pieces and the background of contemporary London and English life which had occasionally appeared in the poems of fifteenth-century writers are first introduced into the tales of courtly and improbable adventures. Thomas Lodge's *Life of Robert second Duke of Normandy* (1591) employs all the paraphernalia of a romance, but purports to be "Famous, true and historicall." His *William Longbeard* (1593) goes a step further, and against the setting of London's underworld, depicts the life and death of "the most famous and witty Eng-

9. One other form of poetry, the elegy, is related to biography through the common aim of furnishing memorials to the dead. Yet although biographies frequently manifest the elegiac spirit in their closing pages, few elegies are entitled to consideration even as imperfect or biassed lives of their heroes.

10. For the popularity of romance, note the large proportion of romance and romance-biographies in the lists of Caxton's, Pynson's or Wynkyn de Worde's printed books given in the Dictionary of National Biography.

lish Traitor," which Lodge draws from Stow's annals.[11] That copious and fascinating writer, Robert Greene, uses the experiences and observations of his own life to give color to his numerous *novelle*, and never more successfully than when, impulsively repentant, he pours out his own confessions in the *Mourning Garment* (1590) and in his *Groatsworth of Witte* (1592). "As a novel writer and an observer of human nature," says Jusserand in his discussion of Greene,[12] "his own portrait is perhaps his masterpiece." The close connection between autobiography and romance is shown in the *Groatsworth of Witte*, wherein Greene begins the tale with "Robertus" as hero, but upon warming to his task throws aside all disguise and speaks in the first person. At times, writers have found it easier to be frank and unrestrained if they hide themselves under assumed names and write their histories in the guise of romance. So George Gascoigne tells his mystical history under the title of "Dan Bartholmew of Bath," and Sir Kenelm Digby unfolds the courtship of his wife as the amorous history of Theagenes and Stelliana. This tendency can also operate in the opposite direction, and the life of a fictitious personage may be rendered more credible if told as an autobiography. Thomas Nashe was one of the first to make capital of this device, and his *Life of Jacke Wilton* (1594) is a dashing and exuberant series of incidents told by its cunning and unscrupulous hero. Such picaresque novels are largely responsible for the increased tendency toward realism noticeable in the romances of the period. They themselves spring from the same popular interest in sensational and strange lives which produced broad-

11. 1605, p. 240.
12. *English Novel in the Time of Shakespeare*, 1890, p. 152.

sides and short pamphlets on the disagreeable deaths of
every murderer and Newgate criminal, and turned over
the pages of old chronicles and foreign histories for lives
incredibly criminal or heroic.[13] With Thomas Deloney
(d. 1600) and his imitators, in the odd, but by no means
rare, publications which were destined for a particular
and limited audience — written and dedicated to the
armorers of London, the famous cloth-workers, the
merchant-tailors, the shoemakers, or the dapper Monsieur Pages of the Court — biography is transformed
into "pleasant history," to use a common title, in order
to render it palatable and flattering. During the reigns
of the first Stuarts, Thomas Heywood continues to write
in the vein of Lodge, Nashe, and Deloney. Heywood's
fondness for romance is best illustrated in "The Generall
History of Women, Containing the Lives of the most
Holy and Prophane, the most Famous and Infamous in
all ages." [14] This large collection of tales and anecdotes
is exactly described, Heywood professes, "not only from

13. The relation of biography to sensational journalism affords an interesting by-path. Some idea of the prevalence of ephemeral and scandalous
tracts may be gleaned from the titles in the Bibliography. Short anonymous
lives of criminals and freaks largely filled the place occupied to-day by the
tabloid newspapers. Specimen titles, sufficiently descriptive, are: "The Displaying of an horrible secte of grosse and wicked Heretiques, naming themselves the Familie of Love, with the lives of their Authours," 1578; "An Historical Account of the Life and Tryal of Nicholas Anthoine, burnt for Judaism
at Geneva in the Year 1632"; "The Phoenix of these late times: Or the
life of Mr. Henry Welby, Esq: who lived at his house in Grub street forty
four yeares, and in that space, was never seene by any," 1637; "A True Relation, of the Lives and Deaths of the two most Famous English Pyrats, Purser,
and Clinton," 1639; "The Penitent Murderer," 1657; "The Memoirs of
Monsieur De Vall," 1670; "The Bloody Murtherer, Or, The Unnatural Son,"
1672; "The Life and Death of Major Clancie, the Grandest Cheat of this
Age," 1680. Each of these extravagant pieces has as a nucleus an actual
figure, but the coarse curiosity that inspired them could not produce any work
important as biography.

14. T. p. 1657 ed. Earlier ed. 1624.

Poeticall Fictions, but from the most Ancient, Modern, and Admired Historians, to our Times." The result is fabulous entertainment rather than a biographical dictionary. His *Nine Worthy Women* (1640) more nearly approaches biography; its heroines range from Judith to Queen Elizabeth. As biographies, most of the productions mentioned in this paragraph are worthless. They are tales based on scraps of history. But as entertaining pieces written from a free sense of style, the works of the Elizabethan pamphleteers are more pleasing than many contemporary accounts with serious claims as biographies.

Such pieces of biographical romance, written by authors of some note and greater copiousness, have not escaped those interested in the development of the English novel. Worthier in themselves, however, and more important as forerunners of the novel, are the autobiographies and memoirs of the seventeenth century, which, principally because they are isolated pieces, have more frequently escaped the vigilance of the historian. A number of these memoirs are filled with events so stirring as to differ little from historical romance. The persecutions and escapes of the Jesuit Father John Gerard (written 1609), Robert Cary's adventures as Warden of the Scottish Marches in the days of Elizabeth (p. 1623) the duels of Lord Herbert of Cherbury and his gallant intrigues (ca. 1643), the exploits of Sydnam Poyntz in the Thirty Years' War (1636), or the martial escapades and continental travels of the entertaining Thomas Raymond (ca. 1658), furnish absorbing instances of the strangeness of truth. The autobiography of Henry Burton (1643) in its straightforward prose, its conscientious absorption in detail, its manly and matter-of-fact account of the most striking incidents, is a direct forerunner of Defoe.

Biography also provides prototypes of the sentimental and the psychological novel. In some instances, such as the memoirs of Lady Anne Fanshawe or Margaret Cavendish, Duchess of Newcastle, biography furnishes the raw materials from which novels might be made. Often, however, not only the matter but the manner is the novelist's. The most outstanding instance is furnished by Sir Kenelm Digby. In a story which engaged Digby's ardent and genuine emotions, his memoirs carry on the artificiality of *Euphues*, introduce into English the *sentiments raffinés* of *L'Astrée* and the French romance writers, and anticipate the elegant sentimentality of Richardson. The discursiveness, the purity and propriety of Digby's Stelliana precede *Pamela* by over a hundred years. Yet Digby wrote for his own pleasure and his manuscript was not published until 1827. If autobiographies had ordinarily been published when written instead of long subsequently, the history of English fiction might have been appreciably altered.

The deep emotion and truthfulness in the love story of John and Lucy Hutchinson carry her memoirs beyond the questions of literary style and periods, and make them, in effect, an historical novel with a sentimental interest. In psychological analysis, one or two memoirs anticipate the novels of later centuries; in this field women are pre-eminent. The daughter of Lady Falkland who wrote her mother's life had some of that dry detachment and power of sharp observation, though little of the wit, which is associated with Jane Austen. Lady Anne Halkett's account of her own life forms, almost without alteration, a satisfactory psychological novel, narrating and analyzing her relations to her various suitors and her conduct in several households. From the field of ecclesiastical biography, the lives of Nicholas Ferrar and Walton's poetic *Life of Herbert* may be singled out as precursors of *The Vicar of Wakefield*.

These principal works, together with others of less direct importance, were influential in the transition from the Elizabethan romance to the eighteenth-century novel. The introduction of realism in setting and background, the substitution of personalities for bald narrations, the presentation of sentiments and emotions somewhat less conventionalized and trite — in a word, the introduction of individual characters into the novel, is largely due to the influence of biography. The forerunners of typical novel forms which developed in periods much later — the historical, the adventurous, the picaresque, the sentimental, the psychological, the idyllic — may be found in the rich field of seventeenth-century memoirs, not only as embryonic and formless hints, but occasionally as finished and complete productions.

Biography, with its elastic and varied possibilities, also served at times as a controversial weapon. As a rule, the tactics of the polemical biographer consist in denouncing a representative enemy of his own cause or party. Valuable contributions are the result of this partisan spirit — such works as Foxe's *Book of Martyrs* or Bale's *Catalogue of Illustrious Writers*. From the defamatory chronicler, few of the prominent figures in political and ecclesiastical conflicts escape untouched. More and Wolsey, Bonner and Laud and Baxter, Charles and Cromwell, suffer alike from their assiduous enemies, and are compensated by the apotheosis of their followers.[15] Where political or religious feeling is intense enough to call forth a biography of untempered praise, a retaliatory piece follows almost inevitably. In these instances the first aim of the writer is not the just reproduction of a life, but the presentation of a figure in such a manner as to aid his own partisan cause. The biographer turns politician.

Even more interesting than these lives of direct timeliness are the biographies of historical figures in the past published as parallels and precedents for present political action.[16] That they were held to have some influence may be judged from Hayward's imprisonment in the Tower upon the publication of *Henry IIII*, a work which the Queen held to be impolitic and disparaging to her own position and tenure of the throne. Cavendish's *Wolsey*, with its emphasis upon the Cardinal's disgrace and death, was first printed, though in a mutilated version, as a weapon to aid the cause of the Commonwealth, and was followed by a parallel between Wolsey and Archbishop Laud, then confined in the Tower. In the decade before the Revolution of 1688, while talk of dethroning the reigning monarch was in the air, the lives of Richard II and Edward II were printed in various forms as significant precedents. Anti-Catholic biographies had been steadily in demand since the Reformation, and ranged from "A Mervaylous discourse upon the lyfe, deedes, and behaviours of Katherine de Medicis" (1575) to "The Life and Death of Pope Joane" (1663), "The Memoires of Mr. James Wadswort, A Jesuit that Recanted" (1679), "The Life of Donna

15. Cf. Bibliography.
16. E. g., *The life of Aelius Seianus*, 1628; Buck's *Richard III*, 1646; Perrinchief's *Agathocles*, 1676. Cf. Bibliography.

Olimpia Maldachini, Who Governed the Church during the Time of Innocent the X" (1666), and "The Devils Patriarck . . . Innocent the Eleventh" (1683). In a few instances,[17] libellous biographers attain a cleverly lurid style which pricks and stings and hammers and cuts by turns, and in which scurrility is raised amost to the level of the liberal arts.

In brief, a leading figure in any national movement was always in danger of becoming identified with and submerged in the movement he headed. A study of defamatory and partisan lives shows that the great of the earth are often represented by their biographers as figureheads, as eikons, and tend to lose their true characters in the rancor of controversy. Controversial lives, therefore, do not occupy an important place in the history of biography, for their tendency towards caricature and heated political argument quickly removes them from the sphere of life-writing.

With the growth of the lives of literary figures and the introduction of brief lives prefatory to collected works, biography assumes some of the functions of literary criticism. Leland in his catalogue of writers did not exclude estimates of their works and descriptions of their style, and the practice he introduced developed through later collections until at the end of the seventeenth century, Blount published his *Censura Celebriorum Authorum* (1690) wherein the short sketches of the authors' lives are subordinate to the criticisms of their works. But if Thomas Pope Blount presents biography which has become almost unmixed literary criticism, the inter-

17. Such as Thomas James's life of the Jesuit Father Parsons (1612), the *Flagellum; Or The Life and Death . . . of O. Cromwell* (1663), or the anonymous *Life and Death of Ralph Wallis The Cobler of Glocester* (1670).

mediate stages are not hard to find. Phillips' *Theatrum Poetarum* and Winstanley's *Lives of the English Poets* are in large part critical, while Langbaine's *Account of the English Dramatic Poets* is far more concerned with cataloguing their works and tracing their literary debts than with their personal adventures. Similarly the life prefixed to Rochester's *Valentinian* (1685) is concerned exclusively with his fame and achievements as a poet. Generally, however, literary criticism is only incidentally introduced into the biographies of the seventeenth century. Walton's attitude is characteristic. Although he takes delight in the poems of Donne and Herbert, the sagacity and statecraft of Wotton and Hooker, the sermons of Sanderson, he does not trouble to give a definite appraisal of their work or a judgment of their merits. Instead he prefers to introduce at random a poem or an epigram, allowing it to speak for itself while it brightens his pages.[18] Probably the best literary criticism in combination with biography produced during the century is Dryden's *Life of Plutarch* (1683). Dryden praises Plutarch for "copiousness of learning, integrity, perspicuity, and more than all this, for a certain air of goodness which appears through all his writings." His style is next considered, and Dryden defends him against criticism levelled at his judgment, his partiality for the Greeks, and his apparently contradictory portraits. The biography closes with a brilliant and enthusiastic parallel drawn between Plutarch and Seneca. Yet this in itself is largely derived from earlier editions

18. Gauden, though his life of Hooker is far inferior to Walton's, must be credited with introducing at an early date (1661) a long analysis of his subject's style and matter, which may be classed as literary criticism welded into the frame of a biography, though the critic is not as discriminating and free from rhetoric as might be desired.

of Plutarch, and shows, as does all the evidence that may be adduced, that biography had not sufficiently developed, during the period under survey, to make it an admirable and adequate vehicle for literary criticism.

To this point the boundaries of biography have been indicated by showing in what respects it approaches other literary forms. Its close alliance to history, its incompatibility with the poetic spirit, its decided influence upon the novel, and its unimportance at this date as a means for literary criticism — in such lights life-writing has been regarded. But early English biography cannot be defined by indicating what it is not, or by establishing its literary neighbors. This survey is preliminary; it has served to show many points of contact with other modes of writing; it has suggested the wide range in theme and treatment which is possible in the biographical art. To some extent it has been a negative consideration, a scrutiny of the periphery of English biography, an examination of instances where the biographical impulse mingles with other currents. There remains the positive definition: What did contemporary writers imply when they spoke of "lives," "histories," and "biographies"? What was their conception of biography, its scope, its purpose, and its method? The preceding chapters have traced the practice of life-writing; it remains to view the theories which produced the separate pieces or tended to determine their form.

A conception of biography is implicit in Bede's work, though it is not formally expressed. Bede wrote the *Vita Sancti Cuthberti* first as a verse life, then as a prose life, and finally as a part of his *Ecclesiastical History*. Yet the treatment in all three versions is the same. The verse life is composed "aliquanto quidem brevius" and is written, as Bede himself describes it, in heroic verse; the account in the history omits the minor miracles and trivial incidents of the prose life; but essentially the three are one. Biography to the Venerable Bede was only history viewed more closely.

Bede's pious chronicles contain the germs of the two conceptions of biography which flourished during the Middle Ages and which in one form or another continued with vigor almost undiminished to the end of the seventeenth century. These conceptions were: first, that biography should furnish examples of holy living and holy dying, and second, that biography should recount historical events as they grouped themselves around one figure. In the first, biography is the servant of religion; in the second, the handmaiden of history. The two tendencies manifest themselves roughly in the saints' lives and in royal biography. The prevalence of these two ideals, the ethical and the political, throughout the entire period here studied, may best be shown from a quotation in the preface to George Mackenzie's *Lives of . . . Eminent Writers of the Scots Nation*: [19]

"The Common Method Observed in Writing the Lives of Illustrious Persons, is either, in Relation to their Moral Conduct, or to History; in the First, a Particular Account is given of all their Actions, and a great many Moral Reflections made upon their Conduct, their Virtues and Vices; but in the Other, the Principal Circumstances of their Lives are only Related, and the Actions that concern their own Persons, that have no Relation to the Public Good, or the History of their Times, are passed over in Silence without any Moral Reflections upon them."

19. 1707, p. xi.

The mediaeval conception of biography as an inspiriting guide to conduct is nowhere better shown than in the writings of John of Tynemouth (14th century), who reverently collects his companies of English saints in order to furnish his readers with *vivendi efficacissima exempla*, the most useful examples of righteous living. "Oh how sweet," he exclaims, "is the story of those saints who lived their lives so gloriously here upon earth! O mortal man, read! and what thou readest, remember, for if the truth be owned, thou canst not do a thing more beautiful."

Biography as an ethical force was not discarded in the English Renaissance. Puttenham [20] in his chapter "Of historicall Poesie, by which the famous acts of Princes and the vertuous and worthy lives of our forefathers were reported," expresses his belief that "Poesie historicall is of all other next the divine most honorable and worthy, as well for the common benefit as for the speciall comfort every man receiveth by it. No one thing in the world with more delectation reviving our spirits then to behold as it were in a glasse the lively image of our deare forefathers, their noble and vertuous maner of life, with other things autentike."

This ideal of biography as an exemplary exercise was so repeatedly expressed, and accepted so wholeheartedly by early biographers, as to take deep root. At a later period, in any discussion of the theory of biography it was tacitly assumed that its purpose was instruction. In ecclesiastical biography this idea was brought over without question and made the foundation for many a pious paper monument. It afforded also the

20. *Arte of English Poesie*, 1589, p. 31.

theoretical justification for a heterogeneous mass of biographical writings.

Side by side with this ethical tradition, there developed the conception of biography as a form of history. Yet this conception is not clearly or frequently expressed in the Middle Ages. Earlier in this chapter, the confusion of history and biography has been emphasized. National and personal annals are hopelessly entangled. There is no difference in treatment, no conscious difference in the meaning of the titles, between the *Historia Henrici Quinti* of Robert Redman and the *De Vita Henrici Septimi* of Bernard André, though both of them were written as late as the sixteenth century.

The Renaissance heralded a new interest in the individual, and only when its curiosity concerning personalities became widespread, are definite theories of biography as a separate art formulated. The historian John Hayward first differentiated biography and history and realized a distinction between "the government of mighty states" and "the lives and acts of famous men." [21] His distinction between "lives" and "Historie" is more than theoretical: his *Lives of the Three Normans* falls definitely into the former class; his *Henry IIII* and *Elizabeth* into the latter.

Bacon (1605) not only considered biography as a

21. Hayward's productions were not written without conscious thought of the problems and functions of the biographer and chronicler. "Since I am entred into this point," he says in the preface to *Henry IIII*, 1599, "it may seeme not impertinent to write of the stile of a history, what beginning, what continuance, and what meane is to bee used in all matter, what thinges are to bee suppressed, what lightly touched, and what to be treated at large: how creadit may be won, and suspition avoyded: what is to bee observed in the order of times, and description of places and other such circumstances of weight; what liberty a writer may use in framing speeches, and in declaring the causes, counsailes and eventes of thinges done: how farre hee must bend himselfe to profit; and when and how hee may play upon pleasure. . . ."

separate and important form, but pointed out the neglect with which it was treated in Britain. His well-known triple partition of history includes biography as one division:

"History, which may be called just and perfect history, is of three kinds, according to the object which it propoundeth, or pretendeth to represent: for it either representeth a time, or a person, or an action. The first we call chronicles, the second lives, and the third narrations, or relations."

With Bacon, the purpose of biography is utilitarian:

"Of these, although the first be the most complete and absolute kind of history, and hath most estimation and glory, yet the second excelleth it in profit and use, and the third in verity and sincerity. . . ."

"Lives," he continues, "if they be well written, propounding to themselves a person to represent, in whom actions both greater and smaller, publick and private, have a commixture, must of necessity contain a more true, native, and live representation [than chronicles]. . . .

"For lives, I do find strange that these times have so little esteemed the virtues of the times, as that the writings of lives should be no more frequent. For although there be not many sovereign princes or absolute commanders, and that states are most collected into monarchies, yet are there many worthy personages that deserve better than dispersed report, or barren elogies. . . .

"We do acknowledge that which Cicero saith, borrowing it from Demosthenes, that *Bona fama propria possessio defunctorum*; which possession I cannot but note, that in our times it lieth much waste, and that therein there is a deficience."

In these remarks Bacon seems a hesitant prophet. Although basing his observations largely upon the formal treatment of classical histories and royal biographies, he marks out the biography of the future wherein not only great and public affairs, but smaller and private actions are mingled, biographies not only of sovereigns and commanders, but of worthy personages of all ranks. The concessions are grudging. Bacon does not exemplify them in his *Henry VII*, and only partially in his *Elizabeth*; but in theory at least, he is a distinguished champion of the extension of biography to all classes, and of its increased cultivation in England.

Chiming perfectly with Bacon's wonder at the rarity of English biography, is the opinion of the author of *The History of Sir John Perrott*.[22] His defence of the value of biography is spirited and logical. Again the note of utility is dominant:

"Yet some perchaunce will say, that to write the Lives of particular Men, is a Thinge as unnecessarie, as it is unusuall: To whom I may answer, that thoe it be somewhat unusual, yet is it nothinge unnecessarie, but rather very proffitable. For as it is a Rule in Philosophie, that we cannot come to Generalls but by Particulars; so it is as true in Reason and Policie, that particular Examples do better informe and instruct us, in the ordering of our selves, and the governinge of others, than the Observation of general Actions; the Groundes whereof are fallible, because the Circumstances are diverse and variable. . . . Therefore this History of a particular Man's Life is here penned."

Edmund Bolton, writing between 1610 and 1618, realizes in his *Hypercritica Or A Rule of Judgment for writing, or reading our History's*,[23] the need for trained historians, for art and style in composition. In his opinion, the writer must be able to combine ethical teaching with analysis of motives, and in this he finds Sir Thomas More for his *Richard III* and Commines for his *Louis XI* to be pre-eminent. The writer of history

22. Written about 1600; p. 8 of preface 1728 ed. Quoted in Chapter V.
23. Ed. Hall, Oxford, 1722.

and of biography must be impartial and above all, must avoid those religious prejudices which cause the "Shipwracks" of narratives otherwise commendable.

Richard Braithwaite in *The Schollers Medley, Or, An Intermixt Discourse upon Historicall and Poeticall Relations* (1614), has little of novelty to add, and harks back to the theory of biography as a guide to life. Doubtless, he says (p. 12), "there is nothing which inflames the minde of man more unto valour and resolution, then the report of the acts of their Auncestors, whose monuments ... must needs stirre up in them a desire of imitation. ... Certainly there is no means better to deter from vice, nor more effectuall inducements unto vertue, then these moral relations. By them we see the lives of Princes, and their employments, etc."

It is evident from the selections already quoted that the theories of biography are largely empirical. They are founded upon current practice, and draw lessons from existing monuments. They are the generalizations from experience rather than the arbiters of an ideal form.

It is natural, therefore, that as the seventeenth century advances and biographies increase in numbers and importance, the theories of biography should be expressed more frequently and with greater cogency. Occasionally new conceptions are developed. Fuller is the first English biographer to admit frankly that entertainment as well as profit may be a legitimate end for biography. The five ends for which he avows he has written *The History of the Worthies of England* (1662) are: "First, To gain some Glory to God. Secondly, To preserve the memories of the Dead. Thirdly, to present Examples to the living. Fourthly, To entertain the

Reader with Delight. And lastly, (which I am not ashamed publickly to profess) To procure some honest profit to my self."

The first three of these reasons mirror faithfully the typical motives repeatedly advanced by biographers as their inspirations. The glory of God was always theoretically foremost with the orthodox Christian writer. "Not out of a vain affectation of my own glory" does Bishop Joseph Hall write his memoirs, "but out of a sincere desire to give glory to my God." *The Life of Robert Blair* is presented to show "God's fatherly leading him in all the most difficult paths of his life and pilgrimage." Philip Stubbes writes (1626):

"Calling to remembrance (most Christian Reader) the finall end of Mans creation, which is, to glorifie God and to edifie one another in the way of true godlinesse: I thought it my duty, as well in respect of the one, as in regard of the other, to publish this rare and wonderfull example, of the vertuous life and Christian death of Mistris Catherine Stubbes."

And Walter Pringle (1662–66) declares that "Since my God gave me children, it hath been much upon my mind to record, for their use, the wonderful goodness of God to me." "In the Lives of Holy Men," writes Baxter in his preface to *Joseph Alleine* (1673), "we see God's Image, and the Beauties of Holiness, not only in Precept, but in reality and Practice; not Pictured, but in the Substance."

The second of Fuller's aims is "To preserve the Memories of the Dead." He continues:

"A good name is an oyntment poured out, smelt where it is not seen. It hath been the lawful desire of men in all ages to perpetuate their memories, thereby in some sort revenging themselves of Mortality, though few have found out effectual means to perform it. For Monuments made of Wood, are subject to be burnt; of Glass, to be broken; of soft stone, to moulder; of Marble and Metal, (if escaping the teeth of Time) to be demolished by the hand of Covetousness; so that in my apprehension, the safest way to secure a memory from oblivion, is (next his own Vertues) by committing the same in writing to Posterity.

"Thirdly, to present examples to the living, having here precedents of all sorts and sizes; of men famous for Valour, Wealth, Wisdome, Learning, Religion, and Bounty to the publick, on which last we most largely insist."

Fuller's phrasing of this third aim — to present examples to the living — is the most embracing, as well as the most succinct, statement of the purpose of early biography. It is echoed in numerous lives.

"How much more then is it mete," concludes John Foxe [24] in his *Actes and Monuments*, "for us to accept and embrace the lyves and doinges, not of roughe warriours, but of moste mylde and constant Martyrs, which may serve, not so much to delight the eare, as to garnish the lyfe, to frame it with examples of great profite, and to enstruct the minde in all kinde of Christian godlyness."

A century later, in *The Life & Death of Dr. James Usher* (1656), Nicholas Bernard declares: "The writing of the lives of Holy and Eminent Men departed, are for us surviving (as a Father sayeth) *Veluti speculum, exemplum, condimentum*, as a Glasse to trimme our lives by, a Copy to improve our hands, a Sauce to sharpen our tastes of the heavenly Gift in them."

Plume in his *Life of John Hacket* (1675) follows Fuller's reasoning closely and sets down his motives for writing as (1) to furnish an example for readers to emulate, (2)

24. 1563 ed. "A declaration concerning the utilitie and profite of thys history."

dutifully to erect a memorial to the dead, and (3) to stimulate posterity in the Christian faith. Similarly, Bishop Burnet says at the conclusion of his *Life of Bedell:* [25] "And as the Lives of the Primitive Christians were a speaking Apology for their Religion, as well as a direction to those that grew up, so it is hoped that the solemn though silent language of so bright an example will have the desired effect both ways." James Fraser says in his memoirs (ca. 1684), "I have in nothing been more refreshed, quickned, and edified, than by hearing and reading of the spiritual Experiences of others of the Lord's People, . . . and in nothing more comforted and sanctified than by a serious recalling to Mind of the Lord's Dealings with me." Richard Baxter (1681) finds the life of his wife so instructive and exemplary that at the conclusion he marshals a list of twenty-one specific ways in which the narrative will be found "useful . . . to considering men."

This group of quotations, which might be extended, has been given at some length at the risk of redundancy, because it represents the general didactic aim which lies at the root of almost all biographies written during the period under survey. Life-writing must be exemplary; it must inspire, illuminate, instruct; and by presenting examples to the living it must teach men better how to live and die.

This high conception of the purpose of biography, though dominant, is by no means the sole motive for writing. One of Fuller's incentives, as he affirms with characteristic candor, was to procure some honest profit for himself. Another was to entertain the reader with delight. In defence of this last motive, so revolu-

25. 1685, p. 219.

tionary in his serious and moral world, the sprightly doctor continues:

"I confess the subject is but dull in it self, to tell the time and place of mens birth, and deaths, and names, with the names of their books, and thereby this bare Sceleton of Time, Place, and Person, must be fleshed with some pleasant passages. To the intent I have purposely interlaced (not as meat but as condiment) many delightful stories, that so the Reader if he does not arise (which I hope and desire) *Religiosior* or *Doctior*, with more piety or learning, at least he may depart *Jucundior*, with more pleasure and lawful delight."

To the success of his ambitions, *The Worthies of England* bears brave witness.

In the discussion of polemical biography, mention has already been made of the conception of life-writing for purposes of defence or defamation. On one side Capgrave (1451) writes his *Life of Gilbert of Sempringham* in order to help effect "the canonizacion of this Seynt," or the *Eikon Basilike* is published as an apotheosis of King Charles. On the other side, the *Flagellum* (1663) scourges Oliver Cromwell, or Thomas Long's *Review of Mr. Richard Baxter's Life* (1697) attacks virulently the non-conformist divine and his theological position.

Again, biography may be written to gratify local pride and interests, as in the chronicle lives of mediaeval monastic foundations, or in the pleasant histories dedicated to various Elizabethan guilds or ambitious town aldermen.

A combination of flattery and respect tempers the class of lives written by dependents. When these biographies are the productions of illiterate but aspiring servitors, as are Broughton's *Pawlet* (1572) or Griffith's *Henry Sidney* (1591), the results are amusing. But far more frequently the position of dependence is ideal for a high type of biography. A secretary, a chaplain, a confidential adviser or *maître d'affaires* frequently merges his own personality with that of his master. His knowledge is detailed and his interest genuine. The best English biographers during the period of written Latin — Eddius, Eadmer, the biographers of Thomas Becket, Adam of Eynsham — were followers attached to the household of their lords. Cavendish was one of Wolsey's gentlemen ushers; Roper and Rawley were secretaries to More and Bacon. A large number of biographies were written by private or domestic chaplains upon the death of their patrons. Among these are Clifford's *Jane Dormer* (p. 1615), *The Lives of Philip Howard and Anne Dacres* (p. 1630), Forrest's *Katherine of Aragon* (1558), Duncon's *Lady Letice* (1647), and Collinges' *Lives of Frances Hobart and Katharine Courten* (1669). Such lives are laudatory and filled with virtuous precepts. In the hands of the Catholics they verge upon the saints' lives, as does Richard Smith's *Lady Magdalen Viscountess Montague* (1627).

A number of the memoirs of the seventeenth century were written because of family pride, to furnish a family guide. They were intended for the sons and grandsons of the noblemen who composed them as a history of the house. Sir James Melville (d. 1593) speaks to his son in the *Memoirs of his own life*, which were written, he says, "to serve for an exempler of lyf and better behaviour to the and thy brether, concerning the service of princes and medling in ther affaires, quhilk I culd not eschew." [26]

"Certainly," says Cherbury in his autobiography (ca. 1643), "it will be found much better for men to

26. 1827, pp. 3-4.

guide themselves by such observations as their father, grandfather, and great-grandfather might have delivered to them . . . for which reason I have thought fit to relate to my posterity those passages of my life, which I conceive may best declare me, and be most useful to them."

Sir Simonds D'Ewes writes his own life (ca. 1649) for similar reasons. "He evidently considered himself a person of no small importance," observes his editor,[27] "and no doubt desired that this account of his life should remain in the hands of his descendants, a memorial of their illustrious ancestor."

Clarendon discloses the aim for which he wrote his autobiography in the heading: [28] "Reflections upon the most material passages which happened after the king's restoration to the time of the chancellor's banishment; out of which his children, for whose information they are collected, may add some important passages to his Life."

Lucy Hutchinson's memoirs of her husband are addressed to her children (ca. 1665), while Lady Anne Fanshawe writes hers for the benefit of her only son (1676). The conception of biography as a family memorial is usually limited, as the above examples show, to titled authors; and family pride is, therefore, not a general incentive to life-writing.

Friendship and love are productive of numerous biographies. The lives inspired by filial, or fraternal, or marital affection are numerous, and range from the pious love of Anthony Walker's *Life of Mrs. Elizabeth Walker* (1690) to the analytical narrative of Lady Elizabeth Falkland (ca. 1655) written by her daughter. The

27. J. O. Halliwell, 1845.   28. 1857, i, 267.

memorials to friendship are noble ones, and include such pieces as Fulke Greville's *Sidney*, Walton's *John Donne*, and Evelyn's *Margaret Godolphin*.

The last motive for writing biography which will here be discussed is purely personal: to pass the time away, or to give expression to grief or passion. Thus Digby whiles away his separation from his wife by setting down in the best manner that he can,[29] "the beginning, progress, and consummation of that excellent love which only makes me believe that our pilgrimage in this world is not indifferently laid upon all persons for a curse." In like fashion, Henry Cary, Lord Falkland, writes his *Life of Edward II* (1627) for his own pleasure, and drives his melancholy pen forward in order "to out-run those weary hours of a deep and sad Passion." Fulke Greville's *Sidney* is written partly as a consolation to himself, who, he says, would "rather seek comfortable ease or imployment in the safe memory of dead men, than disquiet in a doubtfull conversation amongst the living."

English biographies before 1700, therefore, were not invariably inspired with a didactic purpose. Occasionally they were written for the family archives, for consolation, for money, for advancement, for the gratification of local pride, for personal amusement, for love.

And with the repeated expressions of the purposes of life-writing, with the great increase in the practice of biography from the days when Bacon found it strange that the custom of commemorating the dead "in our times lieth much waste," to the year when Thomas Plume [30] notes "the many Volumes of Lives daily published" at home and abroad, criticism of the older

29. 1827, p. 10.   30. *Life of Hacket*, 1675, ii.

methods of life-writing naturally springs up by the side of the analysis of the new.

Thomas Fuller comments on the saints' lives in some detail. He recognizes the worth of individual hagiographers, but attacks their attitude in general, and accuses them of wanting honest hearts and able heads, as well as true matter.[31] Fuller is equally merciless in his criticism of the antiquaries, Bale and Pits, for including mythical material in their catalogues. Thomas Fuller, then, in his conception of biography, rules out all superstitions and unsupported evidence. His criterion is common sense, and his aim the truthful representation of his subjects' careers.

Thomas Stanley follows Hayward and the biographer of John Perrott in recognizing life-writing as a division of history (1655). He goes further, however, and subdivides biography. He distinguishes two principal classes of lives, the active and the contemplative, one having a bearing on public affairs, the other sufficient in itself. He realizes that characters who do not actively enter into history are nevertheless fit subjects of biography, and this appreciation marks, as it were, a declaration of independence. In the lives of philosophers and literary men biography finally breaks away from history.

"Now the life of man being either practick, busied in civill affairs of peace and war, or Contemplative, retir'd from publick businesse to speculation and study of wisdome, divine or humane, it followes that this personall history bee twofold likewise, describing either the actions of such persons as are wholly interested in affairs of state (properly compar'd to the persons of a drammaticall designe, whose single Characters

31. *Worthies of England*, 1662, p. 8. Gilbert Burnet has a similar historical criticism in his *Life of Hale*, 1682.

and parts serve one onely to make up one joint plot. Such are most of those whose lives are related by Plutarch, & the twelve Caesars of Suetonius.) Or the lives of such as have been excellent in some kind of learning; Thus Antipho writ of Poets; Eudemus of Astrologers; Cicero and Plutarch of Oratours, Suetonius of Grammarians. They who writ of philosophers exceeded the rest far in number."
— Stanley, *History of Philosophy*, 1655, Preface.

The voluble Margaret Cavendish, Duchess of New-castle, whom it had pleased God to endow "with a Poetical and Philosophical Genius" even from her birth, employs this philosophical talent, in anticipation of John Dryden, by dividing all of history into three parts.

"Although there be many sorts of Histories," she says in the preface to her life of William Cavendish (1667), "yet these three are the chiefest: 1. a General History. 2. A National History. 3. A Particular History . . . The third is the History of the life and actions of some particular Person . . . it goes not out of its own Circle, but turns on its own Axis, and for the most part, keeps within the Circumference of Truth. The first is Mechanical, the second Political, and the third Heroical. . . . [It should be written] by the Prime Actors, or the Spectators of those Affairs and Actions of which they write, as Caesars Commentaries are."

Her theory that biography should be composed by the actors or spectators of the events recorded is put into practice in the life that follows, which was written not only of a person with whom presumably she was well acquainted —her husband — but was written during his lifetime and published with his approval. The same theory, that biography may best be written by intimate witnesses, produces a further oddity in *The Life & Death of . . . Mr. Joseph Alleine* (1673), which is a joint biography in which at least half a dozen hands may be

discerned, one narrating his early life, another his ministry at Taunton, a third his imprisonment, slow paralysis,
and death. Richard Baxter defends this novel method
in his preface:

" . . . the History is not drawn up by one Hand, nor as by
one that intended rather to shew what he could say, than what
the Person was, and did: But it is the brief Account of the
several parts of his Life, drawn up by several of his most
worthy and judicious Friends, that were present, or most intimate and familiar with him. And I take this to be the best
Advantage to a History, as to the Truth, which should satisfie
the Incredulous, though not as to Uniformity, and a fluid
Stile, which might please the Curious. For a Man's Life is
like a War, or Battle: No dispersed War, no nor any one
particular Battle, can fully be described by the Observations
of any one man alone; But one Man is but in one place, and
seeth only that which is within his own Prospect, which his
proper Station did advantage him to see: But when Intelli-
gent Men from each part of the Army do every one bring in
their several Narratives, all set together, may be a satisfactory History of the whole War, or Fight: So when a Man's
course of Life is transient, and one is his Familiar in his
Youth, and another at riper Age: One in the University, and
another in the Ministry; one in Prison, and another at Home;
one in Health, and another in Death; it is no one of himself
that can creditably report the whole."

This preface of Baxter's marks the first expressed
realization of one of the difficulties of the biographical
art: that it is well nigh impossible for one man to write
from direct knowledge all the major passages in his
hero's life.

Such theories of the sphere of biography had by the
time of the Restoration become current property. David
Lloyd in his "Memoires of the Lives of Those . . . That
Suffered . . . In our late Intestine Wars" (1668) quotes

in his preface Bacon's division directly and in full, and
the popularity of his Royalist collection gave even wider
currency to the doctrine.

Dryden [32] accepts Bacon's three-fold division, modi-
fies and clarifies it:

"History is principally divided into these three species:
Commentaries or Annals; History proper so called; and
Biographia, or the lives of particular men. . . .

"*Biographia*, or the history of particular men's lives, comes
next to be considered; which in dignity is inferior to the other
two, as being more confined in action, and treating of wars
and counsels, and all other publick affairs of nations, only as
they relate to him whose life is written, or as his fortunes have
a particular dependance on them, or connection to them: all
things here are circumscribed, and driven to a point, so as to
terminate in one. . . ."

His description of the effect of a good biography upon
the reader is enthusiastic and far more imaginative than
the conceptions of his predecessors. In history, he says,

"you are conducted only into the rooms of state; here you
are led into the private lodgings of the hero: you see him in
his undress, and are made familiar with his most private actions and conversations. You may behold a Scipio and a
Lelius gathering cockle-shells on the shore; Augustus playing
at bounding-stones with boys; and Agesilaus riding on a
hobby-horse among his children. The pageantry of life is
taken away; you see the poor reasonable animal, as naked as
ever nature made him; are made acquainted with his passions
and his follies, and find the Demi-God a Man."

It will be noted that Dryden approaches very nearly to
the modern conception of biography. The ethical note
is not unduly emphasized; the religious note is absent.
"In all parts of biography," he says, "whether familiar

32. 1683, *Life of Plutarch*, quoted from 1758 ed., p. xlv.

or stately, whether sublime or low, whether serious or
merry, Plutarch equally excelled," and it is the example
of the great classical biographer which dominates Dryden's thought and shapes his conception of ideal biography.

That biography by Dryden's time had gained an
acknowledged place as a separate form of expression is
best shown by a chance paragraph in Joseph Glanville's
Prefatory Answer to Mr. Henry Stubbe (1671).

"If any man hath a design to write his [Stubbe's] Life,"
he says, "and further to describe this Sir Hudibras and
his Steed; He will do well to hold his hand a while, For M.
Stubbe's Friend M. Cross hath writ a Book call'd *Biographia*,
which gives Rules, how Lives are to be writ; This will be
printed, if the Licensers will permit the good man to spoil so
much paper, and so make himself publickly ridiculous. . . .
This Book, it seems, is intended to correct the Learned and
pious Dr. Fell, for his way of writing the Life of Dr. Hammond, and 'tis M. C. revenge upon that excellent person, for
his denying Licence to the scurrilous and non-sensical Book
he writ against me."

Unfortunately, of Mr. Crosse's interesting and indignant monograph, *Biographia*, nothing remains but the
title. The polished school of Dr. Fell evidently continued to exercise its dignified influence over the licens-
ing of ill-mannered and controversial tracts.

Something should here be said of the polite school of
biography. In some ways it is allied with ecclesiastical
biography and springs from the exemplary lives of the
clerics. Yet it became secularized, and dominated the
theory of biography to such an extent that Carlyle in
the nineteenth century may still cry out in rabid wrath:
"How delicate, how decent is English biography, bless
its mealy mouth!"

The tendency among biographers to see, hear, and speak no evil begins innocently enough. Thomas Fuller parries an imagined criticism of his method in *The Worthies of England* with this defence: [33]

"Exception 4. You only report the Vertues, but conceal the Faults of many persons within our own memories.

"Answer. I conceive myself bound so to do, by the Rules of Charity. When an Orator was to praise a person deceased, generally and justly hated for his Viciousnesse, it was suspected that he would for his Fee, force his conscience by flattery to commend him, whose expectations he thus defeated, This dead person (saith he) must in one respect be spoken well of by all, because God made him; and in another respect, should not be spoken ill of by any because he is dead; & *de mortuis nil nisi bonum.* How much more, when men have many good Virtues, with some Faults, ought the latter to be buried in their Graves with forgetfulnesse."

Burnet in his *Life of Rochester*,[34] though he designed it as a moral tract, says: "It is their [Sinners'] Reformation, and not their Disgrace, I desire: This tender consideration of others has made me suppress many remarkable and useful things he told me."

The suppression of faults can easily lead to the suppression of peculiarities, of all characteristics which might be interpreted as detracting from the dignity of the person portrayed. Of the false or exaggerated conception of the biographer as a trustee of his hero's immaculacy, Thomas Sprat is the first apostle. He commends the lives of the humble rather than the annals of the titulary honourable. Yet he does so because they furnish more applicable models for virtuous lives.[35]

33. 1662, chap. 24, p. 73.
34. 1680, p. 27.
35. Sprat's *Life of Cowley*, 1668, p. e 2ᵛº.

"This, Sir, is the account that I thought fit to present the World concerning him. Perhaps it may be judged, that I have spent too many words on a private man, and a Scholar; whose life was not remarkable for such a variety of events, as are wont to be the Ornaments of this kind of Relations. I know it is the custom of the World to prefer the pompous Histories of great Men, before the greatest Virtues of others, whose lives have been led in a course less illustrious. This indeed is the general humour. But I believe it to be an errour in mens judgments. For certainly that is a more profitable instruction; which may be taken from the eminent goodness of men of lower rank, than that which we learn from the splendid representations of the Battels, and Victories, and Buildings, and Sayings of great Commanders and Princes. Such specious matters, as they are seldom delivered with fidelity, so they serve but for the imitation of a very few, and rather make for the ostentation than the true information of humane life. Whereas it is from the practise of men equal to our selves, that we are more naturally taught how to command our Passions, to direct our Knowledge, and to govern our Actions."

This high goal necessitates the exclusion of everything that is not worthy of imitation. The Abraham Cowley depicted by Sprat cannot be identified with the sparkling and confiding personality which appears in the poems and essays. The trivial and the amusing, the errors and failings of the poet, the personal letters, the accidental and the graphic touches, are omitted, since they would not help us to command our passions or govern our actions. This study of eminent virtue includes only typical, not individual, traits, for they alone are to be emulated.

Samuel Clark [36] likewise views his dead heroes as models of supreme goodness:

36. *Lives of Ten Eminent Divines*, 1662, p. A3.

"We must eye them, not to observe their weaknesses, to discover their shame, for this is a poysonous disposition; neither may we observe them thereby to take liberty to the flesh, from what is amiss in them; but we must eye them, as we look into Glasses, to dress, and adorn ourselves thereby.

"We must eye them for imitation: We must look upon the best, and the best in the best."

This cult of perfection in biography seems to appeal peculiarly to churchmen. Bishop Hacket's *Memorial Offer'd to . . . John Williams* (written 1657) is presented "as a Banner at the Shrine of this Renowned Prelate's Memory." Bishop Fell's *Henry Hammond* (1661) is no less pretentious, and it is one of the merits of the distinguished author that he succeeds in attaining dignity without pompousness, and fidelity without the descent to picturesque or intimate descriptions. But the writings of Bishop Burnet best express the theory of formal biography which was in the ascendant during the latter half of the seventeenth century. His hostility to trivial anecdotes and the intrusion of private life into biography is shown in his *Life of Matthew Hale*,[37] where he speaks of certain biographers

"writing lives too jejunely, swelling them up with trifling accounts of the childhood and education, and the domestic or private affairs of those persons of whom they write, in which the world is little concerned: by these they become so flat, that few care to read them, for certainly those transactions are only fit to be delivered to posterity, that may carry with them some useful piece of knowledge to after-times."

He expresses this antipathy to intimate details elsewhere, in *The Lives of James and William Dukes of Hamilton and Castleherald* (written 1673):

37. 1682, p. viii.

"For the Lives of Great Persons, though it might have been expected that after the many excellent Patterns Plutarch had left the World, those should have been generally well written; yet there is no sort of History worse done, they being so full of gross Partiality and Flattery, and often swelled with trifling and impertinent things, so that it is no great wonder if this kind of Writings be much decried and neglected."

His favorite historians and biographers — de Commines, Guicciardine, de Thou, Davila — are noteworthy for their thoroughness and detail. It is therefore natural that he should commend the amplitude and documentation which signalize the biographies of his own time. The brief, unsatisfactory narratives of earlier historians, he says, "have in this last Age made people desire to see Papers, Records, and Letters published at their full length."

Burnet's devotion to the truth and the whole truth, which leads him to commend completeness in presentation and the inclusion of all evidence, also causes him to denounce conscious art and panegyric in life-writing. "Too much Art," he says, "does but disgrace it." And again, in his life of Rochester (Preface):

"The Celebrating the Praises of the Dead, is an Argument so worn out by long and frequent use; and now become so nauseous, by the flattery that usually attends it, that it is no wonder if Funeral Orations, or Panegiricks, are more considered for the Elegancy of Style, and Fineness of Wit, than for the Authority they carry with them as to the truth of matters of Fact."

Or in his life of Bedell (1685): "In writing of Lives all big Words are to be left to those who dress up Legends, and *Make* Lives rather than Write them."

Matter and not manner — matter that does not stoop to domestic and private concerns, matter pre-

sented with dignity, and fullness, and impartiality, —
shall constitute, according to the school of the late
seventeenth century, ideal biography.

To this point some attempt has been made to define
biography by comparisons with allied branches of literature and by considering the conceptions and theories
held by the writers of the period. The scope and purpose
of English biography before 1700 may be further
limited by an analysis of some of the salient characteristics that distinguish the early lives.

Some notion of prevalent conceptions of biography
may be derived from considering how the writers of
lives used their raw materials. The possible forms which
biographical elements may assume are numerous — entries in local registers, official communications, private
letters and published works, diaries, private notebooks
and written meditations, direct and indirect evidence
both written and spoken, records of conversations, extant memorials.

The relations between diaries and biography is much
the same as that between chronicles and history. The
diary makes no attempt to see life steadily and see it
whole. It is focussed on the immediate present, and
finds that the happenings of twenty-four hours are sufficient unto the day. It becomes, therefore, not the record
of a life but the journal of an existence, made up of a
monotonous series of short and similar entries. Furthermore, in a study of biography as a literary form, the
diary has scant claim to consideration, for it makes no
pretence to artistic structure. The diary should therefore be considered as the raw material which may be
re-shaped to form a life. In itself, it is lacking in per-

spective and proportion, and preserves its unity only through a time sequence. Even the diary of Samuel Pepys cannot be considered as a biography. It is without beginning and without conclusions, and in spite of its vivacity and individuality remains a huge and entertaining fragment in social history. The difference in breadth of outlook and in literary finish may best be studied in those instances where a biography and a diary co-exist for the same person, or where a diary shows distinct influence upon an ensuing biography. This last relation is illustrated in Sir Simonds D'Ewes' autobiography (written 1648–50), which was rewritten from a journal in cipher, and transcribed with such slight changes as to circumscribe its outlook and render it a chronicle of trivial outward events. At times D'Ewes becomes as detailed about his health, his movements, and the books he has read as does Pepys.

The rival forms may be compared in Archbishop Laud's *History of his Troubles and Trial* (1695) "to which is prefixed the Diary of his own Life"; in *The Autobiography of Henry Newcome* (1627–95) and his diary; or in Anthony Walker's biography of Mary, Countess of Warwick (1678), her own autobiography, and her diary. In all of these instances the diary possesses the slightest claims to literary merits; where the journal form has influenced an autobiography, it has detracted from unity and clarity in presentation. Yet properly used by the biographer, the diary affords pleasing variety and a direct approach to his subject. To cite several instances, much of the quaintness and vividness in William Hinde's story of John Bruen comes from judicious extracts from that eminent squire's diaries and memoranda. John Evelyn's most poignant touches in the *Life of Margaret Godolphin* are achieved by including entries from her private journal. Staunton's *Mistress Elizabeth Wilkinson* (1659) and Mayo's life of Edmund Staunton (1673) are largely made up of extracts from private diaries. The diary proper, however, remains a raw product and does not in itself constitute biography.

Personal letters have even less claim than the diary to be considered as biography. Dorothy Osborne's letters to Sir William Temple, for example, in spite of their tenderness and intimacy, can be considered only as raw materials for life-writing and not as biography in themselves. And although the preface to *Epistolae Ho-Elianae* [38] claims that "Among these Letters ther goes along a Legend of the Authors life, and of his several employments, with an account of his Forren Travells and Negotiations," nevertheless all such statements must give way to the consideration that the purpose of a letter is not the purpose of a conscious biography. The biographical value of any correspondence is accidental rather than deliberate.

Letters often accurately reflect the subject's character and mirror his inmost thoughts. Judiciously chosen, important letters may be used to illustrate the development of the hero's beliefs; they may show important decisions of policy, and may constitute the landmarks that divide his career into periods. Their value in biography has been recognized from an early date. Eddius, to mention one example at the beginning of the eighth century, includes the letters and addresses of his master Wilfred, and Papal manifestos in reply, as integral parts of his biography. The practice was carried over from the Latin to English. So Stapleton's

38. James Howell, 1655, vol. i.

Latin lives (1588) of Becket and More contain selected letters, which are used to similar purpose in Cresacre More's biography of his great-grandfather and in the anonymous *Life of St. Thomas à Becket* (1639), both in English. George Paule's *John Whitgift* (1612) faithfully and freely quotes the archbishop's letters, with dates and references in the margin. George Carleton's *Bernard Gilpin* (1629), first published in Latin, includes a long letter from Gilpin to his brother George, setting forth his "conversion from the Romane superstition to the light of the Gospell," as well as other letters wisely selected. Richardson's use of letters in *Pamela* to tell an imaginary story has predecessors in the field of biography. So John Duncon in his *Holy Life of the Lady Letice, Vi-Countess Falkland* (1647) narrates her spiritual development through sufferings and trials to a final constant faith, entirely by means of letters addressed to him in his capacity as chaplain.

Izaak Walton's *Lives* show an appreciation of the value of personal letters and a discriminating taste in those which are included. The voluminous school at the end of the century is not sparing in its use of correspondence. Bishop Burnet provides at the beginning of his *Life of William Bedell* (1685) an index for the fifteen letters and sermons which he scatters through the biography, and adds at the conclusion an appendix of miscellaneous Latin papers. Richard Parr includes three hundred of Archbishop Usher's letters as an addition to his life (1686). Richard Baxter's *Narrative of The most Memorable Passages of his Life and Times* is copious in detail, and well documented with his letters, memoranda which he has drawn up, and official communications of various sorts. But the biographers of the late

seventeenth century also made use of less formal documents. John Evelyn includes many of Margaret Godolphin's letters and meditations, which are singularly subjective, nor does he hesitate to set forth her last letter to
her husband written in the tenderest and most intimate
spirit. Similarly Anthony Walker in his loving tribute
to his wife Elizabeth (1690) follows his biography with
selections from her meditations and reveries, and transcribes a letter written to her grandson, which is Polonius
turned grandmother (p. 146):

Dear Johnny, do nothing that looks despicably, childish,
foolish, — twiddling with thy fingers, picking thy buttons,
going with thy hands in thy pockets, or the like, — I pray thee
do none of these unbecoming actions. I love to see thee gen-
teel; keep thy hands and clothes clean."

Against the publication of such letters, written from
the heart and never designed for a general audience,
Thomas Sprat had fulminated in his *Life of Cowley*.
He mentions and praises "one kind of Prose wherein
Mr. Cowley was excellent; and that is his Letters to his
private Friends. In these he always express'd the Native tenderness, and Innocent gayety of his mind. I
think, Sir, you and I have the greatest Collection of this
sort."

"But," he continues, "I know you agree with me, that
nothing of this Nature should be publish'd. . . . The truth is,
the Letters that pass between particular Friends, if they are
written as they ought to be, can scarce ever be fit to see the
light. . . . They may be fit to be seen by one or two in a
Chamber, but not to go abroad into the Streets."

Yet in spite of Sprat's ultra-conservative doctrines
which retarded the development of frank life-writing,
letters continued to be used in their legitimate bio-

graphical function, as authoritative illustrations of the hero's thoughts, and illuminating examples of his intercourse among men.[39]

As a guide to personality, conversations are almost as important as the records left in correspondence. Chance remarks, epigrams and characteristic utterances are, however, ephemeral, and to seize the noteworthy while rejecting the trivial, to reproduce faithfully the spirit and the form of a verbal soliloquy or dialogue, requires the highest biographical skill. A man's conversation may represent the essence of his life and the closest approximation to the texture of his mind. But it is as fleet as the wind, and disappears in a breath. The biographer who can capture it is fortunate. Boswell is usually regarded as the first detailed reporter of his hero's conversation, but this is far from the truth. Eadmer in the twelfth century gives the definite title to his life of Anselm, *De vita et conversatione*, to distinguish the Archbishop's private life from the public career which he sets forth in the *Historia Novorum in Anglia*. Not only do his volumes include Anselm's life, "adeo quicquam in se contineat quod ad privatam conversationem, vel ad morum ipsius Anselmi qualitatem . . . pertinere videatur." Similarly, Adam of Eynsham in the thirteenth century, assiduous and hawk-eyed chronicler of Bishop Hugh of Lincoln, records, he says, only what "aut propriis vidi oculis, aut a sanctis ipsius labiis audivi." The life is concerned with the narration "praecipua gestorum

39. Isolated letters occur in a number of lives; for a more general use of correspondence to supplement and make clear biographical narrations, the reader is referred to Stranguage's *Mary Queen of Scots*, 1624; to the *Life of Philip Howard* (p. 1630), to Hacket's *Scrinia Reserata* (wr. 1657), to Clogie's *William Bedell* (p. 1642), and to James Janeway's life of his brother John (1673).

ejus *atque verborum*"; it is composed "ex ejusdem actibus *et memorabilibus dictis*." Again, much of the vividness of Roper's *Life of Sir Thomas More* arises from the
simplicity and directness of the conversations reproduced between the Lord Chancellor and "Son Roper."
Conversations may be introduced to give a sharply-cut
reality to a narrative, as do Robert Cary's interviews
with Queen Elizabeth, or Walton's rainy day colloquy
with Bishop Sanderson over a tavern fire, or Bernard
Gilpin's confutation of two chaplains defending transubstantiation, again before a fire in the winter season,
or the confidential interview between John Williams,
Lord Keeper of the Great Seal, and Charles I, immediately after the death of James.[40] These faithful and
meticulous records of conversations show a general appreciation among English writers of the direct sources
for biography. "We are indeed uncapable," says the
author of *The Holy Life of Monsieur De Renty* (1658),
"of knowing any thing of a mans interiour, but by his
own declaration; and that which we understand in
Saints of this nature . . . comes by no other way than
their discovering and opening it to some one, and he
afterwards to the publike." In England, biographers
show themselves able and willing to follow this direct
and logical method of procedure.

These exact records fortunately replaced the tendency
of older historians to put appropriate but highly imaginative sentiments in the mouths of their heroes. The
sententious and rhetorical speeches of Robert Redman's *Henry V* and André's *Henry VII* are hardly less
fanciful than Shakespeare's address of Henry V before
Agincourt, or Antony's oration over Caesar. The fu-

40. Hackett's *Scrinia Reserata.*

neral elegy of Edward I by John of London [41] is followed
by a group of supposed speeches by the Pope, Queen
Margaret, and various kings, bishops, barons, soldiers,
clerics, and laymen. It is evident in such examples that
eloquence rather than truth is being pursued. The creation of such fictitious utterance had, however, distinguished precedents in Greek and Latin history and was
accepted as legitimate. An historian as conscientious as
John Hayward will even raise the question, in speaking
of the proper style of a history, "what liberty a writer
may use in framing speeches."

English biography, therefore, improves definitely upon
the practice of the classic historians in its truthful representation of conversations. These exact records are
not the result of one man's efforts and example, but
of a wide number of biographers. Furthermore, it became current practice to include a separate chapter of
weighty or witty utterance. Stapleton's *More* (1588) includes his *Apophthegmata* and *Dicta;* Rawley's *Bacon*
(1657) will describe his dinner-table conversation; the
Life of Lord Burghley (ca. 1600) presents three pages of
his garnered sayings; and the *Life of William Cavendish*
(1667) closes with "several Essays and Discourses
Gather'd from the Mouth of My noble Lord and Husband."

Perhaps the most skilful use of dialogue, during the
seventeenth century, for the purpose of tracing mental
development, is that employed by Gilbert Burnet in his
Life of Rochester (1680), which reproduces in dramatic
detail the long series of conversations between the Anglican Bishop and the dissipated and dying courtier,
leading to Rochester's conversion.

41. *Edward I*, 1883, vol. ii, Rolls Series.

The examples which have been cited tend to show a growing suppleness and diversity in the use of the material from which finished biographies are fashioned. The dependence upon diaries and memoirs, the quotation of letters and conversations, illustrate attempts to understand the subject of a life by an appeal to first authorities. These essays may be partly unconscious; they may be fitful and occasional; but the slow trend toward subjective life-writing is unmistakable.

In discussing subjective biography, a line should be drawn between the legitimate use of original sources, and the more questionable imaginative reconstruction of a life. The saints' lives, told as chronicles of action, were forced to narrate mental conflicts as battles between the saint and hordes of devils. Demons are minutely described in Felix's *Life of Guthlac*; and Dunstan breaks his staff over the devil, who appears to him in the form of a bear.[42] In the Middle Ages, psychological struggles were presented graphically, and sin and exaltation, as well as all mental states, were expressed in concrete images. This symbolical use could not survive in ages when the symbols had become less appealing, and imaginative biography consequently assumed other forms.

John Lydgate in *The Fall of Princes* introduced the heroes as apparitions narrating their lives in the first person. This convention as continued into the seventeenth century by the *Mirror for Magistrates* was invaluable in developing the bold use of the biographical imagination and in compelling biographers to enter into the thoughts of their heroes.

42. For pictorial representations, the sixteen twelfth-century vignettes of such combats included in Birch's *Memorials of St. Guthlac*, 1881, are striking.

Occasional pieces succeed to an astonishing degree in analyzing the inner recesses. Catherine Gascoign's *Life of the Venerable Father Augustin Baker* [43] abounds in conversions, meditations, contemplations, doubts and reconversions subtly distinguished:

"But at the end of that time . . . his Recollections, which had bin formerly profound, became much Distracted, & his heart Cold, Dry & void of all good Affections.

"Upon this change he endeavoured to stir up Devotion, by all the waies & means, he could; seeking out the most moving Books, & pictures, he could hear of; but all in vain. No working of the imagination or Understanding, could any longer produce any Effect upon the Will. Hereby it came to passe, that his Recollections were now so full of Aridities & Distractions, & became so Burthensome to him, that he had not the courage or patience to continue them, but giving over Mentall prayer, he contented himself with his Vocall prayers, & exterior Observances."

The best-known attempt at such capturing of another's personality and thoughts is the *Eikon Basilike* already noticed, which is presented as the autobiography of Charles I, and is told throughout in the first person in order to gain greater freedom and vividness. George Sikes' *Life of Sir Henry Vane* (1662) also throws aside external events and avowedly sketches only the inner life of its hero in an unworthy world (p. 92):

"His Life was not like other mens, nor his Ministry. His wayes were of another fashion, as they reason (Wisd. 2.15) therefore have I writ his Life after another fashion than mens Lives use to be written, treating mostly of the principles and course of his hidden life amongst the sons of God."

The best example of the contrast between the realistic and the imaginative approach to subjective biography

43. 1641, MS. Bodl. Wood⸱B4.

occurs in Walton's *Life of Sanderson*, which illustrates both methods. The graphic last conversation between Izaak and the Bishop has already been mentioned as a predecessor of the Boswellian method of exactitude. Yet elsewhere Walton presents the tenets of the Anglican Church and his own religious conclusions as the opinions of Sanderson. He does so without apology, for, he says, "I desire to tell the Reader, that in this Relation I have been so bold, as to paraphrase and say what I think he (whom I had the happiness to know well) would have said upon the same occasions." Under Walton's pen all the raw materials — letters, conversations, journals — from which biography may be made, are transmuted into those artistic and individual compositions which are unmistakably his own.

Three factors which helped to determine the form of seventeenth-century biography remain to be considered: the influence of lives designed as prefaces to other published pieces, the influence of the character sketch, and the influence of the funeral sermon.

The custom of writing the life of an author to serve as an introduction to his works first becomes common in the seventeenth century. Perfunctory lives had appeared in isolated instances in the century preceding, such as the life of Aesop before his fables (1560); and the form was known to exist, since in Beza's *Life of Calvin*, published separately in English translation in 1564, the printer informs the reader that "the purpose of the Auctor . . . was not to publishe it as an Hystorie, but onely for a Preface to the Commentaries of the saide Calvin uppon the Booke of Iosue."

The first prefatory lives in English, however, were originally not written for this especial purpose but were drawn from other sources. So Foxe published *The Whole workes of W. Tyndall, John Frith, and Doct. Barnes* in 1573, with three prefatory lives "out of the booke of Actes and Monumentes Briefly Extracted." Camden's *Historia Anglica a veteribus scripta* (1603) includes short lives of the historians therein printed taken "ex Centuriis Ioannis Balaei & aliis." The *Historia Anglicana Ecclesiastica* of Nicholas Harpsfield (1622) is introduced by a short life drawn from John Pits.

One characteristic of prefatory lives is that they are written about men of some literary pretensions, an inevitable corollary from the fact that they precede published works. During the seventeenth century, however, these lives were principally concerned with churchmen. In the biographies of figures considered solely as literary artists, a period of sixty years yawns between Speght's *Chaucer* in 1598 and Davies' *Hall* (1656) or Sprat's *Cowley* (1668). These prefatory lives were intended to perform for their subjects the service which earlier biographers — Bede, for example, or Lydgate — had performed for themselves. They were, in other words, to give some conception of the author of the work in a more formal and detailed fashion than the scanty self-notices of previous writers or the short skeleton lives taken from the antiquarian collections. The title of Peter Smith's life of Willet, a study which occupies twenty-four folio pages, shows the general relation of these lives to the works that follow: *Synopsis Papismi . . . with addition of a Preface truly relating the life and death of . . . Doctor Andrew Willet, the Author* (1634).

The prefatory lives tended to increase in importance and acquire independence. This is best illustrated in the study of Izaak Walton, who prepared his *Donne*, *Wotton*, and *Sanderson* as prefaces to the writings of his heroes. His *Donne* was published separately in a second edition. His *Hooker* appeared at first separately, and a year later was used as a preface to his works; it was written to correct a life by Bishop Gauden prefixed to Hooker's collected works; Walton's *Herbert* was issued as an individual piece, and in the same year (1670) appeared a collection of the four lives Walton had to that time composed, a form in which they attained popularity and passed through successive editions. The demand for lives to serve as prefaces caused Walton to write; but the biographies, once written, assumed an independence of their own, and ceased to be prefaces. What is true of Walton's lives is true of seventeenth-century biography in general. Curiosity concerning the authors of popular books, the Renaissance interest in personality as applied to English literature, gave an unprecedented impetus to the production of biography, so that an anonymous writer by the year 1672 can refer to the general "Custom to write the Lives of Authors eminent for their Learning, and to annex them to their Works." [44] These prefatory lives influenced the development of life-writing in general, and included in their number many of the best biographies of the century. They were reprinted in group collections during the decades following the Restoration by such men as Thomas Fuller, Clement Barksdale, and Samuel Clark. In this class will be found such distinctive productions as Harris's *Arthur Lake* (1629), Langbaine's *John Cheke*

44. "Life of Joseph Mede," before his *Works*, 1672.

(1641), Vaughan's *Thomas Jackson* (1653), Rawley's *Francis Bacon* (1657), Fuller's *Henry Smith* (1658), the *Life of Joseph Mede* (1672), Plume's *John Hacket* (1672), Dryden's *Plutarch* (1683), or Fell's *Allestree* (1684). The custom of writing prefatory lives had become so widespread that Abraham Hill in the "Life of Isaac Barrow" prefixed to his *Works* [45] stated, "The affection of Friends, or interest of the Bookseller has made it usual to prefix the life of an Authour before his works."

The influence of these prefatory lives was in the main salutary. Their nature compelled them to be succinct and thus limited them to pure biography.[46] Largely because of the tradition thus established, Bishop Burnet could write in his *Life of Matthew Hale* (1682): "No part of history is more instructive and delighting, than the lives of great and worthy men: the shortness of them invites many readers." These commendable arts of brevity and concentration seem at the present day in danger of disappearing.

Again, the demand for prefatory notices stimulated the production of biographies, developed a familiarity with the biographical form, and established a school of life-writing which supplied the necessary background of warning and inspiring examples to the outstanding biographers of the period.

Last, prefatory lives introduced a new attitude into biography. By their very nature, they were written to interpret to the reader the author of the subsequent work. They were apologies and introductions. In brief

45. 1687, 2d ed.   Written 1683.
46. That prefatory lives actually caused the shortening of biography may be seen in Laurence Humfrey's *Vita & mors Ioannis Iuelli* (1573), whose 269 pages are translated and abridged by Daniel Featley to serve as an introduction to Jewel's works (1609).

space, they were designed to present comprehensively and favorably their subject, and if possible to show his connection with his writings. This purpose, which was tacitly or unconsciously assumed by many writers, is most clearly set forth by Bishop Fell in his "Life of Richard Allestree" prefixed to his friend's *Sermons* (1684):

"In all endeavours of persuasion, the credit of the Speaker being of as great moment as the inherent truth and evidence of what is spoke, it will be reasonable that there should go along with this large collection of Sermons, some account of the Person who was the Author of them; for if it be made out, that they came from one of integrity and knowledge, who neither would deceive others, nor was likely to be deceiv'd himself; one who practic'd what he taught, and preacht to his own soul what he deliver'd to his Auditory, his discourses must carry with them a proportionable weight and value."

Prefatory lives, therefore, served a double purpose: as sympathetic interpretations, and as introductions to authors who had chosen to speak of matters more important than themselves.

The seventeenth century witnessed a heightened interest in personalities. The same curiosity and social instinct which led to the increase of biography also caused the growth of the character sketch. Its relation to biography is close. Yet the two are distinct forms, and the difference between them is not difficult to grasp. Biography essentially is a narrative; the character sketch a portrait. The first is dynamic and progressive; the second static and final. Two types of characters are usually distinguished.[47] One is the Theophrastian or

47. Cf. D. Nichol Smith, *Characters from the Histories and Memoirs of the Seventeenth Century*. Oxford, 1918. Cf., also, Thomas Fuller's *The Holy State* and *The Profane State*, 1642, which include both types.

generic sketch, such as Nicholas Breton's *The Good and the Bad*, Earle's *Microcosmographie*, or the works of Hall, Overbury, and Samuel Butler. This class of characters may be dismissed, since in its retrogression from observed particulars to a generalized type, it represents the antithesis of the biographical impulse. The Theophrastian character readily lends itself to minute observation and mordant satire, as in Earle's "Character of a Grave Divine" or Butler's cruel analysis of an antiquary. On rare occasions biography itself assumed this generalized tone. Bunyan's *Life and Death of Mr. Bad Man* is merely the biographical form of such a character sketch as Breton's "An Atheist, or Most Bad Man." [48]

The other class of character sketch includes the portraits of definite individuals. It embraces such separate pieces as Gabriel Harvey's character of Dr. Perne,[49] Bacon's acute observations on Queen Elizabeth, or the character of King Charles the Second by George Savile, Marquis of Halifax. It includes also such groups of portraits as may be found in Naunton's *Fragmenta Regalia*, in Clarendon's *History of the Rebellion* and *Autobiography*, in Walton's *Lives* or in Burnet's *History of His Own Time*. None of these merits consideration as biography, since the description of a man's character and person cannot be identified with his life. Biography is made up of events, not qualities; the character sketch is composed of immovable traits in a timeless world.

This distinction was not at all times clear during the seventeenth century. So Edmund Vaughan writes the

48. It is interesting to note that in *Grace Abounding to the Chief of Sinners* Bunyan writes an autobiography; in *The Life and Death of Mr. Bad Man* a generalized biography which still retains realism; while in *Pilgrim's Progress* he again writes a generalized biography which reverts to the device of the hagiologists and represents spiritual progress by means of external drama.
49. *Pierces Supererogation*, 1593.

"Life" of Thomas Jackson (1653), yet calls it elsewhere a "Character" and speaks of the biographer's obligation to "draw a face to the Life." One reason for this failure to differentiate character-writing from biography lies in the close alliance of the forms in certain early works. The two letters by Erasmus describing his friends Colet and More very nearly approach biographies in the fullness and accuracy of their detail; yet he himself calls them portraits, and although in the description of personalities they are admirable, they are without incident and all elements of chronology. Or again, such an extended work as *The Life of William Cecil, Lord Burghley* (ca. 1600) is in reality little more than a character sketch, since the chronological actions and events are few, and every page is taken up with illustrative examples of Burghley's qualities.

This confusion of biography and character leads to an even more serious defect in seventeenth-century life-writing. It became conventional to write a life in two sections: a bare chronicle of events in which the hero figures only as a name, and a subsequent character sketch in which his particular virtues and qualities are formally enumerated. Such a method was convenient for the biographer, and its extreme simplicity commended it to writers lacking in biographical skill. Even Bacon divides his *History of Henry VII* into two sections, the first an account of his reign, the second an analysis of his character. [50] Habington adopts the same method in his *Edward IV* (1640) which concludes with a short parallel with Louis XI and a character sketch. Division of labor is carried further in Lord Herbert of Cherbury's *Life and Raigne of King Henry VIII* (1649).

50. 1622: history, 1–232; character, 233–248.

Herbert's work is purely political, but is preceded by "An Analyticall Character or Dissection of Henry the Eighth" by James Howell. The prevalence of this method in royal biography may be deduced from Thomas May's *Reigne of King Henry the Second* (1633), where the seven books of rhymed couplets are followed by a prose "Description of King Henry the Second" which begins: "It has beene a custome of old Historians, when they record the actions of great Princes, to deliver also some Characters of their persons and peculiar dispositions; that the curiositie of succeeding times, who pry deepely into those men, whose lives were of so great moment in the world, might bee fully satisfied and delighted." Anthony Stafford follows the same procedure, which he thus states in his preface to *The Life of Henry Lord Stafford* (1640, p. 6):

"The common method in handling matters of this nature commands me to make the first part of this Discourse the place of his Birth, the Nobilitie of his Race, and Disposition, and to continue and close it up with the Vertues practised in his Life, and the Sanctity expressed in his Death."

The Life of Dr. Thomas Morton (written 1657) furnishes an interesting example of this duality in life-writing. It is divided into two sections, the first a bald narration of facts by Richard Baddily, the second a character sketch by Joseph Naylor.

Richard Mayo defends the character sketch when, after narrating the life of Edmund Staunton (1673) he sets out "methodically and orderly in the close of all, to set down the inimitable graces and practises of this worthy person; it may be the reader will better heed and remember them, then if they had been confusedly scattered up and down the preceding Narrative." Yet ordinarily, the division of a life into chronicles and portrait destroys its unity. Adding a character sketch to a history does not produce a biography; and if the aim of biography is to mirror faithfully a life, then that life should be reproduced in the unity in which it was lived, and not broken up into the two incompatible fragments of an impersonal chronicle and a static character.

Seventeenth-century biography as a whole is marked by this unfortunate convention, which indicates failure to fuse available data into a homogeneous work. The distinguished writers — Carleton in his *Bernard Gilpin*, Walton in all of his productions, and notably the principal autobiographers — carry on the earlier tradition of More, Cavendish, and Roper, and develop character, not by formal separate analysis, but by those incidents and events through which alone personality is made manifest.

One form of commemorating the dead prevalent in the seventeenth century — the printed funeral sermon — markedly influences the development of biography. The form has its beginnings in the sixteenth century, and Oxford and Cambridge, with the publication of addresses by the university orators in memory of their famous sons, took prominent parts in its establishment. Shortly after Ascham's death (1568) appeared the "de vita & obitu Rogeri Aschami ac eius scriptionis laudibus . . . ad adolescentulos latinae linguae studiosos Ed. Grantae oratio." A later biographer of Ascham justly says of its author: [51] "Graunt either avoided the labour of minute inquiry, or thought domestick occurrences unworthy of his notice; or preferring the character of an

51. James Bennet, *Life of Ascham*, 1761.

orator to that of an historian, selected only such particulars as he could best express, or most happily em-
bellish. His narrative is therefore scanty." The criticism would apply equally to such representative funeral
orations as those by John Hales for Sir Thomas
Bodley (1613), by Thomas Goffe for Sir Henry Savile
(1622) and by Degory Wheare for William Camden the
antiquary (1623).

Closely allied in spirit with the published funeral sermon, and preceding it in point of time, are the collections of commemorative elegies and epitaphs.[52] An example of unusually early date is Thomas Wilson's
"Vita et obitus duorum fratrum Suffolciensium, Henrici et Caroli Brandoni prestanti virtute, et splendore
nobilitatis ducum illustrissimorum" (1559). In form
this is a lament and a eulogy, and is followed by numerous *epigrammata*, the voluntary or solicited contributions of the most learned Oxonians "ut nomen Brandonorum tam memorabile in immensum propagaretur."
In particular, the poems of George Whetstone, written
between 1577 and 1587, furnish notable examples of
elegiac biography. Among literary figures honored by
similar tributes, Sir Philip Sidney and Ben Jonson are
prominent,[53] and the custom of prefacing an author's
published works with the eulogies and encomia of his
friends is well known. Naturally the deaths of English

52. Cf. *Select Funeral Memorials*, ed. Sir Egerton Brydges, 1818, for
examples.
53. Sidney may best be studied in *Sidneiana*, ed. S. Lichfield, 1837, for
Roxburghe Club, vol. liii, which contains William Griffith's "Epitaph on Sir
[Henry] Sidney," "The Life and Death of Sir Phillip Sidney" (1587) by John
Philip, and "Amoris Lachrimae, A most singular and sweete Discourse of the
life and death of Sir Philip Sidney Knight" from Breton's *Bowre of Delights*
(1591). See also Whetstone and Greville. A most interesting collection of
elegies from Ben Jonson's friends and admirers is to be found in "Ionsonus
Virbius or, The Memorie of Ben Johnson" (1638).

monarchs furnished opportunities for many lyrical eulo-
gies. The death of Prince Henry in 1612 may be taken
as an example of such tributes, in James Maxwell's
*Laudable Life, and Deplorable Death, of our late peerlesse
Prince Henry* (1612), George Chapman's *Epicede, or
Funerall Song* (1612), Richard Niccol's *The Three Sisters
Teares* (1613), or the anonymous *Funerals of . . . Prince
Henry* (1613).[54]

A minor variation, the single-sheet broadside published immediately after the death of a celebrated character, is common during the period. An example is
James Heath's rhymed *Elegie upon Dr. Tho. Fuller That
most Incomparable Writer, Who Deceased August the
15th* (1661).

The university oration and the metrical elegy or
epitaph both represent in exaggerated fashion the biographical impulse to furnish fit memorials for the dead.
These poetical or oratorical structures are erected in the
desire to fashion a monument more durable than bronze.
Their purpose is not to present faithfully and completely
the lives of their heroes, but to honor their memories in
dignified and worthy phrase. Throughout this group of
biographical writings, the injunction *De mortuis nil nisi
bonum* rules invariably.

The same spirit is evident in the funeral sermon
proper. Delivered as it was before an audience of
friends and relatives, the need for a formal and detailed
account of the life of the deceased was small, whereas
the necessity for praise and panegyric was ever present.
For this reason, the number of lives written in connection with funeral sermons and yet valuable as independ-

54. Although the type waned in popularity, it continued well into the
seventeenth century, as in Francis Wortley's *Characters and Elegies* (1646),
all of which are generic except those written for the King and Queen.

ent pieces of biography is strictly limited. Ordinarily, such lives were published in the seventeenth century in a conventional form: a formal sermon, usually accompanied by a text and stressing certain Christian virtues or dogma, was followed by a brief *résumé* of the life of the departed. At times this little biography was connected loosely to the preceding discourse by an attempt to show how the general Christian qualities praised in the sermon were exemplified in this particular life.[55]

Although in itself the funeral sermon is of slight importance in the history of biography, its influence upon the development of life-writing was great, and the tradition which it established was accepted so widely, particularly in the field of ecclesiastical biography, that frequently no distinction is drawn between the funeral sermon and pure biography. So, for example, William Bates includes, without any differentiation whatever, four funeral sermons among the lives collected in his *Vitae selectorum aliquot Virorum* (1681). Frequently they served as the bases for later biographies. The four decades forming Clement Barksdale's *Memorials of Worthy Persons* (1661–63) "are scribbled," according to Anthony Wood, "from funeral sermons, lives, and characters." Again, such a heterogeneous work as "The

55. This normal duality — sermon and life published together as a last tribute — may be seen in such works as "A Sermon . . . At the Funeralls of Mrs. Margaret Ducke . . . With A short Relation of her Life and Death" 1646; "Gray Hayres Crowned with Grace [a funeral sermon on Mr. Thomas Gataker by Simeon Ashe] . . . Together with his studious, laborious, religious Life, and patient, comfortable Death" 1653; "A Sermon on Mris Elizabeth Wilkinson . . . Whereunto is added a Narrative of her Godly Life and Death" by Edmund Staunton, 1659; "A Sermon Preached . . . at the Funeral of . . . Dr. Brounrig, With an account of his Life and Death" by John Gauden, 1660; "A Sermon Preached at the Funeral Of the Reverend Mr. Thomas Gouge . . . With a brief account of his Life" by John Tillotson, 1682; and "The Life of . . . Edward Rainbow, D.D. Late Lord Bishop of Carlisle. To which is added, A Sermon Preached at his Funeral by Thomas Tully," 1688.

Honour of Vertue, Or The Monument erected by the sorowfull Husband, and the Epitaphes annexed by learned and worthy men, to the immortall memory of that worthy Gentle-woman Mrs. Elizabeth Crashawe" (1620), composed of sermons, elegies and epitaphs, furnishes possibilities which in more skilful hands might have been made into an authentic biography such as Richard Baxter's life of his wife Margaret.[56] Frequently, too, the funeral sermon is the direct inspiration for a long and fairly adequate life. Nicholas Bernard's *Life & Death of Dr. James Usher* (1656) was begun as a funeral sermon, while John Barwick's pretentious life of Bishop Morton (1660) bears the official title of "Hieronikes, Or The Fight, Victory, and Triumph of S. Paul. Accommodated To . . . Thomas Late L. Bishop of Duresme, in a Sermon Preached at his Funeral."

Such definite connections as have been pointed out above are merely the concrete indications of the widespread influence of the funeral sermon upon seventeenth-century biography. It plays an important part in rendering biography exemplary and pious, and helps to explain how lives could be written avowedly "to convince the World . . . that the Religion of our Saviour Jesus Christ is really practicable"[57] or in order that "the commemoration of the dead may best serve to the edification of the living."[58]

If the prefatory sketch may be said to have aided the development of biography in its tendency to be concise,

56. The connection between the funeral sermon and biography may profitably be traced by comparing the biographies which Richard Baxter sponsored or wrote himself, with his funeral sermons gathered in *Biographical Collections; Or Lives and Characters*, 1766.

57. *Life and Death of Mrs. Margaret Andrews*, 1680.

58. *A Patterne of Pietie. Or The Religious life and death of that Grave and gracious Matron, Mrs. Jane Ratcliffe*, 1640, by John Ley.

personal, and critical, and if the seventeenth-century character may be considered a good influence because it fostered deliberate analysis and a bad influence because it tended to separate portrait from chronicle, the funeral sermon must be estimated as almost wholly a harmful factor. It proposed to set forth examples of the good Christian, whatever might be the cost to the individual. Essentially a funeral sermon furnishes edification and consolation; it is not concerned with exact information and the *minutiae* of personality. The praise of the dead is set above judgment. At the funeral of Dr. Brounrig, Bishop Gauden (1660) speaks of his friend as "a Statue and Coloss of learning, piety and prudence," a "bright star," a "florid and fertile soul," "an Angel for his sanctity." "He is," says Gauden, "as a solid mass of gold, pure, precious, and ponderous." This language is extreme, yet it represents in a form only slightly exaggerated the general tone of the funeral sermon and of that large class of biographies which is derived from it. Although in themselves these commemorative elegies and sermons seem valueless, they cannot be overlooked in a study of biographical tendencies, for their influence was profound and far-reaching. During the whole of the seventeenth century they tended to diminish fidelity in individual portraiture and to transform diverse written lives into so many panegyrics of the typical Christian hero. As a result, the development of biographies as personal records was inevitably retarded.

Various characteristics of early English biography have been necessarily suggested in tracing its relation to other literary forms, in outlining the theories that governed the writing of lives, and in considering the influence of such modifying factors as the biographical preface, the character sketch, and the funeral sermon. Furthermore, the historical chapters have shown changes in the fashions of biography. The homiletic fervor of eighth-century saints' lives is transformed into the wondrous tales of the thirteenth century; the mediaeval annals of the English kings are modified under classical influences into the political histories of More and Hayward and Bacon and Herbert; the sixteenth century fosters two types, one treating the falls of princes with conscious art and mournful philosophy, the other narrating adventurous and stirring lives with the Renaissance love of splendor and the Elizabethan delight in action.[59] The progress of biography in the seventeenth century is more varied and complicated. Religious zeal and the growth of the Puritan spirit introduce on a large scale a definite pietistic manner into life-writing. Under the Stuarts, the analytical and critical spirit, the interest in individuals and personalities which produced the character sketch, cause the mediaeval chronicle and the Elizabethan narrative of action to be supplanted by accounts more deliberate in character portrayal. This tendency is furthered by the increase in autobiographies and memoirs, particularly in the ranks of the nobility, by the number of lives written by or about women, wherein national affairs and political or religious controversies, battles and parliaments, are generally subordinate to the personal element, and by the increased interest in the lives of literary figures, wherein external happenings tend to dwindle in pith and moment.

59. Cavendish, Richard Hall, John Josselin, the biographer of Perrott. Continued in the seventeenth century by Cary, Robert Ashley, Raymond.

The expansion of English biography in the seventeenth century is remarkable: Anthony Wood discovers the overwhelming significance of the little fact; Fuller and Aubrey emphasize the value of amusing anecdotes; Cowley reveals the charm of personal confidences; Sprat and Burnet exploit the possibilities of dignified reticence; Bunyan and Burton and Fox and Digby and Anne Halkett develop the biography of intimate confession; Greville and Lucy Hutchinson, Walton and John Evelyn, show the power of love to lift the record of a life into the realm of art.

The pattern of one biography blends with that of another, and the history of a nation is disclosed from a hundred angles. The godfearing country-squire John Bruen and the militant pastor Bernard Gilpin stand opposed to the cavalier, adventurous Cherbury or the light-hearted cynical Thomas Raymond — and foreshadow the Civil Wars. The very fortunes that restore Margaret Cavendish's lord to his ruined estate cast Lucy Hutchinson's republican husband into a fatal prison. Robert Cary sees in the Spanish Armada only the opportunity for an exciting gallop to Portsmouth and a possible fight from a frigate; Charles Croke regards the death and funeral of Cromwell as an excuse to withdraw from his yawning friends at Christ Church; Anne Halkett mentions the escape of James, Duke of York, solely because it prevents her own return to London. Henry Burton, Archbishop Laud, John Bunyan, Joseph Alleine, and George Fox offer no generalizations regarding the ascendancy of Anglican or Puritan, no chronological table of the changing fortunes of the Church. The important facts for them are that at a certain period they are in prison, at another period they are not. This is history as it appears to the participants, history as it is lived. To a realist, perhaps the only history that possesses the virtue of actuality is composed of individual biographies, as many as possible, wherein the course of events is necessarily shown as a series of personal attitudes and experiences. The Civil Wars, as they are presented in the well-ordered pages of a modern historian, never existed. But the Civil Wars of Clarendon and Margaret Cavendish and Ludlow and Walton and Fuller are convincing, because they were seen and felt by actual participants. In this respect, all organized histories are unreal and metaphysical; only the history of separate biographies, Argus-eyed, approximates the truth.

In general, early biographers made little attempt to penetrate beneath the surface actions of their heroes to motives. Only occasionally and accidentally do they endeavor to present emotions and ideas, or to develop character, or to portray the dominating moods and preoccupations of their subjects. It was assumed without question that the story of a man's life is adequately given if the chronicle of his actions is complete. Events were stated, not interpreted; and no apology was offered for failure to delineate intimate traits or to fathom thoughts. There was little consciousness of this omission. Psychology was of slight interest to the biographer. To the tenuous and intangible elements that make up personality, early writers remained indifferent. Broad divisions of good and evil may be drawn; but subtle differentiations in character, or intensive studies of individualities, were seldom consciously made. Among the numerous distinguished lives written before 1700, those that are deliberate analyses of personality are surprisingly few in number. Each individual is considered as a representative of a common humanity, and in consequence, distinctions between one man and all his neighbors may be explained quite simply by narrating the external actions of his life in sequence.

Furthermore, each biography functions as a practical guide, a treatise on ethical or political philosophy exemplified in the life of one man. An individual's life will serve as an applicable pattern for all his fellows. This didactic note prevails in all classes of biography, whether an historian writes the life of a king or statesman, or a nobleman details his own career for the benefit of his heirs, or a cleric records a bishop's saintly ministry, or a pamphleteer sets down the account of famous and worthy men who have been shoemakers. This characteristic is not limited to a single age, but runs steadily through the entire period here studied, from Alcuin's praise of Willibrord in the eighth century — *Videte, fratres karissimi, quanta gloria est Deum sequi* — to Richard Baxter's meditation on Joseph Alleine at the close of the seventeenth century — "To teach me better how to live and die, in Faith, Hope and Love, is that for which I read this narrative."

The subtle analysis of personality, in spite of pioneers in the early periods, was reserved for later times; before 1700 English biography presents, somewhat paradoxically, the life of an individual as if it were lived entirely upon the surface, and the story of a single man as if it were typical of all. The beginnings of penetrating psychological biography, where the aim is to reproduce a life rather than to instruct, may be traced in the seventeenth century and even earlier; but the lonely outposts only serve to throw into sharper contrast the general temper of early biography and to emphasize the persistence of its objective outlook and its moral purpose.

The narrative manner of early English biography was impersonal; its aim was ethical.

This survey should not be brought to an end without a brief glance at the place of written lives in English literature. The growing interest in biography has in recent years tended to increase its relative importance, and scattered biographical pieces have always been considered as ranking among the English classics, though the systematic study of biography as a literary form has steadily been slighted.[60]

The neglect of biography as a literary form is the more remarkable since its scope may be defined with some precision and its natural unity is clearly marked out. Superficially, at least, the representation of an individual life, bounded sharply by the markers of birth and death, offers unlimited possibilities for organized and artistic writing. Unity and logical progress are so natural to biography that they will be found to exist even in lives which otherwise possess few merits in structure or style.

The reason for the neglect of life-writing as a distinct branch of English literature lies largely in the conception of biography as a science rather than an art. Its functions have been limited to the collecting and marshalling of details and the storing of information; its possible relations to philosophy, psychology, and criti-

60. That its place is far from insignificant may be inferred from the fact that out of the first 200 selections in *The Oxford Book of English Prose*, between twenty-five and thirty are excerpts from biographical writings that are considered in this study.

cism, as well as its claims to an independent existence, have been overlooked. Yet many of the best biographies here surveyed are to be esteemed for their treatment and general conceptions rather than for the facts which they contain. Occasionally a writer will view the life of his subject critically and will attempt to invest it with some philosophical significance. So More envisages the career of Richard III as the pursuit of Nemesis, Lydgate and Sackville see their heroes as puppets dangling on Fortune's mighty wheel, Cavendish shapes Wolsey's life as a fatal series of events which cast their shadows before them, Foxe regards his martyrs as the lighters of such a torch as ages will not extinguish, Walton presents Wotton and Herbert completing the circles of their tranquil lives.

In spite of these artistic successes, the writing of lives must remain one of the most exacting branches of literature. The limitations of biography are unescapable. The simple requirement that biography shall reproduce the life of an historical figure restricts imaginative and creative impulses, so that the deliberate attempt of early English biographers to render their portraits faithful and exact has made them less vital than the purely imaginary characters of the Elizabethan stage. In the highest type of life-writing, a great subject must be treated by a great author, and such double stars are rare. The ideal biographer must be observing, patient, and exact; he must also possess sympathy and imagination. Without any one of these qualities, his work will fall short.

In a few isolated instances, and frequently in brief passages from longer works, these severe demands are fulfilled and life-writing rises to the level of great literature. Early English biography was constantly preoccupied with the dignity of human life. In no other branch of literature is the sanctity, the nobility, the stateliness of man's progress so fully realized. The exaltation of great acts pervades its pages, and the desire to instruct posterity through the examples of the glorious dead renders it serious and steady. Imminent and inevitable death tinges each narrative with melancholy grandeur, and in the variegated tissue of lives extending from Saxon England to the England of William and Mary, in the individual careers woven together into a pattern that is the history of England, there may be discerned, at times, a grave and questioning glance upon the destiny of those who tread briefly upon this little stage.

BIBLIOGRAPHY

PART I (pp. 289–366) is a subject-and-author index of early English biographies. The full titles are given under the names of the authors; cross-references are given for the subjects of the biographies. Anonymous works are described under the subjects of the lives. Capital letters denote authors; italics denote subjects. Except in rare instances, the date of the first edition is given, and the date of composition when it differs greatly from the year of publication. For major works, modern editions more easily accessible are mentioned. Brief descriptions of the more important items are inserted when these pieces have not been treated separately in the text. Where the English translator of a biographer is not known, the life is placed under the name of its original author. All works have been examined in the editions specified, except where a secondary authority is given in italics, thus: "Bridget, Saint. 'The life of . . . S. Bridgit.' 1625. By B. B. — *Camb.*" These secondary authorities are given in Part II of the bibliography.

PART II (pp. 367–372) comprises a list of the most important works of reference used in this study.

THE principal abbreviations are: "pr." = printed; "wr." = written; "tr." = translated or translation; "pub." = published; "ascr." = ascribed or ascription; "ed." = edited or edition; "t.p." = title-page; "*D.N.B.*" = Dictionary of National Biography; "E.E.T.S." = Early English Text Society.

BIBLIOGRAPHY

PART I

AN INDEX OF EARLY BIOGRAPHIES

A

ABBO OF FLEURY. "Historia S. Eadmundi Regis Angliae et Martyris." Wr. about 985 and dedicated to Archbishop Dunstan. Surius, *De Probatis Sanctorum Historiis*, vol. vi, 1575.

Adam. "Øe lyff of Adam and Eve." Vernon MS. Repr. Horstmann, *Sammlung altenglischer Legenden*, 1878.
"The Life of Adam . . . Renderd into English by J. S." 1659. From the Italian life by Giovanni Francesco Loredano. Imaginative, wr. in a quaint and sparkling style.

ADAM OF EYNSHAM. "Magna Vita S. Hugonis." Wr. 1212–20. Rolls Series, 1864, ed. J. F. Dimock.

ADAM OF USK. "Chronicon . . . A.D. 1377–1421." Ed. E. M. Thompson. Combination autobiography and chronicle. 2d ed. 1904.

ADAMNAN. "Vita S. Columbae." Wr. 692–97. Pr. *Acta Sanctt. Ord. S. Benedicti*, Paris, 1672. Latin text, William Reeves, 1857, for the Bannatyne Club; J. T. Fowler, Oxf. 1894. Eng. tr. Wentworth Huyshe, 1906.

AELFRIC. "Lives of Saints." Wr. 990–97. Ed. W. W. Skeat, E.E.T.S., 1881, Orig. Ser., vol. lxxvi. Tr. from Latin to Old English. The thirty-nine chapters of his *Homilies* include the lives of several English saints.
"Vita S. Aethelwoldi, Episcopi Wintoniensis." Dedicated to Kenulf, Bishop of Winchester, in 1006. Pr. *Chronicon Monasterii de Abingdon*, ii, 255–266. Ed. Joseph Stevenson, 1858.

Aesop. See Wallye.

Aethelwold. See Aelfric.

Agathocles. See Perrinchief.

AILRED OF RIEVAULX (1109?–66). "De vita et miraculis S. Edwardi regis et confessoris." Pr. in *X Scriptores*, 1652.—*Berkenhout.*

Alan, or Allen, Cardinal William. See Fitzherbert.

Alban, Saint. See Lydgate.

ALCUIN. "Vita S. Willibrordi." Wr. about 782–93. Two parallel versions in verse and prose. *Acta Sanctt. Ord. S. Benedicti*, saec. iii, vol. iii, p. 601; *Monumenta Alcuiniana*, ed. Wattenbach and Duemmler, Berlin, 1873.

Alcuin. Anonymous Latin life. Wr. 823–29. *Monumenta Alcuiniana*, ed. Wattenbach and Duemmler, Berlin, 1873.

Aldhelm. See William of Malmesbury.

Aleman, Matheo. See Mabbe.

Alexander. "Life" in Early English, in E.E.T.S., Ex. Ser., vol. cxliii, 1913.
See Brende.

Alexander VII. See Ayres.

ALEYN, CHARLES. "Historie of . . . Henrie . . . the Seventh." 1638. 152 pp. of ababcc stanzas.

Alfred, King. See Asser, Spelman, Powell.

Alleine, Joseph. "The Life & Death of . . . Mr. Joseph Alleine." 1673. A joint biography. Various chapters by George Newton, Theodosia Alleine his wife, Richard Fairclough and others. 1st ed. between 1668 and 1672. Pref. by Richard Baxter, who declares "no one of himself can creditably report the whole" of a man's life.

Allestree, Richard. See Fell.

Almansor. See Ashley.

Amphabel, Saint. See Lydgate.

ANDERTON, JAMES. "Luthers life collected from the writinges of himselfe." 1624. — *Camb.*

ANDRE, BERNARD. "De vita atque gestis Henrici Septimi Historia." Wr. about 1500–21. Ed. James Gairdner, Rolls Series, 1858. This volume includes "Les Douze Triomphes de Henri VII" in French verse, probably also by André. Oratorical and pseudo-classical style. A mixture of the mediaeval chronicle and Roman historians.

Andrew, Saint. "The Legend of St. Andrew," in Old English verse. Pr. in "The Poetry of the Codex Vercellensis," ed. J. M. Kemble, 1843.

Andrewes, Lancelot. See Isaacson.

Andrews, Margaret. "The Life and Death of Mrs. Margaret Andrews," 1680. Anon.

ANGLESEY, ARTHUR, EARL OF. "Memoirs." 1693. A misnomer.

Anne, Saint. "The Middle English Stanzaic Versions of the Life of Saint Anne." 3 versions, wr. in 14th and 15th cents. Ed. Roscoe E. Parker for E. E. T. S., Orig. Ser., vol. clxxiv, 1928.

Anselm. See Eadmer.

Anthoine, Nicholas. "An Historical Account of the Life and Tryal of Nicholas Anthoine, burnt for Judaism at Geneva in the Year 1632." Anon. Repr. *Harl. Misc.*, ii, 204.

Anthony, Saint. See E. Stephens.

Antichrist. "The byrth and lyfe of Antichrist." W. de Worde. About 1520. — *Camb.*

Apostles. See Cave.

Archangell, Father. See Capucins.

Arminius, James. "The Life and Death of James Arminius and Simon Episcopius." 1672. By J. K.

Arthur. "The Most Ancient and Famous History of . . . Prince Arthur, King of Britaine, Wherein is declared his Life and Death." 1634. From Malory. Anon.

Ascham, Roger. See Grant.

ASHE, SIMEON. "Gray Hayres Crowned with Grace . . . Together with . . . [Mr. Thomas Gataker's] studious, laborious, religious Life, and patient, comfortable Death." 1655.

ASHLEY, ROBERT. "Almansor The Learned and Victorious King that conquered Spaine. His Life and Death." 1627. Tr. from the "Spanish Copie which was printed at Saragoza 1603." A noteworthy and little-known piece of English prose. Intended for King Charles as a supplement to his "Christian patterns for Imitation," it portrays an exemplary life against a bizarre and luxurious background. Should be more widely known.

ASSER. "De Rebus Gestis Aelfredi." Wr. about 893. Archbishop Parker, in first ed. 1574, took liberties with text. Orig. single MS. destroyed in 1731. Best mod. ed., W. H. Stevenson, Oxf., 1904; tr. A. S. Cook, 1906.

Athanasius. "The History of the Life & Actions of St. Athanasius.
. . . By N. B. Catholick." 1664.
  See E. Stephens.

Athenae Oxonienses. See Wood.

AUBREY, JOHN. "Brief Lives." Collected 1669–96. Ed. Andrew
  Clark, Oxf., 1898. 2 vols. See also *Memoir of John Aubrey*, by
  John Britton, 1845.

AUDLEY, JAMES, EARL OF CASTLEHAVEN. "Memoirs . . . His Engagement and Carriage in The Wars of Ireland, From the Year
  1642 to the Year 1651. Written by himself." 1680. Another ed.
  1681.

Augustine. See Goscelin, Capgrave, Sir Tobie Matthews, Watts.
  "The Life of S. Augustine . . . Written by himself." 1660.
  Anon.

AVALE, LEMEKE. "A Commemoration or Dirige of Bastarde Ed-
  monde Boner . . . usurped Bishoppe of London." 1569. Defamatory biography in irregular verse. Repr. by Sir Egerton Brydges,
  Restituta, 1814–16.

AYRES, PHILIP. "A Short Account of the Life and Death of Pope
  Alexander the VII." 1667. Valueless tr.

                                    B

BACON, FRANCIS. "Historie of the Raigne of King Henry the
  Seventh." 1622.
    "A Collection of the Felicities of Queen Elizabeth." A char-
  acter sketch written in Latin and published in translation by
  William Rawley, *Resuscitatio*, 1657. See also *Moral and Histori-
  cal Works of Bacon*, ed. J. Devey, 1852.
    For remarks on early biography, see "The Advancement of
  Learning." 1605.

Bacon, Francis. See Rawley.

Bacon, Nicholas. See Whetstone.

BADDILY, RICHARD. "Life of Dr. Thomas Morton, Late Bishop of
  Duresme. Begun by R. B. Secretary to his Lordship, And Finished
  by J. N. D. D. his Lordship's Chaplain." 1669.

BAGSHAW, EDWARD. "Mr. [Robert] Boltons . . . Foure last Things
  . . . Together with the Life and Death of the Author." 1633.

BAILY, THOMAS. "The Life and Death of . . . John Fisher, Bishop of Rochester." 1655. Taken from Richard Hall, with few changes.

Baker, Augustin. See C. Gascoign.

BALE, JOHN (1495–1563). "A brefe Chronycle concernynge the Examinacyon and death of the blessed martyr of Christ syr Johan Oldecastell the lorde Cobham collected togyther by Johan Bale." 1544.
"Illustrium Majoris Britanniae Scriptorum Summarium in quinque centurias divisum." Ipswich, 1548.
The above item expanded and published as "Scriptorum Illustrium maioris Brytanniae, quam nunc Angliam & Scotiam vocant: Catalogus." Basel, 1557–59.
"The first two partes of the Actes or unchaste examples of the Englysche Votaryes, gathered out of theyr owne legendes and Chronycles by Jhon Bale." 1549.
"The Pageant of Popes . . . Written in Latin by Maister Bale and now Englished with sondrye additions by J.[ohn] S.[tudley]" 1574. Largely derived from the *Scriptorum Illustrium Catalogus.*
"John Bale's Index of British and Other Writers." Ed. R. L. Poole, Oxf., 1902. Transcr. from autograph notebook in Seldon MSS Bodl.
"The Vocacyon of Johan Bale to the Bishoprick of Ossorie in Ireland, his Persecucions in the same, and finall Delyveraunce." Rome, 1553. Repr. *Harl. Misc.*, vol. vi.

BANKS, JONATHAN. "The Life Of . . . Edward Rainbow, D.D. Late Lord Bishop of Carlisle. To which is added, A Sermon Preached at his Funeral by Thomas Tully." 1688.

BANNATYNE, RICHARD. "The Last Days of John Knox By his Faithful Servitor." Wr. shortly after Nov., 1572. Pr. 1913 as No. 35, Knox Club Publications, ed. D. H. Fleming. Important as an early and sustained example in English of moving, vivid biographical narration, but too limited in scope to constitute a life.
Scotch version in Bannatyne's "Memorials of Transactions in Scotland" (1569–73). Ed. 1836.

BARBOUR, JOHN. "The Actes and Life of . . . Robert Bruce." Finished in 1375. 1st ed. Edinburgh, 1570. T. p. from 1616 ed. Poem in four-beat couplets. Claims historical accuracy.
"Legends of the Saints" taken from the *Legenda Aurea.* In MS. Camb. Univ. Lib. — *D. N. B.*

BARCLAY, ALEXANDER (1475?–1552). "Lyfe of the Glorious Martyr saynt George, translated by Alexander Barclay, while he was a monk of Ely." Pynson, n. d. — *D. N. B.*
"The Lyfe of saynte Thomas." Pynson, n. d. — *D. N. B.*
Lives of Margaret, Catharine, and Ethelreda, in verse. Not extant.

BARDNEY, RICHARD. "Vita Roberti Grosthed, Episcopi Lincolniensis." Wr. 1503 (A. Wood). Pr. Wharton's *Anglia Sacra*, ii, 325.

BARKSDALE, CLEMENT. ("Monumenta Litteraria sive, Obitus et Elogia Doctorum Virorum, Ex Historiis . . . Thuani." 1640.)
"Hugo Grotius, His Discourses . . . With . . . the Authours Life." 1652.
"Memorials of Worthy Persons. Two Decads." 1661. Third decade Oxf., 1662; 4th, 1663. Collected from earlier lives.
"A Remembrancer of Excellent Men." 1670. Ten brief reprinted biographies of Protestant churchmen.

BARLOW, WILLIAM. "Vita et Obitus Richardi Cosin." 1598.

BARNARD, JOHN. "Theologo-Historicus, Or the True Life of . . . Peter Heylyn . . . To correct the Errors, supply the Defects, and confute the Calumnies of a late Writer." 1683. The "late writer" was George Vernon, whose life of Heylyn appeared in 1682.

BARNES, JOSHUA. "History of . . . Edward III." Cambridge, 1688. 911 pp. fol. Nothing.

Barnes, Dr. Robert. See Foxe.

Barnestapolius, Obertus. See R. Turner.

Barrow, Isaac. See Hill.

Bartholmew, Dan. See G. Gascoigne.

BARWICK, JOHN. "Hieronikes. Or The Fight, Victory, and Triumph of S. Paul. Accommodated To . . . Thomas [Morton] Late L. Bishop of Duresme, in a Sermon Preached at his Funeral . . . Together, With the Life of the said Bishop." 1660.

Barwick, John. See P. Barwick.

BARWICK, PETER. "The Life of the Reverend Dr. John Barwick . . . Translated into English By the Editor of the Latin Life [Hilkiah Bedford]." 1724. Wr. 1671–91. Latin ed. 1721. Ed. 1903 by G. F. Barwick. Notable for the late date of the Latin life.

BIBLIOGRAPHY

BASSET, PETER (d. 1430). "Acts of Henry V." In English. Interesting for early date. Not now extant. Basset was chamberlain and friend of Henry V. — *Bale.*

BATES, GEORGE. "The Lives, Actions, and Execution of The prime Actors, and principal Contrivers of that horrid Murder of . . . King Charles the first." 1661.

BATES, WILLIAM. "Vitae selectorum aliquot Virorum Qui Doctrina, Dignitate, aut Pietate Inclaruere." 1681. Latin repr. biographies, including funeral sermons. Note late date for biography in Latin.

Baxter, Margaret. See R. Baxter.

BAXTER, RICHARD. Prefaces to lives of Alleine and Janeway, 1673 (q. v.).
    "A Breviate of the Life of Margaret . . . Baxter." 1681.
    For character sketch of Sir Matthew Hale, 1682, see Gilbert Burnet.
    "Reliquiae Baxterianae: Or, Mr. Richard Baxter's Narrative of The most Memorable Passages of his Life and Times. Faithfully Publish'd from his own Original Manuscript, By Matthew Sylvester." 1696. Part I, autobiographical, wr. in 1664. Later sections chiefly historical. Ed. 1925, Dent, by J. M. Lloyd Thomas, is good abridgment.

Baxter, Richard. See Long.

Beaton, David. See Lyndsaye.

Beauchamp, Richard. See Rous.

Beaufort, Margaret. See Fisher.

Becket, Thomas. Seven volumes of materials in Rolls Series, ed. J. C. Robertson, 1875. Becket died 1170, and many biographies written before 1200 are included. Of these, the best are by John of Salisbury, brief, symmetrical and melodramatic; by William Fitzstephen, whose fondness for worldly splendors and lack of a bitter anti-royal prejudice anticipate Cavendish; by Herbert of Boseham, long and satisfying in minute detail; and by William of Canterbury, abundant in miracles performed at Becket's tomb and typical of the capitalization of the miraculous among post-Conquest writers.
    "Life . . . of S. Thomas." 1639. Ded. signed A. B. 396 pp. Nothing original.
    See Stapleton and Wade.

BEDE. "Vita S. Cuthberti Episcopi Lindisfarnensis." Wr. 721–31. Two versions, one in verse and one in prose. "Historia Abbatum." A good early example, in the persons of the abbots of Wearmouth and Jarrow, of grouped biographies. "Historia Ecclesiastica Gentis Anglorum." Wr. 731. All the above repr. in *Baedae Opera Historica*, ed. Charles Plummer, 2 vols., Oxf. 1896. See also *Bede's Historical Works*, Joseph Stevenson, 1887. Latin text and verse life of S. Cuthbert, *Acta Sanctt. Ord. S. Benedicti*, vol. ii, Paris, 1569. *Historia Ecclesiastica* in Old English, with tr. E. E. T. S., Orig. Ser., vols. xcv–xcvi, 1890–91, and Orig. Ser., vols. cx–cxi, 1898.

Bede. "Vita Bedae Venerabilis." Anon. 11th cent. *Acta Sanctt. Ord. S. Benedicti*, saec. iii, vol. iii. Important as a serious attempt at the reconstruction of a life after a lapse of 400 years. Followed by "Elogium Historicum," citing later appraisals of Bede — in this respect a forerunner of biography in the form of literary criticism.

Bedell, Bishop William. See W. Bedell, Clogie, and Burnet.

BEDELL, WILLIAM. "Life of William Bedell, Bishop of Kilmore." (The biographer's father.) Wr. about 1645–60. Pub. Camden Soc., 1872. Repr. Camb., 1902, ed. E. S. Shuckburgh. Largely derived from the Bishop's letters. Descriptions of the homely life of a pious country churchman.

Bedford, Francis, Earl of. See Whetstone.

Bedford, Hilkiah. See P. Barwick.

Bedloe, William. "The Life and Death of Captain William Bedloe One of the Chief Discoverers Of the Horrid Popish Plot." 1681. Anon. Defamatory.

Behn, Aphra. "The Histories and Novels . . . Together with The Life and Memoirs of Mrs. Behn. Written by One of the Fair Sex." 1696. Verges upon scandalous romance.

BENEDICT OF PETERBOROUGH. "Chronicles of Henry II and Richard I." Ed. William Stubbs, Rolls Series, 1867. Good example of the style of the 12th-cent. chronicle.

Bennet, Father. See Capucins.

BERKELEY, JOHN (d. 1678). "Memoirs." Pub. 1702. Negotiations with Cromwell to restore Charles I.

BERNARD, NICHOLAS. "The Life and Death of . . . Dr. James Usher, Late Arch-Bishop of Armagh." 1656. Ed. 1837, T. Jackson, *Lib. Chr. Biog.*

Betun, Robert de. See William of Wycumbe.

BEZA, THEODORE. ". . . the Historie of the life and death of Maister John Calvin . . . Turned out of Frenche into Englishe, by I. S." 1564.

Beza, Theodore. See Crashaw.

BIRCH, COLONEL JOHN. "Military Memoirs . . . 1642-45." Camden Soc. 1873.

BLAIR, ROBERT. "The Life of Robert Blair . . . Minister of St. Andrews, Containing his Autobiography from 1593 to 1636." Wr. 1663. Ed. T. McCrie for Wodroe Soc. 1848.

BLAKMAN, JOHN (fl. 1436-48). "Collectarium mansuetudinum et bonorum morum regis Henrici. vi. ex collectione magistri Joannis blakman bacchalaurei theologie et post Cartusie monachi Londini." N. d. but pr. by Robert Coplande, "said to be 1510." A very early character sketch. Repr. by Thomas Hearne, 1732. Repr., with tr. and notes, by M. R. James. Camb. 1919. Good example of the mediaeval character sketch by rubrics, or qualities of character.

Blood, Thomas. "Remarks on the Life and Death of the Fam'd Mr. Blood." 1680. 2d ed. 1st ed. same year. Topical.

BLOUNT, THOMAS POPE. "Censura Celebriorum Authorum." 1690. Brief Latin lives of writers of all ages.
"Remarks upon Poetry. With Characters and Censures of the Most Considerable Poets, Whether Ancient or Modern. Extracted out of the Best and Choicest Criticks." 1694.

BOCKING, RALPH. Latin life of St. Richard de Wyche, Bishop of Chichester. Wr. 1253-70. *Acta Sanctt.* i (13 Apr.), 273.

BODLEY, THOMAS. "The Life of Sʳ Thomas Bodley, The Honourable Founder of the Publique Library in the University of Oxford. Written by Himself" in 1609. Oxf. 1647.

Boehmen, Jacob. "The Life of one Jacob Boehmen." 1644. A tr. Short and humble.

Boethius. "The Life of Boethius, Recommended to the Author of the Life of Julian." 1683. Political, anti-Catholic. Anon.

BOETHIUS, HECTOR. "Vitae episcoporum Murthlacensium et Aberdonensium." Paris, 1522. "A lame and imperfect work." — *Berkenhout*, p. 28.

BOHUN, EDMUND. "The character of Queen Elizabeth . . . Her Virtues and Defects." 1693.

BOKENAM, OSBERN. "Lyvys of Seyntys." Wr. 1447 in four-beat couplets. Suffolk dialect. Pr. for Roxburghe Club, 1835, vol. l. Also ed. C. Horstmann, 1883. Ten women saints.

BOLTON, EDMUND. "Hypercritica Or A Rule of Judgment for writing, or reading our History's." Wr. 1610–18. Pub. by Anthony Hall, Oxf. 1722. Contains statement on theory of biography.

Bolton, Robert. See Bagshaw.

Boniface. See Willibald.

Bonner, Edmund. See Knell, Avale.

BOREMAN, ROBERT. "A Mirrour of Christianity, Or . . . The Life and Death . . . of Lady Alice, Dutchess Duddeley." 1669.

BOSTON, JOHN OF BURY. "Catalogus Scriptorum Ecclesiae." Boston fl. 1410. Abr. in Tanner, *Bibl.*, 1748. An early antiquarian.

BOURCHIER, JOHN, BARON BERNERS. "The Golden Boke of Marcus Aurelius." 1535. Tr. from a French life of Marcus Aurelius. Originally from Guevara.

BRADSHAW, HENRY. "St. Werburge of Chester." Wr. 1513. Pynson, 1521 ed. Chetham Soc. 1848. E. E. T. S., Orig. Ser., vol. lxxxviii, 1887. In English verse.

Bradwardine. See H. Savile.

BRAGGE, ROBERT. "The Life and Death of the Godly Man, exemplified in a sermon . . . at the funeral of . . . Mr. Thomas Wadsworth." 1676.

BRAITHWAITE, RICHARD. "The Schollers Medley, Or, An Intermixt Discourse upon Historicall and Poeticall Relations." 1614. Shows relation of history to biography and influence of classical models.
   "The Lives of All the Roman Emperors." 1636. Charming anecdotal short lives, from Caesar to "the now reigning Ferdinand the second."

Bramhall, John. See Lymeric.

BRAMSTON, SIR JOHN (1611–1700). "Autobiography." Camden Soc. 1845.

Brandon, Henry, and Brandon, Charles. See T. Wilson.

BRENDE, JOHN. "The Historie of Quintus Curtius, conteining the actes of the great Alexander." 1584. Tr.

Brettergh, Katherin. "Deaths Advantage little regarded, and the Soules solace against sorrow. Preached in two funerall Sermons . . . Whereunto is annexed, the Christian life and godly death of the said Gentlewoman." 1601. T. p. from 5th ed. 1617. Possibly by William Harrison. An early attempt at edifying biography, with an extended death scene narrating in Scriptural phraseology the combat between the devil and this young Puritan gentlewoman.

BRICE, THOMAS. "A compendious Register in metre, containing the names and patient sufferings of the members of Jesus Christ, and the tormented, and cruelly burned within England; since the death of . . . Edward the Sixth, to . . . Elizabeth." 1559. Verse. Repr. vol. iv, Arber's English Garner, 1882.

Bridget, Saint. "The life of . . . S. Bridgit." 1625. By B. B.—Camb.

BROUGHTON, RICHARD. "A brefe discourse of the lyfe and death of . . . Sir William Pawlet." 1572. Repr. Collier, Bibl. Acct., 1865. Verse, but not poetry.

Browne, Sir Thomas. See Whitefoot.

BROWNE, THOMAS. "The Historie of the Life and Reigne of that Famous Princesse, Elizabeth." 1629.

Brownrig, Ralph. See Gauden.

Bruce, Robert. See Barbour.

Bruen, John. See Hinde.

BUCHANAN, DAVID. "Life of John Knox" prefixed to The History . . . of the Church of Scotland. 1644 ed.

BUCHANAN, GEORGE. "Vita, Ab ipso scripta biennio ante mortem." 1580. Incl. in Opera Omnia, 1715. Latin prose. A dry statement of facts.

BUCK, GEORGE. "History of the Life and Reigne of Richard the Third." 1646. Favorable to Richard. A propos of the "school" of royal biography, it may be mentioned that Buck cites Bale, Camden, Giraldus Cambrensis, Commines, Erasmus, Froissart,

Hall, Holinshed, More, Polydore Vergil, Plutarch, William of Salisbury, Stow, Suetonius, and Tacitus, and quotes from their works in the original French, Italian, Latin, and Greek as well as English.

Buckingham. See Sackville.

BUCKLAND, ROBERT. "Lives of Women Saints of our country of England." E . E. T. S., Orig. Ser., vol. lxxxvi, ed. C. Horstmann. In verse. Wr. about 1610.

BUDDEN, JOHN. "Vita . . . Gulielmi Patteni." 1602.

BUNYAN, JOHN. "Grace Abounding to the Chief of Sinners." 1st ed. 1666. T. p. from 7th ed. 1692.
"A Relation of the Imprisonment of Mr. John Bunyan . . . Written by himself." 1765. Repr. in E. C. Baldwin's 1910 ed. of *Grace Abounding.*
"The Life and Death of Mr. Badman." 1680. A generalized character study on a biographical scale.

Burgh, Sir John. See Markham.

Burghley, Lord. See Cecil.

Burley, Sir Simon. See Churchyard.

BURLEY, WALTER (1275–1345). "De vita philosophorum . . . per venerabilem doctorem Walterum burley Anglicum." First pr. in 1467. T. p. from 1472 ed. Cologne. Miniature Latin lives of classical philosophers and poets.

BURNET, GILBERT (1643–1715). "The Memoires of the Lives and Actions of James and William Dukes of Hamilton and Castleherald." 1677. Dedication dated 1673.
"Some Passages of the Life and Death Of . . . John Earl of Rochester, Who died the 26th of July, 1680. Written by his own Direction on his Death-Bed." 1680.
"Life and Death of Sir Matthew Hale, Knight . . . Lord Chief Justice." 1682. T. p. from ed. 1805. "Additional Notes" in the form of a character sketch, by Richard Baxter.
"Life of William Bedell, D.D. Bishop of Kilmore in Ireland." 1685. Drawn from earlier biographies.
"History of His Own Time." 1724. First part completed before 1705. Modelled on de Thou: history told from a personal and contemporary standpoint in great detail. Many character sketches.

BURTON, HENRY. "A Narration of the Life of Mr. Henry Burton . . . According to a Copy written with his owne Hand." 1643.

BURTON, RICHARD. "Englands Monarchs." 1691. Condensed account from William I to William III.
"The History of Oliver Cromwel: Being an Impartial Account . . . Relating only Matters of Fact, without Reflection or Observation." 1692.

BURTON, THOMAS. "Diary of Thomas Burton, Esq. Member in the Parliaments of Oliver and Richard Cromwell, from 1656 to 1659." 1828.

Butler, Nathaniel. See Yearwood.

BYSHOP, JOHN. "Beautifull Blossomes." 1577. Contains discussion of the art of royal biography: a guide to humble conduct as a means to preserve our "brittle blisse."

C

Calvin, John. See Beza.

Camden, William. See Wheare.

Campian, Edmund. See Fenne.

CAPGRAVE, JOHN. "Life of St. Norbert." Wr. 1440 in Troilus stanzas. In MS. (Phillipps Collection, Cheltenham). — *Monro.*
"Liber de Illustribus Henricis." Wr. 1446–53. Ed. J. C. Hingeston, 1858, Rolls Series.
"Nova Legenda Angliae." About 1450. Ed. Wynkyn de Worde, 1516. Abr. tr. by Pynson, 1516. Repr. C. Horstmann, Oxf. 1901.
"Lives of St. Augustine and St. Gilbert of Sempringham." 1451. Ed. J. J. Munro, 1910, E. E. T. S., Orig. Ser., vol. cxl. The *Gilbert* is interesting as being wr. to help bring about Gilbert's canonization (see p. 108). The *Augustine* was written in English "for the solitarye women . . . whech unneth can undyrstande Latyn."
"St. Katherine of Alexandria." E. E. T. S., Orig. Ser., vol. c, 1893.
Bale speaks of a "Catalogus sanctorum angliae" by Capgrave, possibly the *Nova Legenda Angliae.*

Capucins. "The Life of the Reverend Fa. Angel of Ioyeuse Capucin Preacher . . . Together with the lives of the Reverend Fathers,

Father Bennet Englishman, and Father Archangell Scotchman . . . Translated into English by R. R. Catholique Priest." Douai. 1623.

Caraccioli, Galeaceo. See Crashaw.

CARLETON, GEORGE. "The Life of Bernard Gilpin, a Man Most Holy and renowned among the Northerne English." 1629. Latin ed. 1628.

CARY, HENRY, LORD FALKLAND. "The History Of the most unfortunate Prince King Edward II. With Choice Political Observations." T. p. 1680. Wr. about 1627. Conscious and ornate.
"History of The Life, Reign, and Death of Edward II." T. p. 1680. Wr. 1627. A florid elaboration of the first work. Peculiar because in long sections the prose constitutes blank verse, almost regular, and of a high quality. Wr. "to out-run those weary hours of a deep and sad Passion."

CARY, ROBERT. "Memoirs of the Life of Robert Cary, Earl of Monmouth." Wr. shortly after 1626. 1st ed. 1759. Ed. G. H. Powell, 1905.

CAVE, WILLIAM. "Antiquitates Christianae . . . The Lives, Acts and Martyrdoms of . . . [the] Apostles." 1675. Pub. with Taylor's *Life of Jesus.*
"Apostolici: Or, The History of the Lives, Acts, Death, and Martyrdoms of those Who were Contemporary with, or immediately Succeeded the Apostles. As also the Most Eminent of the Primitive Fathers For the First Three Hundred Years." 1677. Shows great industry and some skill in presentation.
"De Vita illorum ac Rebus gestis" in *Scriptorum Ecclesiasticorum Historia Literaria A Christo Nato usque ad Saeculum XIV.* With an *Appendix . . . Ab Anno MCCC ad Annum MDXVII,* by Henry Wharton, 1689.

CAVENDISH, GEORGE. "The Negotiations of Thomas Woolsey, The Great Cardinall of England, Containing his life and Death, viz. 1. The Originall of his promotion. 2. The Continuance in his Magnificence. 3. His Fall, Death, and Buriall." Wr. about 1556. T. p. from 1st ed. 1641. Collated from two MSS. in Lambeth Library by Christopher Wordsworth, *Eccl. Biog.,* vol. i, 1853 ed. Ed. Henry Morley, 1885. Excellent repr. from autograph MS., Kelmscott Press, 1893.

CAVENDISH, MARGARET. "A true Relation of my Birth, Breeding, and Life," in *Natures pictures drawn by fancies Pencil . . . by . . .*

the Lady Marchioness of Newcastle. 1656. See also "CCXI Sociable Letters." 1664.

"The Life of . . . William Cavendishe . . . By the thrice Noble, Illustrious, and Excellent Princess, Margaret, Duchess of Newcastle." 1667. Ed. C. H. Firth, 1886. Wr. and pub. while the Duke was still living.

Cavendish, William. See M. Cavendish.

CAWTON, THOMAS. "The Life and Death of . . . Mr. Thomas Cawton, Sometime Minister of the Gospel at St. Bartholomew's." 1662. A typical ecclesiastical biography by a pious son.

CAXTON, WILLIAM. For list of his published books with dates, see *D. N. B.* Valuable to show proportion of biographies and pseudobiographies in English literature at the close of the fifteenth century.

Tr. of Saint Jerome's *Vitae patrum*, 1491.

Cecil, William, Lord Burghley. "The Life of that Great Statesman William Cecil, Lord Burghley . . . Publish'd from the Original Manuscript wrote soon after his Lordship's Death [1598]." 1732. Anon. An extended character sketch, remarkably full for such an early date, and concentrated on the Lord Treasurer, who "had seen and tasted so much both of the sweete and sower of the world."

"The Compleat Statesman, Exemplified in the life & actions of Sir William Cecil, Lord Burghley . . . written by one who lived in the house with him during the last xxv years of his life . . . Now first published from a MS. of that age." Pp. 1–49 in Francis Peck's *Desiderata Curiosa*, 1779 ed.

Cecilia, Saint. "The Life of St. Cecilia." By Bertha Ellen Lovewell. 1898. A valuable study for prevalence of saints' lives in Middle English.

Chaderton, Lawrence. See Dillingham.

Chandos, John. See Wyrley.

CHAPMAN, GEORGE. "An Epicede or Funerall Song On . . . Henry Prince of Wales." 1612.

CHAPPELL, WILLIAM. "Vita Guilielmi Chappel Episcopi Corcagiensis & Rossensis." Wr. 1641–49. In Hearne's *Appendicis ad J. Lelandi . . . Collectanea*, 1770. Three-hundred-line Latin metrical autobiography by Milton's tutor.

Charles I. See G. Bates, Gauden, Heylyn, Milton, Perrinchief, W. Sanderson, E. Walker, L. Wood.
"The None-such Charles His Character . . . Published by Authority." 1651. Anon. Scurrilous.

Charles II. See Charleton, D. Lloyd, G. Savile, Tuke.
"Eikon Basilike Deutera. The Pourtraicture of his Sacred Majesty King Charles II. Found in the Strong Box, With his Reasons for turning Roman Catholick." 1694. Anon. A poor imitation of Gauden's work.

CHARLETON, WALTER. "An Imperfect Pourtraicture of . . . Charls the II." 1661.

Charter, Henry. See Robertson.

CHAUCER, GEOFFREY. "The Seconde Nonnes Tale, of the lyf of Seinte Cecile." Wr. 1373–74(?). Good example of the late romantic hagiographies in verse.
"The Monkes Tale, de Casibus Virorum Illustrium." Chaucer's version, in 17 brief examples, of the fall of the great. The theme is drawn largely from Boccaccio and is expanded by Lydgate and the sixteenth-century *Mirror for Magistrates* school. It demonstrates
> "that fortune alwey wol assaille
> With unwar strook the regnes that ben proude."

Chaucer, Geoffrey. See Speght, Thynne.

Cheke, Sir John. Short anonymous life prefixed to his "The True Subject to the Rebell . . . with the Authors life." 1641. Attr. by Anthony Wood to Gerald Langbaine. Pretentious.

CHERBURY, EDWARD, LORD HERBERT. "Autobiography." Wr. about 1643, treating his life to the year 1624. Pub. by Walpole in 1764. Ed. Sidney Lee, 1886.
"Life and Raigne of King Henry the Eighth." 1649. Justifies the sub-title "A generall History of the Times." Many original papers and much unrelated material. Political.

Chichele, Henry. See Duck.

Christina of Sweden. See John Howell.

Christopher, Saint. "Life of St. Christopher." Old English prose, supposedly in script of Beowulf scribe, in *Three Old English Prose Texts.* E. E. T. S., Ex. Ser., vol. clxi, 1924.

CHURCHYARD, THOMAS. Verse lives of Jane Shore and Cardinal Wolsey in 1563 ed. *Mirror for Magistrates*. Above the level of the collection as a whole.

"Churchyardes Chippes." 1575. This includes his melancholy metrical autobiography of considerable interest. Also "Syr Symon Burleis Tragedie," drawn from Froissart and narrated in first person, like a *Mirror for Magistrates* life.

CHUTE, ANTHONY. "Beawtie dishonoured written under the title of Shores Wife." 1593. Repr. by W. Budig, 1908, *Untersuchungen über 'Jane Shore.'* 197 ababcc stanzas. Dramatic monologue.

Clancie. "The Life and Death of Major Clancie, the Grandest Cheat of this Age." 1680. Topical.

CLARK, SAMUEL. "A Mirror for Saints." 1646; 1655; 1657.

"Marrow of Ecclesiastical History." 1649–50; 1654.

"A Martyrologie . . . Whereunto are added the Lives of Jasper Coligni . . . And of Joane Queen of Navarre . . . With the Lives of ten of our English Divines." 1652.

"Life of Tamerlane." 1653. Unrestrained in lavish ornament.

"General Martyrology." 1660.

"A Collection of the Lives of Ten Eminent Divines . . . Whereunto is added, the Life of Gustavus Ericson, King of Sueden." 1662.

Three additional collections of lives in 1662 and 1671.

"The Life & Death of . . . Sir Francis Drake." 1671.

"The Marrow of Ecclesiastical History," 1675, reprinting many of the above.

"The Lives of sundry Eminent Persons in this Later Age. In Two Parts. I. Of Divines. II. Of Nobility and Gentry of both Sexes. By Samuel Clark . . . To which is added His own Life." 1683.

Clark's expressed theory was that "When many excellent Lives are collected into one or more Volumes, they do continue, and will so do, till Printing shall be no more." A professional biographer, displaying industry and piety without judgment.

Claymond, John. See Shepery.

Cleveland, John. The edition of his *Works*, 1687, contains "the Life of the Author." Dedication signed J. L. and S. D. Inadequate.

CLIFFORD, HENRY. "The Life of Jane Dormer Duchess of Feria." Wr. about 1615–20. Existing MS. wr. 1643 or earlier. Ed. Joseph Stevenson, 1887. Catholic, with some good sections by Lady Jane's chaplain regarding her domestic affairs.

Clinton, Edward. "A True Relation, of the Lives and Deaths of the two most Famous English Pyrates, Purser, and Clinton." 1639. Anon.

Clitherow, Margaret. See Mush.

CLOGIE, ALEXANDER. "Speculum Episcoporum, or The Apostolick Bishop." A contemporary life of William Bedell (d. 1642), included in *Two Biographies of William Bedell*, ed. E. S. Shuckburgh, Camb., 1902.

CODRINGTON, ROBERT. "The Life and Death of the illustrious Robert, Earl of Essex." 1646. Repr. 1744 ed., *Harl. Misc.*, i, 211. Not impressive.

Colbert, Jean Baptiste. "The life of the famous John Baptist Colbert, late minister . . . of state to Lewis XIV . . . Done into English from a French copy [by G. Courtilz de Sandras]." Anon. 1695.

COLES, ELISHA. "History of the Life and Death of . . . Jesus Christ." 1680. Verse. — *Pickering and Chatto.*

Colet, John. See Erasmus.

Coligny, Jasper. See Golding and Clark.

COLLIER, JEREMY. "The great Historical, Geographical, Genealogical and Poetical Dictionary; being A Curious Miscellany of Sacred and Prophane History. Containing, in short, The Lives and most remarkable Actions Of the Patriarchs, Judges, and Kings of the Jews; Of the Apostles, Fathers, and Doctors of the Church; Of Popes, Cardinals, Bishops, &c. Of Heresiarchs and Schismaticks, with an Account of their Principal Doctrines; Of Emperors, Kings, Illustrious Princes, and Great Generals; Of Ancient and Modern Authors; Of Philosophers, Inventors of Arts, and all those who have recommended themselves to the World, by their Valour, Virtue, Learning, or some Notable Circumstances of their Lives." 1st ed. 1694 in English, derived largely from Louis Moreri's encyclopaedia. T. p. from 1701 ed. This is Collier's revision to the year 1688. Later volumes, 1705 and 1721. Illustrates the encyclopaedic tendency at the close of the 17th century — the ultimate distension in biographical collections.

COLLINGES, JOHN. "Par Nobile . . . With the Narratives of the holy Lives and Deaths of those two Noble Sisters [the Lady Frances Hobart and the Lady Katharine Courten]." 1669.

Columba, Saint. See Adamnan and Patrick.

Commines, Philippe de. See Danett.

COMPTON, HENRY. "The Life of Donna Olimpia Maldachini, Who Governed the Church during the Time of Innocent the X. Which was from the Year 1644. to the Year 1655. Written in Italian by Abbot Gualdi: And faithfully rendred into English." 1667.

Constantine. See Saltonstall.

Cooper, Anthony Ashley (1621–83). "Memoires of the Life of Anthony Late Earl of Shaftsbury . . . Offered to the Consideration of the Protestant Dissenters." 1683. Anon. Derogatory.
"Some Memoirs . . . of . . . the Earl of Shaftsbury." 1681. Anon. Favorable.
"Memoirs . . . of Anthony Ashley Cooper, First Earl of Shaftesbury." Autobiography, extending from 1621 to 1639, wr. late in his life. Ed. W. D. Christie, 1859. Contains some of the most vivid passages in 17th-cent. memoirs.

CORKER, JAMES. "Stafford's Memoires: Or, A Brief and Impartial Account of . . . William, late Lord Viscount Stafford." 1681. Attr. to Corker by Wood.

CORNWALLIS, SIR CHARLES. "A Discourse of the most Illustrious Prince, Henry, late Prince of Wales." Wr. 1626. Pr. 1641. Repr. *Harl. Misc.*, iv, 319–325. Just, accurate, and distinctive.

Coryate, Thomas. "The Character of . . . Thomas the Coryate," wr. "by a charitable friend." Prefixed to his *The Odcombian Banquet.* 1611. A gay little portrait, abounding in conceits and wit.

Cosin, Richard. See Barlow.

COTTON, CHARLES. "The History of the Life of the Duke of Espernon . . . Wherein the history of France is continued from . . . 1598 where D'Avila leaves off." 1670. Tr. from Guillaume Girard.
"Memoirs of the Sieur De Pontis." 1694. Tr. from Pierre Thomas Du Fosse. — *Halkett and Laing.*

Cotton, John. See Norton.

COTTON, SIR ROBERT. "A Short View of the Long Reign of King Henry the third." T. p. 1642. 1st ed. 1627. Critical and philosophical.

Cotton, Sir Robert. See T. Smith.

Courten, Lady Katharine. See Collinges.

COWLEY, ABRAHAM. "Of Myself." Autobiography, pp. 143–145 of his *Works*, 1668.

308 BIBLIOGRAPHY

Cowley, Abraham. See Sprat.

Cranmer, Thomas. See Harpsfield, Morice, Sanders, Strype.
Also historical fragments and the anonymous "Lyfe and Death of Thomas Cranmer, late Archebushope of Caunterbury " are included in "Narratives of the Days of the Reformation." Camden Soc., vol. lxxvii, 1859.

Crashaw, Elizabeth. See W. Crashaw.

CRASHAW, WILLIAM. "The Honour of Vertue. Or The Monument erected by the sorowfull Husband, and the Epitaphes of that worthy Gentle-woman Mrs Elizabeth Crashawe." 1620.
"The Italian Convert, Newes from Italy of A Second Moses, or The Life of Galeacius Caracciolus the Noble Marquesse of Vico. Containing the story of his admirable conversion from Popery, and forsaking of a rich Marquesdome for the Gospels sake." Wr. before 1609. T. p. from 1635 ed. From Beza's Latin tr. of original Italian version. Admirable for its forceful unity.

CROKE, CHARLES. "Fortune's Uncertainty, or Youth's Unconstancy. Wherein is contained A true and impartial Account of what hapned in the space of few Years to the Author, whom you will know in this ensuing Discourse by the name of Rodolphus." 1667. Assigned to Croke by Wood.

Cromwell, Oliver. "The Pourtraiture of his Royal Highness, Oliver Late Lord Protector &c In His Life and Death." Anon. 1658. Possibly by Carrington (cf. *Cat. Lib. T. Hearne,* 1735). Laudatory.
"Flagellum; Or The Life and Death, Birth and Burial of O. Cromwell, The late Usurper." T. p. 3d ed. 1665. Anon. Derogatory. Possibly by Sir Samuel Tuke, as 1st ed., 1663, is "By S. T. Gent." Assigned by *D. N. B.* to James Heath, who pub. a *different* biography of Cromwell in the same year. An outstanding example of defamatory biography, plausible and realistic in its cool attempts at detraction.
Also see R. Burton, T. Burton, Dawbeny, Flecknoe, H. Fletcher, Heath, le Wright.

Cromwell, Thomas. See Drayton.

Crook, Samuel. "The Life and Death of Mr. Samuel Crook by W. G." 1651.

Crosse, Robert. See Glanvill.

Curtius, Quintus. See Brende.

BIBLIOGRAPHY

Cusack, George. "The Grand Pyrate: Or, the Life and Death of Captain George Cusack The great Sea-Robber." 1676. Anon.

Cuthbert, Saint. See Bede.
"The Life of St. Cuthbert, In English Verse, c. A.D. 1450." Ed. J. T. Fowler for Surtees Soc., 1891, with two other versions.
"The Legend of St. Cuthbert. With the Antiquities of the Church of Durham. By B. R. Esq." 1663.

CYNEWULF. "Guthlac." Wr. 8th cent. Pr. in Thorpe's *Codex Exoniensis*, 1842; E. E. T. S., vol. civ. *Anglo Saxon Version of the Life of St. Guthlac*, C. W. Goodwin, 1848. Eng. tr., *The Poems of Cynewulf*, C. W. Kennedy. Dutton, 1910. Important as an early example of the saint's life in English. Local color and the pagan spirit superposed on the hagiographical form.
"Juliana." Ed. William Strunk, Belles-Lettres Series, 1904. A subjective struggle told objectively.

D

Dacres, Anne. See P. Howard.

DANETT, THOMAS. "The History of Comines." 1596. Repr. Tudor Translations, 1897, 2 vols. A tr. of Philippe de Commines' study of Louis XI.

DANIEL, SAMUEL. "Civill Warres." 1609, complete ed. Metrical history in 8 books of the conflicts between the houses of Lancaster and York.

DARCIE, ABRAHAM. "Annals of Elizabeth." 1625. A pretentious chronicle. From Camden.

DAUNCY, JOHN. "The History Of . . . Henrietta Maria de Bourbon, Queen of England." 1660.
"The History of . . . Charles the II . . . from the Murder of his Royal Father . . . to this present year, 1660." 1660.
Tr. Perefixe's "Histoire de Henri le Grand." 1663. — *D. N. B.*

David, Saint. See Giraldus Cambrensis.

DAVIES, JOHN. "An Account of the Author of this Translation, and his Works," in *Hierocles Upon the Golden Verses of Pythagoras . . . Englished by J.[ohn] Hall.* 1657.
"The Life, and Philosophy, of Epictetus." 1670.

DAWBENY, H. "Historie and policie re-viewed in the heroick transactions of Oliver late Lord Protector from his cradle to his tomb." 1659. Anon. — *Halkett and Laing.*

310　　　BIBLIOGRAPHY

Dee, John (1527–1608). "Diary." Ed. J. O. Halliwell, Camden Soc. 1842. Disappointing.

Defamatory Biography. For specimens of sensational and topical lives, accounts of murders, and broadsides of criminal trials, see "A Handlist of Printed Books in the Wood Collection," Bodleian Library, Nos. 365–373 and 424–428.
"A Cat May look upon a King." 1652. Anon. Brief calumniatory lives of all English kings from William to Charles I.
See Chandler. Bibliography, Pt. II.

Deloney, Thomas (1543?–1600?). "The Works of Thomas Deloney," ed. F. O. Mann, Oxf., 1912, include:
"The pleasant Historie of Iohn Winchcomb, In his yonguer yeares called Iack of Newbery, The famous and worthy Clothier of England." Wr. 1596. T. p. from 1626 ed.
"The Gentle Craft . . . Shewing what famous men have been Shoomakers in time past in this Land." Wr. 1597–1600. Two parts. T. p. from 1648 ed.
"The Pleasant History of Thomas of Reading." Wr. 1597–1600. T. p. from 1672 ed. Shows the appeal to a popular audience and the grafting of a realistic biographical form upon the romance.

Dempster, Thomas. "Historia ecclesiastica gentis Scotorum." 1627. Bologna. Latin. Inaccurate lives, including his own rather lurid autobiography (Art. 1210).

Devereux, Robert. "A briefe and compendious Narrative Of the renowned Robert, Earle of Essex . . . With a Summary Chronicle of his life." 1646.

Devon, Worthies of. See Prince.

D'Ewes, Sir Simonds. "Autobiography and Correspondence." Wr. 1648–50. Ed. J. O. Halliwell, 1845, 2 vols. Rewritten from a journal in cipher. Composed as a family memorial by one who considered himself of no small importance. Among many tiny, dry incidents and political anecdotes, this piece has some passages of true emotion (e. g., ii, 146).

Dickenson, Jonathan. "A Journal of the Travels and Sufferings of several Persons, who were Shipwreck'd in the Gulph of Florida." Wr. 1696–97. T. p. 4th ed. 1759.

Digby, Sir John. See Walsingham.

Digby, Sir Kenelm. "Private Memoirs." Wr. before 1633. Pub. from original MS. 1827.

DILLINGHAM, WILLIAM (d. 1689). "Vita Laurentii Chadertoni . . . Una cum Vita Jacobi Usserii." 1700. Cambridge. Survival of Latin lives at a late period.

Diogenes. See A. Stafford.

Donne, John. See Walton.

Dormer, Jane, Duchess of Feria. See Clifford.

Douglas, Margaret. See J. Phillips.

Dove, Robert. See Nyxon.

Drake, Sir Francis. See Clark and Fitz-Geffrey.

Dramatic Poets. See Langbaine and Gildon.

DRAYTON, MICHAEL. "Englands Heroicall Epistles." T. p. 1599 ed. "The Barrons Wars." 1603. Metrical history, as are "Piers Gaveston," "Matilda," and "Robert of Normandy" (1593–96). "The Historie of the Life and Death of the Lord [Thomas] Cromwell." 1607. T. p. 1609. Repr. in 1610 ed. of *Mirror for Magistrates.* Singularly competent in a well-known form. Shows a grasp of policies and motives, a good use of small incidents, a sense of social wrongs, and a use of psychology and irony.

DRUMMOND, WILLIAM (d. 1649). "History of the Lives and Reigns of the Five James's, Kings of Scotland." 1st ed. 1655. T. p. 1711 ed.

DRYDEN, JOHN. "Life of Plutarch" as introduction to Plutarch's *Lives.* 1683. "The Life of St. Francis Xavier, of the Society of Jesus . . . Written in French by Father Dominick Bohours." 1688.

DUCK, ARTHUR. "The Life of Henry Chichele, Archbishop of Canterbury. In which There is a Particular Relation of many Remarkable Passages in the Reigns of Henry the V and VI . . . Written in Latin by Arth. Duck . . . Now made English." 1699. Latin ed. 1617.

Ducke, Margaret. "A . . . Sermon . . . At the Funeralls of Mrs. Margaret Ducke . . . With A short Relation of her Life and Death written by a Friend." 1646.

DUDITH, ANDREW. "Vita Reginaldi Poli, Britanni, S. R. E. Cardinalis." 1563. Tr. from Italian of Becatelli.

Dudley, Lady Alice. See Boreman.

DUGDALE, WILLIAM. "Monasticon Anglicanum," 3 vols., 1655–73, contains Latin saints' lives, such as Gilbert (1083?–1189) and St. William of York (d. 1154).
"Antiquities of Warwickshire." 1656.
"The Baronage of England, Or An Historical Account of the Lives and most Memorable Actions of Our English Nobility." 1675.

DUGRÈS, GABRIEL. "Jean Arman Du Plessis, Duke of Richelieu, and Peere of France: His Life, &c." 1643.

DUNCON, JOHN. "Holy Life and Death of the Lady Letice, Vi-Countess Falkland." Wr. 1647. 2d ed. 1649. T. p. 3d ed. 1653. Ed. M. F. Howard, 1908.

Dunstan, Saint. "Memorials of Saint Dunstan," ed. William Stubbs, Rolls Series, 1874, contains six lives, including those by Osbern (q. v.), Eadmer (q. v.), William of Malmesbury, Capgrave, a biography by a Saxon priest "B" (c. 1000) and another by Adelard (a. 1012). Bishop Stubbs' introduction is of value in the study of hagiography.

DUNTON, JOHN. "Dunton's Remains . . . To this Work is Prefixt the Author's Holy Life and Triumphant Death [by his son John]." 1684.
"Religio Bibliopolae . . . By Benj. Bridgwater." 1691. An intimate profession of faith. Bridgwater was one of Dunton's associates; this narrative is autobiographical.

DUPPA, BRIAN. "The Authors Life" prefixed to *The History of the Church of Scotland* by John Spotswood. 1655. Attr. to Duppa by Wood. Counter-Puritan spirit.

DURHAM, WILLIAM. "The Life and Death of . . . Robert Harris, D. D. Late President of Trinity Colledge in Oxon." 1660.

Duval, Claude. See Pope.

Dyer, Sir James. See Whetstone.

E

Eadburga. See Osbert.

EADMER (d. 1124?). "Vita S. Wilfridi." Rolls Series, *Historians of York*, vol. i, 1879.
"Vita S. Anselmi Archiepiscopi Cantuariensis." Antwerp, 1551. Also Rolls Series, 1884. The *Vita Anselmi* may profitably be com-

pared with Eadmer's "Historia Novorum," Rolls Series, 1884, which covers the same period.
"Miracles of St. Anselm." In *Ungedruckte Anglo-Normannische Geschichtsquellen*, F. Liebermann, 1879.
"Vita S. Oswaldi." Rolls Series, *Hist. York*, vol. ii. Comparison with the earlier life of Oswald upon which Eadmer draws shows his literary ability and psychological insight.
"Vita S. Dunstani." Wharton's *Anglia Sacra*, 1691, vol. ii.

EDDIUS STEPHANUS. "Vita S. Wilfridi." Wr. about 710–20. Mabillon, *Acta Sanctt. Ord. S. Benedicti*, saec. iv, pt. i, Paris, 1677; A. Gale, *Scriptores XV Historiae Brit.*, Oxf. 1691. Also *Historians of York*, vol. i, ed. James Raine, Rolls Series, 1879. Excellent tr. and notes, ed. Bertram Colgrave, Camb. 1927. Wr. from intimate personal knowledge, but remaining a dry and exact historical record. Important for early use of original sources in form of letters, testaments, papal bulls, etc.

Edmund, Saint (841–70). See Abbo of Fleury and Osbert.
"Miracles of St. Edmund." Wr. about 1070. In *Ungedruckte Anglo-Normannische Geschichtsquellen*, F. Liebermann, 1879.

Edmund, Saint (1170?–1240). "Vita S. Edmundi Archiepiscopi Cantuariensis." Possibly by Robert Richy and Robert Bacon. Last half of 13th cent. Surius, *De Probatis Sanctorum Historiis*, 1575, vol. vi.

EDMUNDSON, WILLIAM (1621–1712). "Journal of his Life, Travels, Sufferings and Labour of Love in the Work of the Ministry." 2d ed. 1774. Quaker. — *Fitch*.

Edward the Confessor. Lives in Latin prose and metre, and an Anglo-Norman metrical life. Rolls Series, 1858, ed. H. R. Luard. All anon.
See Osbert.

Edward I and Edward II. "Chronicles of the Reigns of Edward I and Edward II." 2 vols. Rolls Series, ed. William Stubbs, 1882–83. Contains two *vitae* of Edward II and a "Commendatio Lamentabilis" for Edward I by John of London.
For Edward II, also see Lord Falkland, R. Howard, Hubert, de la Moore.

Edward III. See J. Barnes and May.

Edward IV. See Habington.

Edward V. See T. More.

Edward VI. See Godwin.

Edwin, Saint. "Vita S. Eadwin, Regis et Martyris, ad an. 633. MS. Bodl. Tanner 15. f. 206. Pr. in Capgrave's *Nov. Leg. Angl.*

Egwin, Saint. "Vita S. Egwini Episcopi Wigorniensis." Anon 11th cent. *Acta Sanctt. Ord. S. Benedicti,* saec. iii, vol. iii.

Eikon Basilike. See Gauden.

Elizabeth, Queen. "The life and death of Queen Elizabeth, From the wombe to the Tombe, from her Birth to her Buriall . . . Written in Heroicall Verse." Anon. 1639.
  See F. Bacon, Bohun, Thomas Browne, Darcie, Heywood, R. Niccols, Naunton, F. Osborne.

ELLIOT, ADAM. "A Narrative of My Travails, Captivity and Escape from Salle, In the Kingdom of Fez." In his "A Modest Vindica-tion of Titus Oates." 1682. Thrilling anecdotes of slavery in Africa and of escapes from the Moors, wr. in a direct, manly style. A forerunner of *Robinson Crusoe.*

ELLWOOD, THOMAS. "History of the Life of Thomas Ellwood. Writ-ten by his own Hand." 1714. Autobiography from 1639 to 1683, shortly after which it was probably composed. One of the out-standing Quaker memorials.

Emperors, Roman. See Braithwaite, Hellowes, Knolles, Traheron.

England's Champions. See Ricraft.

England's Monarchs. See R. Burton.

"*England's Worthies*: Under Whom all the Civill and Bloudy Warres, since Anno 1642 to Anno 1647 are related." 1647. Repr. 1819. Anon.

Epernon, Jean-Louis, Duc d'. See C. Cotton.

Epictetus. See Davies.

ERASMUS. Latin short lives of More and Colet in "Virorum qui superiori nostroque seculo eruditione . . . et doctrina illustres atque memorabiles fuerunt, Vitae." Frankf., 1536, 1st ed. earlier. This ed. also includes his own "Vita . . . ex ipsius manu fideliter repraesentata."
  "The Life of Dr. Colet, writ by Erasmus." Camb. 1661. Tr. by Thomas Smith.

Essex, Robert, Earl of. See Codrington, Pricket, Wotton.

Etheldred. See Thomas of Ely.

Ethelwold. See Wulfstan.

Eusebius. See Saltonstall.

EVELYN, JOHN. "Diary," 1641–1705/6. 1st ed. 1818.
"The Life of Mrs. [Margaret] Godolphin." Wr. shortly after
1678. Ed. S. Wilberforce, 1847.

F

FAIRFAX, THOMAS, LORD. "Short Memorials . . . Written by Himself." 1642–44. Pub. 1699. Dedication by Brian Fairfax is
thumb-nail biography of some beauty.

Falkland, Lady Elizabeth. "The Lady Falkland: Her Life. From a
MS. in the Imperial Archives at Lille." Wr. before 1660 by one of
her four daughters. Ed. 1861.

Falkland, Lady Letice, Viscountess. See Mayne and Duncon.

Falkland, Lord. See H. Cary.

FANSHAWE, ANNE, LADY. "Memoirs." Wr. 1676. First pr. 1829–30.
Repr. from original MS. 1907.

Farr, Richard. "The Cheating Solliciter Cheated: Being A True and
Perfect Relation of the Life and Death of Richard Farr." 1665.

Faustus. "The historie of the damnable life, and deserved death of
doctor John Faustus . . . translated into English by P. F. gent."
T. p. from 1592 ed. A well-known example of the influence of the
realistic biographical method upon romance.

Featley, Daniel. See Humfrey and Fuller.

FELIX OF CROWLAND. "Vita S. Guthlaci." Wr. about 715–30. *Acta
Sanctt. Ord. S. Benedicti*, saec. iii, vol. iii, p. 263. Also *Memorials
of St. Guthlac*, ed. W. de G. Birch, 1881. A good example of the
mediaeval attempt at subjective biography: mental struggles are
made objective, and the saint lives in a world of devils and good
angels.

FELL, JOHN. "The Life of . . . Dr. H.[enry] Hammond." 1661. Ed.
T. Jackson, 1837, *Lib. Chr. Biog.*
"The Life of Richard Allestree D.D. sometime Regius Professor
of Divinity in the University of Oxford, and Provost of Eton."
Prefixed to *Forty Sermons* by Allestree, 1684. T. p. from 1848
repr.

FENNE, JOHN. "Vita et Martyrium Edmundi Campiani." In *Concertatio Ecclesiae Catholicae in Anglia*, 1583, which also contains the "Vita et Martyrium Domini Radulphi Schervini" and "D. Alexandri Brianti." Assigned to Fenne and John Gibbon by Wood. Probably by Robert Turner.
"The Life of the Blessed Virgin, Sainct Catharine of Siena . . . now translated into Englishe . . . by John Fen Priest & Confessar to the Englishe Nunnes at Louaine." 1609.
See Robert of Shrewsbury.

FERRAR, JOHN. "The Life of Nicholas Ferrar." Wr. about 1655. Ed. J. E. B. Mayor, 1855.

Ferrar, Nicholas. See J. Ferrar and Jebb.

FINCH, LEOPOLD WILLIAM. "Life of Corn. Nepos," prefixed to "The Lives of Illustrious Men. Written in Latin By Cornelius Nepos and Done into English by Several Hands." 1684.

FISHER, JOHN. "a mornynge remembraunce . . . of the noble prynces Margarete countesse of Rychemonde & Darbye." Wynkyn de Worde, n. d. A sermon comparing Margaret to Martha, delivered in the year 1509 and repr. E. E. T. S., Ex. Ser., vol. xxvii. This also contains (p. 268) Fisher's funeral sermon for King Henry VII.

Fisher, John. See Baily and R. Hall.

FITZ-GEFFREY, CHARLES. "Sir Francis Drake his Honorable lifes commendation, and his Tragicall Deathes lamentation." 1596. Drake's much-travelled splendor narrated in fiery verse. Outstanding among verse biographies.

FITZHERBERT, NICHOLAS. "De Antiquitate & Continuatione Catholicae Religionis in Anglia, & De Alani Cardinalis Vita Libellus." 1608.

FITZSTEPHEN, WILLIAM. See Becket.

Fitzwalter, Robert. See Vallans.

FLECKNOE, RICHARD. "The Idea of His Highness Oliver . . . with certain brief Reflexions on His Life." 1659.
"The Portrait of the Author." In *Heroick Portraits*, 1660. A static character sketch of one whom Dryden preserved in more perennial bronze.

FLETCHER, GEORGE. "The Nine English Worthies." 1606. Derived from Capgrave's *De Illustribus Henricis*. Wr. for Prince Henry.

FLETCHER, HENRY. "The Perfect Politician: Or, A Full View of the Life and Actions . . . of O. Cromwell." 1660. Moderate in outlook.

FORMAN, Dr. SIMON. "Autobiography and Personal Diary of Dr. Simon Forman the celebrated Astrologer, From A.D. 1552 to A.D. 1602." Autobiography wr. 1600. Ed. J. O. Halliwell, 1849.

FORREST, WILLIAM. "The History of Grisild the Second." 1558. Pr. Roxburghe Club, vol. xcvii, 1875, ed. W. P. Macray. Life of Katherine of Aragon in ababbcc stanzas. An arresting and detailed verse life, showing influence of Chaucer rather than Lydgate.

FOX, GEORGE. "A Journal or Historical Account of the Life, Travels, Sufferings, Christian Experiences and Labour of Love in the Ministry of . . . George Fox." Wr. from dictation after 1674–75. Pub. with above t. p. 1694. Diplomatic ed. Norman Penney, Camb., 1911, from MSS. which do not contain the 1694 ed. account of Fox's youth, which was added by William Penn and other Friends.

FOXE, JOHN. "Actes and Monuments of these latter and perillous dayes, touching matters of the Church, wherein ar comprehended and described the great persecutions and horrible troubles, that have bene wrought and practised by the Romishe Prelates, speciallye in this Realme of England and Scotlande, from the yeare of our Lorde a thousande, unto the tyme now present." 1563. Latin ed. 1559, Basel.
"The Whole workes of W. Tyndall, John Frith, and Doct. Barnes," 1573, has three prefatory lives "out of the booke of Actes and Monumentes Briefly Extracted." Pref. by John Foxe. Early examples of lives used as prefaces to works.

France, Kings of. "An Epitome of All the Lives of the Kings of France. From Pharamond . . . to . . . King Lewis the thirteenth . . . Translated . . . by R. B. Esq." 1639.

FRASER, JAMES. "Memoirs of the Life Of . . . Mr. James Fraser of Brea, Minister of the Gospel at Culross. Written by Himself." Wr. about 1684. Pub. 1738. A complete record of God's mercies toward him, his trials and victories, wr. as an inspiriting example to Christians.

Frith, John. See Foxe.

FRITHEGODE. Metrical Latin life of S. Wilfred. Wr. before 950. *Acta Sanctt. Ord. S. Benedicti,* iii, 173; Rolls Series, *Historians of York,* vol. i, 1879.

FULLER, THOMAS. "The Holy State" and "The Profane State." Camb. 1642. Generic characters followed by brief illustrative lives. A unique biographical work.
  "Abel Redevivus or The dead yet speaking. By T. Fuller and other Eminent Divines. The Lives and Deaths of the Moderne Divines." 1651. Draws particularly on Daniel Featley, Thomas Gataker, and Henry Holland.
  "The Sermons of Mr. Henry Smith . . . With a Memoir of the Learned Author By Thomas Fuller." 1658. Brief.
  "The History of the Worthies of England." 1662. Contains lives of the worthies of each shire interspersed among his choro-graphical descriptions. Usually short, and tinged with his restless wit and inquiring spirit.

Fuller, Thomas. See Heath.
  "The Life of That Reverend Divine, and Learned Historian, Dr. Thomas Fuller." 1661. Anon. An excellent example of the typical 17th-cent. ecclesiastical biography.

FULWELL, ULPIAN. "The Flower of Fame. Containing the bright Renowne and moste fortunate Raigne of King Henry the VIII." 1575. *Harl. Misc. Suppl.* 1813. A panegyric in prose and verse.

G

GADBURY, JOHN. "The Life and Death Of the late Famous Mathematician and Astrologer, Mr. Vincent Wing." 1670.

Gage, Sir Henry. See Walsingham.

GAINSFORD, THOMAS. "The true and wonderful History of Perkin Warbeck." 1618.
  "The true, exemplary, and remarkable History of the Earle of Tirone: Wherein the manner of his first presumption, affrighting both England and Ireland with his owne and the King of Spaines Forces, and the misery of his ensuing dejection, downefall, and utter banishment is truely related." 1619.

GALE, THEOPHILUS. "The Life and Death of Mr. John Rowe of Crediton in Devon." 1673. Pref. signed Theophilus Gale, to whom the life is ascribed by Halkett and Laing.

GASCOIGN, CATHARINE. "An Account of The Life of the Venerable F. [ather] Augustin Baker, Monk, of the English Congregation of S. Benedict. Who Died in England, upon the 9th of August A. Dom. 1641. Aetatis suae 63." MS. Wood B4, Bodleian. Anon., but probably by this nun at Cambrai. Contemplative and devotional, standing almost by itself.

GASCOIGNE, GEORGE. "Dan Bartholmew of Bath." Autobiographical. Pr. in Gascoigne's *Works*, vol. i, ed. J. W. Cunliffe, 1907. Wr. 5545 years after the creation of the world, which would seem to make it a youthful work (Gascoigne b. 1525?). Centres on a complicated love affair, which is "mistical and not to bee understoode but by Thaucthour him selfe."

Gascoigne, George. See Whetstone.

Gataker, Thomas. See Ashe, Fuller.

GAUDEN, JOHN. "Eikon Basilike. The Pourtraicture of His Sacred Majestie in his Solitudes and Sufferings." 1648. Ostensibly an autobiography of Charles I, to whom certain critics assign it on evidence not negligible. Guizot mentions 47 eds.
"A Sermon Preached . . . at the Funeral of . . . Dr. [Ralph] Brounrig, With an account of his Life and Death." 1660.
"The Works of Mr. Richard Hooker . . . With an account of his Holy Life, and Happy Death, Written by Dr. John Gauden." 1662. Essays some literary criticism of its subject.

GAUFRIDUS (OF COLDINGHAM?). Latin "Life of Bartholemew the Hermit of Farne." Wr. about 1200. *Symeon of Durham*, Rolls Series, vol. i, Appendix II. The temptations of Saint Anthony in an English setting. Interesting for certain grotesque and spiteful miracles which show the deterioration of the original conception of hagiography.

Geoffrey, Archbishop of York. See Giraldus Cambrensis and Roger of Howden.

George, David. See Meuse.

George, Saint. "The Life and Death of The Famous Champion of England, St. George." N. d. Verse. Anon.
See Lydgate.

GERARD, FATHER JOHN. "Autobiography." Wr. in Latin 1609. Tr. by G. R. Kingdon; pub. in 1886. A fascinating series of adventures wr. by a Jesuit.

GERVASE OF CANTERBURY. "Actus Pontificum Cantuariensis Ecclesiae." Wr. about 1200. *Hist. Ang. Scriptores X*, 1652. Rolls Series, vol. ii, 1880, ed. William Stubbs.

Gesta Pontificum Anglorum. See William of Malmesbury.

Gesta Regum Anglorum. See William of Malmesbury.

GETHIN, GRACE. "Reliquiae Gethinianae, Or, Some Remains of . . . Grace Lady Gethin." 1700. 2d ed. Little essays and a funeral sermon by Dr. Birch.

Gibbon, John. See Fenne.

Gilbert of Sempringham. See Capgrave.
Anon. Latin life, wr. about 1200. Pr. in Dugdale's *Monasticon Anglicanum*, 1655–73.

Gildas, Saint (d. 512). Latin *Vita* in "Gildas," ed. Joseph Stevenson, 1838. Date uncertain. Wr. "before Geoffrey of Monmouth."

GILDON, CHARLES. "Lives and Characters of the English Dramatick Poets." 1698. Langbaine revised and brought up to date.

Gilpin, Bernard. See Carleton.

GIRALDUS CAMBRENSIS. "Vita S. David." Ed. J. S. Brewer, Rolls Series, 1863, vol. iii.
"Vita S. Remigii," wr. about 1196–99, and "Vita S. Hugonis," wr. about 1200–10. Ed. J. F. Dimock, Rolls Series, 1877, vol. vii.
"Vita Galfridi Archiepiscopi Eboracensis." Wr. 1212–20. *Anglia Sacra*, Henry Wharton, ii, 375; 1691; Rolls Series, 1861–77, ed. J. S. Brewer, vol. iv.
"De Rebus a se gestis." Wr. before 1220. Fragmentary autobiography with all chapter heads preserved. *Anglia Sacra*, ii, 457–513. Also in Rolls Series.

GLANVILL, JOSEPH. "A Prefatory Answer to Mr. Henry Stubbe." 1671. Page 211 for reference to Crosse's "Biographia, which gives Rules, how Lives are to be writ."

Glascock, Christopher. See Shelton.

Gloucester, Henry Duke of. See Manley.

GODET. "Chronicle." 1560.—*Haslewood*, 1815 ed. *Mirror for Magistrates.* Important as showing influence of *Mirror for Magistrates*: contains prose lives of English kings to Harold; but from William to Elizabeth is wr. in octave stanzas.

Godolphin, Margaret. See Evelyn.

Godric. See Reginald.

GODWIN, FRANCIS. "Annales of England Containing the Reignes of Henry the Eighth. Edward the Sixt. Queene Mary." 1630. Tr. by Morgan Godwyn. Latin ed. 1616. Sprightly, annalistic, anecdotal.

"A Catalogue of the Bishops of England . . . together with a briefe History of their lives and memorable actions." 1601. A Latin ed. in 1616. Painstaking and valuable. Biographies are not uniform, and the whole is largely indebted to Archbishop Parker.

GOLBURNE, J. ". . . the lives of the Popes and their doctrine." 1600. Tr. from Cipriano de Valera. — *Br. Mus. Cat.*

GOLDING, ARTHUR. "The Lyfe of . . . Jasper Colignie Shatilion, sometyme great Admirall of Fraunce. Translated out of Latin." 1576. Latin ed. 1575.

GOSCELIN (fl. c. 1110). "Vita S. Augustini Anglorum Apostoli." *Anglia Sacra*, ii, 55, ed. Wharton, 1691.
　　Latin life of Saint Swithin. Surius, *De Sanctorum Historiis*, iv, 46.

GOUGE, THOMAS. "A Narrative of the Life and Death of Dr. [William] Gouge," before his *Commentary on the Epistle to the Hebrews.* 1655.

Gouge, Thomas. See Tillotson.

Gouge, William. See Thomas Gouge.

GOWER, JOHN. "Cronica Tripertita" concerns King Richard II, with incidents of his life. Wr. in Latin hexameters, 1399–1408. First pr. 1850, Roxburghe Club. Also in *Works*, 1902.

GRAFTON, RICHARD. "An abridgement of the Chronicles of England." 1563. Drawn from Edward Hall.

Gralhy, Sir John. See Wyrley.

GRANT, EDWARD. "de vita & obitu Rogeri Aschami," as a preface to Ascham's *Familiarum Epistolarum libri tres.* 1576.

GRATTON, JOHN. "Journal of the Life of John Gratton," 1720, contains an autobiography from 1642 to 1694. Quaker.

Grecian Poets. See Kennet.

GREENE, ROBERT. "Greenes Mourning Garment." 1590.
　　"Greenes Groatsworth of Wit bought with a Million of Repentance." 1592. Autobiographical. See *Works*, ed. Grosart, 1881–86.

Gregory the Great. "A Life of Pope St. Gregory the Great Written by A Monk of the Monastery of Whitby (Probably about A.D. 713)." 1904. Ed. by F. A. Gasquet from MS. Gallen 567. Many details in history of early English church. Many miracles. Scant in facts, but is first extant life of Gregory.

Grenville, Richard. See G. Markham.

GREVILLE, SIR FULKE. "The Life of the Renowned Sr Philip Sidney." Wr. 1610–12. T. p. from 1st ed. 1652. Ed. Nowell Smith, Oxf. 1907.

GRIFFITH, WILLIAM. ". . . an excellent Epitaph of the life and death of . . . [Sir Henry Sidney]." 1591. Repr. Brydges, *Cens. Lit.*, ii, 49. Verse. The adjective in the title is misapplied.

GRIMESTON, EDWARD. "The Heroyk Life and Deplorable Death Of the most Christian King Henry the fourth . . . By P. Mathieu." 1612. Tr.

Grosteste, Robert. See Bardney.

Grotius, Hugo. See Barksdale.

Guevara, Antonio da. See Hellowes.

GUMBLE, THOMAS. "The Life of General Monck." 1671.

Gundulf. "Vita Gundulfi Episcopi Roffensis." Anon. Early 12th cent. In Wharton's *Anglia Sacra*, ii, 273.

Gustavus of Sweden. See Clark.

Guthlac. See Felix of Crowland and Cynewulf.

Guy of Warwick. See Rowlands.

Guzman. See Mabbe.

GWYNNE, JOHN. "The Military Memoirs of John Gwynne." Wr. after the Restoration. Pub. 1822.

H

HABINGTON, WILLIAM. "Historie of Edward the Fourth." 1640.

HACKET, JOHN. "Scrinia Reserata: A Memorial Offer'd to . . . John Williams . . . Containing a Series of the Most Remarkable Occurrences and Transactions of his Life, in Relation both to Church and State." 1693. Wr. before 17 Feb. 1657.

Hacket, John. See Plume.

Hainam, Richard. "The witty Rogue . . . Or, The History Of that incomparable Thief Richard Hainam." 1656.
"The English Villain: Or the Grand Thief. Being A full Relation of the desperate Life, and deserved Death of . . . Richard Hanam." N. d. Anon. About 1656.

HALE, SIR MATTHEW. "Life and Death of Pomponius Atticus." 1677. Tr. from Cornelius Nepos. — *Halkett and Laing.*

Hale, Sir Matthew. See Burnet and R. Baxter.

Hales, John. See Pearson.

HALKETT, ANNE, LADY. "Autobiography." Wr. 1678. Ed. J. G. Nichols, 1875.

HALL, EDWARD. "Chronicles of England." 1548. Henry IV to Henry VIII.

Hall, John. See Davies.

HALL, JOSEPH. "The Shaking of the Olive-Tree. The Remaining Works of . . . Joseph Hall, D.D. Late Lord Bishop of Norwich. With Some Specialties of Divine Providence in his Life. Noted by His own Hand." Wr. about 1647. T. p. 1660.

HALL, RICHARD. "The Life of Fisher." Wr. about 1559 in English. Pr. from MS. Harl. 6382 for E. E. T. S., Ex. Ser., cxvii. 1921.
Previously pr. with alterations by Thomas Baily (q. v.) in 1655 as "The life and death of that renowned John Fisher, bishop of Rochester."

Hamilton, James and William, Dukes of Hamilton and Castleherald. See Burnet and Needham.

Hammond, Henry. See Fell.

HARDYNG, JOHN (1378–1465?). "The chronicle of Jhon Hardyng." 1543. Verse to Edward IV; prose to Henry VIII. Additions by Richard Grafton.

Harold, King. "Vita Haroldi. The Romance of the Life of Harold, King of England . . . With Notes and a Translation." Ed. W. de G. Birch, 1885. Anon. Wr. probably about 1200. The most interesting example of history verging upon romance.

HARPSFIELD, NICHOLAS. "Historia Anglicana Ecclesiastica a primis Gentis Susceptae Fidei Incunabulis ad nostra fere Tempora Deducta." Wr. about 1575. Pub. 1622.
Also wrote a life of Cranmer (in MS.) and a life of More which add little to Roper's account except a character sketch, and which is quoted in part in Wordsworth's *Eccl. Biog.*, vol. ii, 1818 ed.

Harrington, James. See Toland.

HARRIS, JOHN. "Sermons . . . by . . . Arthure Lake, late Lord Bishop of Bath and Wells. Whereunto is prefixed by way of

Preface, a short view of the Life and Vertues of the Author."
1629. Attr. to Harris by Wood.

Harris, Robert. See Durham.

HARRISON, WILLIAM. See K. Brettergh.

HARVEY, GABRIEL. "Character of Dr. Perne, Master of Peterhouse,
Cambridge, and Dean of Ely." In *Pierce's Supererogation*, 1593.
A brilliant character sketch. Repr. Brydges, *Cens. Lit.*, x, 327.

HATFELD, EDMUND. "Life of St. Ursula." Wr. before 1509 at the
command of Lady Margaret Beaufort. First ed. Wynkyn de
Worde, n. d. Repr. Roxburghe Club, vol. xxiv, 1818. Shows connection of saints' lives and romance. Eighty 8-line stanzas.

Hatton, Sir Christopher. See John Phillips.

Hawkewood, Sir John. "The Honourable Prentice . . . Shewed in
the life and death of Sir John Hawkewood." 1616. By W. U.
See Vallans. Followed by history of Robert Fitzwalter.

HAWKINS, HENRY. "The Lives of Saint Paul The First Hermite, Of
Saint Hilarion the first Monke of Syria, and of S. Malchus."
Paris, 1630. Tr. from St. Jerome.
"The History of St. Elizabeth." 1632. — *D. N. B.*
"The Life of St. Aldegunda." Paris, 1636. — *D. N. B.*

HAYNE, THOMAS. "Life and Death of Dr. Martin Luther. The Passages whereof have bin taken out of his owne and other Godly and
most Learned, mens writings, who lived in his time." 1641.

HAYWARD, JOHN (d. 1627). "The First Part of the Life and raigne
of King Henrie the IIII." 1599.
"The Beginning of the Reigne of Queene Elizabeth." N. d.
Repr. Camd. Soc. 1840.
"The Lives of the III. Normans, Kings of England: William the
first. William the second. Henrie the first." 1613.
"The Life and Raigne of King Edward the Sixth." 1630.

HEAD, RICHARD. "Jackson's Recantation, or, The Life & Death of
the Notorius High-Way-Man." 1674.
Also composed the "Life and Death of Mother Shipton." 1677.
— *D. N. B.*

HEATH, JAMES. "An Elegie upon Dr. Tho. Fuller That most Incomparable Writer, Who Deceased August the 15th." 1661.
"The History of the Life and Death of Oliver Cromwell, the
late Usurper . . . truly collected and published, for a Warning to
all Tyrants and Usurpers." 1663. Repr. in *Harl. Misc.*

"New book of English Martyrs." 1663.

"England's Chronicle: Or, The Lives & Reigns of the Kings and Queens." 1689. T. p. from 1691 ed. Extends from Julius Caesar to William and Mary. Possibly the work of a different Heath. (James Heath: 1629–64.)

Hector. See Lydgate.

HEIGHAM, JOHN. "The Lives of Saints. Written in Spanish by . . . Alfonso Villegas." 1621. 2d ed.

HELLOWES, EDWARD. " . . . the lives of tenne Emperours of Rome." 1577. From Spanish of Antonio da Guevara.

Henricis, Liber de Illustribus. See Capgrave.

Henrietta Maria. See Dauncy.

"The Life and Death of . . . Henrietta Maria de Bourbon." 1669. Anon.

Henry II. See Benedict, May, William of Newbury.

Henry III. "The Troublesome Life and Raigne of King Henry the Third. Wherein five Distempers and Maladies are set forth . . . Sutable to these unhappie times of ours." 1642. Anon. Political.

"A Short View of the Long Life and Raigne of Henry the Third . . . Presented to King James." 1627. Anon. Affected style.

"A brief Survey . . . of the Life and Reign of Henry the III." 1680.

Henry V. See Basset, Thomas of Elmham, Redman.

Also "Versus Rhythmici de Henrico V°" by an anonymous contemporary. Rolls Series, 1858, ed. Cole. A well-rounded verse biography of less than three hundred lines.

"The First English Life of King Henry The Fifth written in 1513 by an anonymous Author known commonly as The Translator of Livius." Oxf. 1911, ed. C. L. Kingsford.

Henry VI. See Blakman.

Henry VII. See Aleyn, André, Bacon, Fisher.

Henry VIII. See Cherbury, Fulwell, Godwin, James Howell.

Henry, Prince of Wales. See Chapman, Cornwallis, Maxwell.

Henry IV, Emperor. See Roberts.

Henry IV of France. See Grimeston.

Herbert, George. See Oley, Walton.

HERBERT, PHILIP. "The Life and Death of Philip Herbert, the late Infamous Knight of Barkshire." N. d. but about 1649–50. (Herbert d. 1650.) Derogatory. Anon.

HEYLYN, PETER. "Short View of the Life and Reign of King Charles." 1658. Favorable. Anon., but assigned to Heylyn in MS. note in Bodleian copy.

"Cyprianus Anglicus: Or, The History of the Life and Death of . . . William Laud . . . Lord Archbishop of Canterbury . . . Containing also The Ecclesiastical History of the Three Kingdoms of England, Scotland, and Ireland from His first rising till His Death." 1668. Good example of the voluminous type of ecclesiastical biography peculiar to the late 17th cent.

Heylyn, Peter. See Barnard and Vernon.

HEYWOOD, THOMAS. "Englands Elisabeth: Her life and troubles, During Her Minoritie, from the Cradle to the Crowne." 1631.

"Hierarchy of the Blessed Angels." 1635. Note on Lib. 5, p. 245, refers to his intention to write the lives of the poets.

"The Exemplary Lives and Memorable Acts of Nine the most worthy women of the world: Three Iewes. Three Gentiles. Three Christians." 1640.

"The Life of Merlin . . . His Prophesies, and Predictions Interpreted . . . Being a Chronographicall History." 1641.

"The Generall History of Women, Containing the Lives of the most Holy and Prophane, the most Famous and Infamous in all ages, exactly described not only from Poeticall Fictions, but from the most Ancient, Modern, and Admired Historians, to our Times." 1657. Earlier ed. 1624.

Heywood's works make an interesting study of classical and romantic anecdotes told as biography.

Hildebrand. See Roberts.

HILL, ABRAHAM. "The Works of . . . Isaac Barrow, D.D. Late Master of Trinity College in Cambridge." 1687. 2d ed. contains a life of Barrow. Wr. in April, 1683. Amusing, with intimate details.

Hind, James. "The English Gusman; or the History Of that Unparallel'd Thief James Hind . . . Written by G. F." 1652.

". . . the Merry Life, and Mad Exploits of Captain James Hind, The Great Robber of England." Anon. N. d., but about 1657.

HINDE, WILLIAM. "A Faithfull Remonstrance of The Holy Life and Happy Death, of John Bruen . . . Exhibiting variety of many Memorable and Exemplary passages of his Life, and at his Death, usefull for all sorts and sexes, but principally intended as a Path and President of Piety and Charity for the Inhabitants of the Famous County Palatine of Chester." Wr. 1625–27. T. p. from 1st ed. 1641.

Historia Abbatum. See Bede.

Historia Ecclesiastica Gentis Anglorum. See Bede.

Hobart, Lady Frances. See Collinges.

HOBBES, THOMAS. "Vita Authore Seipso." 1679. 400-line auto-biography in Latin metre, with dignified and moving peroration. "The Life of Mr. Thomas Hobbes of Malmesbury . . . now Translated into English." 1680. Verse. A translation of his own autobiography.

HOCCLEVE, THOMAS (1368–1450?). "La Male Regle de T. Hoc-cleve," wr. 1406; "Hoccleve's Complaint," and the introduction to "The Regement of Princes," wr. 1411–12. All largely auto-biographical. Repr. E. E. T. S., Ex. Ser., vols. lxi and lxxii.

HODDESDON, JOHN. "The History of the Life and Death of Sr. Thomas More . . . by J. H. Gent." 1652. T. p. ed. 1662.

HODGSON, CAPTAIN JOHN. "Autobiography." Wr. about 1683. Ed. 1882. Military memoirs of the Civil Wars.

HOLINSHED, RAPHAEL. "Chronicles of England, Scotlande, and Irelande." 1577. Shows, as do all the Elizabethan chroniclers listed in this bibliography, close connection between current his-tories and earlier biographies.

HOLLAND, HENRY. "Baziliologia. A Booke of Kings. Beeing the true and lively Effigies of all our English Kings from the Conquest untill this present . . . And a briefe Chronologie of their Lives and Deaths." 1618.
"Heroologia Anglica, Hoc est Clarissimorum et Doctissimorum Aliquot Anglorum qui Floruerunt ab Anno Cristi MD Usque ad Presentem Annum MDCXX Vivae Effigies Vitae et elogia Duo-bus tomis." 1620. Patriotic and Protestant. Heroes, such as Essex, Sidney, Grenville, Hawkins, and Drake, as well as church-men. Widening of the field for biography.
See Fuller.

HOLLAND, HUGH. Autobiographical metrical sections in "To my Mayden Muse," prefixed to his *Pancharis*, 1603. Humorous, and rich in local allusions. This is the Holland whose commendatory verses are in Shakespeare's First Folio.

HOLLAND, PHILEMON. Tr. of the *Roman Emperors* of Suetonius. 1606.

HOLLAND, ROBERT. "The holy History of our Lord and Saviour Jesus Christ . . . Gathered into English metre." Dedication dated 1594. See Brydges *Restituta*, 1814–16.

HOLLES, DENZIL. "Memoirs of Denzil Lord Holles . . . From the Year 1641, to 1648." 1699.

Hooker, Richard. See Gauden, Walton.

HORNANUS, HADRIAN JUNIUS. "The lives of excellent Philosophers and worthy Oratours. Written in Greeke by Eunapius of Lydia." Dedicated to the Queen, "From Harlem. the Kal. of March. 1568."

Howard, Philip. "The Lives of Philip Howard, Earl of Arundel and of Anne Dacres, His Wife." Anon. Possibly by Lady Anne's chaplain. Wr. about 1630, and pub. 1857. Catholic.

HOWARD, SIR ROBERT. "The History of the Reigns of Edward [II] and Richard II. With Reflections. . . ." 1685. Pub. 1689. T. p. from 1690 ed. (— *Halkett and Laing.*) Ascribed to George Savile, Marquis of Halifax, by Walpole and Wood. Political theory justifying deposition.

Howard, Thomas. See E. Walker.

HOWELL, JAMES. "Analyticall Character" prefixed to Cherbury's *Henry VIII* (q. v.), 1649.
  "Lustra Ludovici, or The Life of . . . Lewis the XIII." 1646. (1643 — *D. N. B.*) This also contains (pp. 155–188) "The Life of Armand John de Plessis Cardinal of Richelieu." Unique in the collecting of favorable and unfavorable criticisms of Richelieu.
  "Epistolae Ho-Elianae." 1655. Autobiographical sections.

HOWELL, JOHN. "A Relation of the Life of Christina Queen of Sweden . . . Translated out of French, by J. H." 1656. Ascr. (*Halkett and Laing*) to "John" (?) Howell.

HUBERT, FRANCIS. "The Deplorable Life and Death of Edward the Second." 1628. 580 Troilus stanzas. Anon. Attr. to Hubert by J. P. Collier. Important as a revolt against the *Mirror for Magis-*

trates tradition, and disbelief in the sway of "Fortune, which wise men make to wait on them." Yet it retains the dramatic monologue and the verse form.

Hugh of Lincoln. See Adam of Eynsham and Giraldus Cambrensis.

HUMFREY, LAURENCE. "Ioannis Iuelli Angli, Episcopi Sarisburiensis vita & mors." 1573. Tr. by Daniel Featley and pr. as pref. to Jewel's works, 1609.

Humphrey, Duke of Gloucester. See Middleton.

Hutchinson, John. See L. Hutchinson.

HUTCHINSON, LUCY. "Memoirs of the Life of Colonel [John] Hutchinson." Wr. 1664–71. 1st ed. 1806. Ed. C. H. Firth, 1885.

HYDE, EDWARD, EARL OF CLARENDON. "Life . . . Written by himself." Wr. 1668–72. First pub. 1759. 1857 ed. 2 vols.
  Cf. his "History of the Rebellion" (pr. 1702–04, 1826, and 1888, ed. W. D. Macray) for relation of history and biography.

I

Innocent XI. See Nesse.
  "The Life and Reign of Innocent XI." 1690. Anon.

ISAACSON, HENRY. "Life and Death of . . . Lancelot Andrewes, Late Bishop of Winchester, Which may serve as a Pattern of Piety and Charity to all Godly disposed Christians." 1650. Repr. 1829. Cardinal virtues incarnate.

J

Jackson. See Head.

Jackson, Thomas. See Vaughan.

JAMES I OF SCOTLAND (1394–1437). "The Kingis Quair." 197 autobiographical Troilus stanzas. Attr. to James. MS. 1488–1513. Mod. ed. A. Lawson, 1910. Begun about 1423, according to W. W. Skeat in ed. for Scottish Text Soc., 1911. An early example of subjective, half-imaginative, poetical autobiography, which became increasingly common during the latter part of the 16th cent.

James I. See Drummond, F. Osborne, W. Sanderson.

James II. "Some Historical Memoires of the Life and Actions of His Royal Highness . . . James Duke of York and Albany." 1683. Anon. Military and adulatory.

"Original Papers containing the secret history of Great Britain from the Restoration to the Accession of the House of Hanover." Ed. James Macpherson, 2 vols. 1775.
"The Life of James the Second." J. S. Clarke, 2 vols. 1816. Both of the above are based on James's original memoirs, now destroyed.
Also "Papers of Devotion of James II." Roxburghe Club, 1925. Diplomatic repr. of original MS.

JAMES, THOMAS. "John Wickliffs life collected out of diverse Auctors," at conclusion of *Two Short Treatises, against the Orders of the Begging Friars.* 1608. Interesting for its faint attempt to trace influences of earlier writers on Wycliffe.
"The Jesuits Downefall . . . Together with the Life of Father Parsons." 1612. Cleverly lurid recrimination.

JANEWAY, JAMES. "Invisibles, Realties, Demonstrated in the Holy Life and Triumphant Death of Mr. John Janeway." 1673. Pref. by Richard Baxter. Repr. 1837, T. Jackson, *Lib. Chr. Biog.* An ascetic Christian who died young. Approaches subjective biography in accounts of religious rhapsodies and letters included.

Janeway, John.   See James Janeway.

JEBB, DR.   Life of Nicholas Ferrar, included in *Nicholas Ferrar. Two Lives,* 1855, ed. J. E. B. Mayor, who attributes this version to "Dr. Jebb" on a MS. note.

Jermin, Michael.   See Nicolls.

Jerome.   See Hawkins.
His *Vitae Patrum* tr. in 1491 according to Maunsell's *Catalogue.* Pr. by Caxton, 1495. — *Camb.*

Jessey, Henry.   "The Life and Death of Mr. Henry Jessey, Late Preacher of the Gospel." 1671. Anon.

Jesus Christ.   See R. Holland, Parkhurst, Jeremy Taylor, Wesley.
"A Stanzaic Life of Christ." 1926. Ed. Frances A. Foster. 14th-cent. poem compiled in Middle English from Higden's *Polychronicon* and the *Legenda Aurea.* E. E. T. S., Orig. Ser., vol. clxvi.

Jewel, John.   See Humfrey.

Joan of Navarre.   See Clark.

Joan, Pope. "The History of the Life and Death of Pope Joane: Who was elected to the Papacy, An. 855 . . . by H. J. Gent." 1663.

JOCELIN OF BRAKELOND. "Chronica . . . de rebus gestis Samsoni Abbatis Monasterii Sancti Edmundi." Wr. after 1203. Ed. J. G. Rokewode for Camden Soc., 1840. See also *Memorials of St. Edmund's Abbey*, 1890–96, 3 vols. Rolls Series, ed. T. Arnold. Eng. tr. Sir Ernest Clarke, 1903, King's Classics. In Carlyle's phrase, a "Boswellian narrative," which from the Sage of Chelsea would be highest praise. Minute and homely details concerning a bluff and blunt churchman, similar to Adam of Eynsham's *Hugh of Lincoln*, which is almost contemporaneous. Important.

JOCELIN OF FURNESS (fl. 1200). Lives of St. Patrick (1624 first pr.; tr. 1809), St. Kentigern, first Bishop of Glasgow, and King David of Scotland. — *D. N. B.*

JOHN OF LONDON (d. 1311). Funeral elegy on Edward I, "Commendatio Lamentabilis in transitum magni Regis Edwardi." Pr. in vol. ii of *Materials for Edward I and Edward II*, Rolls Series, 1883. Begins with photographic picture of his life and habits, followed by imaginary lamentations by the king's principal mourners.

JOHN OF SALISBURY. See Becket.

JOHN OF TYNEMOUTH. "Sanctilogium, sive de Vitis et Miraculis Sanctorum Angliae, Walliae, Scotiae et Hiberniae." Wr. about 1350. In Cotton MS. Tiberius E. i. Original of Capgrave's *Nova Legenda Angliae*.

JOHNSON, RICHARD. "The Famous History of the Seven Champions of Christendom." N. d. Oldest dated copy 1597. (Sts. George, Denis, James, Anthony, Andrew, Patrick, and David.)
  "A Remembrance of the Honors due to the Life and Death of Robert Earle of Salisbury, Lord Treasurer of England." 1612. Wr. in prose because he finds "the Muses lippes lockt up." A significant straw that shows the prevalent belief in the adequacy of verse as a biographical vehicle.

Jones, Captain. See D. Lloyd.

Jones, Henry. "The Bloody Murtherer, Or, The Unnatural Son," who "was prest to Death, his Sister burnt, and his Boy Hang'd" for the murder of his mother. 1672. Sensational.

Jonson, Ben. "Ionsonus Virbius or, The Memorie of Ben Johnson." 1638. Elegies by various authors published shortly after his death.

JOSSELIN, JOHN. "The life off the 70. Archbishop off Canterbury [Matthew Parker] presentlye Sitting Englished and to be added to the 69. lately Sett forth in Latin." 1574. Tr., Strype conjectures, by John Stubbs.

Joyeuse, Father Angel. See Capucins.

Juliana. "Life of Juliana" in Middle English versions, two in prose, one in rhyme; wr. about 1230; pr. in E. E. T. S., Orig. Ser., vol. li.

JURDAIN, IGNATIUS. See Manton and Nicolls.

K

Katherine of Aragon. See Forrest.

Katherine of Siena. See Fenne, Vineis.

Katherine, Saint. Old English metrical version of a life of St. Katherine, wr. about 1200, in E. E. T. S., Orig. Ser., vol. lxxx.

KENNET, BASIL. "The Lives and Characters Of the Ancient Grecian Poets." 1697.

KETTLEWELL, JOHN. "The Life of a Christian." 1695. Extracted from his *Measure of Obedience*, 1681. Generic.

KNELL, THOMAS. "An Epitaph, or rather a short Discourse made upon the Life and Death of Dr. Bonner, sometime unworthy Bishop of London, whiche dyed the Fifth of September in the Marshalsie. Imprinted . . .1569, Sept. 14." Repr. *Harl. Misc.*, i, 595. Verse, describing this Catholic adept in persecution. See Story.

KNOLLES, RICHARD. "Generall Historie of the Turkes . . . Together with The Lives and Conquests of the Othoman Kings and Emperours unto the yeare 1621." *Hist.*, 1st ed. 1603; with *Lives*, 1610; t. p. from 3d ed. 1621. Had important influence on development of biographies of romantic figures. Elizabethan delight in opulence. The lives abound in details of royal wars and intrigues but are not individual.

Knox, John. See Bannatyne, D. Buchanan.

L

Lake, Arthur. See J. Harris.

Langbaine, Gerald. See Cheke.

LANGBAINE, GERARD. "An Account of the English Dramatick Poets, or, Some Observations And Remarks On the Lives and Writings. . . ." 1691. Oxf.

LARKIN, EDWARD. "Speculum Patrum: A Looking-Glasse of the Fathers . . . To which are added, The Characters of some of the Chief Philosophers, Historians, Grammarians, Orators, and Poets." 1659. Drawn from Burley, a Latin *Patrologia*, and classical authorities.

LATIMER, HUGH. "Sermons," ed. for Parker Society, 1844, contain autobiographical passages in first sermon before Edward VI, 8 March, 1549. Pr. by John Day, 1562.

LAUD, WILLIAM. "Diary of his own Life" prefixed to Wharton's *History*, 1695 (q. v.). Contains numerous minutely detailed entries of psychological and dramatic interest.

Laud, William. See Heylyn, Wharton.
    "Rome for Canterbury: Or, a true Relation of the Birth and Life of William Laud, Archbishop of Canterbury." 1641. Anon. Repr. *Harl. Misc.* iv, 359–364.

LAVARDIN, JACQUES DE. "The Historie of George Castriot, Surnamed Scanderbeg, King of Albanie . . . Newly translated by Z. I. Gentleman." 1596. Illustrative of the growing popular desire for romantic biography.

Legendary. "Early South English Legendary." MS. before 1280. E. E. T. S., Orig. Ser., vol. lxxxvii, 1887. This, with the North English Cycle (c. 1300) and the Scottish Legendary (c. 1400), shows the popularity of saints' lives in the vernacular.

LEGH, EDWARD. "Selected and Choice Observations concerning the Twelve First Caesars." 1635.

Leicester, Earl of. "Leycesters Common-wealth." 1641. Attr. to the Jesuit Father Parsons. Derogatory. 1st ed. 1584.

LELAND, JOHN. "Commentarii de Scriptoribus Britannicis." Wr. about 1534–43. Known to Bale and other antiquaries in MS. Ed. from autograph MS. under above title by Anthony Hall, Oxf. 1709.

LEY, JOHN. "A patterne of Pietie. Or The Religious life and death of that Grave and gracious Matron, Mrs. Jane Ratcliffe. Widow and Citizen of Chester. Of whom the discourse is framed and applied so as the commemoration of the dead may best serve to the edification of the living." 1640.

Leyden, John. See Rowlands.

LILLY, WILLIAM. "History of His Life and Times, From the Year 1602, to 1681. Written by himself." Wr. 1681. Pub. 1715. The astrologer.

Lisle, Sir George. "The Loyall Sacrifice: Presented In the Lives and Deaths of those two Eminent Heroick Patternes . . . Sir Charles Lucas, And Sir George Lisle." 1648. Anon.

Lives of the Saints. See Aelfric, Bokenam, Buckland, Legendary, Mabillon, Messingham, Porter, Ribadeneyra, Villegas.

LIVINGSTONE, JOHN. "Life of John Livingstone, Minister of the Gospel . . . Written by himself." Wr. about 1663–64. Ed. 1848. Contains an impartial self-study (pp. 143–146). Such an appraisal is sufficiently rare in early English biography to render this life of some importance.

LLOYD, DAVID (1597–1663). "The Legend of Captain Jones." 1st ed. 1631. T. p. 1648. In verse. A witty and exuberant travesty.

LLOYD, DAVID (1635–92). "Eikon Basilike Or, The True Pourtraic-ture of his Sacred Majesty Charls the II." 1660. A sanctification at odds with its subject.
  "Memoires of the Lives, Actions, Sufferings & Deaths of Those . . . That Suffered . . . For the Protestant Religion, And the great Principle thereof, Allegiance To their Soveraigne, In our late Intestine Wars, From the Year 1637, to the Year . . . 1666. With the life and Martyrdom of King Charles I." 1668. Oppor-tune journalism, drawn from a multitude of sources.
  "The Statesmen and Favourites of England since the Reforma-tion." 1665–70. — D. N. B.
  "The Worthies of the World." 1665. Abridged from Plu-tarch. — D. N. B.

LLOYD, RICHARD. "A briefe discourse of the most renowned actes and right valiant conquests of those puisant Princes, called the Nine worthies." 1584. In verse. Includes Joshua, Hector, David, Alexander, Judas Maccabaeus, Julius Caesar, Arthur, Charle-magne, and Guy of Warwick.

LODGE, THOMAS. "The Famous, true and historicall life of Robert second Duke of Normandy, surnamed for his monstrous birth and behaviour, Robin the Divell." 1591. Mod. repr. in Works, 1883, vol. ii.
  "The Life and Death of william Long beard, the most famous and witty English Traitor, borne in the Citty of London." 1593. Repr. J. P. Collier, Illustrations of Old English Literature, vol. ii, 1860.

Long, Thomas. "A Review of Mr. Richard Baxter's Life." 1697. An attack upon the *Reliquiae Baxterianae*. Polemical, not biographical.

Longbeard, William. See Lodge.

Louis XIII. See James Howell.

Loyal Martyrology. See Winstanley.

Loyola, Ignatius. "The Life of B. Father Ignatius of Loyola . . . Translated out of Spanish . . . By W. M." 1616.

Lucas, Sir Charles. "The Loyall Sacrifice: Presented In the Lives and Deaths of those two Eminent Heroick Patternes . . . Sir Charles Lucas, And Sir George Lisle." 1648. Anon.

Ludlow, Edmund. "Memoirs . . . 1625–72." Wr. 1663–73. First pub. 1698. Ed. C. H. Firth, 1894. Military and political.

Lupton, Donald. "The History of the Moderne Protestant Divines, Containing their Parents, Countries, Education, Studies, Lives, and the yeare of our Lorde in which they dyed." 1637.

Luther, Martin. See Hayne and Anderton.

Lydgate, John (1370–1451). "The Fall of Princes." Wr. 1431–39. Eds. 1494, 1527, 1554, 1558. Ed. Henry Bergen, E. E. T. S., 1924, Ex. Ser., 3 vols.
   Minor Poems, ed. H. N. MacCracken, 1911, for E. E. T. S., Ex. Ser., vol. cvii. Has saints' legends of interest. Includes "the lyf of Saint George . . . made . . . at the request of tharmorieres of London for thonour of theyre brotherhoode and theyre feest of Saint George." A definite and unusual reason for the writing of saints' lives: popularization of hagiography.
   "The Legend of St. Edmund and Fremund." Pr. in Horstmann's *Sammlung Altenglischer Legenden*, 1878.
   "The Life of St. Giles" and "The Life of St. Margarete." Wr. 1430. In Horstmann.
   "The glorious Lyfe and Passion of Saint Albon, Prothomartyr of Englande, and also the Lyfe and Passion of Saint Amphabel." Wr. 1439. T. p. 1533 ed. Verse.
   "The Life and Death of Hector." 1594 fol.
   "The Life of Our Lady." Wr. for Henry V. Pr. by Caxton, 1484.
   "The testament of John Lydgate," Pynson, n. d. Repr. J. P. Collier, *Cat. Early Eng. Lit.*, 1837, pp. 175–178. Autobiographical.

LYMERIC, JOHN. "The Life of the Author" prefixed to "The Works of . . . John Bramhall D.D. Late Lord Archbishop of Ardmagh." Dublin,1677. 54 fol. pp. Controversial.

LYNDSAYE, SIR DAVID. " . . . the Tragedy of the late most reverende father David [Beaton], by the mercie of God Cardinall and archbishoppe of sainct Andrewes . . . ." 1546. Important as showing the direct influence of Lydgate in the decade preceding the *Mirror for Magistrates*.

For Scotch version, see Lyndsaye's *Works*, ed. D. Laing, 1879, i, 139–155, which also contains "The History of ane nobill and vailyeand squyer, William Meldrum." Boisterous and satirical.

Lyvys of Seyntys. See Bokenam.

M

MABBE, JAMES. "The Rogue: Or The Life of Guzman de Alfarache. Written in Spanish by Matheo Aleman." 1622. Typical picaresque novel in biographical form.

MABILLON, JOHN. "Acta Sanctorum Ordinis Sancti Benedicti." Ed. in 9 fol. vols. with d'Achery, 1668–1701. Original sources.

Machor, Saint. See Ninian.

MACHYN, HENRY. "Diary." 1550–63. Ed. J. G. Nichols for Camden Soc. 1848.

Magdalene, Mary. See T. Robinson.

Mahomet. See Raleigh.

MAIDSTONE, RICHARD DE (d. 1396). "Deposition of Richard II" in English alliterative verse. Camden Soc., vol. iii. Unimportant.

MALORY, SIR THOMAS (fl. 1470). "Le Morte Arthur" in Caxton 1485 ed. has also the title "The byrth, lyf, and actes of kyng Arthur."

MANLEY, THOMAS. "A short View of the Lives of . . . Henry, Duke of Gloucester, and Mary Princess of Orange . . . Collected by T. M. Esq." 1661. (Attr. from *Lowndes*.)

MANTON, THOMAS. Character sketch of Ignatius Jurdain in the "Life and Death of Jurdain," 1654, by Ferdinand Nicolls (q. v.).

MARBECKE, JOHN. "The lyves of holy Sainctes, Prophetes, Patriarches, and others, contayned in holye Scripture." 1574. A Biblical biographical dictionary.

Marcus Aurelius. See Bourchier.

Margaret, Countess of Richmond and Derby. See Fisher.

Margaret, Saint. "Seinte Marharete ϸe Meiden Ant Martyr In Old English Now First edited from the Skin Books By the Rev. Oswald Cockayne." 1865. E. E. T. S., Orig. Ser., vol. xiii. Two versions, 1200 and 1330.

MARKHAM, GERVASE. "The Most Honorable Tragedie of Sir Richard Grinvile, Knight." 1595. Verse.

MARKHAM, ROBERT. "The Description of that ever to be famed Knight, Sir John Burgh . . . with his last service at the Isle of Rees, and his unfortunate death." 1628. Repr. Brydges, *Cens. Lit.*, vi, 213. In verse. An entertaining, if unconscious, parody of the grand manner, which treats of "Arch-dutchesses, and such heroicke things."

Marshal, Stephen. "The Life of . . . Mr. Stephen Marshal, Sometime Minister of the Gospel at Finchingfield in Essex." 1680. Anti-presbyterian satire. Anon.

MARTINDALE, ADAM. "Life of Adam Martindale Written by himself." Wr. about 1685. Pub. 1845 for Chetham Soc. Ed. R. Parkinson.

MARTYN, DR. THOMAS. "Historica Descriptio Complectens Vitam, ac Res Gestas Beatissimi Viri Gulielmi Wicami." 1597. T. p. 1690 ed.

MARTYN, WILLIAM. "Historie, and Lives, of Twentie Kings of England." 1615. Patriotic biography, proved popular in successive eds. in 1628 and 1638.

Martyrology. "An Old English Martyrology." Wr. about 850. Drawn from Bede, Gregory of Tours, Roman Martyrology, etc. Pr. E. E. T. S., Orig. Ser., vol. cxvi.
"The English Martyrologe Conteyning A Summary of the Lives of the . . . Saintes of . . . England, Scotland, and Ireland, By a Catholicke Priest." 1608.
See also Watson, Whytford.

Mary of Anjou. "The Unequal Match: or The Life of Mary of Anjou Queen of Majorca. An Historical Novel." 2 parts, 1681 and 1683. Dedication signed "F. S." An elegant romance.

MARY, QUEEN (1662–94). "Memoirs of Mary, Queen of England, (1689–93)." Ed. R. Doebner. 1886. Pious reflections. See Manley.

Mary Stuart. See Sanderson and Stranguage.

Mary Tudor. See Godwin.

Mary the Virgin. See Pinelli, A. Stafford, John Taylor.

MATHER, COTTON. "Ecclesiastical History of New-England, From . . . 1620 . . . unto . . . 1698." 1702. In 7 books. Book II "Containing the Lives of the Governours, and Names of the Magistrates of New-England." Book III, "The Lives of Sixty Famous Divines, by whose Ministry the Churches of New-England have been Planted and Continued." English biography crosses the Atlantic.

Mathieu, Pierre. See Grimeston.

MATTHEW, SIR TOBIE. Augustine's *Confessions,* tr., 1st ed. 1620. 2d ed. Paris, 1638.
    "The Penitent Bandito: Or the History Of the Conversion and Death of . . . Signor Troilo Savelli." 1663. 2d ed.

MAUNSELL, ANDREW. "Catalogue of English Printed Bookes." 1595. In two parts, dealing with divinity and the sciences respectively. Valuable for occasional titles.

MAXWELL, JAMES. "The Laudable Life, and Deplorable Death, of our late peerlesse Prince Henry." 1612. 44 ababcc stanzas. A laudatory character sketch with amusing marginal guides.

MAY, THOMAS. "Reigne of King Henry the Second." 1633. Seven books of rhymed couplets.
    "Victorious Reigne of King Edward the Third." 1635. Late date for verse lives. Barren rhymed historical annals.

MAYNE, JASPER. Character sketch in heroic couplets preceding Duncon's *Lady Letice,* 1647 (q. v.).

MAYO, RICHARD. "Life & Death of Edmund Staunton." 1673. An intimate ecclesiastical biography, charming in style and tone.

Mede, Joseph. "The Works of . . . Joseph Mede," 1672, has a prefatory life "written by some of great acquaintance with him, and that always had a just esteem for him."

Medicis, Catharine de. "A Mervaylous discourse upon the lyfe, deedes, and behaviours of Katherine de Medicis, Queene mother, wherin are displayed the means which she hath practised to atteyne unto the usurping of the Kingedome of France, and to the bringing of the estate of the same unto utter ruine and destruction." Heidelberg. 1575. Anon. tr.

Meg. "The Life and Pranks of Long Meg of Westminster." 1582, and many succeeding editions. Rogue pamphlet. — *Chandler.*

Meldrum, William. See Lyndsaye.

MELVILL, JAMES. "Diary... 1556–1601." Ed. for Bannatyne Club, vol. xxxii, in 1829. A God-fearing minister is well sketched in this autobiography, which becomes in its later sections a history of the Scottish Church.

MELVILLE, SIR JAMES. "Memoirs of his own life" (1549–93). 1st ed. 1683. Ed. from orig. MS. 1827, Bannatyne Club, vol. xvii.

Merlin. See Heywood.

MESSINGHAM, THOMAS. "Florilegium Insulae Sanctorum Seu Vitae et Acta Sanctorum Hiberniae." 1624. Paris. Shows persistence of the Latin hagiological tradition.

MEUSE, CONRAD. "The Life and Heresie of David George." Basel, 1560. From Latin life, 1559. — *Maunsell.*

Mexia, Pedro. See Traheron.

MIDDLETON, CHRISTOPHER. "The Legend of Humphrey Duke of Glocester." 1600. Repr. in Brydges, *Cens. Lit.,* ii, 162. In verse.

MILTON, JOHN. Autobiography in preface to "Second Defence of the People of England," 1654, in Latin. "Jo. Miltoni pro se defensio" (1655 ed.). Good example of the impersonal autobiography of the 17th cent. Other autobiographical notices may be found in *An Introduction to Milton, Comprising all the Autobiographical Passages in his Works,* by Hiram Corson, 1899.
"The Life and Reigne of King Charls, Or the Pseudo-Martyr discovered." 1651. (Attr. *Halkett and Laing.*) An attack on the *Eikon Basilike.*

Milton, John. See E. Phillips, Toland.
"The Earliest Life of Milton." Repr. from "The English Historical Review," January, 1902. Ed. Edward S. Parsons. Used by Anthony Wood. Anon. Sympathetic. Deals especially with his political writings.

Mirror for Magistrates. Ed. 1555 suppressed; 1559 1st ed.; supplements to 1610. 1587 standard ed. Ed. Joseph Haslewood, 1815.

MOLIERE, HENRIETTA SYLVIA. "The Memoires of the Life and Rare Adventures of Henrietta Sylvia Molière. Written in French by her Self." 1671 and 1677. Tr. Anon.

340 BIBLIOGRAPHY

MONIER, PHILIP. "The History of Painting, Sculpture, Architecture, Graving; and Of those who have Excell'd in them. . . ." 1699. Not, however, the lives of the painters, but the history of the arts.

Monk, General George. See Gumble, Skinner.

Monmouth, James, Duke of. "The Heroick Life and Magnanimous Actions of . . . James Duke of Monmouth." 1683. Military. By "S. T."

Monmouth, Earl of. See R. Cary.

Montague, Viscountess. See R. Smith.

DE LA MOORE, THOMAS. "Vita et Mors Edwardi II." (Moore fl. 1327–47.) Rolls Series, 1883, ed. William Stubbs, who disproves Moore's widely accepted authorship.

MORE, CRESACRE. "The Life and Death of Sir Thomas Moore." 1st ed. pub. abroad, n. d., but about 1631. Assigned to its true author by Joseph Hunter in 1828 ed. repr. The fullest early biography of More, with many very good anecdotes not in Roper. Acknowledges debt to Roper and Stapleton. Cresacre was More's great grandson and writes with evident family pride. Includes several miraculous incidents following More's death.

MORE, SIR THOMAS. "Lyfe of Johan Picus, Erle of Mirandula." Tr. from Italian life by Giovanni Francesco Pico. Wynkyn de Worde, about 1510. Also in 1557 ed. of his *Works*. Ed. J. M. Rigg, 1890.
"History of King Richard III." Wr. about 1513. Pub. in 1557 ed. of his *Works*. Pr. in part in Hall's *Chronicles*, 1548, and later histories. First part pub. for political purposes in 1641 as ". . . the Pitifull Life, and unfortunate Death of Edward the fifth."

More, Sir Thomas. See Erasmus, Harpsfield, Hoddesdon, C. More, Rastell, Roper, Stapleton.
Also a life wr. about 1600 is repr. in Wordsworth's *Eccl. Biog.*, ii, 1818 ed., 57.

MORICE, RALPH. "Anecdotes and Character of Archbishop Cranmer." Wr. 1563–76. Pr. in "Narratives of the Days of the Reformation." Camden Soc., vol. lxxvii, 1859.

Morrell, William. "The Notorious Imposter, Or the History of the Life of William Morrell." 1692.

Morton, Thomas. See Baddily and J. Barwick.

Mossom, Robert. "A Narrative Panegyrical Of the Life, Sickness, and Death, of George [Wilde], By Divine Providence, Lord Bishop of Derry in Ireland." 1665/6. Shows transition from funeral sermon to biography, and is, in fact, an oral biography.

Munday, Anthony. "The English Romayne Lyfe. Discovering The lives of the Englishmen at Roome." 1582. Not individual biographies; but picturesque details in the life of Munday are given, "sometime the Popes Scholler in the Seminarie among them."

Mush, John. "Vita & Martyrium D. Marg. Clithoroae." Wr. 1586 (*D. N. B.*); pub. 1612 (*Pits*). Catholic.

N

Nashe, Thomas. "The Unfortunate Traveller. Or, The life of Jacke Wilton. Newly corrected and augmented." 1594. Influence of the biographical form in introducing realism into romance.

Naunton, Sir Robert. "Fragmenta Regalia: Or, Observations on the late Queen Elisabeth, her Times and Favourites." Wr. about 1630. Pub. 1641. Repr. *Harl. Misc.*, ii, 72–95, from 1653 ed. Good historical character sketches and gossip.

Naylor, Joseph. "Life of Dr. Thomas Morton, Late Bishop of Duresme. Begun by R.[ichard] B.[addily] Secretary to his Lordship, And Finished by J. N. D.D. his Lordship's Chaplain." 1669.

Needham, Marchamount. "Digitus Dei: Or, God's Justice upon Treachery and Treason; Exemplifyed in the Life and Death of the late James Duke of Hamilton." 1649.

Neot, Saint. Old English and Latin lives in "The History . . . of Eynesbury and St. Neot's." G. C. Gorham, 1824.

Nepos, Cornelius. See Finch.

Nerius, Philip. "The Holy Life of Philip Nerius . . . Translated out of a French Copie published at Paris. 1656." 1659. Latin ed. Rome 1645. Miraculous account of the founder of the Congregation of the Oratory.

Nesse, Christopher. "The Devils Patriarck, Or A Full and Impartial Account Of the Notorious Life Of this Present Pope of Rome Innocent the Eleventh." 1683.

NEWCOME, HENRY. "Autobiography." Wr. before 1695. Pub. Chetham Soc. 1852. For relations between diaries and biographies, see "Newcome's Diary, 1661–63," also in Chetham Soc.

NICCOLS, RICHARD. "England's Eliza." In Pt. V of *Mirror for Magistrates*, 1610. 463 stanzas of Elizabethan history. Niccols also wrote other *Mirror* histories.

NICOLLS, FERDINAND. "Life and Death of Mr. Ignatius Jurdain, One of the Aldermen of the City of Exeter." 1654. T. p. from 2d ed. 1655. (Wood also attributes a life of Jurdain to Michael Jermin.)

NICOLSON, WILLIAM. "The English Historical Library . . . Giving a Short View and Character of most of our Historians either in Print or Manuscript." 1696–99. T. p. 2d ed. 1714. More a catalogue than a biographical collection.

Nine English Worthies. See G. Fletcher, R. Lloyd.

Nine Worthy Women. See Heywood.

Ninian, Saint. "The Legends of SS. Ninian and Machor From an Unique MS. in the Scottish Dialect of the 14th Century." Ed. W. M. Metcalfe, 1904. Ascribed to John Barbour. In 4-beat couplets.

NORTH, THOMAS. Tr. of Plutarch's *Lives*, 1579.

NORTON, JOHN. "The Life & Death of . . . Mr. John Cotton, Late teacher of the church of Christ at Boston in New-England." 1658.

Nova Legenda Angliae. See Capgrave.

"*Numerus Infaustus.*" 1689. A collection of short topical lives to show the misfortunes of English kings bearing the title of "the Second." Political.

NYXON, ANTHONY. "London's Dove: or A Memoriall of the life and death of Maister Robert Dove, Citizen and Marchant-Taylor of London." 1612. Centred on his charity.

O

Odo, Bishop. See Osbern.

Offa, King. See Paris.

Oldcastle, Sir John. See Bale, Weever.

OLEY, BARNABAS. "A Prefatory View of the Life of Mr. Geo. Herbert." Prefixed to *Herbert's Remains*, 1652. A triple parallel between Herbert, Dr. Thomas Jackson, and Nicholas Ferrar. Known to Walton.
See Vaughan.

Olimpia, Donna. See Compton.

O'Neill, Hugh, Earl of Tyrone. See Gainsford.

Ortell, Abraham. "The Life of Abraham Ortell, Cosmographer to Philip the Second . . . written first in Latine by Francis Sweert . . . and now translated . . . by W. B." in *Theatrum Orbis Terrarum*, 1606. Early example of a prefatory life of a layman.

OSBERN OF CANTERBURY. "Vita S. Odonis Archiepiscopi Cantuariensis." Wr. about 1090. *Acta Sanctt. Ord. S. Benedicti*, saec. v, 1685. (According to *D. N. B.* this Life is not Osbern's, but may have been wr. by Eadmer.)
"Vita Dunstani." In *Anglia Sacra*, Wharton, vol. ii, 1691. Good example of vivid incidents combined without discrimination with devil plagues and miraculous manifestations.

OSBERT OF STOKE CLARE. "Passio Sancti Athelberti, Regis et Martyris." (Fl. 793.) Osbert also composed lives of Edward the Confessor, Edmund the Martyr, and Eadburga. Osbert himself lived ca. 1136. — *Hardy*.

OSBORNE, DOROTHY. "The Love Letters of Dorothy Osborne to Sir William Temple." 1903. 1st pub. 1888. Wr. during Civil Wars Interesting as showing possible biographical elements in a collection of letters.

OSBORNE, FRANCIS. "Historical Memoires on the Reigns of Queen Elizabeth, and King James." 1658.

Oswald, Saint. See Eadmer.
Also anon. life, wr. about 995–1005, in *Acta Sanctt. Ord. S. Benedicti*, vii, 727, and in Rolls Series, *Hist. York*, i, 399. Includes trivial miracles: a church mouse chokes on a piece of the *panis benedictus*.

P

Painters. "The Lives of the Painters . . . from the French of Monsieur [Roger] De Piles [1681]." 1706. A further extension of the biographical field just after the close of the century. Cf. Philip Monier.

344 BIBLIOGRAPHY

Par, Thomas. See John Taylor.

PARIS, MATTHEW. "Vitae duorum Offarum . . . et Viginti trium Abbatum S. Albani." Wr. before 1259. Lives of various kings and church leaders in his *Chronica Majora*, Rolls Series, ed. H. R. Luard, 1883.
Fragment from "Vita S. Stephani Cantuariensis" in *Ungedruckte Anglo-Normannische Geschichtsquellen*. F. Liebermann, 1879.

PARKER, HENRY. "The True Portraiture of the Kings of England." 1688.

PARKER, HENRY, BARON MORLEY (1476–1556). Tr. into English from Plutarch, in MSS. Tr. of Anselm's "Life of Mary and Our Saviour." — *D. N. B.*

PARKER, MATTHEW. "De Antiquitate Britannicae Ecclesiae & Privilegiis Ecclesiae Cantuariensis, cum Archiepiscopis eiusdem 70." 1572. At Lambeth by John Day. 1605 ed. Hanover. Biographies from Augustine to Parker himself, arranged chronologically by sees. Not uniform in length or quality. See also Godwin.

Parker, Matthew. See Josselin.

PARKHURST, JOHN. "Vita Christi." 1578. In verse. — *Berkenhout*, p. 347.

PARR, RICHARD. "The Life of . . . James Usher, Late Lord Arch-Bishop of Armagh . . . With a Collection of Three Hundred Letters." 1686.

Parsons, Father Robert. See T. James.

Patrick, Saint. Tripartite Life in Rolls Series, 1887, 2 vols. Fine collection of hagiological fables.
"The life of . . . S. Patricke . . . with the lives of . . . S. Bridgit and . . . Saint Columbe." 1625. By B. B. — *Camb.*
"The Delightful History of the Life and Death of . . . St. Patrick, Champion of Ireland." 1685. Anon.

Patten, William. See Budden.

PAULE, GEORGE. "The Life of . . . John Whitgift, Archbishop of Canterbury." 1612.

Pawlet, William. See Broughton.

Pazzi, Mary Magdalen of. "The life of the holy and venerable mother Suor Maria Maddalena de Patsi, translated into English by G. B." Cologne, 1619.
Another life tr. by Dr. Thomas Smith, 1687.

PEARSON, JOHN. Life of Hales prefatory to the *Golden Remains of . . . Mr. John Hales of Eton College.* 1659.

PEPYS, SAMUEL. "Diary." 1660–69. 1st ed. 1825. Interesting in a comparative study of the diary and autobiography.

Perne, Andrew. See Harvey.

PERRINCHIEF, RICHARD. "The Royal Martyr: Or, The Life and Death of King Charles I." 1676.
"The Sicilian Tyrant: Or The Life of Agathocles." 1676. Intended as a parallel to Cromwell.

Perrott, Sir John. "The History of That most Eminent Statesman, Sir John Perrott, Knight of the Bath, and Lord Lieutenant of Ireland." Wr. about 1600. T. p. from 1st ed. of 1728. MS. in Bodl. Wood D. 33. (Ascribed erroneously to Richard Rawlinson, 1690–1755, by Halkett and Laing.)

PHELPS, THOMAS. "True Account of the Captivity of Thomas Phelps, at Machaness in Barbary, and Of his strange Escape." 1685.

"PHILANAX MISOPAPPAS." "Rawleigh Redivivus: Or The Life & Death of . . . Anthony Late Earl of Shaftsbury. Humbly Dedicated to the Protesting Lords." 1683. Political and anti-Catholic. Epistle Dedicatory signed "S. N."

PHILLIPS, EDWARD. "Theatrum Poetarum." 1674.
"Letters of State, Written by Mr. John Milton," 1694, contains "An Account of his Life" by Phillips.

PHILLIPS, JOHN. "A Commemoration of the Right Noble and vertuous Ladye, Margrit Duglas . . . Countis of Lenox . . . Wherin is rehearsed hir godly life." 1578. Repr. Collier, *Bibl. Acct.*, ii, 157. In verse. Dramatic monologue and dream form.
"The Life and Death of Sir Phillip Sidney." 1587. Verse. Repr. for Roxburghe Club, vol. liii. 1837.
Commemorative poem on Sir Christopher Hatton. 1591. — *D. N. B.*
Three other epitaphs in single folio sheets, to the wife of Alexander Avenet (1570); Sir William Garrat (1571); and Henry Wriothesley, Earl of Southampton (1581). — *D. N. B.*

Philosophers. See W. Burley, Hornanus, Stanley.

Pim, John. "A Short View of the life and actions of . . . Iohn Pim." Anon. About 1644–45.

PINELLI, LUCAS. "The Virgin Maries Life . . . translated into English by R. G." Douai, 1604.

PITS, JOHN. ". . . Relationum Historicarum de Rebus Anglicis Tomus Primus." Paris, 1619. An antiquarian collection of lives of Englishmen written to offset Bale and state the position of the Catholics. Pits announces it is to include "non solum Theologos aut Ecclesiasticos Doctores, sed etiam Iurisconsultos, Medicos, Philosophos, Mathematicos, Historicos, Oratores, imo etiam Grammaticos insigniores." This ambitious plan, inspired by the precedents of Cicero and Suetonius, is incompletely realized.

PLUME, THOMAS. "An Account of the Life and Death of the Author" in "A Century of Sermons . . . by John Hacket, Late Lord Bishop of Lichfield and Coventry." 1675.

Plutarch. See Dryden, North.
For a biography of Plutarch, see 1612 ed. of North's tr. of the *Lives.* Also see Dryden.

Poets, Lives of the. See Heywood, E. Phillips, Winstanley.

Pole, Reginald. See Dudith.

Pomponius Atticus. See Hale.

Pontis, Louis de. See C. Cotton.

POPE, DR. WALTER. "The Memoires of Monsieur Du Vall, containing the History of his Life and Death." 1670. (Attr. *Ath. Oxon.*, iv, 724.)

PORTER, JEROME. "The Flowers of the Lives of the most Renowned Saincts of the three kingdoms England, Scotland, and Ireland. . . . By the R. Father, Hierome Porter Priest and monke of the holy order of Sainct Benedict." Douai, 1632.

POWELL, ROBERT. "The Life of Alfred . . . Together with a Parallell of our Soveraigne Lord, King Charles." 1634.

POWELL, VAVASOR. "Life and Death of Vavasor Powell." Largely an autobiography wr. before 1670. Pub. 1671. Ed. T. Jackson, *Lib. Chr. Biog.* 1837.

POYNTZ, SYDNAM. "The Relation of Sydnam Poyntz, 1624–36." Wr. 1636. Ed. A. T. S. Goodrick, 1908.

PRESTON, THOMAS. "A lamentable tragedy mixed ful of pleasant mirth, conteyning the life of Cambises king of Percia." 1570. Verse. — *Br. Mus. Cat. Early Printed Books.* Demonstrating the impracticability of biography in King Cambyses' vein.

PRICKET, ROBERT. "Honors Fame in Triumph Riding. Or the Life and Death of the late Honorable Earle of Essex." 1604. Repr. Collier, *Bibl. Acct.*, ii, 187. In verse.

PRINCE, JOHN. "The Worthies of Devon." 1701. Antiquarian scholarship, showing the tendency of collectors toward specialization in this period.

PRINGLE, WALTER. "Memoirs." 1662–66. Ed. Walter Wood, 1847. Fragments addressed to his children designed to show God's goodness.

Purser. "A True Relation, of the Lives and Deaths of the two most Famous Pyrats, Purser, and Clinton." 1639. Anon.

PUTTENHAM, RICHARD. "The Arte of English Poesie." 1589. Critical. See particularly Book I, chap. 19, "Of historicall Poesie."

Q

QUARLES, FRANCIS. "The History of Queen Ester," 1642; "Job Militant," 1642; "The Historie of Sampson," 1642. In verse. Illustrations of the re-working of Biblical stories in biographical form.

Quarles, Francis. See U. Quarles.

QUARLES, URSULA. "A Short Relation of the Life and Death of Mr. Francis Quarles, by Ursula Quarles, his sorrowfull Widow." In *Solomons Recantations*, 1645.

QUIN, WALTER. "The Memorie of the most worthie and renowned Bernard Stuart, Lord D'Aubigni renewed." 1619. Repr. Collier, *Bibl. Acct.*, ii, 213. In couplets.

R

Rainbow, Edward. See Banks.

RALEIGH, SIR WALTER (?). "Life and Death of Mahomet." 1637. A brief, pleasant, and somewhat fanciful biography, attr. to Raleigh on the title-page.

Raleigh, Sir Walter. See Shirley.

RASTELL, WILLIAM. Life of Sir Thomas More. — *Wood.* Pub. 1557 folio of More's works.

Ratcliffe, Mrs. Jane. See Ley.

Ratsey, Gamaliel. "The Life and Death of Gamaliel Ratsey, A famous Thief of England." 1605. Mod. repr. by J. P. Collier.

Rawdon, Marmaduke. "Life of Marmaduke Rawdon of York." Wr. mainly before 1668. Anon.; possibly autobiography, though Robert Davis suggests the author is Rawdon's son, in 1863 ed. for Camden Soc. The complacent account of the travels of a success-ful wine-merchant, a Royalist who enjoyed the peacefulness of the Canary Islands during the Civil Wars.

RAWLEY, WILLIAM. "The Life of the Honourable Author," as a pref. to the *Resuscitatio* of Francis Bacon. 1657. Conscientious and detailed rather than discriminating.

RAYMOND, THOMAS. "Autobiography." Born 1610. Last entry 1658. First pr. Camden Soc., 3d ser., vol. xxviii, 1917.

Reading, Thomas of. See Deloney.

REDMAN, ROBERT. "Historia Henrici Quinti." Wr. 1536–44. Rolls Series, 1858, ed. C. A. Cole.

REGINALD OF DURHAM. "De vita et miraculis S. Godrici, Heremitae de Finchale." Late 12th cent. Ed. 1847 for the Surtees Soc. Miracles and apparitions.

Remigius, Saint. See Giraldus Cambrensis.

Renty. "The Holy Life of Mon^r De Renty . . . Written in French by John Baptist S. Jure. And Faithfully translated into English, By E. S. Gent." 1658. Repr. in John Wesley's abridgment, *Lib. Chr. Biog.*, 1837, T. Jackson. The story of a French nobleman who could not serve both his Court and his God. A saint's life on the scale of Plutarch, exceptionally powerful.

RERESBY, SIR JOHN. "Memoirs." Finished in 1689. First pub. 1734. Ed. J. J. Cartwright, 1875.

REYNOLDES, RICHARD. "A Chronicle of all the noble Emperours of the Romaines, from Iulius Caesar, orderly to this most victorious Emperour Maximilian, that now governeth." 1571. Ample and well written.

Rhodes, Benjamin. See Samwaies.

RIBADENEYRA, PETER. "The Lives of Saints . . . translated into English By W. P." St. Omers, 1659.

Rich, Mary. See M. Warwick.

Richard, Saint. See Bocking.

Richard I. See Benedict.
 Also "Kynge Rycharde cuer du lyon." Wynkyn de Worde, 1509. Verse romance.

Richard II.   See Gower, R. Howard, Maidstone.
"Vita Ricardi Secundi." Wr. about 1402–04 by a monk of
Evesham. Ed. T. Hearne, 1729.
"The Life and Reign of King Richard The Second. By a Person
of Quality." 1680. Political, justifying deposition, and published,
according to a note in the Bodleian copy, "for example for the
fanatical crew of the times to imitate."

Richard III.   See Buck and T. More.

RICHARD OF HEXHAM (fl. 1138–54). "De Gestis Regis Stephani."
— *Hardy.* Good example of the royal chronicle for a single king.

Richelieu.   See Dugrès, James Howell.

RICRAFT, JOSIAH. "A Survey of Englands Champions, and Truths
faithfull Patriots." 1647. Adulatory sketches of Royalist leaders
in the Civil Wars.

Robert, Saint (d. 1216?). "The Metrical Life of St. Robert of
Knaresborough." Roxburghe Club, 1824. In Middle English.

Robert of Normandy.   See Lodge.

ROBERT OF SHREWSBURY. "The Admirable Life of Saint Wenefride
Virgin, Martyr, Abbesse. Written in Latin above 500 yeares ago,
by Robert, Monke and Priour of Shrewsbury . . . translated . . .
By J. [ohn] F. [enne]" 1635.

ROBERTS, JOHN. "The lyfe of Hyldebrande, called Gregory the
.vii. pope of that name: with the lyfe also of Henry the fourth,
emperour of Rome and Almayne." Wynkyn de Worde, 1534.
From the Italian of Benno.

ROBERTSON, GEORGE, and CHARTER, HENRY. "De vita et morte
Roberti Rollok, Academiae Edinburgense Primarii, Narrationes."
1599. Repr. 1826.

ROBINSON, MATTHEW. "Autobiography." Wr. before 1680. Completed after 1694 by George Grey. Ed. J. E. B. Mayor, 1856.
Tells with disarming self-appreciation the story of a sporting par-
son who was also an anatomist, a horse-breeder, a fellow at Cambridge, a hunter, a student of the civil law and a correspondent of
Sir Thomas Browne.

ROBINSON, DR. THOMAS. "Life and Death of Mary Magdalene."
Wr. about 1621. Spenserian stanzas and classical allusions.
E. E. T. S., Ex. Ser., vol. lxxviii.

Rochester, John Wilmot, Earl of. See Burnet and Wolsley. "Valentinian . . . Together with a Preface concerning the Author and his Writings. By one of his Friends." 1685. An argumentative essay denying Rochester's licentiousness.

DE ROCOLES, J. B. "The Lives and Actions of Several Notorious Counterfeits." 1686.

ROGER OF HOWDEN. "Vita Gaufridi Archiepiscopi Eboracensis." Wr. before 1201. In Rolls Series, 1868–71, ed. William Stubbs.

ROGERS, JOHN. "The displaying of an horrible secte of . . . heretiques, naming themselves the Familie of Love . . . with the lives of their authours [David Joris and H. Niclas]." 1578.

ROLLE, RICHARD OF HAMPOLE (c. 1300–50). Autobiographical sections in his works. Ed. C. Horstmann, 1895. This also describes an anonymous *vita* of Rolle.

Rollok, Robert. See Robertson.

Roman Emperors. See Reynoldes.

ROPER, WILLIAM. "The Mirrour of vertue in worldly greatness, or the life of Syr Thomas More Knight, sometime Lo. Chancellour of England." Wr. about 1558. T. p. 1626 1st ed. Paris. Hearne's ed. 1722. King's Lib. ed., 1902, elaborate but inaccurate.

ROUS, JOHN (1411–91). "Life of Richard Beauchamp, Earl of Warwick." In Cotton MS. Jul. E. iv. — *Camb. Hist. Lit.*, vol. ii, chap. 17.
 "Diary." 1625–42. Ed. M. A. E. Green for Camden Soc. 1856.

Rowe, John. See Gale.

ROWLANDS, SAMUEL. "Hell's Broke Loose . . . The Life and Death of John Leyden." 1605. Verse. Powerful. Gruesome and picaresque variation of the *Mirror for Magistrates* tradition. Quotes *Hamlet*.
 "The Famous History of Guy Earl of Warwick." 1607. Both in his *Works*. 1880 ed. for Hunterian Club, 3 vols.

ROY, WILLIAM. "Satire Against Cardinal Wolsey." 1st ed. n. d. but before 1530. 2d ed. Wesel, 1546. Repr. *Harl. Misc. Suppl.*

Rupert, Prince. "Historical Memoires of the Life and Death of . . . Rupert, Prince Palatine of the Rhine . . . Containing A brief but Impartial Account of his great and Martial Atchievements." 1683.

S

SACKVILLE, SIR THOMAS. "Complaint of the Duke of Buckingham." In 1559 ed. *Mirror for Magistrates.* Wr. about 1557. Also the "Induction" to the *Mirror.*

Sadler, Thomas. "Sadler's Memoirs: Or, The History of the Life and Death Of that Famous Thief Thomas Sadler." 1677.

Saints' Lives. See Aelfric, Bokenam, Buckland, Legendary, Mabillon, Messingham, Porter, Ribadeneyra, Villegas.

SALTONSTALL, WYE. "Eusebius His Life of Constantine." 1637. Indicative of the patristic influence upon 17th-cent. ecclesiastical biography.

Sampson, Abbot of St. Edmund's. See Jocelin of Brakelond.

SAMWAIES, PETER. "A Narration of the Exemplary Death of Mr. Benjamin Rhodes, Steward to . . . Thomas Earl of Elgin, &c. Briefly Touch'd in a Funeral Sermon." 1657. A mirror for menials.

Sanctilogium Angliae. See John of Tynemouth.

SANDERS, NICHOLAS. "De vita & moribus Thomae Cranmeri haeritici." 1580. See Wells' *Manual.* Also Pits.

Sanderson, Robert. See Walton.

SANDERSON, WILLIAM. "Compleat History of the Lives and Reigns of Mary Queen of Scotland, and of Her Son and Successor, James The Sixth." 1656. Reigns, not lives.
"Compleat History of the Life and Raigne of King Charles." 1658.

Sarpi, Paolo. "The Life of . . . Father Paul . . . Authour of The History of the Counsell of Trent." 1651. Anon.

Savage, Thomas. "The Wicked Life and Penitent Death of Tho. Savage . . . Written as an Example for Youth." Anon.; n. d. but about 1688.
"The Murtherer Turned True Penitent; Or, An Account of the Wicked and Notorious Life of Tho. Savage." N. d. Anon.

Savelli, Troilo. See Matthew.

SAVILE, GEORGE, MARQUIS OF HALIFAX (1633–95). "A Character of King Charles the Second." 1750 ed. Also *Works,* ed. W. Raleigh, 1912.

Savile, George. See R. Howard.

SAVILE, SIR HENRY. "The Life of Agricola." 1591. Joseph Barnes, Oxf. Tr. from Tacitus with 4 books of his *History.* 2d ed. 1598 with Richard Greneway's tr. of the *Germania* and the *Annals.*
Short Latin biography as a preface to Thomas Bradwardine's *De Causa Dei*, 1618. Valuable as an early attempt at the historical and scholarly reconstruction of a life buried in the past.
"Rerum Anglicarum Scriptores Post Bedam Praecipui." 1596. Latin chronicles.

Scanderbeg. See Lavardin.

SCARISBROOK, EDWARD. "The Life of the Lady Warner . . . Written by a Catholick Gentleman." 1696. (Ascr. *Halkett and Laing.*)

Scrinia Reserata. See Hacket.

Sejanus, Aelius. "The Powerfull Favorite, Or, The life of Aelius Seianus. By P. M." Paris, 1628. Wr. to discredit the Stuart régime.

Selby, James. "The unhappy citizen. A . . . narrative of the life and death of James Selby." 1691.

Seven Champions of Christendom. See Johnson.

Shaftesbury, Anthony, Earl of. See "Philanax Misopappas."

SHEFFIELD, JOHN, DUKE OF BUCKINGHAM (1648–1721). "Memoirs." Wr. by himself, in vol. ii of his *Works*, 1723.

SHELTON, WILLIAM. "A Sermon at the Funeral of Mr. Christopher Glascock." 1690.

SHEPERY, JOHN. "De vita Joannis Claimundi." Wr. 1537–42. — Pits. See also Leland.

Sherwin, Robert. See Fenne.

Shipton, Mother. See Head.

SHIRLEY, JOHN. "The Life of . . . Sir Walter Raleigh." 1677.

Shoemakers, Lives of. See Deloney.

Shore, Jane. See Churchyard, Chute.

Sidney, Sir Henry. See Griffith.

Sidney, Sir Philip. See Greville, J. Phillips, Whetstone.

SIKES, GEORGE. "The Life and Death of Sir Henry Vane, Kt. or, A short Narrative of the main Passages of his Earthly Pilgrimage; Together with a true account of his purely Christian, Peaceable,

Spiritual, Gospel-Principles, Doctrine, Life, and Way of Worshipping God, for which he Suffered Contradiction and Reproach from all sorts of Sinners, and at last, a violent Death, June 14. Anno 1662." 1662. Anon. Attr. to Sikes by Wood. A pious attempt at subjective biography.

Simon Episcopius. "The Life and Death of James Arminius and Simon Episcopius." 1672. By J. K.

SKINNER, THOMAS. "The Life of General Monk." 1723. Wr. about 1677–79.

SLINGSBY, SIR HENRY. "Diary." 1638–48. Ed. 1836.

Smith, Henry. See Fuller.

Smith, Major General John. See Walsingham.

Smith, Miles. See J. Stephens.

SMITH, PETER. "Synopsis Papismi . . . with addition of a Preface truly relating the life and death of . . . Doctor Andrew Willet, the Author." 1634. Intimate details in the midst of extended panegyrics. Shows influence of patristic biographies. Typical ecclesiastical life.

SMITH, RICHARD. "The Life of . . . The La. Magdalen Viscountesse Montague." Wr. in Latin about 1610. Tr. "by C. F." 1627.

SMITH, THOMAS. "The Life of Dr. Colet, writ by Erasmus," 1661, Cambridge. Tr.
"The life of Mary Magdalen of Pazzi." 1687. Tr.
"Gulielmi Camdeni Vita." 1691, as Latin pref. to a volume of letters addressed to Camden.
"Vita D. Roberti Cottoni." In *Catalogus . . . Bibliothecae Cottonianae.* 1696.

Smith, Thomas. See Strype.

Socinus (1539–1604). . . . "The Life of Faustus Socinus Senensis by a Polonian Knight." Tr. pr. in 1653.

Speculum Patrum. See Larkin.

SPEED, JOHN. "Historie of Great Britaine." 1611. Painstaking.

SPEGHT, THOMAS. "The Life of Geffrey Chaucer," prefixed to 1598 ed. of Chaucer's poems. Corrected and extended in 1602 ed.

SPELMAN, SIR JOHN. "Life of King Alfred." Wr. about 1642. Pub. in Latin 1678. Rhetorical.

Spenser, Edmund. Works, 3d fol. ed., 1679, contains "An Account of his life." — *D. N. B.*

Spotswood, John. See Duppa.

SPOTTISWOOD, JAMES. "Breefe Memoriall of the Lyfe and Death of Doctor James Spottiswood, Bishop of Clogher in Ireland." Wr. before 1664. Editor of 1811 ed. considers it autobiographical.

SPRAT, THOMAS. "An Account of the Life and Writings of Mr. Abraham Cowley," prefixed to Cowley's *Works*, 1668. Latin life prefixed to ed. of Cowley's Latin poems, 1668.

STAFFORD, ANTHONY. "The life, and death of that great Cynicke Diogenes." 1615.
"The Female Glory: Or, The Life, and Death of our Blessed Lady, the holy Virgin Mary." 1635.
"Honour and Vertue, Triumphing over the Grave. Exemplified in a faire devout Life, and Death, adorned with the surviving perfections of Henry Lord Stafford." 1640. Influence of ecclesiastical upon secular biography.

Stafford, Henry, Lord. See A. Stafford.

Stafford, William, Lord. See Corker.

STANLEY, THOMAS. "The History of Philosophy." 1655. With lives of the ancient philosophers, making good use of original sources. Outstanding for its defence of the biography of thought rather than of action.

STAPLETON, THOMAS. "Tres Thomae." Douai, 1588. Lives of the Apostle, Thomas à Becket, and Sir Thomas More.

STAUNTON, EDMUND. "A Sermon . . . on M^rls Elizabeth Wilkinson, late Wife to Dr. Henry Wilkinson Principall of Magdalen Hall: Whereunto is added a Narrative of her Godly Life and Death." 1659.

Staunton, Edmund. See Mayo.

Stephen, King. See Richard of Hexham, William of Newbury.

STEPHENS, EDWARD. "The life of St. Anthony, translated out of the Greek [of Athanasius] by D. S." 1697. (Attr. *Halkett and Laing* and Bodl. Cat.)

STEPHENS, JOSEPH. Life of Miles Smith prefixed to his *Sermons.* 1632.

STORER, THOMAS. "The Life and Death of Thomas Wolsey Cardinall. Divided into three parts: His Aspiring, Triumph, and

Death." Oxf. 1599. Ed. 1826 with notes. The poetical climax of the Lydgate-*Mirror for Magistrates* tradition. Classical and balanced artificial style, but opulent and impressive.

Story, John. "A Declaration of the Lyfe and Death of John Story, late a Romish Canonicall Doctor." 1571. Repr. *Harl. Misc.*, ii, 98–105. Attr. to T. Knell in *D. N. B.*

STOW, JOHN. "Chronicles of England, from Brute unto this present yeare of Christ. 1580." Makes direct use of earlier royal chronicles and biographies.

STRANGE, RICHARD. "The life and gestes of S. Thomas Cantilupe . . . collected by R. S. S. I." Ghent, 1674. Catholic.

STRANGUAGE, WILLIAM. "The Historie of the Life and Death of Mary Stuart Queene of Scotland." 1624. An extended study, with Plutarch quoted as a model. Letters and speeches interspersed, and a clear conception of Mary's essential femininity brought out through her actions.

STRYPE, JOHN (1643–1737). "Memorials of . . . Thomas Cranmer." 1694.
 "The Life of . . . Sir Thomas Smith . . . Principal Secretary of State to King Edward the Sixth, and Queen Elizabeth." 1698.
 (Also lives of Aylmer, 1701; Cheke, 1705; Grindal, 1710; Parker, 1711; and Whitgift, 1718.)

Stuart, Bernard. See Quin.

Stubbes, Katherine. See P. Stubbes.

STUBBES, PHILIP. "Christal Glasse for Christian Women . . . the Godly Life and Christian Death of Mistris Katherine Stubbes." 1st ed. 1592. T. p. from ed. 1626. Exemplary and didactic, but the portrait of the author's wife is inspired by tenderness and tinged with a sense of regret and loss. Important for its early date and unusual subject in English.

STUBBS, THOMAS (fl. 1360–75). "Actus Pontificum Eboracensium." In *Historiae Anglicanae Scriptores X*, 1652.

Studley, John. See Bale.

Stukely, Thomas (d. 1578). "The Famous History of Stout Stukley: Or, His Valiant Life and Death." N. d. Verse.

Suetonius. See P. Holland.

Summers, Will. "A Pleasant History Of the Life and Death of Will Summers." 1676. Earliest known copy, though evidently a repr. of previous editions. Anon. Frivolous.

SURIUS, LAURENTIUS. "De Probatis Sanctorum Historiis." 7 vols. 1576–81. Cologne. Saints' lives, including many by Englishmen.

Sussex, Thomas, Earl of. See Whetstone.

Sweert, Francis. See Ortell.

SWINNOCK, GEORGE. "The Life and Death of T.[homas] Wilson [minister of Maidstone, Kent]." 1672.

Swithin, Saint. See Goscelin.

T

Tacitus. See H. Savile.

Tamerlane. See Clark.

TASWELL, WILLIAM. "Autobiography." 1651–82. Ed. G. P. Elliott for Camden Soc., 1852.

TAYLOR, JEREMY. "The Great Exemplar of Sanctity, and Holy Life according to the Christian Institution. Described In the History of the Life and Death of . . . Jesus Christ . . . with Considerations and Discourses upon the several parts of the story." 1649. Philosophical, exemplary, and extended.

TAYLOR, JOHN. "The Booke of Martyrs." 1617. Verse.
"The Life and Death of . . . the Virgin Mary." 1620. Verse.
"The Old, Old Very Old Man: or, The Age and long Life of Thomas Par." 1635. Verse. Curious for its subject. The biographies of freaks are less common than the lives of knaves, but are nevertheless quite frequent in the 17th cent.
"The Whole Life and Progresse of Henry Walker the Ironmonger." 1642.
John Taylor, the Water Poet, represents the popularizing of biography and its extension in metrical pseudo-biographies to odd characters and topical lives of burghers. See also his collected works, ed. 1630. Repr. 1868–69, in 3 vols. Ed. C. Hindley, 1872.

TEMPLE, SIR WILLIAM. "Memoirs." 1672–79. Pub. 1692.

Terence. "Terence's Comedies: Made English With his Life." 1694. Anon.

Teresa, Saint. See Woodhead.

Thauler, John. "The History of the Life of . . . Dr. Joh. Thauler." 1660. From Latin.

Thomas Cantilupe, Saint. See Strange.

THOMAS OF ELMHAM. "Liber Metricus de Henrico V⁰." Wr. about 1414. Rolls Series, ed. C. A. Cole, 1858.

THOMAS OF ELY. Latin "Life of Etheldred." Wr. after 1174, in Wharton's *Anglia Sacra*, 1691.

THOMAS OF MONMOUTH. "The Life and Miracles of St. William of Norwich." Last half of 12th cent. Ed. Augustus Jessopp and M. R. James, 1896. Shows deterioration of saints' lives, the blending with romance, and the coarsening of the miracles.

THORNTON, MRS. ALICE. "The Autobiography of Mrs. Alice Thornton, of East Newton, Co. York." 1875. Wr. after 1669. Told to show God's mercies to her in saving her from rickets, smallpox, and dangerous falls. The troubles of her children engross her. One after another she buries them; and at the end her husband.

THYNNE, FRANCIS. "Animadversions upon . . . Chaucers Workes." 1598. Repr. in H. J. Todd's *Illustrations of Gower and Chaucer*. 1810.

TILLOTSON, JOHN. "A Sermon Preached at the Funeral Of the Rev. Mr. Thomas Gouge . . . With a brief account of his Life." 1682.

TOLAND, JOHN. Life of Milton prefixed to his *Works*. Amsterdam, 1698.
    "The Oceana of James Harrington . . . With An Exact Account of his Life Prefix'd." 1700.

TRAHERON, WILLIAM. "The Historie of all the Romane Emperors . . . First collected in Spanish by Pedro Mexia." 1604. From Julius Caesar to Rodulph II.

Translations. For important early translations of classical and Continental biographies into English, see *Camb. Hist. Eng. Lit.*, vol. iv, chap. 1, bibliography.

Tregosse, Thomas. "The Life and Death of Thomas Tregosse Late Minister of the Gospel." 1671. Anon.

TUKE, SIR SAMUEL. "A Character of Charles the Second Written By an Impartial Hand." 1660. Wood attr. this to Tuke; *Camb. Hist. Eng. Lit.*, to George Morley.

Tully, Thomas. See Banks.

Turner, Colonel James. ". . . the Life and Conversation of C. Iames Turner." 1663.
    "The Life and Death of James, Commonly called Collonel Turner." 1663. Sensational pamphlets.

TURNER, SIR JAMES. "Memoirs of his own life and times . . . 1632–1670." 1st ed. 1829. Military.

TURNER, ROBERT. "Maria Stuarta . . . Continet haec epistola historiam pene totam vitae." 1588. By "Obertus Barnestapolius." Included, with other sources, in "De Vita & rebus gestis . . . Mariae Scotorum Reginae." 1725, ed. Samuel Jebb.
    See also Fenne.

TUSSER, THOMAS. "Metrical Autobiography." First pr. in his "500 Points of Good Husbandry." 1573. Repr. 1846.

Twelve Caesars. See Legh.

Tyndall, William. See Foxe.

U

Ursula, Saint. See Hatfeld.

Usher, James. See Bernard, Dillingham, Parr.

V

Valera, Cipriano de. See Golburne.

VALLANS, WILLIAM. "The Honourable Prentice: or this Taylor is a man. Shewed in the life and death of Sir John Hawkewood . . . with the famous history of the noble Fitzwalter, Lord of Woodham in Essex." 1615. By "W. U." Ascr. through note in Bodleian copy.
    Variant: "The Honour of the Taylors: Or, The Famous and Renowned History of Sir John Hawkwood." 1687.

Vane, Sir Henry. See Sikes.

VAUGHAN, EDMUND. "The Works of . . . Thomas Jackson . . . With the Life of the Author." 1653. Enthusiastic pref. by Barnabas Oley.

VERE, SIR FRANCIS. "Commentaries." Pub. by William Dillingham, 1657. Influence of Caesar. Wr. before 1609.

Verney. "Memoirs of the Verney Family During the Civil War." 1892. Private letters.

VERNON, GEORGE. "The Life Of . . . Dr. Peter Heylyn." 1682.

Villegas, Alfonso. See Heigham.

Villiers, George, Duke of Buckingham. See Wotton.

VINEIS, RAINMUNDUS DE. ". . . the lyf of saint Katherin of senis." 1493 (?). — *Camb.*

Virgil. ". . . of the lyfe of Virgil and of his death, and many other marvayles that he did in his lyfe-tyme by witchcrafte and nygromancy, through the develles of hell." Anon. N. d. About 1500.

W

WADE, LAURENCE. "Life of Becket," in verse, 1497. MS. Bennet Col. Camb. — *Ritson, Bibl. Poet.*

Wadsworth, James (d. 1623). "The Memoires of Mr. James Wadswort, A Jesuit that Recanted . . . Faithfully published to the World out of the Authors own Original Notes." 1679. Probably spurious. Unfavorable to the Jesuits.

Wadsworth, Thomas. See Bragge.

WALKER, ANTHONY. "Eureka, Eureka. The Virtuous Woman found . . . A Sermon . . . At the Funeral of . . . Mary, Countess Dowager of Warwick . . . With so Large Additions as may be stiled the Life of that Noble Lady." 1678.
"The Holy Life of Mrs. Elizabeth Walker: Giving a modest and short account of her exemplary piety and charity. Chiefly designed to be given to her friends." 1690. Repr. 1823.

WALKER, SIR EDWARD. "The Life and Actions of Thomas Howard, Earl of Arundel and Surrey." Wr. 1651.
"The Life and Actions of King Charles I." Wr. 1655. Both pub. in *Historical Discourses*, 1705. Defence against imputations of tyranny.

Walker, Mrs. Elizabeth. See A. Walker.

Walker, Henry. See John Taylor.

Wallace, William. "The Acts and Deeds of the most famous and valiant Champion, Sir William Wallace." 1620 ed. 1645 ed. says first wr. in Latin by John Blair, and "turned in Scots meeter by one called Blind Harry, in the dayes of king James the fourth." Henry the Minstrel flourished 1470–92. Approaches the romance in treatment.

Wallis, Ralph. "The Life and Death of Ralph Wallis The Cobler of Glocester." 1670. Anon. Scurrilous, with Anglican bias. A witty libel.

WALLYE, MASTER. "The Fables of Esope in Englysshe with all his lyfe and Fortune." N. d. or author, but possibly the ed. licensed to master Wallye in 1560. (Arber's *Stationers' Register*, i, 48.) Like the Lives of Virgil, this is an attempt to give verisimilitude to romantic and entertaining anecdote through an appeal to historical figures in antiquity.

WALSINGHAM, EDWARD. "Britannicae Virtutis Imago. Or, The Effigies of True Fortitude, Expressed to the life, in the famous actions of that incomparable Knight, Major Generall Smith." Oxf. 1644.

"Hector Britannicus or Sr John Digby." Attr. by C. H. Firth to Walsingham and first pub., ed. G. Bernard, in 1910 for the Camden Soc., 3d ser., vol. xviii.

"The Life of Sir Henry Gage, Governor of Oxford." 1645. Oxf.

WALTON, IZAAK (1593–1683). "The Life and Death of Dr. Donne, Late Deane of St. Pauls London" as pref. to Donne's *LXXX Sermons*. 1640.

"The Life of Sir Henry Wotton," as pref. to *Reliquiae Wottonianae*. 1651.

"The Life of Richard Hooker." 1665. "The Works of Mr. Richard Hooker . . . With an account of his Life and Death." 1666.

"The Life of Mr. George Herbert." 1670.

"The Life of Dr. Sanderson, Late Bishop of Lincoln . . . To which is added, Some short Tracts or Cases of Conscience, written by the said Bishop." 1678.

First collected ed. of first 4 lives in 1670; 2d ed. in 1674. *Walton's Lives*, ed. by Thomas Zouch, 1796. 3d ed., 1817, has good biography of Walton; pub. separately 1823. *Walton's Lives*, ed. A. H. Bullen, 1884; ed. Austin Dobson, 1898. With an introduction by George Saintsbury, 1927.

Warbeck, Perkin. See Gainsford.

WARE, SIR JAMES. "De scriptoribus Hiberniae." 1639. English tr. by Walter Harris, 1746.

Warner, Lady. See Scarisbrook.

WARNER, WILLIAM. "Albions England." 1586, 1589, 1592. Metrical history which, in complete edition (1612), extends from Noah to James I.

WARWICK, MARY [RICH], COUNTESS OF. "Autobiography." Entries to 1674; d. 1678. Ed. for Percy Soc. 1848. See also her diary from 1666 to 1672 in "Memoirs of Lady Warwick," 1847, for comparison of biography and journals. A tale of loyalty and affliction, which brings out both her maternal competence and her sweet religious fervor.

Warwick, Mary, Countess of. See A. Walker.

WARWICK, SIR PHILIP. "Memoires Of the reigne of King Charles I. With a Continuation to the Happy Restauration of King Charles II." Wr. 1675–77. Ed. 1701.

WATSON, JOHN. "English Martyrologie; containing a Summary of the Lives of the Saintes of England, Scotland, and Ireland." 1608. — *Gerould.*

WATTS, WILLIAM. "Saint Augustines Confessions translated." 1631.

WEBB, JAMES. "An Encomium or Short Character of the Gracious and Virtuous Mrs. Lucy Webb." Dublin, 1698–99.

Webb, Lucy. See J. Webb.

WEEVER, JOHN. "The Mirror of Martyrs, or The life and death of . . . Sir John Oldcastle." 1601. Verse. Influence of *Mirror for Magistrates* tradition, applied to an unusual subject.

Welby, Henry. "The Phoenix of these late times: Or the life of Mr. Henry Welby, Esq: who lived at his house in Grub-street forty-four yeares, and in that space, was never seene by any. Aged 84." 1637. Anon. New biographical possibilities.

Wentworth, Sir Thomas. "A Short and True Relation of the life and death of Sir Thomas Wentworth Knight." 1641. Unfavorable and trivial account of the proto-martyr.
"The Downfall of Greatnesse . . . A Poem: Or, A short Survey of Thomas Lord Wentworth, Late Earle of Strafford . . . His History and Tragedy." 1641. Boccaccio and Lydgate in mid-seventeenth cent.

Werburge, Saint. See Bradshaw.

WESLEY, SAMUEL. "The Life of . . . Jesus Christ. An Heroic Poem." 1693. Ten books of heroic couplets.

WHARTON, HENRY (1664–95). "Excerpta ex vita MS. Henrici Whartoni, A.M. a seipso scripta." Pp. 105–154, D'Oyly's *Life of William Sancroft*, 1821. Extracts from a Latin original now destroyed.
"Anglia Sacra, Sive Collectio Historiarum, partim Antiquitus, partim recenter scriptarum de Archiepiscopis & Episcopis Angliae,

a prima Fidei Christianae susceptione ad Annum MDXL." 1691. 2 vols. Vol. ii particularly valuable for Latin lives of bishops after the Conquest. Contains Osbern's *Dunstan*, Malmesbury's *Wulfstan*, the *Life of Gundulf*, Wycumbe's *Robert de Betun*, Bardney's *Grosteste*, and others.

"The History of the Troubles and Tryal of . . . William Laud, Lord Arch-Bishop of Canterbury. Wrote by himself, during his Imprisonment in the Tower. To which is prefixed the Diary of his own Life." Wr. 1641–43. Pub. 1695. Also see Cave.

WHEARE, DEGORY. "Commemoratio Vitae et Mortis V. C. Gulielmi Camdeni Clarentii, facta Oxoniae in Schola Historica statim a funere. Ann. 1623." Included in his *Hist. Camdeniani*, 1623.

WHETSTONE, GEORGE. "A Remembraunce of the wel-imployed life, and godly end, of George Gaskoigne Esquire." 1577. An elegy in ababcc stanzas, told mainly in the first person.

"A Remembraunce of the woorthie and well imployed life of . . . Sir Nicholas Bacon, Knight; Lorde Keeper of the Greate Seale . . . who deceased the 20th daye of Februarie 1578." Dated March 4.

Similar opportune verse biographies were issued for "Sir James Dier," 1582; "Thomas Earl of Sussex," 1583; and "A Mirror of Treue Honnour and Christian nobilitie, exposing: The life, death, and devine vertues, of the most noble, and godly Lorde Frauncis Earle of Bedford," 1585.

"Sir Phillip Sidney, His Honorable Life, His Valiant Death, and True Vertues." 1587.

Whitaker, William. "Vitae et mortis Doctiss. Sanctissimique Theologi Gulielmi Whitakeri . . . vera descriptio: Socio eiusdem Collegii [St. John's, Cambridge] authore." Appended to vol. i of *Opera*, 1610, and followed by numerous elegies in Latin and Greek.

WHITCOMBE, ROBERT. "Janua Divorum: or, The Lives and Histories of the Heathen Gods." 1678. — *Pickering and Chatto*.

WHITEFOOT, JOHN. Character sketch of Sir Thomas Browne (1605–82) in Browne's *Posthumous Works*, 1712. Whitefoot first knew Browne about 1637. Formal.

WHITELOCK, BULSTRODE (1605–75). "Memorials of the English Affairs from the Beginning of the Reign of Charles the First to the happy Restoration of King Charles the Second." 1682. Repr. 1853, 4 vols. Political annals with occasional personal notes.

Whitgift, John. See Paule.

Whittingham, William. "The life and death of Mr. Will Whittingham Deane of Durham who departed this life A^o D^{ni} 1579. Iune 10." Bodl. MS. Wood E 4. Repr. Camden Soc., vol. cxiv. *D. N. B.* dates this about 1603. Possibly earlier. Biography not finished. Author probably a Calvinist. Important for its early date among English ecclesiastical lives.

WHYTFORD, RYCHARD (fl. 1495–1555?). "The Martiloge in englysshe after the use of the chirche of salisbury." 1526.

Wilde, George. See Mossom.

Wilfred, Saint. See Eadmer, Eddius, Frithegode.
Anonymous Latin life in *Historians of York*, Rolls Series, vol. i, 1879.

Wilkinson, Elizabeth. See Staunton.

Willet, Andrew. See P. Smith.

William III. "The History Of the most Illustrious William, Prince of Orange." 1688. Anon.

WILLIAM OF CANTERBURY. See Becket.

WILLIAM OF MALMESBURY. "Gesta Regum Anglorum." Wr. before 1125. Includes vivid sketches for the Norman kings and leaders.
"Gesta Pontificum Anglorum," with appendix of "Vita S. Aldhelmi." 1125. Both in Rolls Series, 1870. The *Gesta* a good early example of grouped biographies. The *Vita* includes original letters. One of the four parts, treating the *sanctissimi viri . . . genus et scientiam*, closely approaches significant biography.
"Vita S. Wulstani Episcopi Wigorniensis." In Wharton's *Anglia Sacra*, ii, 241.

WILLIAM OF NEWBURGH (1136–98?). "Historia Rerum Anglicarum," Rolls Series. Contains possibilities of good lives of Stephen and Henry II.

William of Norwich. See Thomas of Monmouth.

WILLIAM OF RAMSEY (fl. 1219). Wrote Latin lives of Waltheof, Guthlac (metrical), Edmund, and others. — *D. N. B.*

WILLIAM OF WYCUMBE (fl. 1160). "Vita Domini Roberti de Betune, Herefordensis Episcopi." Wharton's *Anglia Sacra*, ii, 295.

William of York (d. 1154). Anonymous Latin life included in Dugdale's *Monasticon Anglicanum*, 1655–73.

Williams, John. See Hacket.

WILLIBALD. "Vita S. Bonifacii." Wr. about 755–86. *Opera Bonifacii*, ed. J. A. Giles, 2 vols. 1844.
Latin autobiography wr. about 755–86. — *D. N. B.*

WILSON, ARTHUR (1595–1652). "Some Account of Arthur Wilson, written by himself; Entitled, 'Observations of God's Providence, in the Tract of my Life.'" First pub. 1735 in vol. ii of Francis Peck's *Desiderata Curiosa.* Also in *The Inconstant Lady* by Wilson, 1814. A queer mixture of piety and recklessness.
"The History of Great Britain, Being the Life and Reign of King Iames The First." 1653. Title shows confusion of history and biography.

WILSON, THOMAS. "Vita et obitus duorum fratrum Suffolciensium, Henrici et Caroli Brandoni prestanti virtute, et splendore nobilitatis ducum illustrissimorum, duabus epistolis explicata." 1559. Interesting as an early biography neither ecclesiastical nor royal. A memorial garland rather than an organized life.

Wilson, Thomas. See Swinnock.

Wilton, Jack. See Nashe.

Winchcomb, John. See Deloney.

Wing, Vincent. See Gadbury.

Winifred, Saint. See Robert of Shrewsbury.

WINSTANLEY, WILLIAM. "England's Worthies." 1660. — *D. N. B.*
"The Loyal Martyrology: or Brief Catalogues and Characters of the most Eminent Persons who Suffered for their Conscience during the late times of Rebellion . . . as also, Dregs of Treachery: With the Catalogue and Characters of those Regicides . . . with others of that Gang, most Eminent for Villany. For encouragement to Virtue, and determent from Vice." 1665. Wr. for bread, not for posterity.
"The Lives of the most Famous English Poets." 1687. Trivial, containing for Elizabethan and contemporary poets uneven and prejudiced accounts.
"The Honour of Merchant-Taylors . . . Their Honourable Loves, and Knightly Adventures . . . Together with their Pious Acts and large Benevolences." 1668. Hack-writing.

Wolsey, Thomas. See Cavendish, Churchyard, Roy, Storer.

WOLSLEY. "Valentinian . . . Together with a Preface concerning the Author [John Wilmot Earl of Rochester] and his Writings. By one of his Friends." 1685. Assigned by Malone catalogue to "Mr. Wolsley." Scant.

Women, History of. See Heywood.

WOOD, ANTHONY. "Athenae Oxonienses. An Exact History of all the Writers and Bishops who have had their Education in . . . Oxford from 1500, to the end of the year 1690." 2 vols., 1691 and 1692. Standard ed. Philip Bliss, 1813–20.
"The Life of Anthony à Wood From the Year 1632 to 1672, Written by Himself" in 1683. Included in vol. ii, 1772, of Thomas Hearne's "Lives of . . . Leland, Hearne and Wood." Begins as a life in the third person, and becomes diary notes in first person to the year 1695. Also ed. in full by Andrew Clark, as *Life and Times of Anthony Wood.* 5 vols., Oxf., 1891–1900. Exhaustive.

WOOD, LAMBERT. "Life and Raigne of King Charles." 1659. Ascr. to Peter Heylyn erroneously. Temperate.

WOODHEAD, ABRAHAM. "The Life of the Holy Mother S. Teresa." 1669–71. Tr. from Spanish. Crynes cat. notes an ed. of 1611, probably the Spanish ed. of same year.
"Life of Gregory Lopez, a Spanish Hermit in the West Indies." 2d ed. 1675. — *D. N. B.*
"An historical Narrative of the Life and Death of . . . Jesus Christ." Oxf. 1685.

WORTHINGTON, DR. JOHN. "Diary." 1637–67. Chetham Soc., vols. xiii and xxxvi. Unimportant.

WORTLEY, FRANCIS. "Characters and Elegies." 1646. Generic except for King and Queen.

WOTTON, HENRY. "A Parallell betweene Robert late Earle of Essex, and George late Duke of Buckingham." 1641.
"The Life and Death of Geo. Villiers, Duke of Buckingham." 1642. T. p. from 1654 *Reliquiae Wottonianae*, which also includes the parallel between Buckingham and Essex. Also characters of Charles I, Doge Giovanni Bembo, and Ferdinando di Medici.

Wotton, Henry. See Walton.

LE WRIGHT, THOMAS. "An Exact Character or, Narrative of the late right Noble, and magnanimous Lord, Oliver Cromwell." 1658. Laudatory.

WULFSTAN. "Vita S. Ethelwoldi Episcopi Wintoniensis." Wr. about 1000. Pr. *Acta Sanctt. Ord. S. Benedicti*, saec. v, p. 606.

Wulfstan, Bishop of Worcester. See William of Malmesbury.

Wycliffe, John. See T. James.

Wykeham, William of. See T. Martyn.

WYRLEY, WILLIAM. "The glorious life and honourable death of Sir John Chandos, Lord of St. Salviour, le Viscount, great Seneschall of Poyctou." In *The true use of Armorie,* 1592.
"In pomp and glory though brave days we spend,
Yet happy none, until be known his end."
This also includes "The Honourable life and languishing death of Sir John de Gralhy Capitall de Buz . . . sometime one of the principall Governors of Guyen." Both in verse. Repr. Brydges, *Cens. Lit.,* ii, 40. Influence of *Mirror for Magistrates* acknowledged.

X

Xavier, Saint Francis. See Dryden.

Y

YEARWOOD, RANDOLPH. "The Penitent Murderer. Being an Exact Narrative Of the Life and Death of Nathaniel Butler; Who (through Grace) became a Convert, after he had most cruelly murdered John Knight." 1657. Pub. as an object lesson by the Lord Mayor's chaplain.

YONGE, WALTER. "Diary." 1604–29. Ed. J. G. Nichols for Camden Soc., 1848.

PART II

A LIST OF THE MOST IMPORTANT WORKS OF REFERENCE FOR THE STUDY OF EARLY ENGLISH BIOGRAPHY

ARBER, EDWARD. "An English Garner in Gatherings from our History and Literature." 8 vols. 1877–96. Repr. of old tracts.

BANNATYNE CLUB. Pub. of biographical material for Scotland. 1823 ff.

BARING-GOULD, S. "The Lives of the British Saints." With John Fisher, 4 vols., 1907. 1st pub. 1872.

BERKENHOUT, JOHN. "Biographia Literaria; Or a Biographical History of Literature: Containing the Lives of English, Scottish, and Irish Authors. From the Dawn of Letters . . . to the Present Time." 1777. Contains caustic criticisms of earlier antiquaries.

BIOGRAPHIA BRITANNICA. 6 vols. 1747–66.

"BIOGRAPHICAL COLLECTIONS: OR LIVES AND CHARACTERS." 1766, 2 vols. Interesting as showing connections between funeral sermons and brief biographies. Repr. sermons by Baxter (1660–82), Bates (1677 and 1694), Howe (about 1677), and others.

BOLLANDISTS. Society of Belgian Jesuits, who have pub. valuable original material in the *Acta Sanctorum*, intermittently from 1643 to the present time.

"BRITISH MUSEUM CATALOGUE OF EARLY ENGLISH BOOKS TO 1640." 3 vols. 1884.

BRYDGES, SIR EGERTON. "Select Funeral Memorials." 1818. Contains verse epitaphs of early 17th cent. Shows the elegiac approach to biography.
"Censura Literaria. Containing Titles, Abstracts, and Opinions of Old English Books." 10 vols. bound as 5. 2d ed. 1815. Valuable sources.
"British Bibliographer." 4 vols. 1810–14.
"Restituta." 4 vols. 1814–16.
"Archaica." 2 vols. 1815. Repr. of scarce tracts.

BURR, ANNA ROBESON. "The Autobiography. A Critical and Comparative Study." 1909. An enthusiastic pioneer work.

CAMBRIDGE. "Early English Printed Books in the University Library Cambridge (1475 to 1640)." 4 vols. Camb. 1900–07.

CAMBRIDGE HISTORY OF ENGLISH LITERATURE. Particularly valuable for its bibliographies.

CAMDEN SOCIETY. Pub. of important materials; numerous letters and diaries. 1838 to present date.

CHANDLER, FRANK WADLEIGH. "The Literature of Roguery." 1907. 2 vols. Vol. i is important for reference, particularly chap. 4, "The Criminal Biographies," which relates picaresque with biographical literature.

CHETHAM SOCIETY. Pub. of valuable materials relating to Lancaster and Chester. 1844 on.

COLLIER, J. P. "A Bibliographical and Critical Account of the Rarest Books in the English Language." 2 vols. 1865. Largely an amplification of his Bridgewater Catalogue. Repr. selections from old verse lives.

CROSS, WILBUR L. "An Outline of Biography From Plutarch to Strachey With a Bibliography." Holt and Co., 1924. From an address at Columbia Univ., 1921. Discusses briefly the principal problems of the biographer and contains a good representative bibliography at the end.

DELEHAYE, HIPPOLYTE. "Les Légendes Hagiographiques." 1905. Interesting as showing parallels in Continental hagiography and connections with popular romance.
"Les Origines du Culte des Martyrs." 1912.
"Les Passions des Martyrs et les Genres Littéraires."
"The Work of the Bollandists." (Tr.) 1922.

DICTIONARY OF NATIONAL BIOGRAPHY. Founded in 1882 by George Smith. 63 vols. and 3 vols. supplement. Indispensable.

DUNN, WALDO H. "English Biography." Dent, 1916. Historical and critical survey of the entire field, from the earliest instances to modern times. A serious and extended attempt to establish biography as a definite branch of English litereaure. Of great value as a pioneer study in this field.

EARLY ENGLISH TEXT SOCIETY. 1864 to the present year. Invaluable pub. of original materials.

EDWARDS, EDWARD, and CHARLES HOLE. "A Handbook to the Literature of General Biography." 1885. Contains interesting and convincing discussions of the philosophy of biography.

ENCYCLOPAEDIA BRITANNICA. Article on "Biography" by Edmund Gosse.

GEROULD, GORDON HALL. "Saints' Legends." 1916. New York. Valuable bibliography. The saint's legend is here treated as a form of literature rather than as biography.

GILES, JOHN ALLEN. "Vitae quorundam Anglo-Saxonum." Caxton Soc. 1854. Repr. of early Latin biographies.

GRIFFITHS, A. F. "Bibliotheca Anglo-Poetica: or, A Descriptive Catalogue of a rare and rich collection of Early English Poetry in the possession of Longman, Hurst, Rees, Orme, and Brown." 1815.

GROSS, CHARLES. "Sources and Literature of English History from the Earliest Times to about 1485." 1900. Valuable bibliography.

GUIZOT, FRANCOIS P. "Collection des Mémoires relatifs à la Révolution d'Angleterre." 24 vols. 1827. Tr. into French. Important as reference.

HALKETT, SAMUEL, and LAING, JOHN. "A Dictionary of the Anonymous and Pseudonymous Literature of Great Britain." 4 vols. 1883. Useful in identifying authors of minor pieces.

HALLIWELL, J. O. "The Literature of the Sixteenth and Seventeenth Centuries. Illustrated by Reprints of very rare Tracts." 1851.

HARDY, THOMAS DUFFUS. "Descriptive Catalogue of Materials relating to the history of Great Britain and Ireland, to the end of the reign of Henry VII." 4 vols. in Rolls Series, 1862–71. Invaluable for sources.

HARLEIAN MISCELLANY. "a collection of scarce, curious, and entertaining tracts . . . interspersed with historical, political, and critical notes" (by William Oldys). 8 vols. 1744–46. Another ed., 10 vols., 1808–13, used as reference in Pt. I of this Bibliography. Contains valuable repr.

HASKINS, CHARLES HOMER. "The Renaissance of the Twelfth Century." Cambridge, U. S. A., 1927. Chap. 7, "Historical Writing," is of some interest in connection with this survey.

HEARNE, THOMAS. "A Catalogue of the Library of Thomas Hearne." 1735. Useful as source book.

HOLWECK, F. G. "A Biographical Dictionary of the Saints With a General Introduction on Hagiology." 1924.

HORSTMANN, CARL. "Sammlung Altenglischer Legenden." 1878. Contains Old English verse translation from the Legenda Aurea and miscellaneous verse romances. Also ed. in E. E. T. S., vols. xvii, lxxxvi, and lxxxviii.

JACKSON, THOMAS. "A Library of Christian Biography." 12 vols. 1837. Includes repr. of a number of the best or most edifying 17th-cent. lives.

JOHNSTON, JAMES C. "Biography: The Literature of Personality." The Century Co. New York, 1927. Theoretical study and classification of types of biography. Valuable bibliography of available works on biography.

JUSSERAND, J. J. "The English Novel in the Time of Shakespeare." 1890. Valuable in comparative study.

KINGSFORD, C. L. "English History in Contemporary Poetry . . . 1399 to 1485." 1913.
"English Historical Literature in the 15th Century." Oxf. 1913.

KURTZ, BENJAMIN P. "From St. Antony to St. Guthlac. A Study in Biography." Univ. of California Publications in Modern Philology, vol. xii, No. 2, 1926. Traces debts of mediaeval biography, particularly Felix's Guthlac and Bede's Cuthbert, to the Vita Antonii of Athanasius.

LAING, JOHN. See Halkett.

LEE, SIDNEY. "National Biography: A Lecture." 1896.
"Principles of Biography." 1911. Cambridge.
"The Perspective of Biography." 1918. Theories of a practised biographer.

LOWNDES, WILLIAM THOMAS. "The Bibliographer's Manual of English Literature." 4 vols. 1834. Revised ed. 6 vols. 1857-64.

MACKENZIE, GEORGE. "Lives and Characters Of the most Eminent Writers of the Scots Nation with an Abstract and Catalogue of Their Works; Their Various Editions; and The Judgment of the Learn'd concerning Them." 3 vols. 1708-22.

MACRAY, W. D. "A Manual of British Historians to A.D. 1600." 1845.

MAUROIS, ANDRE. "The Modern Biographer," The Yale Review, Jan. 1928. A discriminating appraisal of the differences between old and modern biography. The old wrote exemplary lives; the modern reactionary or self-expressive. Differences in method: the modern writer considers biography a work of art. Stress upon modern (1) chronological organic development, (2) moral aloofness, (3) collection of all available details. Important.

"Aspects of Biography." Tr. by S. C. Roberts. Camb. Univ. Press, 1929. Originally a series of 6 lectures. Shows debt to Dunn, Strachey, Nicolson, and E. M. Forster. Largely theoretical, but well arranged and intuitively accurate.

MISCH, GEORG. "Geschichte der Autobiographie." Berlin, 1907. 1st vol. *Das Altertum.*

MORLEY, HENRY. "Character Writings of the 17th Century." 1891. Type characters only.

NICHOL SMITH, DAVID. "Characters from the Histories and Memoirs of the 17th Century." Oxf. 1918. Valuable selection for the study of relations between characters and biography.

NICOLSON, HAROLD. "The Development of English Biography." Hogarth Press, 1927. Six lectures, largely based on Dunn. Biography is the "truthful and deliberate record of an individual's life written as a work of intelligence." Provocative and stimulating opinions and judgments throughout.

NORTHUP, C. S. "A Register of Bibliographies of the English Language and Literature." 1925. New Haven, U. S. A.

PICKERING AND CHATTO CATALOGUES. Valuable for occasional references.

PINKERTON, JOHN. "Vitae Antiquae Sanctorum qui habitaverunt in . . . Scotia." 1789. Revised and enlarged by W. M. Metcalfe, 1889, Paisley. Repr. of sources.

RITSON, JOSEPH. "Bibliographia Poetica: A Catalogue of Engleish Poets, of the 12, 13, 14, 15 and Sixteenth Centurys." 1802. Sources and titles.

ROLLS SERIES. Fountain head for original materials in the study of English history or biography in the early centuries. Contains important prefaces and introductions.

ROXBURGHE CLUB. Important for original biographies. 1835 ff.

SCHELLING, FELIX. "The English Chronicle Play." New York, 1902. Interesting in study of relations of Elizabethan drama to biography.

SCOTTISH TEXT SOCIETY. 1883 to date.

SPINGARN, J. E. "Literary Criticism in the Renaissance." 1899. "Critical Essays of the Seventeenth Century." 3 vols. 1908. Interesting, in several cases, as showing the border line between criticism and biography.

STEPHEN, LESLIE. "Studies of a Biographer." 1898. Vol. i has chapter on biographical theories.

STUART, DUANE REED. "From New Biography Back to Old." *Princeton Alumni Weekly*, March 9, 1928. A stimulating and convincing essay. Discusses the bewildering field of modern biography with discrimination and shows classical prototypes or parallels.
"Epochs of Greek and Roman Biography." Univ. of California Press, Berkeley, 1928. An authoritative study, with a first chapter that contains fruitful suggestions for a correlation of classical and English biography.

STUBBS, BISHOP WILLIAM. "Historical Introductions to the Rolls Series." 1902. Ed. Arthur Hassall. Valuable for background.

SURTEES SOCIETY. 1834 to date. Valuable for originals and repr. pertaining to the history of Northern England.

TANNER, THOMAS. "Bibliotheca Britannico-Hibernica: Sive, de Scriptoribus qui in Anglia, Scotia, et Hibernia ad saeculi xvii initium floruerunt . . . Commentarius." 1748. Drawn from Bale, Leland, Pits, and others. Reference.

THAYER, WILLIAM ROSCOE. "The Art of Biography." New York, 1920. A simple and brief critical survey wr. from a personal standpoint.

WELLS, JOHN EDWIN. "A Manual of the Writings in Middle English 1050–1400." Yale Univ. Press, 1916. Comprehensive survey.

WOOD, ANTHONY. "A Hand-List of Wood Printed Books." Catalogue of Anthony Wood's library now in the Bodleian. Invaluable.

WORDSWORTH, CHRISTOPHER. "Ecclesiastical Biography; or, Lives of Eminent Men, connected with the history of religion in England from the commencement of the Reformation to the Revolution." 1st ed. 1810. T. p. from 1853 (4th) ed. 6 vols. Repr. of original biographies, some of which are only here readily accessible.

WRIGHT, THOMAS. "Biographia Britannica Literaria, Or Biography of Literary Characters, Anglo-Saxon Period." 1842. Valuable for sources.
"Biographia Britannica Literaria . . . Anglo-Norman Period." 1846. Shows decline in biography under the Normans.

CHRONOLOGICAL TABLE OF THE MOST IMPORTANT ENGLISH BIOGRAPHIES BEFORE 1700

THE purpose of this table is to present in brief space the most significant developments in English biography to the year 1700.

Only those biographies of some literary value in themselves or of some importance in the history of biography as an art are here included.

Lives before 1400 are in Latin, after 1400 in English, except where the letters "L." and "E." indicate otherwise.

Dates before 1500 indicate date of composition. Dates after 1500 indicate year of publication. After 1500, lives marked with an asterisk were written in the year specified, but not published.

Abbreviations: p. = *post*   a. = *ante*   c. = *circa*

700

c. 692–697	Adamnan's Columba
710–720?	Eddius' Wilfred
c. 713	Life of Gregory the Great, by a monk of Whitby
715–730	Felix's Guthlac
721–731	Bede's Cuthbert, Lives of the Abbots of Wearmouth and Jarrow
8th cent.	Cynewulf's O. E. Juliana, Guthlac, etc.
755–786	Willibald's Boniface
c. 782–789	Alcuin's Willibrord

800

c. 823–829	Vita Alcuini
c. 850	O. E. Martyrology
c. 893	Asser's Alfred

900

a. 950	Frithegode's Wilfred
985	Abbo's King Edmund
995–1005	Vita Oswaldi

1000

c. 1000	Anon. Life of Dunstan; Wulfstan's Aethelwold
c. 1006	Aelfric's Lives of Saints, O. E.; Aelfric's Vita Aethel-woldi
c. 1090	Osbern's Dunstan

1100

1109–1124?	Eadmer's Anselm
c. 1110	Goscelin's Augustine the Missionary
1125	William of Malmesbury's Aldhelm
1150–1200	Thomas of Monmouth's S. William of Norwich
1170–1200	The Becket biographies
Late 12th cent.	Reginald of Durham's Godric

1200

c. 1200	Life of St. Katherine, E. verse; St. Margaret, E. verse
p. 1203	Jocelin's Abbot Sampson
1212–1220	Magna Vita Sancti Hugonis
1212–1220	Gerald's Geoffrey of York
	" autobiography
a. 1280	Early South English Legendary, E.
a. 1300	North English Legendary, E.

1300

a. 1345	Burley's Vitae Philosophorum
a. 1350	John of Tynemouth's Sanctilogium
1375	Barbour's Bruce, E.
p. 1373–1374	Chaucer's St. Cecilia and Monk's Tale, E.
c. 1375–1400	Lives of St. Ninian and St. Machor, E.

1400

1406–1412	Hoccleve's autobiographical poems
c. 1410	John Boston of Bury's Catalogus Scriptorum Ec clesiae, L.
c. 1423	King's Quair commenced
a. 1430	Adam of Usk's Chronicon, L.
1431–1439	Lydgate's Fall of Princes; also Albon, Hector, the Vir gin, Edmund and Fremund; Lydgate's autobio graphical fragments
1436–1461	Two versions of John Hardyng's Chronicle
1436–1448	Blakman's Henry VI, L.
1447	Bokenam's Lyvys of Seyntys (Margaret 1443)

1450 Life of St. Cuthbert
1446–1453 Capgrave's Liber de Illustribus Henricis, L.
    " Katherine of Alexandria
    " Nova Legenda Angliae, L.
    " St. Gilbert (1451) and Augustine
1470–1490 Blind Harry's William Wallace
a. 1500 Bradshaw's St. Werburge

1500

*1503 Richard of Bardney's Grostete (L. verse)
c. 1510 More's Pico della Mirandola
*1513 More's Richard III
c. 1510–1520 Barclay's St. George and other saints' lives
1534 Roberts' Gregory VII and Henry IV
*1533–1552 Leland's collections, L.
1544 Bale's Oldcastle
1548 Bale's Ipswich Catalogue, L.
*1549 Latimer's autobiographical notices.

1550

1553 Bale's Vocacyon
*c. 1556 Cavendish's Wolsey
*c. 1558 Roper's More
*1558 Forrest's Grisilda (Katherine of Aragon)
1559 Bale's Catalogue, L.
1559 Wilson's Vita . . . Henrici et Caroli Brandoni, L.
1559 1st ed. Mirror for Magistrates
*1559 Hall's Life of Fisher
1563 Foxe's Acts and Monuments (L. ed. 1559)
1564 Tr. of Beza's Calvin
1568 Hornan's Lives of the Philosophers
1573 Humfrey's Jewel, L.
1573 Thomas Tusser's metrical autobiography
1574 Eng. tr. Josselin's Matthew Parker
1574 Marbecke's Holy Saints
1575 Churchyard's Chippes
1576 Golding's Coligny
1577–1587 Whetstone's Gascoigne, Bacon, ·Bedford, Sussex, Sidney
1577 North's tr. of Plutarch
*a. 1579 Life of William Whittingham
1587 Standard ed. Mirror for Magistrates
1588 Stapleton's More, L.

1590–1592	Robert Greene's autobiographical tracts
1591	Savile's Agricola
1592	Katherine Stubbes' Life
*a. 1593	Melville's memoirs
1593	Lodge's William Longbeard
1596	The Historie of Scanderbeg
1596	Fitz-Geffrey's Drake
1598	Speght's Chaucer
1599	Storer's Wolsey
1599	Hayward's Henry IV

1600

*c. 1600	Life of Cecil, Lord Burghley
*c. 1601	Life of Sir John Perrott
1601	Godwin's Bishops of England
*p. 1601	Mr. James Melvill's Diary
1603	Hugh Holland's verse autobiography
1604	Traheron's Roman Emperors
1607	Drayton's Cromwell
1609	Featley's Jewel, tr.
*1609	Bodley's autobiography
*c. 1610	Lives of Women Saints, verse (Buckland)
1610	Last supplement to Mirror for Magistrates
*1610–1612	Fulke Greville's Sidney
1612	Nyxon's Robert Dove
1612	Paule's Archbishop Whitgift
1612	Life of Plutarch
1613	Hayward's Three Normans
1618	Savile's Bradwardine, L.
1619	Pits' Catalogue, L.
*c. 1620	Clifford's Duchess of Feria
1622	Bacon's Henry VII
1624	Stranguage's Mary Queen of Scots
1624	Heywood's General History of Women
1624	Messingham's Florilegium, seu Vitae Sanctorum, L.

1625

1617–1635	John Taylor's miscellaneous verse lives
1626	1st ed. Roper's More
*1626	Hinde's John Bruen (pr. 1641)
*p. 1626	Robert Cary's memoirs
1627	Ashley's Almansor

*1627	Falkland's Edward II
1628	Hubert's Edward II
1629	Carleton's Bernard Gilpin (L. 1628)
*c. 1630	Naunton's Fragmenta Regalia (pr. 1641)
*1627–1633	Kenelm Digby's memoirs
c. 1631	Cresacre More's Thomas More
1631–1641	Heywood's romantic biographies
1634	Smith's Andrew Willet
1635	Crashaw's Caracciolus Marquis of Vico
*1636?	Sydnam Poyntz's memoirs
1637	Lupton's Protestant Divines
1640	Walton's Donne
1640	Habington's Edward IV
1641	1st ed. Cavendish's Wolsey
1642	Wotton's Duke of Buckingham
1642	Fuller's Holy and Profane States
1643	Henry Burton's autobiography
*c. 1643	Herbert of Cherbury's autobiography to the year 1624
1644	Walsingham's Major General Smith
1646	Howell's Louis XIII
1647	Bodley's autobiography printed
1648	Eikon Basilike
*1648–1650	Simonds D'Ewes' memoirs
1649	Duncon's Lady Letice, 2d ed. (wr. 1647)
1649	Herbert of Cherbury's Henry VIII

1650

1651	Fuller's Abel Redevivus
1651	Walton's Henry Wotton
1652	Greville's Sidney published
*a. 1652	Arthur Wilson's autobiography
1652	Oley's Life of Herbert
1654	Nicoll's Jurdain
*1655	Life of Lady Falkland
*c. 1655	John Ferrar's Nicholas Ferrar
1655	Stanley's Philosophers
1656	Davies' John Hall
1656	Margaret Cavendish's autobiography
1657	Rawley's Francis Bacon
*1657	Hacket's Archbishop Williams
*c. 1658	Raymond's memoirs.

1660

1660	Lloyd's Charles II
1658–1665	Cromwell biographies
*c. 1660	William Bedell's William Bedell
1661	Fell's Henry Hammond
1661	Anon. Life of Thomas Fuller
1646–1683	Clark's collections of lives
1662	Fuller's Worthies
*1663	Robert Blair's autobiography
*1663–1664	John Livingstone's autobiography
1661–1670	Barksdale's collections of lives
*1664–1671	Lucy Hutchinson's memoirs
1665	Winstanley's Loyal Martyrology
1665	Walton's Hooker
1666	Bunyan's Grace Abounding
1667	Life of William Cavendish by his wife Margaret
1667	Charles Croke's autobiography
*a. 1668	Life of Marmaduke Rawdon
1668	Heylyn's Laud
1668	Lloyd's royalist lives
1668	Sprat's Cowley
1668	Cowley's autobiographical essay
*1668–1672	Clarendon's autobiography

1670

1670	Walton's Herbert
1671	Vavasor Powell's autobiography
1673	Mayo's Staunton
1673	Baxter's Alleine and John Janeway
1674	Phillips' Theatrum Poetarum
*c. 1674	Memoirs of Mary Rich, Lady Warwick
*p. 1674–1675	Fox's Journal
1675	Plume's Bishop Hacket
1675–1677	Cave's Lives of the Apostles
*1676	Anne Fanshawe's autobiography
1678	Walton's Sanderson
*1678	Anne Halkett's autobiography
*p. 1678	Evelyn's Margaret Godolphin
1679	Thomas Hobbes' autobiography, L.
*a. 1680	Matthew Robinson's autobiography

1680

1680	Burnet's Rochester
1681	Baxter's Margaret Baxter
1682	Burnet's Hale
1682	Adam Elliot's autobiography
1683	Dryden's Life of Plutarch
*1683 and later	Anthony Wood's autobiography
*p. 1683	Thomas Ellwood's autobiography
1684	Fell's Richard Allestree
1685	Burnet's Bedell
1686	Parr's Usher
1687	Winstanley's English Poets
*1689	Sir John Reresby's memoirs

1690

1690	Blount's Censura Literaria, L.
1691	Langbaine's Dramatic Poets
1691–1692	Wood's Athenae Oxonienses
1693	Hacket's Archbishop Williams published
1694	Phillips' Milton
1694	Blount's Characters of the Poets
1694	Strype's Cranmer
1695	Wharton's History of William Laud (including Laud's diary, 1641–1643)
1696	Reliquiae Baxterianae (parts wr. as early as 1664)
1696	Life of Aphra Behn
1698	Strype's Thomas Smith

INDEX

INDEX